An Advanced
Geography of
Northern and
Western Europe

An Advanced Geography of Northern and Western Europe

R. J. Harrison Church, B.Sc.(Econ.), Ph.D.(London)
*Professor of Geography in the University of London at the
London School of Economics and Political Science*

Peter Hall, M.A., Ph.D.(Cambridge)
*Reader in Geography with reference to Regional
Planning, University of London, London School of
Economics and Political Science*

G. R. P. Lawrence, M.Sc. (London)
Lecturer in Geography, King's College, University of London

W. R. Mead, M.Sc.(Econ.), Ph.D.(London), F.D.(Uppsala)
*Professor of Geography in the University of London at
University College*

Alice F. A. Mutton, M.A., Ph.D.(London)
*Senior Lecturer in Geography, Queen Mary College,
University of London*

HULTON EDUCATIONAL PUBLICATIONS

© 1967 R. J. Harrison Church
Peter Hall
G. R. P. Lawrence
W. R. Mead
Alice F. A. Mutton

First published 1967 by Hulton Educational Publications Ltd.,
55–59 Saffron Hill, London, E.C.1

Phototypeset and printed by BAS Printers Ltd., Wallop, Hampshire

Contents

Preface

A reviewer of five comparable textbooks on Europe, writing in *Geography* (January 1965), p. 95, concludes

> '*A future author might, like Unstead, read more of the detailed sources, and come up with a shorter, more demanding, more selective, original, new and attractive book.*'

This we have tried to produce. We have written about countries or aspects with which we are most familiar, and which we have taught for many years.

We have tried to follow an agreed order of treatment and content, although there are some necessary variations. For the countries and their regions, we begin with areas of ancient rocks, and so with Northern Europe. This order is also followed, as far as possible, for each country. Our maps have, perforce, been drawn in different departments, each with their own styles and techniques; it would have been frustrating to our cartographers to insist upon one style. We are grateful to them for their patience and skill. Furthermore, each author has selected different aspects for cartographic and photographic illustration; this likewise reflects interests, the nature of the area analysed, and the availability of source material. We have tried to give feeling and depth to both the general, national and regional aspects and to convey the real character of this diverse part of Europe.

English names have been used where these are well established. Temperatures have been given first on the Centigrade scale, following current British practice; other figures have been given in English measurements followed by metric ones—again following a growing British custom. A select list of references for further reading is given in most chapters; it has been confined to references which should be readily available to students or teachers from their own libraries or on inter-library loan. We have avoided the citation of statistics, preferring rather to convey the order of magnitude. The latest statistics can be found in the annual United Nations *Statistical Digest*, *Demographic Yearbook*, F.A.O. *Trade Yearbook* and *Production Yearbook*, and United Nations *Economic Survey of Europe* and *Economic Bulletin for Europe*, most or all of which are in public libraries. National publications including statistical and other year books are available in university libraries or from the embassies. Another valuable source is George Philip's annual *Geographical Digest*. There is also a very comprehensive Statistical Appendix at the end of our volume.

R.J.H.C.

Acknowledgements

Thanks are due to the following for permission to reproduce photographs: Finnish Foreign Ministry (Plates 1, 2, 3); Enso-Gutzeit OY. (Plate 4); Karhumäki OY. (Plate 5); Swedish State Railways (Plate 6); Luossavaara-Kiirunavaara A.B. (Plate 7); Swedish Tourist Traffic Association (Plates 8, 9); Royal Norwegian Embassy (Plates 11, 12); The Export Council of Norway (Plates 13, 14); Mats Wibe Lund Jr. (Plates 15, 16, 17, 18, 19); National Travel Association of Denmark (Plates 20, 21, 22, 23, 24); German Tourist Information Bureau (Plates 25, 26, 27, 28, 29, 30, 31, 32, 33, 35); German Embassy (Plates 34, 36); Lex Hornsby & Partners (Plates 37, 39, 40, 41, 42); German Tourist Information Bureau and Lex Hornsby & Partners (Plate 38); Beringer and Pampaluchi, Zürich (Plate 43); H. Rüedi, Lugano (Plate 44); Swissair (Plates 45, 50, 51); Swiss National Tourist Office (Plates 46, 48, 49); Frido, Sierre (Plate 47); Luxembourg National Tourist Office (Plates 52, 53); Luxembourg Embassy (Plate 54); Belgian Embassy (Plates 55, 62); Institut Belge (Plates 56, 57, 58, 59, 61); Belgian National Tourist Office (Plates 60 and 63); Aerofilms (Plates 64, 66, 67); K.L.M. (Plates 65, 68, 69, 70); French Government Tourist Office (Plates 71, 74, 77, 78, 79, 80, 82, 83 (left and bottom right), 84, 86, 87, 90); French Embassy (Plate 72); Société Nationale des Pétroles d'Aquitaine (Plate 73); Dunkirk Chamber of Commerce (Plate 75); French Embassy and French Government Tourist Office (Plate 76); Marseilles Chamber of Commerce and Industry (Plates 88, 89); J. Allan Cash (Plate 10); Renault Ltd. (Plate 85).
The following photographs are the authors' copyright: Plates 81, 83 (top right).

Maps and Diagrams

Plates

By W. R. Mead

Introduction to North-West Europe

The twelve countries considered in this book do not form a geographical region; they are part of an indivisible whole that is Europe. They include France, Germany (West and East), the Benelux Countries (Belgium, the Netherlands, and Luxembourg), Switzerland and the Scandinavian lands (Denmark, Norway and Sweden) together with the eastern and western outliers of 'Norden'—Finland and Iceland respectively. The British Isles, which are an integral part of north-western Europe, are treated in a separate volume.

A Varied Environment

North-West Europe includes much of the Pre-Cambrian Fennoscandian Shield, Caledonian and Hercynian Europe as well as parts of Alpine Europe. As a result, almost all rocks in the geological succession are encountered within its compass. For good measure it has its share of vulcanicity and, in the Icelandic islands of Surtsey and Surtling, new land is being born of molten rock in the North Atlantic Ocean. Three-quarters of the surface area of North-West Europe has been substantially modified by the direct action of the Quaternary Ice Sheet. Sizable glaciers occur in Iceland, Norway, France and Switzerland. The pronounced variations in relief in relatively short distances associated with the Secondary and Tertiary orogenies are complemented by extensive areas of relatively featureless lowlands. Between Hercynia and Scandinavia is the north-western part of the North European Plain, much modified by erosion, deposition and along the coastal margins by both eustatic and isostatic adjustment. A diversity of soils, varying from the rich wind-borne *loess* (or *limon*) of the Rhine Rift Valley terraces and the Börde to the heavily podsolised soils of northern Scandinavia and Alpine Europe, is spread over the area. In general, the diversity of the physical landscape is least in Denmark and Finland: most, in France.

All parts of North-West Europe are affected to a greater or lesser extent by the sea. The maritime effect is most pervasive in the climate. Continental 'controls' may take local and seasonal precedence but they are subject to continuous modification by maritime influences. These influences are a reflection of the powerful mid-latitude airstreams which move from west to east across the North Atlantic Ocean. Much of the weather of North-West Europe is generated in Greenland and Iceland— with Iceland a virtual synonym for 'Low Pressure'. The maritime fringes of western Europe have high humidity, precipitation, cloud-cover and windiness. When land meets sea in pronounced relief, these characteristics are reinforced. When coastlands are in high latitude, cloud and fog, as well as winter darkness, exaggerate what an American writer has called the 'crepuscular' in North-West Europe's climate. Much of north-western Europe is 'umbrella' country, while the very word 'mackintosh' was born within its shores. Because of its proverbial instability, it is said that much of North-West Europe has no climate, only weather. By way of compensation, most of the area is free from climatic extremes and enjoys a high positive thermal advantage in winter.

As a result of these humid temperate conditions, the area is one of the most favoured parts of the world for vegetative growth. Deciduous woodland is the climax plant association for the greater part of it. The variety of indigenous trees, shrubs and plants is great; the growing season is relatively long for the latitude. For plant life, tolerance diminishes northwards, eastwards and altitudinally. Broad-leaved deciduous woodland, with their oaks and beeches, yield to coniferous forests, the spruce and pine of which give way latitudinally and altitudinally to the tundra vegetation with its dwarfed birches and willows, its mosses and lichens. The natural vegetation of North-West Europe has been more fundamentally changed by men than that of most parts of the inhabited world. Woods have been cleared, swamps drained, heathlands reclaimed, saltmarshes empoldered. Their natural vegetation has been subsequently replaced by new plant associations and new species. These have been brought from homoclimes throughout the world: they have also been bred and hybridised *in situ*.

Indigenous fauna has undergone even more fundamental changes than flora. The lesser rodents and herbivores remain, sometimes to be assailed by new diseases (such as the rabbit by myxomatosis). Carnivores appear intermittently in the extreme north and rather more along Finland's Russian border. But bird populations are vast; though density and diversity diminish from the littoral to the eastern marshlands. Some species, such as the starling, have thrived in association with man. Others, such as the stork, have suffered reduction in food supply as marshes have been drained. Europe still has some of the greatest concentrations of seabirds in the world. They crowd—and cloud—the immense bird cliffs of Norway and the Faeroes. Offshore waters (increasingly incorporated within territorial limits) are among the most heavily fished in the world. Yet the North Atlantic—and especially the territorial waters of Iceland and Norway—still claim some of the world's most productive breeding grounds.

Relief conditions are such that most of North-West Europe drains to the shallow North Sea or its tributary basin, the Baltic Sea. As with Europe at large, the North-West is a peninsula of peninsulas. An irregular coastline underlines the intimacy of association between land and sea. Inter-relations between the two elements reach a maximum in the skerries and fiords of Norway; but each country has its share of fragmented shores. Estuarine features are an integral part of these, the relatively high precipitation guaranteeing that the land is generally well-watered and that it is endowed with abundant rivers. These are of varying maturity. In the north, where the continental ice sheet retired at a relatively late stage, an immature drainage pattern prevails. Elsewhere, North-West Europe enjoys its fair share of substantial and mature waterways; among them, the Seine, Rhine, Elbe, and Oder are the longest.

This varied environment is occupied by a heterogeneous people, so that generalisation about the inhabitants of North-West Europe is no easier than it is about their homeland. Roundhead types of Alpine stock dominate in south-central Europe and in the Celtic 'fringe' lands; longheaded Nordic peoples take precedence elsewhere. Ural-Altaic peoples are encountered in Finland and among the Lapp community of northern Scandinavia. Within the countries of North-West Europe, as well as between them, there may be pronounced ethnographic differences. And in both settlement and field patterns as well as place-names, students of history and toponymy have found evidence for the ethnographic evolution of North-West Europe's countryside.

The Past in the Present

Civilisation was late to emerge in North-West Europe by comparison with the Mediterranean lands. Yet much of the land bears abundant signs of long occupation. These signs diminish rapidly beyond the northern plains and are hard to identify in the coniferous woodlands. Stone Age, Bronze Age, Iron Age and Dark Age (with their sub-divisions and local chronologies) have left their marks upon the face of the land. The grassy ramparts of man's strongholds and cattle kraals in Schleswig-Holstein, the clustered megaliths of Brittany, the piles of kitchen middens around Jutish Himmerland, the boat burial mounds of the Swedish island of Gotland, the suites of cultivation terraces in the Aquitaine Basin preceded the mosaics of villas, roadbeds, bridges and amphitheatres that endure from Roman settlements on the edge of the then barbarian world. The use of stone for building, where stone was available, gave permanence to the remains of early cultures; but North-West Europe lacks anything to compare with the wealth of monuments of the Mediterranean world. Over much of North-West Europe, especially in Scandinavia, where timber was the common constructional material, both fire and decay have destroyed its testimony. The story of its permanent occupation is patiently pieced together by historian and philologist, adding speculation about place-name before the evidence of document can replace the archaeologist's artifact.

In North-West Europe military and ecclesiastical relics are the principal structures persisting from the Middle Ages. The rounded Norman arch, supporting fortress and church alike, spread slowly northwards in monastic cloister (as seen in the Cistercian ruins at Lysekloster in western Norway) and bastioned churches (as at Østerlars on the Danish island of Bornholm), before it soared in the high Gothic style of Chartres, Rheims, Cologne,

Freiburg and a multitude of other mainland cathedrals. 'Gothic', with all its overtones, is still one of the uniquely descriptive words that can be truly applied only to North-West Europe. 'Feudal', with all its undertones of vassalage and rigidly defined social classes, is a second adjective that adheres.

All of North-West Europe did not escape simultaneously from feudalism to freedom, or from a subsistence to a commercial economy. Yet specialisation became an early characteristic of production over most of the area—and intense local specialisation has become a distinguishing feature. This was both born of and gave birth to trade. In most of Europe, the names of places and areas became synonymous for products at an early stage. In North-West Europe, the name of the product is frequently better known than its place or area of origin—Limoges and Meissen, Gouda and Gruyère, Charollais and Friesian, Burgundy and Champagne.

Specialisation encouraged a proliferation of market towns and ports, at favourable points for exchange, and a functional differentiation between and within them. Many of the commercial settlements, with their crafts and infant industries, their burghers and burgesses, grew around the core of material and spiritual strongholds. Ports had their charters, markets their privileges, and they jealously guarded them. Commodity fairs strengthened their positions and trade routes focused upon them. Meanwhile, the towns of North-West Europe were woven into a fabric of administration that repeated itself in a complex of ephemeral principalities, duchies, margravates and provinces—the toponymical relics of which still survive. From the thirteenth century onwards, where stone was not available for construction, red brick and pantile (made from local clays) and cross timbering (from local hardwoods) were given a new importance. They have stood the test of time in some of the most pleasing domestic architecture of the Low Countries and North-West Germany, and some of the most formidable church façades, in Hanseatic cities such as Lübeck and Rostock. The rise of arts such as music, no less than of crafts, such as building, is closely connected with the growth of places of civic assembly.

While towns and political units grew and changed their shape and form, the country folk ploughed and plodded on. They were responsive to the rhythm of the seasons (as medieval monks recorded in their colourful Books of the Hours), and sensitive to the limitations of the soil. Field was added to field, intake to intake—first from the firm lands out of the forests, next from the peatlands out of the swamps, finally from the heathlands out of the sand. Each country had its own particular problems to overcome with the Dutch becoming the specialists on the wetlands, while the Saxons, with their experiences on the Lüneburgerheide, were exemplars on the drylands.

Layer upon layer of past tillage operations have left their marks in the fields of the present landscape from charcoal layers in the soils that tell of an earlier Brandwirtschaft, in balk and bank, wall and fence, ditch and dike, fragmented open field or diminutive enclosure—to hamper progressive farming or to prompt academic controversy. Associated custom and institution contribute to the richly differentiated landscapes of North-West Europe; while climate casts over them a richly varied seasonal mantle. The long and strong traditions have their lighter manifestations as well as their heavier complications: from the midsummer bonfires of Scandinavia, the burning of the Winter in Zürich, through the sauerkraut festivals of the Rhineland to the vendages of the French vineyards. Nowhere have the pastoral and the bucolic appealed more strongly to the imagination of the graphic artist than in North-West Europe, though patronage and purse have played a powerful rôle in attracting the centre of gravity of painting from the Mediterranean to the shores of the North Sea.

A Hearth of Enquiry and Invention

The people who have practised their urban crafts and rural arts in North-West Europe have been of a continuously restless disposition. Earlier geographers ascribed this restlessness to the stimulus of climatic instability. Restlessness has also been a response to long-period changes of climate, as with the Dark Age migrations of Goth and Hun from northern Europe to the gates of Rome. These overland movements were complemented at a later period by the overseas Viking movements—in purposeful settlement as well as purposeless plundering, for they colonised Iceland and Greenland and settled in Muscovy as well as sacking Lindisfarne. Sometimes, emigration has been an expression of revolt. For North-West Europe is a territory of revolt as well as of tradition. North-West Europe bred Luther and Calvin, Voltaire and Rousseau. 'Liberty, equality, fraternity' is a phrase that was born in North-West Europe and has had great consequences in human geography.

Restlessness is also expressed in curiosity. Curiosity has enticed explorers to the four corners of the earth and, when there were only the ice-caps to conquer, men like Nordenskiöld and Nansen set scientific siege to them. Curiosity, bred of observation, was disciplined in the natural world by men such as Linnaeus. Through their endeavours North-West Europe has been a forcing house of scientific enquiry. Not surprisingly, many of the tools of geography have been forged or refined here. Tools of measurement were invented or developed—the thermometers of Fahrenheit, Réaumur and Celsius; surveying instruments; the metric system. Cartographic projections, recalled by such names as Mercator and Mollweide, were conceived. National topographic map series were initiated, with Cassini in France as a progenitor, followed by Dufour and Siegfried in Switzerland, a country which has pioneered the intricate apparatus for plotting contours from air photographs. Scientific enquiry has been matched by the tradition of technical discovery. North-West Europe was the hearth of 'revolutions' in industry and transport. Steam power and the factory system in their modern form were nurtured here. And North-West Europe had abundant supplies of thermal energy which could be used to drive its machines. From France, through Belgium, into the Ruhr, along the Hercynian edge to Upper Silesia and in Bohemia lay the vital coal measures. The organisation and accumulation of capital in its contemporary sense belongs to the area. Until the financial centre of gravity crossed the Atlantic Ocean, it reposed somewhere on the north-west European seaboard, with Amsterdam a North Sea counterpart to Venice, and the Fuggers of Augsburg anticipating the Rothschilds of Vienna. The barons of industry and of a new feudalism, which were the complement of the capitalist order, gave rise to the revolutionary reaction of Engels and Marx, other offspring of North-Western Europe.

For the world, this third of a continent has been a hearth of invention and innovation—from garden and field crops, through domesticated stock, through the tremendous group of technical skills that have revolutionised motive power, industry and transport, to the 'light baggage' of ideas that has transformed society. North-West Europe, the most progressive part of Europe since the Reformation, could claim for several centuries to be the most progressive part of the world. Its peoples conquered with their merchant shipping and their money, on the rare occasions when their navies failed. Through restless energy and easy mobility, their inhabitants and their ideas came to occupy, control and, eventually, to transform many other lands a little into the likeness of themselves. In the process, the countries of North-West Europe have racked themselves in rivalry and sacked themselves in war. If they have taken much to themselves, they have given no less of themselves.

They remain of world stature. Together with the North-Eastern U.S.A., they are the world's greatest producing and consuming area. They continue to search for integration but traditional divisions regularly disrupt their efforts. The core of the 'Inner Six' or the Common Market Countries reposes in Benelux, West Germany and France; while the Scandinavian countries as well as Switzerland form powerful limbs of the 'Outer Seven' or European Free Trade Area. Of the twelve countries treated in this book, six have common membership of the N.A.T.O., three (Sweden, Finland and Switzerland) follow a policy of non-alignment, and one (East Germany) continues the European schismatic tradition.

A Home of Geography

The study of geography was not born in North-West Europe but it has matured here. The area has been a natural breeding ground for its practitioners. Atlas-makers such as Blaeu and Ortelius gave a new appreciation to maps. French naturalists, such as Guettard (with his observations on basalt and vulcanicity) and Cuvier (the fossil palaeontologist) gave a new meaning to rocks. In such as them and in the discourses of philosophers such as Kant, scientific geography took its roots. North-West Europeans also began to speculate upon physical phenomena and to conceive the rudiments of theories that are today's commonplaces—glaciologists such as de Geer in Sweden, meteorologists such as Bjørknes in Norway, geophysicists such as Wegener in Germany. A handful of geographers took the world as their province before the world became too much for a single geographer. Humboldt (1769–1859) gave his name to geographical features in the four corners of the earth. Through Ritter (1799–1859) with his general comparative geography *Erdkunde*, and Ratzel (1844–1904) with his *Anthropogeographie*, German geography attracted wide intellectual attention. Internationally renowned scientific societies, proliferating in the capitals and university cities of North-West Europe, actively encouraged geographical enquiry before specialist geographical societies were born. Paris led the way with the Geographical Society in 1821; Berlin followed in 1828. Against this background emerged the 'national schools' of geography that began to focus attention upon the detail of the homeland. They are illustrated in France by Gallois, proselytising the *pays* as the unit of study, Demangeon walking every lane in Picardy, Vidal de la Blache giving the lead in regional studies. National schools of geography began to conceive national atlases: the first was published in Finland in 1899.

It was natural that the method and vocabulary of geography should be enriched in such a milieu. Geographers in North-West Europe borrowed methods from political scientists and sociologists such as Le Play. North-West Europeans christened the systematic branches of geography with their own peculiar adjectives—Economic Geography, (attributed to Götz in Berlin in 1887), Physiography (to Cortambert in 1836). They conceived a variety of other terminology—from Humboldt's 'isotherm' (*c.* 1816) to Galton's 'anticyclone' (1863), and Haekel's 'Ecology' (1876). To North-West Europe belong certain type areas—the area of Jurassic rocks (from the Jura), Hercynian or Armorican (for the later Palaeozoic folded areas deriving their names from the Harz mountains and Brittany respectively). A host of words indigenous to the area have been woven into the fabric of geography—*plateau* from France, *polder* from the Netherlands, *fjord* from Norway, *ås* from Sweden, *hinterland* from Germany, *cirque* from Switzerland and *geysir* from Iceland. Not surprisingly, the rudiments of place-name study had their origins here, with leadership coming from Ekwall in the Swedish University of Lund.

Terra Matris

A knowledge of the countries that this book reviews is critical for British people as well as for the geographical understanding of the British Isles. The countries of North-West Europe remain the most important and influential part of Europe for Britain.

The human geography of these islands—from its prehistoric stirrings to its current political expressions—makes sense only by reference across the narrow seas. The British are, unavoidably, Europeans; but, all too often, they are reared on a theory of distinctiveness, as a result of which they look for the differences that divide rather than the likenesses that unite Britain and North-West Europe. Even geographers contrive to get along without reference to those who work on kindred themes across the Channel and the North Sea; nowhere are the consequences of this more unfortunate than in the approach of the British to the lands of their nearest neighbours. Yet their curiosity and inventiveness, their varied environments, their richness in *nuances*, their juxtaposition of past and present—all themes of this brief introduction—are one with those of the British Isles. The countries of North-West Europe, Britain's *terra matris*, merit the closest examination.

FURTHER READING   G. Chabot, *L'Europe du nord et du nord-ouest*, 1958.

V. Gordon Childe, *The dawn of European civilisation*, 1950.

R. J. Chorley, A. J. Dunn etc., *The history of the study of land forms*, Cambridge, 1964.

J. G. D. Clark, *Prehistoric Europe: the economic basis*, Cambridge, 1952.

R. E. Dickinson, *The West European City*, 1951.

T. W. Freeman, *A hundred years of geography*, 1961.

W. L. Thomas (ed.), *Man's rôle in changing the face of the earth*, Chicago, 1962.

The Physical Environment

Geology and Structure

The rocks of North-West Europe are representative of the entire geological column; almost every rock type is to be found in the area. Structurally, too, there is great diversity—ranging from the ancient shield region of Fenno-Scandinavia to the fold mountains of Alpine France and Switzerland and the regions of recent deposition such as the Netherlands and the Aquitaine Basin.

The oldest rocks are those of the Pre-Cambrian shield complex of Finland and the Scandinavian Peninsula. These were consolidated upwards of 600 million years ago and are chiefly hard metamorphosed strata. Most of the later rocks have been removed from that area by erosion but are present in pockets within the shield. South-eastwards the oldest rocks pass beneath younger strata. It is usual to regard this block as the primeval core of Europe against which later rocks and earth movements have been piled.

The geological record continues with the rocks of Palaeozoic age. In North-West Europe these are to be found in two principal groups of areas.

Fig 1   Major features of the Geology of North-West Europe

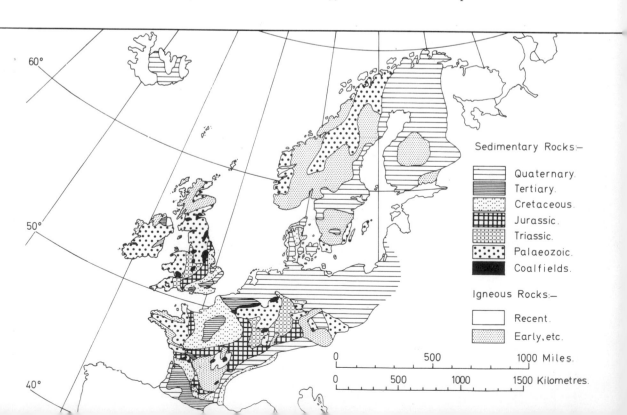

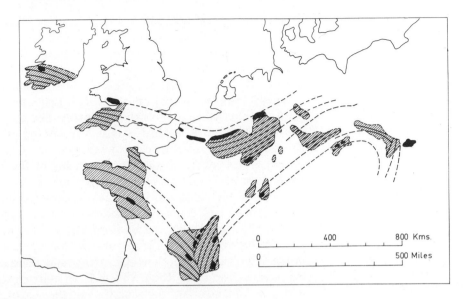

Fig 2   Hercynian lands and structural trends
(After S. W. Wooldridge and R. S. Morgan, *An Outline of Geomorphology*)

The older marine sediments of early Palaeozoic times (Cambrian to Ordovician) were involved in the folding and thrusting of the Caledonian orogeny. These rocks lie mainly in the extreme north-west, underlying much of the Norwegian section of the Scandinavian peninsula and with a structural 'grain' from south-west to north-east. Later Palaeozoic rocks were also affected by the Hercynian earth-movements and their surface extent is confined to a number of areas in western and central Europe. The largest single block is formed by the Ardennes–Rhenish Uplands; isolated areas of similar strata occur in France and Germany. Rocks of both earlier and later Palaeozoic age are chiefly consolidated resistant sediments but in some areas they have been metamorphosed, for example as aureoles surrounding igneous intrusions in the Central Massif. Sandstones, grits, quartzites, conglomerates and schists are typical of the older Palaeozoics. Limestones and marls do occur, in particular in the younger Carboniferous groups, and give rise to distinctive landforms. One such area lies on the south side of the Famenne depression, in the Ardennes.

The Hercynian or Armorican earth movements marked the close of the Palaeozoic period, some 280 million years ago, but the structural trends of the mountains then formed are still evident. Two major trend lines may be distinguished (Fig. 2)—one having an orientation from west towards south-east which characterises Brittany. It then swings to north-west to south-east in the Central Massif. The other trend is from south-west to north-east and this can be traced in certain parts of the Central Massif, the Vosges, the Black Forest, the Rhenish Uplands, and the Central Uplands or Mittelgebirge of Germany.

Of the many valuable raw materials contained within the earth's crust, probably those of the Coal Measures have been associated with the most extensive alterations to the natural landscape. The basins in which these deposits are found in Europe are associated with the borders of the 'Hercynian lands'; thus, the great series of coalfields stretching discontinuously from northern France through Belgium and the extreme south of the Netherlands to Western Germany lies on the northern flank of the Ardennes and Rhenish Uplands. Continuing eastwards, the Hanover, Zwickau and Dresden fields also lie north of the Hercynian uplands of central Germany. In France the coalfields of the Central Massif lie on the edge or within pockets of the Hercynian rocks.

Rocks of Mesozoic and later age are confined mainly to the basins of accumulation and deposition lying between the older blocks. Such areas include the Paris Basin, the Basin of Aquitaine, the North Sea Lowlands and the North German Plain. Jurassic and Cretaceous strata occur also in the scarplands of southern Germany, and there are extensive Tertiary deposits in the middle Rhine Valley. Even more closely associated with the Rhenish Uplands are such basins as the Cologne embayment, with Oligocene lignite beds reaching a thickness of 600 feet.

The main basins of North-West Europe have received deposits of either sea- or river-borne materials at intervals during and since the Jurassic period. Erosion has removed rocks to a greater or lesser extent; while various earth movements, in particular the outer ripples of the Alpine orogeny, have had some effect upon these areas. Thus have been sculptured the scarps and vales of the Paris and Aquitaine basins and of south Germany. Later deposits have been less affected by movements and the resulting landforms are those of terraces, plateaux and flat plains. Recent deposition is more typical of the lowlands of north Belgium, the Netherlands, Scandinavia and Germany. In these areas, rocks of the later Tertiary as well as the Quaternary (Pleistocene and Recent) tend to dominate the scene. In particular, areas of sands and gravels have given rise to the low plateau features of the Campine, the Veluwe, the Lüneburg Heath, and many others.

Rocks of both Palaeozoic and Mesozoic age were involved in the most recent mountain building episode affecting North-West Europe—that of the Alpine orogeny.

The Alpine area is structurally the most complex region in North-West Europe; in terms of relief it stands out from other areas but in area it is less than that of the Scandinavian mountains and possesses mountainous features compacted into a small region. However, these structures form part of a vital mountain system which crosses central Eurasia and represents the most recent mountain-building episode in geological history, little more than a million years ago.

The great accumulations of sediments dating from Mesozoic and early Tertiary times in the Tethys geosyncline were involved in the later Tertiary in a complex series of folding and thrusting movements. These were chiefly the result of pressure from the south squeezing the trough against the stable blocks to the north. The resulting landforms show considerable contortions, faulting and over-thrusting and the complex fold features known as *nappes* (Pl. 43). The mountains so produced were immediately subjected to strong erosive forces; it is noteworthy that the isolated northern mountains such as the Rigi, 5,747 feet (1,752m.) consist entirely of almost horizontal sediments derived from the mountains to the south. Late Tertiary deposits are known as *molasse* and, as well as characterising the foreland trough zone of the Swiss-Bavarian Plateau they are to be found in the tectonic depressions of the Rhine Rift Valley and the Rhône-Saone Valley.

Mountain-building episodes are frequently accompanied by volcanic activity. Characteristic landforms and igneous rocks marking such a phenomenon occur widely in North-West Europe. Iceland represents an entire island in which such activity is still in progress. Unmistakable evidence of earlier volcanism is provided by the *puys* of the Central Massif. Although this area may be classed as a Hercynian region, in which Palaeozoic strata predominate, the igneous intrusions are of much later date and are related to the Alpine orogeny. The Eifel, Rhön and Vogelsberg intrusions in the Central Uplands of Germany arc also comparatively recent geologically, post-dating the principal Alpine movements.

The Pleistocene period has left its mark on the face of North-West Europe in several different ways; it can be said to have made the most marked contribution to many present-day landforms. The Scandinavian ice-sheet at its maximum extent covered a large proportion of the North German Plain and the eastern Netherlands. By contrast, the ice cap of the Alps extended only as far as the Jura and the line of the Danube. Thus the Hercynian uplands and much of France lay outside the direct influence of the Pleistocene ice, except for local ice caps such as those of the Central Massif. Conditions of extreme cold were experienced by these regions but, more important, it was then that the *loess* or *limon* deposits of the French and Belgian plains were accumulated. The full diversity of the glacial epoch is well represented in the superficial rocks of the Netherlands, where ground moraine deposits are responsible for the sandy heathlands of the north-east; limon in the extra-glacial areas covering the higher terraces of the Rhine near Maastricht, and outwash gravels and pre-glacial materials folded by ice-pressure ('push-moraines') can be distinguished in the Veluwe. The record is simpler than in Scandinavia and north Germany since the Netherlands experienced the Scandinavian ice sheet only once, during the Riss glaciation. In the remaining areas of the North European Plain the onset of successive ice-sheets and their subsequent waning has resulted in such features as the *Urstromtäler* of Germany.

River deposits of recent times are important in the detailed geography of many areas. The distributaries of the Rhine, the river and sea clays of the Netherlands, together with the dunes of this and the North German coast, are the most extensive examples of the younger deposits in the geological column of North-West Europe.

SURFACE FEATURES   A three-fold classification of the configuration of North-West Europe is easily made: thus it is possible to distinguish between the high mountains and lowland plains, leaving a middle category of intermediate plateaux. In terms of altitude the mountains of the area rise to a maximum of 15,711 feet (4,807 m.) in the Alps, and to over 8,000 feet (2,640 m.) in Scandinavia. The highest parts of the Central Uplands do not generally much exceed 4,500 feet (1,380 m.), although the higher peaks of the Central Massif of France attain 6,000 feet (1,840 m.). The lowland areas, below 1,000 feet (300 m.), exhibit great variations. These are often very significant, and it is necessary to sub-divide the lowland areas carefully. Thus, the polder lands of Belgium and the Netherlands are below the 26 foot (8 m.) contour and may even be more than this amount below sea-level. The heathlands of southern Scandinavia and the North German Plain reach varying altitudes but it is only in the latter that heights of 600 feet (185 m.) are exceeded over large tracts of country.

The surface configuration of North-West Europe causes serious obstacles to movement in only a few areas. The alignment of the high mountains is twofold; the south-west to north-east line of the Scandinavian mountains and the broadly west-east axis of the Alps. On morphological grounds it is only the Alps that can be grouped as mountains of high relief—the remainder of the area consisting of plateaux and plains.

Very little of North-West Europe is occupied by flat plains. The principal lowland areas are better regarded as glacially roughened plains (southern Sweden, Finland, the Netherlands and parts of north Germany). The western Netherlands fall into a category of lake-and-marsh plains, and so, too, do sections of the North German Baltic coastlands.

The erosional history of most of this area has resulted in much of the land surface being broken into various plateaux sections. These units in some cases show considerable relief and many have been tilted. The Fenno-Scandian shield is, perhaps, the best example of this. Nevertheless, in many parts of the Hercynian massifs, comparatively uniform crest-lines and upland plains at various altitudes demonstrate planation by denudational processes. In the areas of younger rocks—the basins and plains of North-West Europe, the landscape reflects the erosional history in a series of scarps and vales. Thus clays of the Mesozoic and Tertiary periods underlie the Flanders Plain, and limestones of Jurassic and Cretaceous age form the scarps of Lorraine, Swabia and Franconia.

Drainage   Almost the entire area of North-West Europe drains westwards to the Atlantic either directly or via the English Channel, North Sea or Baltic; however, southern Bavaria and Württemberg in south Germany are drained by a series of streams flowing to the Danube, while the Rhône-Saône basin flows into the Mediterranean.

A number of different catchment basins can be distinguished. Some, such as the Paris Basin, the Netherlands and western Germany, have important trunk streams into which most other rivers empty. Elsewhere, as in eastern Sweden, the pattern is of many parallel rivers flowing directly to the sea. An entirely different pattern, unique to the area and the result of glaciation, is presented by Finland with its indeterminate pattern of innumerable lakes which cover nearly 20% of its total area. Iceland's drainage is radial.

It is clear from topographic maps of this area that the pattern of the drainage is the product of a complex history. This pattern has emerged as a result of many interruptions to the erosion cycle. Thus the Rhine basin owes its present extent to a fusion during Miocene and later geological periods of originally separate rivers.

An important feature of the drainage of much of the area is the fact that many of the rivers may be classed as 'major' streams. The Rhine is the longest with a length of about 700 miles (1130 km.). It is not alone, however, as the trunk streams in the basins shown on Fig. 3 may also be called major rivers. This is indicated by the extent to which these rivers are used for inland transport and the carriage of bulk goods.

The lake and marsh plains of the Netherlands present a special feature in the drainage pattern of North-West Europe, necessitating a dense network of drainage channels.

Fig 3   Drainage Basins of North-West Europe

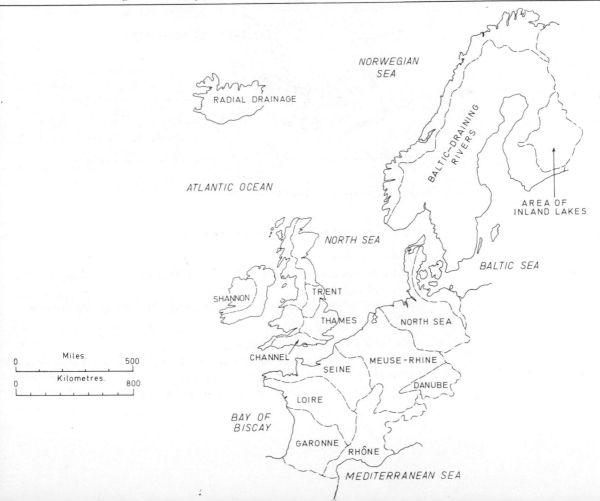

Physical Regions of North-West Europe

The foregoing summary description of the geology, surface features and drainage of North-West Europe leads to a broad regional sub-division as shown in Figure 4.

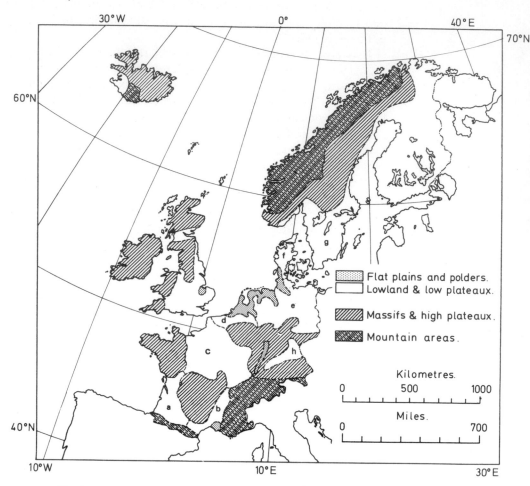

Fig 4   Physical Regions of North-West Europe

In descending order of relief forms these are:

I.   The mountain regions:
Alpine mountain areas. e.g. The young fold mountain chains of the Alps and Pyrenees.
Scandinavian mountains. The remnants of the Caledonian structures in Norway.

II.   The massifs and high plateaux:
The Hercynian blocks of Brittany, the Central Massif, the Rhenish Uplands, the Vosges—Black Forest massif.
The Pre-Cambrian shield of Fenno-Scandinavia.

III. The lowlands: These are probably best sub-divided into areas broadly determined by dominant drainage patterns, as follows:

1. The flat plains and polders of the Netherlands and north-west Germany.

2. The lowlands and low plateaux of:
   (a) The Aquitaine Basin.
   (b) The Rhône Basin and Languedoc.
   (c) The Paris Basin.
   (d) The uplands of northern France and middle Belgium.
   (e) The North German Plain.
   (f) The Jutland Peninsula and Danish islands.
   (g) Southern Scandinavia.
   (h) The South German Scarplands.
   (i) The Alpine Foreland.

Climate The North-West European climate is a type referred to in many simple climate divisions of the earth. The area designated North-West Europe in this book embraces a succession of climatic regions of which only one can be strictly called 'North West European'. The area stretches from the shores of the Arctic Ocean, north of latitude 71°N, to the shores of the Mediterranean Sea at latitudes 43°N. Similarly, the area extends from the exposed coasts of western France for a distance of nearly 1,000 miles (1,600 km) to the frontiers of eastern Germany. Nevertheless, this is only the western part of the great longitudinal extent of the land mass of Eurasia. No part of the region is more than 300 miles (4,800 km) from any coastline. It is therefore true to say that most of North-West Europe experiences a climate which has at least some maritime influence.

However, as Europe extends into the great landmass of Eurasia the continental influence is ever present and so liable to affect weather patterns at any time. There is also a zone of transition between the areas of Europe under maritime and under continental influence. The factors which largely control the climate of North-West Europe are shown in Figure 5. Here are indicated the generalized pressure distribution and air masses, the interaction of which latter produce the day-to-day weather of the region.

The source regions of the air masses are five in number. These masses are summarised in tabular form below:

	Air Mass	*Source Region*	*Characteristics*
A	Arctic	Arctic Sea	Very cold
mP	Polar maritime	North Atlantic	Cold, wet
cP	Polar continental	Siberia	Cold, dry (winter)
			Warm, dry (summer)
mT	Tropical maritime	Central Atlantic	Warm, wet
cT	Tropical continental	Asia Minor, Africa	Warm, dry

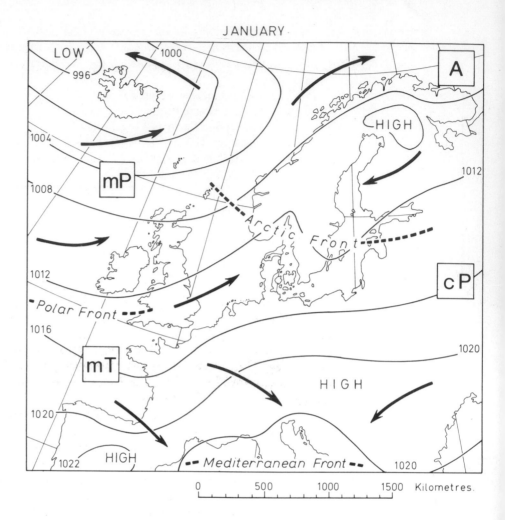

The frontal zones which separate these air masses are of prime significance in the daily weather pattern of North-West Europe. Two such
frontal systems are especially notable; the Arctic front which marks the
southern boundary of the Arctic air mass and the Polar front which lies
between the Polar and Tropical air masses. This generally lies in a west-
south-west/east-north-east direction over the Low Countries and
Scandinavia. It swings north of this in summer, and in winter may be
further south, even extending into the Mediterranean. The Arctic front
generally affects only the northern regions of Scandinavia in winter.
Exceptionally, it may move south into central Germany and be associated
there with severe wintry conditions.

It is along the Polar front that the cyclones or depressions form which
dominate much of the weather pattern of the area. These, moving in a
general west-east direction, usually involve maritime air masses, Polar
and Tropical. The rainfall of North-West Europe is thus chiefly cyclonic

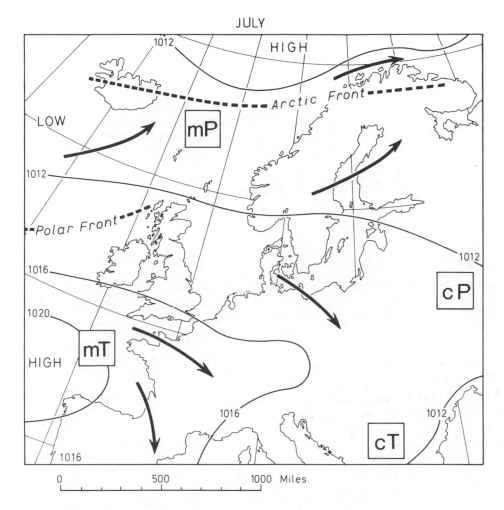

Fig 5 Air Masses and Frontal Patterns. Arrows show generalized circulation.

in type. In addition there is an orographic effect and any map of annual precipitation shows this quite clearly.

In view of the latitudinal spread of the area, a great range in temperature between the extreme north and south might be expected. This is to a considerable extent mitigated by the Atlantic influence so that only in central Sweden and Finland are severe winter conditions experienced. Similarly, the moderating influence of the Mediterranean itself results in the south of France having summer temperatures that are not excessively hot, e.g. Marseilles July mean temperature 22·2°C (72°F). The range in temperatures between winter and summer conditions shows a marked increase across North-west Europe away from the maritime influence; the most 'continental' areas being eastern Germany and Finland.

C

North-West Europe may be divided into major climatic regions on the basis of temperature patterns and rainfall regimes. These regions are shown in Figure 6 and are as follows:

a   The West Coast Marine region
b   The transitional Central region
c   The Continental eastern region
d   The Tundra region
e   The region of Mediterranean climate
f   The Mountain climate region

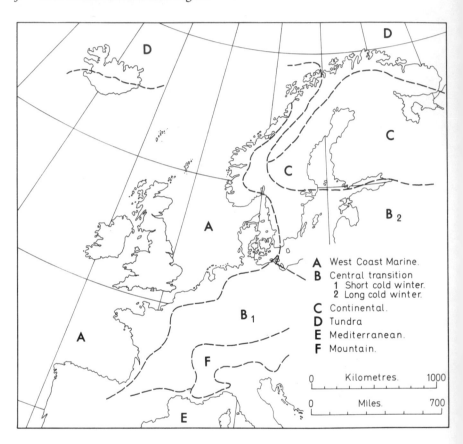

Fig 6   Climatic Regions

The lines between these regions are in many cases extremely arbitrary; transition zones may be distinguished between all climatic regions in North-West Europe and the diagnostic factors only become clear in the core of the region. Probably the clearest and most well-defined region is that of the Mediterranean climate, with its virtual absence of rainfall during the summer period. The principal characteristics of these climatic types must now be briefly summarised:

a   The West Coast Marine areas are the areas dominated by the Atlantic maritime influence. Rainfall is evenly distributed throughout the year, cloud cover is seldom broken for long periods and relative humidity is generally high. Temperatures show a low annual range although there is a tendency for an autumnal maximum. Because of the great spread of this region, from the Biscay area to the northern shores of Scandinavia, it is sometimes necessary to make sub-divisions on the basis of temperature patterns. Thus the Norwegian coast, exemplified by figures for Bergen, shows a range of 13·3°C (24°F.) from 1·1°C. (34°F.) in January to 14°·4°C. (58°F.) in July whilst Brest has a range of 11·1°C. (20°F.) with figure of 7·2°C. (45°F.) and 18·3°C. (65°F.) for January and July respectively.

b   The Transitional central region can be divided into two sub-regions based on the characteristics of the winter. Thus in the north, the transitional area between maritime and continental conditions is marked by a long cold winter, whilst the winters of areas to the south-west are comparatively short, albeit cold. Stockholm's figures indicate nearly five months with a mean temperature below freezing whereas Berlin has only one such month. Rainfall amounts are generally between 25 and 30 inches per annum; the northern areas having a marked dry winter season with no part of southern Sweden, for example, receiving more than 10 inches during the winter half of the year.

c   The truly continental conditions of Finland and central and northern Sweden are in fact more nearly sub-Polar. Temperatures in winter are severely cold, descending well below freezing point. Rainfall is low and the 20-inch mean annual isohyet crosses this area.

d   Tundra conditions are experienced in upland areas of central and northern Scandinavia and near the shores of the Arctic Ocean. Winter conditions and rainfall are similar to those of the last region but the main difference lies in the coolness of the summers; this region includes the area of permafrost conditions.

e   The region of Mediterranean climatic conditions is a clearly-defined one with the well-known characteristics of sub-tropical temperatures and a marked summer drought. The section of southern France that falls within this division does, however, receive some summer rainfall, chiefly of a thundery nature, and the figures for Marseilles are 0·7 and 0·8 inches for July and August respectively.

f   The region of central Europe which is separately distinguished as having a mountain climate is characterised by a high total annual precipitation comparable to the wetter areas of the West Coast Marine region. There is a marked summer rainfall maximum but precipitation is adequate throughout the year. Temperature characteristics are very variable in this region since this is a region of contrasts of relief and sites. Climatic features, of cold winters and snowfall in particular, are responsible for the rôle of many parts of this region as tourist areas for winter sports.

VEGETATION
AND SOILS

The natural vegetation of much of North-West Europe cannot be properly described as so much of the area has been altered by man's activities. It is possible to ascribe general vegetation zones to the area, and it is also possible to recognise areas where the vegetation is still 'natural'; areas which, for some reason, are of little economic value to man.

The zones of natural vegetation which cross Europe in a west-east direction are four in number: the zone of tundra vegetation, the coniferous forest belt, the deciduous forest belt and the region of Mediterranean scrub vegetation. Within the last three zones little natural vegetation remains, although there are considerable stretches of *maquis* scrub in Mediterranean France. Elsewhere the chief areas of natural vegetation are found in one of two localities—the upland heaths and the coastal margins.

The North Sea and Baltic coastlines provide many areas of dune and marsh which support a natural vegetation of a special nature. The chief distinction is between those parts which support fresh-water plants and those which allow only salt-tolerant plants. The heathlands of North-West Europe, whose vegetation is natural, occur at different altitudes. Firstly, there are the dune heathlands of the coastlands such as those of the Netherlands, Frisian Islands, etc. The second group of heathlands is found on the sands and gravels of the glacial outwash materials of the North European Plain; these are being reduced in total area by reclamation processes. Finally, there are the upland heaths of the Hercynian massifs. These are generally at altitudes in excess of 2,000 feet (610 m.) and their vegetation is the result of a combination of altitude, exposure and soil conditions. The total area of these heaths is also being reduced by the reclamation of peat bogs and the planting of conifers.

The arrangement of vegetation in zones or belts occurs as a result of increasing severity of winter weather conditions; as well as being a feature from south to north across Europe, it is also produced by increasing altitude in mountain areas. The pattern of vegetation zones in the Alps and Pyrenees begins on the lower slopes with mixed forests in which beech and spruce are dominant. This is succeeded, at about 2,000 feet (610 m.), by a markedly more coniferous association, with pine and larch; the tree line, or upper limit of tree growth, occurs at between 5,000 and 6,000 feet above sea-level (1,500 to 1,800 m.) in these areas and above this a scrub vegetation with grasses and shrubs is to be found. Finally, on the higher summits, a tundra vegetation gives way to bare rocks and to snow or ice. The tree line descends in altitude northwards until it reaches sea-level on the shores of the Arctic Ocean. In Alpine areas the natural vegetation above the tree line is often known as Alpine meadow and includes grasses and low flowering plants; ecologically similar summer-flowering plants are typical of the 'fjell' of the Scandinavian highlands. True tundra conditions with lichen and mosses are only revealed when the last of the winter snow has melted.

The detailed soil map of North-West Europe (Fig. 7) is a complex document, but it is possible to recognise four major categories. These are

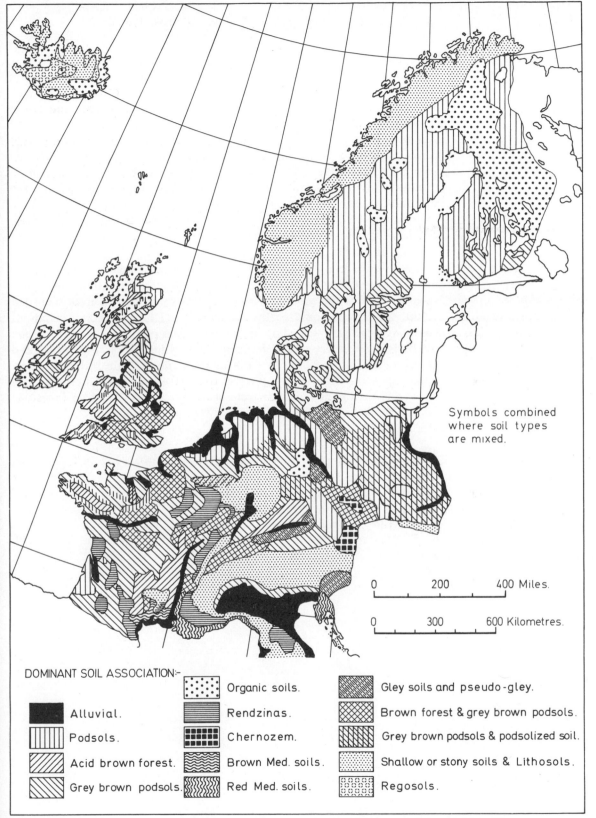

Symbols combined where soil types are mixed.

0   200   400 Miles.

0   300   600 Kilometres.

DOMINANT SOIL ASSOCIATION:-

Organic soils.

Gley soils and pseudo-gley.

Alluvial.

Rendzinas.

Brown forest & grey brown podsols.

Podsols.

Chernozem.

Grey brown podsols & podsolized soil.

Acid brown forest.

Brown Med. soils.

Shallow or stony soils & Lithosols.

Grey brown podsols.

Red Med. soils.

Regosols.

Fig 7   Soil map of North-West Europe
(Based on 'Soil Map of
Europe' at 1/2,500,000, F.A.O., 1966)

the alluvial, podsols, brown earths and Mediterranean soils. This leaves the smaller groups developed in the mountain and tundra areas. The podsols may be sub-divided into a number of different groups, depending on such features as the degree of leaching, the parent material, etc., and also a number of intermediate types occur within the brown earths.

The soil groups also occur in a series of zones extending west-east across the area, with the zone of tundra soils in the extreme north. Podsols, with a higher degree of leaching, are found on the moister and more exposed regions of Scandinavia, Denmark and the Low Countries, but the higher regions have mountain soils. The brown earths are particularly important in a zone from central France across southern and central Germany. Between these two zones the chief soil type is a podsol with only slight leaching.

There are a number of distinctive and locally important soil groups, in which the character of the parent rock plays an important rôle. Soils such as those of the sea-marsh and reclaimed polderlands form one such group. Moor soils, only partly podsolised, of the glacial heathlands of Germany, form another. The higher limestone plateaux of, for example, the Paris Basin, carry typical rendzina soils, while heavy alluvial clay and gravel soils floor the broad valleys of the central Rhine, Rhône, Loire, lower Seine and other rivers. West of the Saale river in the Leipzig-Halle embayment is a region of chernozem or black-earth soils and the limestone hills of Mediterranean France frequently carry terra rossa soils.

FURTHER READING   R. Brinkmann, *Geologic Evolution of Europe* (translated from German by J. E. Sanders), New York, 1960.

A. Holmes, *Principles of Physical Geology*, 2nd ed., 1960.

W. G. Kendrew, *The Climates of the Continents*, 5th. ed., 1961.

A. A. Miller, *Climatology*, 9th. ed., 1953.

S. W. Wooldridge and R. S. Morgan, *An Outline of Geomorphology*, 1959.

The Population of North-West Europe

North-West Europe contains one of the world's greatest concentrations of population. The population of the countries included in this survey totals 165 millions. It is not much less than the population of the U.S.A. The distribution of this population is very uneven. In Belgium and Iceland respectively, North-West Europe contains the most populous and the least populous state in the continent. Belgium is, in addition, one of the most densely peopled states in the world, with 798 inhabitants per square mile (30·7 per sq. km.). North-West Europe also includes the most extensive area of high population density in the Old World. By contrast, Iceland and northern Scandinavia offer contrastingly extensive areas with little or no population.

The countries of North-West Europe also include old-established population concentrations. An urban civilisation had been established in the Netherlands by the fifteenth century when, for example, it is estimated that one-third of the population of Brabant lived in towns. But the great contrasts in population density emerged in much more recent historical times. They sprang principally from the age of intensified technical change in agriculture, industry and transport associated with the nineteenth century. The new provisions for improved nutrition and health which accompanied these helped to sustain if not to generate the 'population explosion' associated with Europe, and especially with North-West Europe at that time.

The technical changes promoted the development of marked variations in population distribution within the countries of North-West Europe as well as between them. Originally for reasons of resource distribution and subsequently for reasons of inertia and capital investment, some of the greatest population concentrations in the temperate world have evolved within a few dozen miles of thinly peopled and almost empty country. This is especially true of the coalfield settlements of West Germany and adjacent Belgium. Reasons of political geography have hitherto prevented the emergence of any continuous settlement feature comparable to what Jean Gottman has called *Megalopolis* on the eastern seaboard of the U.S.A.; though the Ruhr bids fair to become one.

The emergence of North-West Europe's present pattern of population distribution implies that its peoples have been much on the move. Movement has been prompted at different times and in different places by political, economic and social forces. Political forces have played an important rôle in the past because of the ethnography of the peoples of

North-West Europe and the distribution of political boundaries. Indeed, by comparison with the U.S.A., population mobility in north-western Europe has been far less because of the intercepting boundaries. In all of the countries of North-West Europe, rural-urban migrations have been impressive. They reached their climax in Germany, France and Belgium before they affected the more marginal parts of the continent. The time lag in the Scandinavian countries is such that Sweden and Norway have only just passed through it and the process is still active in Finland. The drift from the land, hitherto accounted by north-west Europeans as an undesirable feature, is now more generally regarded as a positive means of adjustment between an overpopulated countryside and industrial and servicing concentrations.

There is a long tradition of population movement between the countries of the mainland of North-West Europe and lands beyond the seas. The prehistoric and Dark Age settlement waves to the offshore islands were succeeded in historic times by the movement to the temperate open spaces. The great waves to these overseas lands which reached their climax in the early years of the twentieth century have ceased. They have been subject to restriction by immigrant quotas imposed in particular by the U.S.A. For north-west Europeans emigration has become a much more selective process. The movement is more narrowly restricted to skilled workers and trained technical staff. The so-called 'brain drain' from North-West Europe's mainland is numerically as great as that from Britain.

Migration between the countries of North-West Europe and into them has been greater in recent years than formerly. France has always re-cruited population from Italy and from its former colonial territories across the Mediterranean. The break-up of overseas empires has also prompted a retreat to the motherland. The Netherlands has witnessed a substantial return stream of population from its former possessions in south-east Asia. The war years, in particular, resulted in immense migra-tions. West Germany received 9·7 millions from its lost territories in the east: East Germany received 2·8 millions. The rehabilitation of these refugees caused major population changes in West Germany after the Second World War. At the same time, more than 420,000 displaced people left Finland's ceded territories to be resettled in the remaining nine-tenths of the country. Sweden has received tens of thousands from the former Baltic states of Estonia, Latvia and Lithuania. Migration within North-West Europe has been eased in recent years by the emergence of regional economic blocs such as the European Common Market. The five Scandinavian countries have a common labour market. Here, migration has been especially pronounced into Sweden. The geography of the migratory millions who constitute the great seasonal currents of tourists remains to be written.

Population concentration and population mobility in North-West Europe, as in the continent at large, is inseparable from ethnographic diversity. The peoples of North-West Europe are marked by their heterogeneity. The fact of this heterogeneity has frequently been less important in the history of Europe's peoples than the interpretation of the fact. Until the 1930's, many school atlases used to include ethnographic maps of Europe. Such maps are now largely omitted from atlases, because they tend to degenerate into linguistic maps, the frontier zones of which are in any case largely a matter of conjecture. Cartographic representation of ethnographic data assumed an especially volatile character in the 1930's, when a number of European countries employed them for political and emotive purposes.

Ethnographic issues are not easy to treat scientifically and objectively, because they are so much the stuff of which nations are made. The population of Europe remains acutely sensitive to nationality. Irredentisms, which have been among Europe's most common causes of war, have not been eliminated from north-western Europe although their significance may have been reduced in international perspectives. Inside the countries of North-West Europe, domestic tensions are still stirred by ethnographic issues. Belgium provides an illustration of a state where Flemish-speaking and French-speaking groups stand in pronounced antithesis. The language issue remains an underlying feature in Finnish domestic politics, though the Swedish language is yielding in many areas to the Finnish. The peoples of North-West Europe have hitherto been racked by religious differences and the European boundary between the areas dominated by the Catholic and the Protestant faith passes through the heart of the area. The historic tensions which gave rise to so much disturbance in the Netherlands are still alive.

Because of these intra-European tensions, there has been a sensitiveness to national rates of population growth and development. Partly for this reason, the study of population among the nations of North-West Europe has long been an object in itself. Modern censuses were initiated in Sweden —a country anxious to assess its manpower in the face of eighteenth century Russian pressure on its eastern flank. Counting heads became a significant administrative exercise in Napoleonic France. Juxtaposing population growth and food supply, Thomas Malthus depressed Europe with his theories of eventual starvation, so that political economy became even more entrenched as a 'dismal science'. The graphical representation of population data was initiated in North-West Europe and the first modern population maps were published in Sweden by Sten de Geer during the First World War.

The age of *laissez-faire* was scarcely conducive to family planning; but the loss of life in the First World War and the uncertainties of the inter-war years led to a variety of population policies in the states of North-West Europe. The blood-letting suffered by France had pronounced effects on the subsequent generation of population development in France. Apprehension about population decline was a marked feature in north-western Europe in the 1930's. A programme of active population expansion was initiated by the Fascist regime in Germany. Elsewhere, less direct methods were employed; but family allowances and other artificial

c*

inducements to encourage an increase in births characterised most countries of Western Europe, especially France. Population trends can be partly modified by political measures, though there is something in the spirit of the age which operates independently of legislation.

Urban Development

There is almost no record of town development in western Europe before the arrival of the Romans; though the Celtic inhabitants of France and the North Sea coastlands had produced a considerable culture, it was not an urban one. Urban life was therefore an importation from the Mediterranean, where it had existed for some thousand years, having been brought in turn from Mesopotamia and Egypt. As the Roman advance into North-West Europe was halted, at circa A.D. 100, along a diagonal line running from Regensburg on the Danube north-west to Koblenz on the Rhine, and thence down the Rhine to its mouth, the earliest urban tradition is restricted to the areas south and west of this line: south-western Germany including the upper Rhine Valley, the lower German Rhinelands, the southern part of the Low Countries, and France. Here the Romans soon established a well-defined hierarchy of towns, linked by routeways, for various purposes of an administrative and defensive nature: military garrisons, colonies of veterans, administrative capitals. The subsequent fate of these towns has been very varied. Though some have decayed completely and some have lapsed into relative obscurity as small market towns, many have survived to become major cities of modern Europe: they include Bordeaux, Lyons, Paris (where a pre-urban, pre-Roman settlement had existed), Cologne, Mainz, and Augsburg.

Most of these successful Roman foundations illustrate a critical point about city development in Europe, which was underlined in later centuries. Towns might often be founded in the first instance purely for defensive or administrative purposes. That would demand that they were located either at strategic defensive positions on lines of movement, or at easily accessible points where a province or region could easily be governed. But once the town was established, almost inevitably there would be a growth of trade and thence of industry. The very facts that had governed the location of the town—its relationship to corridors of movement, its situation at a critical crossing-point of a river, its central location in a lowland basin—made it the natural centre of trading movements.

This was already evident in Roman times; the larger cities, like Cologne or Paris, were already emporia and centres of handicraft industry. After the Romans evacuated north-western Europe in the fifth century, for a time trade and industry almost disappeared. The centuries that followed, the Dark Ages, were a period of 'an economy without markets', in the words of the economic historian Henri Pirenne. The economy of western Europe relapsed to a self-sufficient agrarian basis, with each village supplying its own needs. Some of the towns of western Europe were almost certainly depopulated when the Romans left; in others, a few people lived on, using the town as an agricultural village.

Slowly, the need for an urban form of organisation developed again. In point of time, the first bases for town development were the ones that had obtained in Roman times: the defensive and political. As western Europe emerged from political chaos, and as larger and better-formed political units developed in the eighth and ninth centuries, fortified places were developed both for defence and for the administration of the surrounding territory; at the same time, the increasing influence of the Roman Catholic church demanded a scheme of territorial administration. The expression of all this on the ground was a series of small and heavily-fortified settlements, based on a fortress (Lille, Münster, Hanover), on a king's or a prince's palace (Blois, Frankfurt-on-Main), or on a cathedral (Laon, Chartres, Beaune, Osnabrück). Such places sprang up all over Europe between A.D. 700 and A.D. 850, that is just before the coronation of Charlemagne as first Holy Roman Emperor and then during the period of his reign. They were not towns as we would know them, rather the nucleus or embryo of towns. They were given a name which is common to all western European languages: borough or burgh in Britain, bourg in France, burg in Germany, borg in Sweden; a fortified place.

For a short time their functions remained restricted, for in the still unsettled conditions of the time trade was limited. Then, in the tenth century, more stable conditions appeared. In the northern seas, the Norsemen turned from piracy to settlement and even to trade. In the Mediterranean, a campaign began against the Moors which was eventually to clear the southern trade routes from their threat. Trade blossomed, especially along the overland route between the great inland seas of Europe where seaborne commerce became concentrated: from the North Sea lands of Flanders and from the Paris Basin, this trade led either down the Rhône Valley to Marseilles, or via the Rhine and south Germany through the Alpine passes to the Mediterranean ports of north Italy. The earliest great cities of medieval Europe reflect this concentration of activity. Many of them, Paris, Lyons, Marseilles, Cologne, Mainz, were built on Roman foundations. Others, especially in Germany—Essen, Frankfurt, Stuttgart, Nuremberg, Munich—were new foundations of the Middle Ages, developed round fortified nuclei which were established either by Charles the Great or by the host of small territorial princedoms which followed the gradual disintegration of his empire. In the later Middle Ages, between the eleventh and thirteenth centuries, the same process followed in the northern lands. Great trading cities like Stockholm, Copenhagen and Oslo were creations of this time. They reflected the growing importance of the trade between the primary producing countries of northern and eastern Europe, via the Baltic Sea, and the more developed countries such as England, the Low Countries, northern France and north-west Germany.

Though medieval cities were in most cases established first for defensive and administrative reasons, their later fortunes depended largely upon the strength of their trading links. The great cities were invariably either seaports (Hamburg, Bremen, Lübeck, Bruges, Antwerp and later Amsterdam, Rouen, Marseilles) or inland transport nodes where routes met (Cologne, Frankfurt, Hanover, Munich). Because of the general difficulty and slowness of inland transportation in medieval Europe, inland waterways were, if anything, even more important, relatively, than they are today. Consequently, many of the major cities were found at bridging points of rivers, which were used for navigation then even if they may not be so used today. Here overland routes, often following tributary river valleys, would gather at the bridging point, which might also be the head of navigation, and transhipment would take place. Here too industry would naturally coalesce. The guiding principle for medieval industry was that transportation costs, both for raw materials and finished products, were high. Therefore the early stages of production (sawing of timber, smelting of iron and other metals) would normally take place near the source of the raw material; the later stages of production were strongly oriented towards local markets, pools of skilled labour and transport facilities, and so they naturally concentrated in the major trading cities.

Medieval Europe of course had many towns which were far from major trading centres. The later Middle Ages in particular saw a very widespread growth of very small market towns set in the midst of the agrarian countryside. As agriculture slowly became more productive, the more fertile areas in particular found that they could produce a surplus for sale, using the proceeds to buy manufactured town goods. The natural result was the small market town, acting as a local market for agricultural produce and supplying the basic local needs of the farm population for a limited range of manufactured goods. More sophisticated demands, which were limited, would be met by bigger market towns set at greater intervals apart; and so a hierarchy of towns developed. But it was observable that the bigger towns in this hierarchy were dependent, in greater or lesser measure, on interregional and even international trading exchanges too; the local market function, even if it served a large and populous region, was not enough to explain the importance of these major centres.

The pattern of town development which resulted from this period, between the eighth and the fourteenth centuries, has proved decisive for western Europe. To a remarkable degree the hierarchy of towns then established, their location and spacing and relative importance, has remained in later centuries, relatively uninfluenced by forces like the industrial and transportation revolutions of the age since 1800. To the British student, who is accustomed to the phenomenon of towns which mushroomed in the Industrial Revolution, this may seem very anomalous. But although these towns are a significant element in the urban geography of Britain, it must be remembered that outside the coalfields, in south-eastern and south-western England and in East Anglia, the older medieval market towns still represent the dominant element in the modern urban pattern, and that furthermore the relative ordering of these towns has often changed little since the Middle Ages.

In Britain the anomalous feature is the phenomenon of the coalfield towns. In continental western Europe this phenomenon is relatively less important, for two reasons. In the first place, there are only two major bituminous coalfields in western Europe which can rank with the major British fields: they are the Franco-Belgian field and the Ruhr coalfield of Germany. Here, towns and industrial villages mushroomed during the nineteenth century just as in their English equivalents. Secondly, and most importantly, the industrial revolution came much later to most of continental western Europe than to Britain. The railways were already established, and this fact made it easier to carry heavy industrial raw materials away from the coalfields to the existing towns. Railways in continental Europe were sometimes built by the state (as in parts of Germany), sometimes by private enterprise in accordance with a national plan (as in France), sometimes by small private enterprise groups financed by merchant capital which had accumulated in the cities (as in parts of Germany). In any event, the general policy was to build railways to connect existing major cities, so that the new rail pattern tended to reproduce the older pattern of road and water routes. The natural effect then was to concentrate the rapid industrial growth, which followed the exploitation of the coal and the building of the railways, into the existing urban centres. Here a variety of raw materials could be readily assembled, here distribution to national and international markets was easiest, here surplus labour from the countryside naturally migrated to form the biggest labour pools. So the great ancient trading cities of medieval Europe, often after centuries of relative stagnation since the end of the Middle Ages, suddenly became modern centres of industry; within a few decades from 1850 to 1914 their populations might swell two, three or four times.

Up to 1914, and even to a large degree up to 1939, this urban growth took a form very different from that observable in most British cities. In continental western Europe as in Britain, it is true that the advent of modern urban transportation methods allowed cities to spread somewhat outside a walking radius from the town centre, within which they had been confined for centuries. Particularly important here was the electric tram, which appeared around 1900 and which has remained a dominant form of transport in many continental cities, retaining its own against the competition of the motor bus as in Britain it failed to do.

Yet even when outward expansion was feasible, the characteristic form of growth was the high density, specially-constructed apartment block rather than the single family house which was typical of even the poorer English urban areas. Up to the outbreak of the Second World War, therefore, most continental cities were contained within a much smaller area than their English counterparts. (Scottish cities are closer to continental than to English examples in this respect.) Despite extensive war damage and reconstruction at lower densities in the inner areas of many cities (especially in Germany and the Low Countries), and despite the growth of single family suburbs on the English and American models in the post-war period, the differences may still be striking. The average density of population in the municipality of Paris for instance is nearly three times that of its nearest English equivalent, Inner London.

Despite this, the populations of several urban areas of Europe have swollen to such a size that serious problems of regional planning result. The conglomeration of cities at the entrance of the Rhine into the North European Plain, extending into the Ruhr coalfield, includes over 10 million people in an area measuring forty miles from north to south and fifty from east to west; the Paris region, which added over a million to its population between 1954 and 1962, numbered nearly nine million in the mid-1960s, while the highly urbanised region of the western Netherlands, known as the *Randstad* (Ring City) *Holland*, numbered 4·3 million. The continued growth of such areas is all the more striking when it is compared with the relative stagnation or decline of such peripheral regional areas as the eastern borderlands of the German Federal Republic, the Massif Central or Brittany in France, or the provinces of Groningen and Friesland in north-east Netherlands. Despite vigorous attempts to steer more growth into these areas and, in the case of France, to limit the growth of the metropolitan region, this remains a problem as puzzling and as difficult for most continental European nations as it is for Britain.

FURTHER READING   R. E. Dickinson, *The West European City*, 1951.
R. E. Dickinson, *City and Region*, 1964.
Peter Hall, *The World Cities*, 1966.
William Petersen, *Population*, 1961.
Alfred Sauvy, *Fertility and Survival*, 1961.

Economic Development

AGRICULTURE
AND FORESTRY

Agriculture in North-West Europe is an important economic activity and the lands of North-West Europe are the highest-yielding, per unit area, of any region in the world. Most of Europe is well sited for varied agricultural activities—both as regards relief and climate. With the exception of the more exposed and colder northern lands, and the higher parts of France and Switzerland, some agricultural pursuit is possible everywhere in the area. In very few parts of North-West Europe are rainfall amounts dangerously low for agriculture. A little over one-third of the area is classified as agricultural land and much of the remainder is in productive forest.

Some nine different crop belts may be recognised in North-West Europe, and these are shown on Figure 8. The five main cereals (wheat, maize, rye, barley and oats) are cultivated but mixed livestock farming is also practised in all regions. Extensive areas of grassland occur in the Central Massif, Normandy and eastern France, the Low Countries and Scandinavia: yet only 10% of Denmark's agricultural land is under permanent grass; 40% is occupied by coarse grains.

A number of significant concentrations of agricultural activity may be noted in North-West Europe; Germany, north of the Central Uplands, possesses a unique area in which potatoes are a significant crop. The northern limit of the vine is indicated on Figure 8, and extensive areas of vineyards occur in France and, to a lesser extent, in Germany. The principal areas are associated with river valleys, the Garonne and its tributaries, the Rhône, Loire, Rhine and Moselle being the chief. The Mediterranean coastlands of France form a further region and here another concentration may be noted, that of market gardening, and fruit and flower growing. There are many concentrations of market-gardening activity in North-West Europe, especially around Paris, in the Brussels-Antwerp region, the central districts of South Holland, the Rhine Rift Valley, the Copenhagen area, etc.

Industrial crops are chiefly represented by tobacco and flax. The central and eastern Aquitaine Basin and the Rhine Rift Valley are notable for tobacco, whereas flax is a speciality of the Belgian Flanders Plain. Orchards with a concentration on cider apples are a distinctive feature of Brittany, Normandy and northern France nearly as far east as the Somme. Hops for the brewery industries, mainly of regions north of the limit of the vine, are quite widely grown but there is a notable concentration of this crop in southern Germany, north of Munich.

The agricultural industry in most of the area is operated mainly in

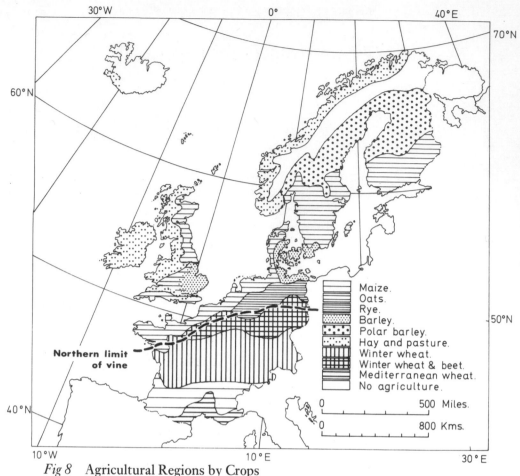

Fig 8 Agricultural Regions by Crops
The regions are delimited by reference to the dominant cereal crop, where appropriate. (After Stamp, Shackleton and O.E.C.D. publications)

small units. At least 10% of the total population of these countries is occupied in agriculture, compared with about 4% in Great Britain. The figure rises to some 20% in France and Luxembourg.

The process of farm consolidation is under way in many countries in Europe. The small family farm is generally not an economically viable unit and in order to make it more productive it is necessary to re-group fields, instead of having a large number of small isolated strips comprising one farm. In parts of West Germany this has also involved the building of new farmsteads adjacent to the field groups, instead of being in the old nucleated settlement. In some regions of France and the Low Countries the farm is little more than a smallholding and provides merely a subsidiary income. Some holdings in the Netherlands are too small for there to be any hope of turning them into a successful unit, and there the best policy is to persuade some of the agricultural community to leave the land. The consolidation of holdings or the re-allocation of land is virtually complete in Finland, is well under way in France, Germany and the Swiss Mittelland, but has barely started in Belgium.

The forestry resources of North-West Europe are significant and are to be found in every country except Iceland. The forested areas in Denmark and the Netherlands (10% and 8% respectively) are small compared with the 50% of Sweden's surface area which is so covered. Timber in Scandinavia is coniferous and more than half of the total North-West European wood production for industrial purposes comes from here. Hardwoods are found in southern France but much of the timber product of the Landes, the Ardennes of France and Belgium, the central uplands of Germany and the Dutch heathlands is of coniferous softwoods. Wood enters international trade chiefly in the form of pulp as well as sawn and in veneer and the chief exporters to other countries are Sweden and Finland.

Mining and Industry

The power-basis of industry in North-West Europe is divided between supplies of coal, oil, natural gas, hydro-electric power and atomic power. In the early days of industrial growth, domestic production of coal reigned supreme: since the 1920's, however, coal supplies have needed supplementing, both from imports of coal and from supplies of oil and other fuels. Since the Second World War the increase in imported oil supplies has resulted in reduced domestic use of coal.

The main coal reserves of the area are located in the fields of northern and eastern France, Belgium and Germany. Other fields of bituminous coal occur in the Netherlands and the French Central Massif. Locally significant supplies of lignite are found in Denmark, Sweden and the Netherlands, but Germany is the leading producer of this fuel. Important fields are located west of Cologne, near Magdeburg and south of Leipzig. It is used for electricity production in power stations sited on the coalfield and also in the form of briquettes for industrial and household consumption.

Oil is produced in small quantities in some districts of North-West Europe, but represents a small fraction of total needs. The Emsland field near Hanover produces less than one-tenth of Germany's needs. France produces about 7% of her oil needs, chiefly from the Aquitaine fields, while the Schoonebeck field in the eastern Netherlands forms a further source within the area. Oil for industrial needs, together with refined products from imported oil, form an increasing element in the power requirements of North-West Europe and these are obtained from the world's major fields. Refineries are sited at or near the chief ports, Marseilles, Bordeaux, Le Havre, Rotterdam, Bremen, Stockholm, etc. Natural gas is a further power source, especially for French and Dutch industrial and domestic purposes. Extensive fields in North Africa are the source for some of the gas fed into the pipelines of France but home deposits are tapped in the Aquitaine Basin. Home production in the Netherlands is derived from the gas field near Groningen. Gas obtained as a by-product of the iron and steel industry is locally important in Belgium, Lorraine and other industrial centres.

Hydro-electric power accounts for much industrial power in Fenno-Scandinavia, Switzerland and France. Elsewhere it is of secondary importance, supplementing demands at peak occasions. Areas of high potential for the production of hydro-electric power outside the northern lands still exist in France, Germany and Switzerland.

Other sources of energy include peat and wood in Denmark, Finland and Sweden, geo-thermal power (for central heating) in Iceland, and nuclear power. Installations for the latter are established at a number of localities in France, West Germany and the Low Countries, and uranium deposits are worked in several districts of the Central Massif of France.

Many industrial raw materials are produced within the countries of North-West Europe. Iron ore in significant quantities is mined in central and north Sweden, Lorraine, Normandy, the Siegerland, and in smaller quantities elsewhere. The characteristic of the iron and steel industry of the region is the internal movements of the basic materials. Thus Swedish iron ore plays an important rôle in the German industry, and Ruhr coking coal is vital to the Lorraine, Belgian and Luxembourg iron and steel industries.

The ferro-alloy minerals (Nickel, Cobalt, Molybdenum) are found only in the old shield areas of Fenno-Scandinavia. Non-ferrous ores such as Copper, Lead and Silver are more widely distributed but the chief areas for these are the Hercynian lands.

Quarrying activities are widely scattered in the upland areas of all the countries and important building stones come especially from the Hercynian lands. Certain limestones and sandstones of younger age have also been used, for example the Jurassic Caen stone of Normandy. The granites and other igneous rocks of the Central Massif, the Rhenish Uplands and Scandinavia provide the setts and cobblestones found in many urban stretches of roads in those countries, and polished slabs are used for decorative panels in some architectural styles throughout Europe.

The raw materials of the building industry—sands, gravels, limestone for cement manufacture, are plentiful as is the dolomitic limestone formerly in great demand for the manufacture of bricks for the lining of basic steel furnaces.

Sands of value to the glass industry, and kaolin for the chinaware industry are somewhat more specialised raw materials. Examples of both occur and have led to well-established industries of international repute. The Danish kaolin of Bornholm and the glass-sands of Charleroi, Fontainebleau and Mol are well-known examples.

Primary concentrations of industry are associated with the older established coalfield areas of North-West Europe. Other concentrations are adjacent to the mineral deposits, especially of iron ore as in Central Sweden, or to route centres, especially ports such as Hamburg, Copenhagen, etc. These last-named groups include some of the older industries and owe their origin to the trade established before and at the time of the Hanseatic league.

There are, however, a large number of industrial concentrations within the countries of North-West Europe in which it is either not possible to designate a particular specialism or in which the industries are varied and principally market-oriented. These areas are largely a product of the twentieth century, although some may have an older origin.

The widespread distribution of industrial activities is shown in Figure 9, from which it can be seen that the industrial landscape is a significant feature of the North-West European scene.

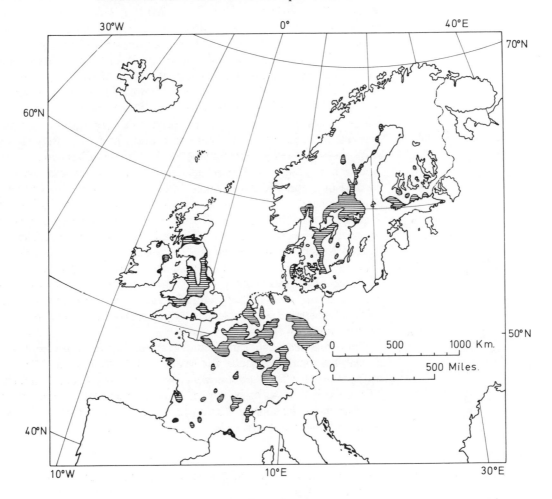

Fig 9   Industrial areas of North-West Europe

European Organisation   Since the Second World War the countries of Europe have come together in various ways for strategic and economic purposes. The grouping became crystallised when seventeen countries accepted the American post-war offer of aid under the Marshall Plan. These were Austria, Belgium, Denmark, France, West Germany, Greece, Iceland, Ireland (Eire), Italy, Luxembourg, the Netherlands, Norway, Portugal, Sweden, Switzerland, Turkey and the United Kingdom. For many subsequent purposes these countries have been referred to as the Western European group. With the exception of Austria, Eire, Sweden and Switzerland they comprise the European partners in N.A.T.O., and, together with Spain, they formed the Organisation for European Economic Co-operation. This became the Organisation for Economic Co-operation and Development in 1964.

The countries of eastern Europe are grouped under the terms of the Warsaw Pact and the Council for Mutual Economic Aid (Comecon). Economic groupings within Western Europe have also emerged. The initial grouping in 1947 was of the three countries which form the Benelux Customs Union. This was followed in 1953 by the launching of the European Coal and Steel Community linking these industries in France, West Germany, Italy and the Benelux lands. The success of this grouping led to the same countries signing the Treaty of Rome in March 1957 which established the European Economic Community (the Common Market) in 1958. The aims were to reduce, and ultimately to abolish all restrictions on trade, capital and labour movement between the countries. A common policy on agriculture, transport and external trade is being worked out, and the countries of 'The Six' are sometimes referred to as 'Little Europe'. For various reasons other nations of the O.E.C.D. group declined to sign the Treaty of Rome. Seven of these remaining countries—Austria, Denmark, Norway, Portugal, Sweden, Switzerland and the United Kingdom established the European Free Trade Area (E.F.T.A.), a looser economic grouping so that they would be placed in a less disadvantageous position for possible future negotiations with the Common Market group. These seven countries agreed to create a free-trade area by 1970. The external tariffs of each country remain, and there is no weakening of sovereignty of the member states.

Trade between the European Economic Community and the 'Outer Seven' has increased since the latter's establishment in 1960 and some of the reasons which, for example, prevented the United Kingdom from joining the E.E.C. at its inception, have lost their significance. Meanwhile, the European Economic Community has greatly increased its internal trade and economic strength.

FURTHER READING

J. F. Dewhurst, J. O. Coppock and P. L. Yates, *Europe's Needs and Resources*, 1961.

A. M. Lambert, 'Farm Consolidation in Western Europe', *Geography*, 1963, pp. 31–48.

P. L. Yates, *Food, Land and Manpower in Western Europe*, 1960.

Finland

Finland, in area 130,000 square miles (337,000 sq. km.) is about the same size as Great Britain. Most Finns call Finland *Suomi* and its inhabitants *Suomalaiset*. The fact was recorded in English encyclopaedias a century ago, but the world continues to use the historic name Finland. 'Finland, the land of a thousand lakes', is a well-known epithet; there are officially 55,000 lakes and they cover one-tenth of the country's surface. But there are as many swamps in Finland as there are lakes. One-third of its surface area consists of swamp (*suo* in Finnish), and some parishes register as much as 80% bogland. Finland is also a land of tens of thousands of islands. They comprise lacustrine as well as maritime archipelagoes. There are also islands of firm land in the seas of swamps. The most telling adjective used to describe this country of lakes, swamps and archipelagoes was employed by L. D. Stamp in 1931—'amphibious'.

Amphibious Finland is no static concept; its land and water relations are in a state of continuous flux. 'Finland is a daughter of the Baltic Sea', declared Zachris Topelius in his history course for students at the University of Helsinki in 1867. Elsewhere, he demonstrated with the aid of Finland's first contour map that the country was originally a great *skärgård* or skerry. The neptunist theme is repeated visually beside the harbour in Helsinki, where a fountain symbolises the rise of the city from the sea.

It is commonly held that isostatic emergence is a mechanical adjustment which follows the release of the great weight of ice that hitherto depressed the area. But adjustment is no simple process. Within a general pattern of land upheaval there may be many local differences in degree. And while adjustment is markedly demonstrated around the coasts, it also operates differentially across the granite face of Finland. Lines of equal intensity of adjustment are marked on maps and they give a maximum uplift of 39 inches (100 cms.) per century in the Vaasa Archipelago. Inland, the effects of uplift are detected in slow changes in the levels of the shallow lakebeds and even along old-established railway tracks. Isostatic adjustment is a physical process that has tangible consequences in everyday life. Three score years and ten are sufficient to transform into cornfields the shallows where boats formerly sailed. In the lives of city ports, adjustment must be paid for in persistent dredging of channels or in the construction and maintenance of new outports, as at Pori (Sw. Björneborg). Amphibious Finland is therefore sensitive to this delayed effect of the Ice Age. It is paradoxical that a country set against the background of one of the great stable shield areas of the world should display such pronounced and continuous uplift.

The Physical Environment
GEOLOGY AND RELIEF

The Fennoscandian Shield, of which Finland occupies a substantial part, is a basement complex of Pre-Cambrian rocks. Finland is a country of granites and of metamorphic rocks. There is a complete absence of rocks between the Pre-Cambrian and the Quaternary. Peneplanation of Finland's bedrocks took place at an early geological stage; but although the surface of its rock plain is remarkably even, north-west, south-east trend lines and fault mosaics are readily discernible in the lake district and the south-west archipelago. Finland shares its peculiar terrain with Russian Karelia to the east, and with Sweden, beyond the depression of the Bothnian Gulf, to the west. Its North American counterpart is the Laurentian Shield. Finland's different granites and metamorphic rocks possess varying degrees of resistance. Least resistant are the so-called *rapakivi* granites; where moulded by the sea, their shapes may range from turtle-back hummocks to facies reminiscent of sculptures by Henry Moore. Granite is a widespread element in the landscape—breaking through the thin crust of surface deposits in gnarled mound or ridge in the crevices of which the pine roots crawl. Among the other rocks, Ordovician limestones were much sought after by early mineralogists. Finland's largest limestone quarry, at Pargas south-west of Turku, has been worked for two centuries; it has a cement plant as have Lohja (between Turku and Helsinki) and Lappeenranta (in the south-east). Ordovician limestone is also known to floor the shallow Lumparland Bay in Central Åland.

Superimposed upon the Baltic Shield are glacial and post-glacial sediments. Two still-stands of ice, each lasting some 250 years, occurred towards the end of the Goti-glacial stage of retreat (*c.* 8000 B.C.) of the ice sheet. They produced a complex rampart of moraine, sands and gravels known as Salpausselkä. Salpausselkä extends from beyond the border of the Karelian U.S.S.R. in the south-east to the Hankö Peninsula in the south-west. Seaward, elements of it emerge as islands—the outermost of which is Jurmo. While the morainic ridges of Salpausselkä were being deposited, the southern edge of Finland lay beneath the waters of the Baltic Ice Lake. Subsequently, the continental ice receded in a north-westerly direction, depositing additional chains of eskers which pick out the direction of its retreat. Finland possesses some of the most impressive eskers in the world. They rise 200 feet (60 m.) above the surrounding countryside, and their serpentine character is frequently exaggerated by a lakeland setting.

A rise of sea level followed the recession of the continental ice sheet. It produced the saltwater Yoldia Sea, the waves of which, together with those of succeeding water bodies, etched high-water marks around the Baltic margins, so that a depositional, pedological and vegetational distinction can be traced between those parts that were submerged and those

Fig 10   Four maps of features essential to the appreciation of the geography of Finland
(Based on the *Atlas of Finland*, the *Geography of Norden* and I. Hustich, *Land i Förvandling*, Stockholm)

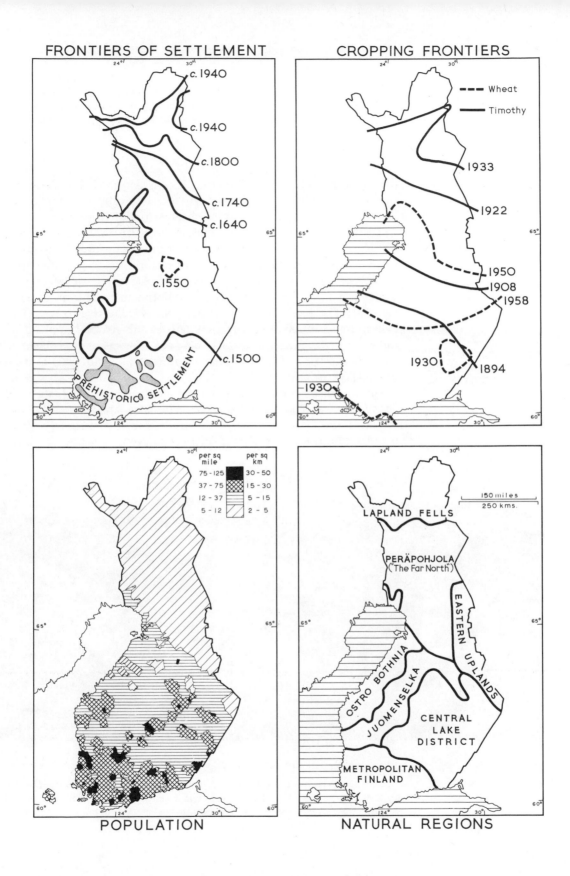

FRONTIERS OF SETTLEMENT

c.1940
c.1940
c.1800
c.1740
c.1640
c.1550
c.1500
PREHISTORIC SETTLEMENT

CROPPING FRONTIERS

- - - Wheat
——— Timothy

1933
1922
1950
1908
1958
1930
1894
1930

POPULATION

per sq mile | per sq km
75 - 125 | 30 - 50
37 - 75 | 15 - 30
12 - 37 | 5 - 15
5 - 12 | 2 - 5

NATURAL REGIONS

150 miles
250 kms.

LAPLAND FELLS

PERÄPOHJOLA
("The Far North")

EASTERN UPLANDS

OSTRO BOTHNIA

JUOMENSELKA

CENTRAL LAKE DISTRICT

METROPOLITAN FINLAND

which lay above the level of the waters. Subsequent land upheaval has exposed extensive marine clays, sometimes several scores of miles in width, along the south and west coasts. Through this sea change some of Finland's best soils have resulted.

RELIEF AND DRAINAGE Both glacial and marine deposits mask a naturally low-lying country; two-thirds of Finland are less than 650 feet (200 m.) above sea level. Finland rises in a shallow amphitheatre to the Balto-Arctic watershed. In the south, the terminal moraine of the Salpausselkä attains heights of 500 feet (150 m.), though an illusion of greater altitude is given from ski jumps, observation towers and forest rangers' treetrop platforms. In the archipelago, the rocky eminences of north Åland rise to 400 feet (120 m.) and command impressive views of the Bothnian Sea beyond their fiorded foreland. The bald Koli heights in north Karelia rise to over 1,100 feet (340 m.) and anticipate the treeless fells of sub-Arctic Lappland. Finland thrusts an arm north-westwards between Norway and Sweden towards the Atlantic coast. Here, in Haltiatunturi (Sw. Haldefjäll) is its highest peak (1,312 m.).

For the most part, Finland's watersheds are confused, its valleys ill-defined and its lake basins shallow. The lakes are frequently complexes of lakes; the rivers, strewn with rapids and low waterfalls, frequently broaden into ribbon lakes. The lakes are unevenly distributed. The largest

Plate 1 The Port of Oulu (Uleåborg) in northern Finland.
The port is typical of the major softwood processing centres which have grown up at the estuaries of Finland's principal rivers. The approaches to the port are shallow, for this is an area of active land upheaval. A hydro-electric barrage spans the lower reaches of Oulu River.

of the lake systems is Saimaa in eastern Finland, lying at 250 feet (76 m.) above sea level. It drains by way of the Vuoksi River to Lake Ladoga (now wholly in the boundaries of the U.S.S.R.). The Imatra Rapids, to which early Baedeker guides accorded one of their few Finnish stars, have been transformed by a hydro-electric power installation. The Päijänne lake system, in the south centre, has its outlet by way of the Kymi (Sw. Kymmene) River to the Gulf of Finland. The parallel drainage systems of Ostrobothnia provide a mirror image of the larger Swedish rivers that drain to the west coast of the Bothnian Sea. In the north the great network of tributaries gathered together by the Kemijoki constitutes Finland's longest river system.

After the bold orchestration of Norway's scenery, that of Finland seems to be composed for muted instruments. To foreign eyes, much of it is monotonous. The same elements are repeated, but closer inspection reveals that if the themes are common each repetition displays a variation.

CLIMATE   The high latitude location of Finland implies first, a hard climate in which the impact of winter is greater than that of summer, although the severity of winter is partly ameliorated by the Atlantic Ocean. But continental controls generally take precedence over oceanic in Finland's weather picture. Maritime influences are greatest in the south-west—Peninsular Finland. In the second place, high latitude means a pronounced seasonal rhythm of daylight and darkness. In northernmost Finland the sun does not rise above the horizon for six weeks at midwinter—'twilight pinched between two darknesses', is one countryman's description of December days. By contrast, about one-fifth of Finland sees the midnight sun; while the 'light nights' of summer make an aesthetic as well as an agricultural impact. Spring is delayed. Even in the south it is the beginning of May before winter's drab colours are relieved by signs of green.

The archipelagoes of Åland and Åboland enjoy the most favoured temperatures. Helsinki has a July mean of 17°C (63°F) and a February mean of −6°C (21°F); corresponding temperatures for Rovaniemi are 15°C (59°F) and −11°C (12°F). Average climatic conditions do not vary significantly over the greater part of the country.

Precipitation is generally light, averaging 26 inches (650 mm.) in the southern coastal areas and 20 inches (500 mm.) in Lapland. It is fairly well distributed seasonally and occurs on over 100 days in most parts of the country. In keeping with Finland's continental setting, there is a July-August maximum. Convectional thunderstorms average 12 days annually in the south. About one-third of the precipitation falls as snow, reaching about a foot in depth in the south and $2\frac{1}{2}$ feet in the north. Snow is a critical feature of Finland—for winter movement, for the protection of arable land, for replenishing the lakes and water courses. Snow covers the ground for about four months in the south, and for seven months in the north. It is eagerly awaited and helps to illumine the gloomy month that precedes the midwinter solstice.

Lakes and surrounding sea are usually frozen from December until late April in the south, and longer in the north. The intensity of the winter freeze varies greatly from year to year. Exceptionally mild winters, such as 1960–61 may be succeeded by severe winters, such as 1962-3. Exceptionally hard winters occurred in 1940, 1942 and 1966. Icebreakers are able to keep open winter channels to the ports of Turku and Hanko; while Helsinki, Kotka and Pori are not usually more than temporarily inaccessible. Ports such as Oulu and Kemi are usually closed for a lengthy period. Ice forecasting has become a fine art and weekly charts are compiled of the distribution of different categories of ice. Winter calls for strengthening ships against ice, for snow ploughing and snow clearance, for heavy fuel and lighting bills.

On land, winter routes take short cuts across the frozen surfaces of lakes and coastal waters. They are recorded on Finnish topographical maps and their carefully marked courses are followed by public as well as private transport. While they ease movement at the height of the winter, they are hazardous in the 'spring' winter or 'autumn' winter, when the ice neither bears nor breaks. For older country people, it is 'half-ski, half-boat weather'. Rotten ice takes its annual toll of postmen on their island rounds, priests and doctors on their errands of mercy, and of incautious lorry drivers.

VEGETATION   The natural vegetation of Finland does little to dispel the illusion of scenic monotony. Over seven-tenths of its surface is covered with trees and the dark blanket of conifers prevails. Several broad generalisations may be made about the vegetation. First, woodland elements seem to have derived principally from the east; meadow elements, from the south-west. Secondly, pine dominates the drier land; spruce, the moister land. Thirdly, the frontier of the pine advances higher latitudinally and altitudinally than that of the spruce. Fourthly, the most ubiquitous tree is the birch. It attains almost optimum conditions of growth in the south and declines into birch scrub in the north before it is transformed into a dwarf species. Fourthly, the speed of growth and reproduction of timber trees is much more rapid in the south than in the north. Softwood trees are ready for sawn timber after about 80 years in the south, but only after a century or more in the north. Density of timber stands is less there than in the south. Fifthly, alder and willow are widely distributed, and there is a narrow oak zone in the south. Protected relics of the severely denuded oakwoods persist in a few parklands and nature reserves; though place names recall their former extent. Sixthly, light conditions reduce undergrowth; but regardless of the canopy of shade the blueberry and wortleberry grow profusely on the wetter and drier lands respectively. Heather cloaks wide stretches of the sandy heaths.

The number of plant species is relatively small—a reflection of environmental restraints. The northern limits of over 200 familiar West

European vascular plant species are found in Finland. The most prolific and varied plant growth is associated with the meadow and grove lands that fringe the maritime margins of the south-west. It is partly explained by a lime constituent in the soil; partly by a milder local climate. Over extensive areas marsh and swampland species take precedence. Peat bogs have their own classification—the principal types of which are spruce and birch bog, pine bog, open, wet sphagnum bog, and treeless fen. Where land merges into sea or lake, reeds such as the feathery *Phragmites* flourish. The salinity of the Baltic Sea falls so low to the east of Porvoo (Sw. Borgå) and to the north of Pori, that familiar seaweeds such as the *Fucus* disappear from its rocky edges. A great variety of mosses and lichens cushion or encrust the rock outcrops. Reindeer moss (*Cladonia rangiferina*), distinctively milky-green in colour, provides extensive pasturage in the north.

Natural vegetation has been substantially modified by man, although much of the woodland conveys an illusory primeval appearance. In the past, forests have been subjected to widespread firing. Rotational burning for cultivation has operated selectively against conifers. Although it has been prohibited for over a century, extensive areas of birch and alder around the southern shores of Lake Saimaa recall the practice, and indicate the slow regeneration of the conifers. Ostrobothnia and its hinterland were widely cut over in former times for tar and pitch distillation. In addition, the peatlands of Ostrobothnia were subject to burning-and-paring. Improvement of natural vegetation has been most actively promoted by drainage, which has enabled the colonisation of mossland by timber and has speeded its growth on formerly saturated soils. Finland's forests have been more thoroughly surveyed than those of any country in the world save Sweden.

The forest was formerly a great hunting ground. Each settlement had its forest wilderness, from which game and furs were obtained. As late as the 1880s wolves were likely to appear anywhere in Finland and bears could intrude upon one-half of the country. Wild life has generally retreated to the innermost recesses of the border country; although the occasional bear is shot and the intermittent wolf pack is hunted (unfairly, perhaps, by helicopter in Lappland). Wild reindeer and elk provide less game for the table than the domesticated reindeer (which is frozen, smoked and even processed for sausages).

The forest, which envelopes and obliterates prehistoric settlement sites, enlivens the daily life of Finland. Its residual trees and groves remind the town dweller that even he is ultimately a man of the trees. By comparison with most of North-West Europe, the natural world is close at hand in Finland. Finns use the woodlands for personal enjoyment as well as commercial profit. Their children are brought up in a Linnean tradition to identify its plants, birds and animals. They are sensitive to the changing colours of the seasonal round—winter drawn in black and white, the fierce green of the late May flush of growth, the blaze of the autumn which is brightest in the north.

**Population
Distribution**

The Finnish population totals 4,600,000. Numbers have grown substantially in recent decades; there were 420,000 inhabitants in 1749 and 2,000,000 in 1879. There are about half a million Finns of emigrant stock overseas (mostly in North America) and about 50,000 Finnish nationals in Sweden. Density is 35 per square mile (14 per sq. km.). Finland's population records, together with those of Sweden, are more complete than those of any other country in the world.

Peoples of Finnish stock probably began to move into present-day Finland from the south and east rather more than 2,000 years ago. Others of Swedish origin crossed from the west and occupied the coastal fringes, and descendants of Swedish immigrants continue to speak Swedish. The Finnish language, completely different in vocabulary and structure from either Swedish or Russian, is used by 92% of the population. By paragraph 14 of its constitution, Finland is a bilingual country—and the south-westernmost province of Åland is almost exclusively Swedish-speaking. Swedish-speaking elements both tend to contract in the face of the pressure of Finnish-speaking peoples and to be absorbed by them. There are regional differences among the Finnish-speaking peoples—the Ostrobothnians, Karelians, peoples of Savo and Häme each harbouring their own particular dialects and customs. In addition, the Orthodox faith is associated with Karelians; it has 80,000 adherents in an otherwise Lutheran community. In the north, Finland has about 2,500 Lapps. Their language is closely related to Finnish, but they are different from Finns in physical appearance.

The Finns have been as much concerned with their ethnography as with their demographic record. Few nations have assembled such detailed information about the distributional features of their ethnography. *Kalevala*, the great collection of folk lore of the Finns, taken down in the early nineteenth century from orally transmitted poetry, provided a great stimulus for ethnographic enquiry. As may be seen in Figure 10, colonisation of Finland in historic times was from coast to interior (principally along the river valleys) and from south to north. The oldest historical monuments are the fine medieval stone churches, and they are concentrated in the south-west. Population has always been unevenly distributed and there remain extensive unpeopled areas in the northern third. Concentration is predominantly coastal and rather more than one-half of the population lives in the south-western quarter of the country. Greater Helsinki, including such satellite suburbs as Tapiola (Sw. Hagalund), has some 750,000 inhabitants. It has an ex-centric situation in relation to the shape of the country. Turku (Åbo), the old capital of the Swedish period, has under one-fifth that number. It runs neck and neck in the population race with Tampere (Sw. Tammerfors). The population drift continues strongly towards the south-west.

Beside the regional drift, there is an urban drift. 58% of Finland's population still occupies rural areas, so that by comparison with the rest of Scandinavia, there is a time lag in rural depopulation. Townward migration is partly a reaction to overpopulation in rural areas. Migration runs side by side with a changing occupational structure. Mobility is greatest in and to the southern third.

Population distribution underwent considerable change as a result of the Russo-Finnish Wars of 1939–40 and 1941–44. Over 420,000 inhabitants, or one-tenth of Finland's population, left the territories that had been ceded to the U.S.S.R. Resettlement took eight years. Thousands of new town flats and homes had to be built, and over 30,000 new farms had to be created.

Rural settlement is dispersed and its dispersal started partly with the land reorganisation laws of the mid-eighteenth century. The detached farmstead, frequently bearing the same name as its owner, is the basic unit of settlement. The church village is the lowest constituent in the hierarchy of nucleated settlement.

Economic Development

AGRICULTURE AND FISHERIES

Finnish agriculture is closely associated with forestry and the forest usually frames the farm. Farmland has been won principally from the woodland and most farms usually combine silvicultural and agricultural operations. Almost two-thirds of Finland's forests are privately owned, chiefly by farmers. In the agriculturally slack winter season, thousands of farmers take to work in their own forests. The proportion of farm income deriving from forests averages about a third of the total in southern Finland

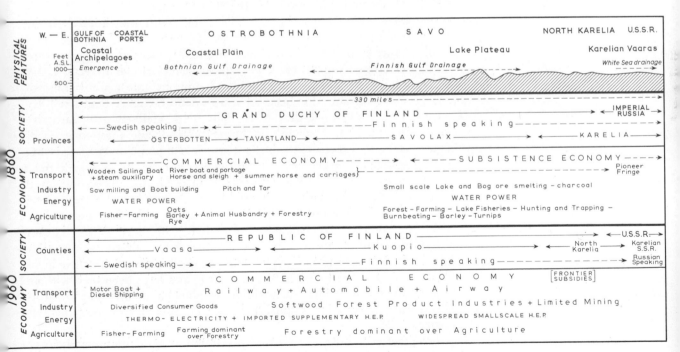

Fig 11   A transect diagram of Finland, indicating aspects of historical evolution

and as much as three-quarters in Oulu province. Some 40,000 lumberjacks also migrate to the scores of logging camps. Pioneer farming continues as a subsidiary though declining feature of Finnish agriculture. Forest maintenance grows increasingly important as Finnish trade in softwood products expands. It is estimated that by effective forest drainage alone, a 30% increase in output would result after 50 years. Statistics of farm numbers and farm sizes are inclined to mislead. Most of Finland's farms are in the category 13–38 acres (5–15 ha.) of cultivated land; but the country must not be regarded as a land of dwarf holdings, because a forest holding several times as big may be appended. Finland has published agricultural statistics for over a century. The successive volumes would indicate that from 1930 the number of large holdings or estates has diminished steadily. In general the size of holdings increases from south to north; but the area of cultivated land per farm diminishes in the same direction.

Climatic control of farming in Finland is powerful. The growing season averages 175 days in Uusimaa (Nyland): 120 days, in Lappland. But averages are dangerous in Finland, where summer frosts as well as late spring and early autumn frosts are frequent hazards. It has been observed that crop failure due to frost occurs regionally in Finland in one year out of four. Bad crop failures occurred in 1948, 1952, 1959 and 1962.

The range of crops grown also reflects the length of daylight, temperature and precipitation conditions. The length of the summer day in the high north partly compensates for the shorter growing season. The prolonged snow cover (which, in turn affects the depth and duration of the frozen ground) results in a closed season for farming.

Finland looks principally to animal husbandry, so that its chief crops are fodder crops. Animals are kept indoors from October to May. Dairy cows predominate and they number 1·18 millions; most are of Finnish stock, but the Ayrshire has been bred in Finland for more than a century and constitutes about one-third of the dairy herd. Yields of dairy cattle are much the same as in Denmark or the Netherlands and three-quarters of the herds do not exceed ten animals. Pigs are complementary to dairying, as in Denmark. Large flocks of sheep are not found, although most farms, especially in the east, have a few. They are usually an improved Finnish breed. In the north, reindeer husbandry remains a feature, and a figure of 170,000 is given, though it is notoriously difficult to assess their numbers. Poultry have increased substantially in recent years. Horses have declined in numbers, but are still widely bred—partly because they are indispensable to forestry operations. Finnish horses, with their great blonde manes and tails, are light and sinewy, and have been bred with an eye to economy in fodder consumption, to manoeuvrability and to hardiness in the face of cold. Viipuri had royal permission to export them as early as 1348.

The chief crop grown in Finland is rotation grass. Timothy and clover are commonly sown in a long ley. The rapid spread of improved timothy grass can be seen from Figure 10. Most of the grass is converted into hay, but ensiling is widespread. Rootcrops also make their contribution to animal fodder. Potatoes, introduced to Finland in the middle eighteenth century, are grown almost everywhere, but sugar beet and fodder beet are restricted to the south-west. Rape is also grown.

The pattern of grain cultivation has changed appreciably in recent decades. Among bread grains, rye has been subordinated to spring-sown wheat, but oats and barley occupy the greatest area. Finland is only self-sufficient in bread grains in good years. It imports considerable quantities of fodder grains, chiefly maize from the U.S.S.R.

Plate 2   Mallasvesi in the Finnish Lake District.
The interplay of land and water is counterbalanced by the interplay of farming and forestry. This is mixed farming country developed principally against the background of lake terraces. The pattern of open ditches stands out clearly. Sub-surface drainage progresses steadily.

Farming has taken a great technical leap forward in the last twenty years. Improved fertiliser programmes have contributed much to increased yields (Finland has its own nitrogen fertiliser plants, e.g. at Oulu; but potassium and phosphates are imported). Drainage claims increasing investment. Over seven-eighths of Finland's cultivated land is drained by open ditches, but sub-surface drainage advances swiftly. Stone and boulder clearance assumes an especially prominent rôle in south-east Finland. Farm buildings represent a heavy capital outlay, and improvement costs are high if older properties are to be rationalised. Above all, mechanisation exerts an appeal; the multiplication of tractors in Finland has transformed field operations since 1950. A great range of appliances, from combine harvesters through potato lifters to motor saws and log barkers, has been produced for the domestic market and even for export. Prestige as well as practical value enters into the possession of many of them. Very large-scale equipment, such as ditch-digging machines and bull-dozers, can be hired from commercially-operated pools.

Over 80% of the farms on which these technical changes are taking place are owner-operated. The Finnish farmer may be a smallholder, but he is rarely a tenant. Limited availability of capital has encouraged Finns to follow the example of the Danes in rural cooperation; cooperatives, purchasing from the farmer and for the farmer, are as numerous in Finland as anywhere in the world. Dairies, mills and slaughteries process food for export as well as for domestic consumption.

Woven into the fabric of farming are local variations on the broad design. There are apple orchards in south-west Finland and Åland, but pear and plum are rare because they are very sensitive to the severe winters. Fur farming is concentrated on the coasts and islands, and mink of diverse colours attract the growing interest of overseas buyers. Greenhouse cultivation, especially of tomatoes, is prominent in the coastal parishes of southern Ostrobothnia and around the capital. Climate forbids great garden enterprise, but in a country where windows are jungles of flowering plants, horticulturalists are in appreciable demand. The woodlands offer a significant harvest for the gathering. The wortleberry alone yields a commercial harvest of 2 million litres, liqueurs are made from the cloudberry and Arctic strawberry, and scores of varieties of edible fungus are harvested by the ton.

Fishing and farming still go hand in hand, but the last generation has witnessed the growth of increasing professionalism. The fishing fleet, the larger vessels of which are operated by five or six man crews, is concentrated in the south-western archipelagoes, ranges over the central Baltic, and looks principally to a small variety of herring. The harvest reaches its peak in spring. Northern rivers are relatively rich in salmon. The whitefish is also much esteemed; while a lesser relative especially abundant in the northern reaches of Lake Saimaa is the basis of the traditional fish pie of Savo province. Pike are trapped around the reedy edges of the lakes; while ice-hole fishing remains a favourite winter sport. The seal, which used to be seasonally hunted from the Vaasa archipelago, is still common.

Farming has a variety of government supports, so that its distributional features are in part artificial. Transport and price subsidies ease the lot of the farmer in the northern third of Finland. Pioneer farming and land clearance are also underwritten. The resettlement of refugee farmers caused major disturbances in the structure and distribution of farming activity after the Second World War. There is a substantial representation of farmers in the Finnish parliament where the Agrarian Party plays a powerful rôle in shaping farming policy. One-tenth of the state budget goes to agriculture in one form or another. Opinion is much divided over the wisdom of artificially extending agricultural development in the north-land, when the greatest returns from investment can clearly be obtained by intensifying activity in the south-western third.

MINING AND INDUSTRY
Manufacturing industry, which has been traditionally associated with timber and which has commonly responded to the attraction of coastal location, is relatively well-distributed in contemporary Finland. Diver-sification has been retarded because of the limited variety of indigenous raw materials, and development was delayed by the absence of coal and oil. But ingenuity has largely overcome these obstacles and manufacturing industry has been transformed in recent years. Transformation represents escape from the restraints of the domestic environment, though at the cost of dependence upon external sources of supply.

Four stages can be identified in the evolution of Finland's industry. In the first, activity was restricted to processing the products of farm, forest and mine. Dairy produce, hides, saltpetre, pitch, tar, resin, potash, rough sawn goods, ships' timbers and bar iron were produced by small-scale enterprises, principally in the coastal zone. Lake ore and bog ore were smelted with charcoal; wind and water provided energy. Many place names bear the suffix *koski* (waterfall); they include prominent industrial centres such as Myllykoski and Valkeakoski.

The second stage dates from the introduction of steam power in the mid-nineteenth century, generated with imported coal as a source of energy. Cheaper sea transport encouraged the growth of softwood plants, to which were added mechanical and chemical pulp, plywood and veneer production. At the same time, railways penetrated into the interior. The third stage belongs to the era of independence after 1918, with hydro-electricity as the new source of energy. Most of Finland's leading industrial establishments were in existence by then, but a new set of trading relations confirmed their locations. Yet primary, or at best secondary, industry ruled the day. Output of consumer goods was modest, that of capital goods extremely restricted.

In the fourth and contemporary stage, Finnish industry has assumed a West European complexity, with refinement and ingenuity. It has some of Europe's largest factories—not only softwood plants such as Kaukopää sulphate pulp and cardboard mill at Imatra or Veitsiluoto saw mill near Kemi, but Arabia—the porcelain factory—at Helsinki. The 1947 Treaty requirement to pay reparations to Russia gave impetus to the metallurgical and engineering industries, which are the principal employers of industrial labour today. They can draw on the rich copper ores of Outokumpu in eastern Finland and of Pyhäsalmi in central Ostrobothnia but, as with all Finland's large-scale industries, they underline the energy shortage.

D

Plate 3   Pyhäkoski power station on Oulu River.
Oulu river's hydro-electric energy is now completely developed. This generating station occupies the site of one of the best known falls on the river.

Finland meets only 60% of its power requirements. Russia is the chief source of petroleum imports. Finland has two large refineries at Naantali (Sw. Nådendal) near Turku, and Sköldvik by Porvoo (Sw. Borgå).

Neither increasing specialisation nor new post-war locations for industrial plants moved from areas ceded to Russia has promoted excessive concentration of manufacturing. Helsinki is the largest single industrial city, with electrical industries, ship-building, printing, food processing (including chocolate manufacture), the headquarters of the state alcohol monopoly, brewing and sugar refining. Textiles were established in Tampere and Turku six generations ago, and Tampere is the largest textile town in Norden. Tampere also has engineering and locomotive-assembly shops, while Turku has added agricultural machinery, milling and porcelain to shipbuilding. Textile manufacture is associated with other towns of western Finland—from Hyvinkää with century-old woollen textile mills, through Forssa to Vaasa (both making cottons). Finnish glassware, paralleling Swedish in quality and design, and with a tradition established in the eighteenth century, is manufactured in a number of smaller towns—Riihimäki, Karhula and Nuutajärvi (Sw. Notsjö). Furniture manufacture, competing with the rest of Scandinavia in originality of design, has expanded rapidly in Lahti.

In general, the traditional wood manufacturing industries of Finland are located away from the south-west. Softwood processing reaches its fullest expression towards the heads of the Gulfs of Finland and Bothnia. On the shores of the Gulf of Finland, Kotka (with the valley of the Kymi) and Hamina (with the Imatra hinterland) lie in close juxtaposition, and provide the largest stream of exports from any part of Finland. Pori, in the south-west, draws on the hinterland of the Kokemaki River; but the scale of its operations is modest compared with those of the north Bothnian ports of Oulu (Sw. Uleåborg) and Kemi. A growing range of interior industrial sites—extending as far east as Joensuu and as far north as Kajaani and Kemijärvi—furthers the policy of dispersal and carries the economic frontier of processing deep into the countryside. In the interior, the 'company town' is a distinguishing feature of settlement, with its several thousands of inhabitants directly dependent upon the softwood plant in its midst. Jämsänkoski and Juankoski provide examples. Paper products, their principal concern, account for one half of Finland's exports.

Mining and ore processing were formerly located mostly in the south-west, where Swedish prospectors sought to create a second Bergslag. The legacies of past localising forces remain there, e.g. at Dalsbruk and Fiskars, and new developments can also be seen, e.g. iron mining on Jussarö, with associated smelting on Hanko Peninsula. But the centre of gravity of mineral interest has shifted northwards. In addition to the copper developments at Outokumpu and Pyhäsalmi in Savo province (with refining at Pori and Harjavalta), magnetite-ilmenite ores are mined at Otanmäki. To meet domestic requirements, and fed mostly by domestic ores, an iron and steel plant has been established at Raahe (Sw. Brahestad), which will parallel those of Luleå (Sweden) and Mo i Rana (Norway).

Much of Finland remains unprospected. There are plenty of known iron ore resources in Finnish Lapland and other valuable metals must exist in a country only 5% of which has been investigated by modern prospecting methods. Raajärvi, the open cast pit east of Rovaniemi, which produces concentrates for Raahe, was discovered by aeromagnetic methods. Finland's nickel mines in the Petsamo corridor, lost to the U.S.S.R. in 1944, have been offset by a new mine at Kotalahti in the lake region. Zinc is mined at Vihanti and lead at Korsnäs, both in Ostrobothnia. Chemical by-products derive from mineral as well as softwood processing. Domestically, these enterprises diversify Finnish industry, though they are small-scale by international standards.

TRADE AND INTEGRATION

Finland must trade or die, for it lacks self-sufficiency in many essential products. It is most dependent upon essential fuels, two-thirds of which come from the U.S.S.R. Physical conditions impose their own rhythm of trading; though they are not transmitted to the flow of currency or credits. Most of Finland's commerce moves across the sea. Its traditional trading partners have been the United Kingdom and Germany. The United Kingdom is still Finland's principal market and the German Federal Republic is the leading source of supply. Finland is an associate member of E.F.T.A. The U.S.S.R. has become a leading market in the last twenty years, developed from reparations paid by Finland after 1944. Finland's industrial structure, partly modified to meet Russia's reparations requirements, has been correspondingly geared to the Russian market. For example, two-thirds of the exports of its metallurgical and engineering industries go to the U.S.S.R. The U.S.A. also figures prominently in Finnish trading. As with the rest of Scandinavia, Finland also assembles entire plants for export, e.g. paper-making plants (equivalent in intricacy and cost to a substantial cargo vessel), plywood plants, hydro-electric units and pre-fabricated houses.

Just over one-half of this trade is carried in foreign ships, although a million tons of merchant shipping flies the blue and white Finnish flag. Kotka and Hamina are the chief export harbours, and Helsinki is the chief import harbour. One-third of Finland's tonnage is registered in the little Åland port of Mariehamn (F. Maarianhamina), and is inseparable

Plate 4   Log rafts at an assembly point on Lake Saimaa.
Movement of timber across the great lakes systems of central Finland is still an active process, although overland transport competes increasingly strongly. Bundle floating is the most economic means of movement.

from traditions established in its historic clipper ship days. Turku is the principal ferry port for Sweden, handling over half a million passengers annually.

The need for a winter icebreaker service, already established in the 1890s, has encouraged a special ship-building industry in the Sandviken yards of Helsinki, where icebreakers of up to 26,000 h.p. are constructed, and output reaches over one-tenth of the world's total.

Domestic trade moves principally over a trunk road system that has been transformed since 1955. Finland is still building railways—broad gauge in contrast to Sweden—and domestically built diesel-powered loco-motives operate on them. Limited electrification is contemplated. Finland has also one of the most intensive domestic air networks of any country in Europe. An enormous volume of timber moves over the waterways during the open season, bundle-floating of logs being especially important. In 1962, an agreement was signed with the U.S.S.R. to reopen the Saimaa Canal (which was completed in 1856, but closed after bisection by the new boundary in 1944).

As a country with limited capital, Finland has been forced to husband its investment resources with care. One result is the tradition of planning that has been embraced at all levels. There are plans for individual industrial plants to succour northern Karelia, for trading estates on the margins of Helsinki. There are city plans, such as that for Rovaniemi, whose inhabitants had to rebuild the completely ruined town left at the end of the war. In the Imatra area, industry and inhabitants have been regrouped subsequent to the 1944 boundary change and against the background of a plan initiated by one of Finland's leading industrial organisations—Enso-Gutzeit O/Y. Still larger in scale is the integrated development of the Kumo Valley, planned by Alvar Aalto.

The Regions of Finland

Gathering together the diverse facets of Finland's physical and human geography, it is possible to distinguish a number of regions, though there are few clear-cut boundaries between them. One of the most valid divisions of Finland was proposed by the Finnish regionalist, J. G. Granö. He distinguished between *Kultur* Finland and *Natur* Finland; in the former, the hand of man takes precedence in the landscape and in the latter, the natural world is still supreme. The frontiers of the natural world are shifting—shrinking northwards and eastwards. Figure 10 illustrates a simple regional division of Finland. A variety of other regional divisions is given in the *Atlas of Finland*.

A Young State and an Old Nation

Finland displays a blend of ancient and modern in all aspects of its geography. Its Archaean shield is the oldest part of Europe, while the marine plains superimposed around its edges are among the most youthful

Plate 5 Kemijärvi in north-east Finland.

Kemijärvi lies in the eastern half of the Kemi river basin. It is in 'colonial' Finland and on the edge of the fell country. Kemijärvi is in the throes of active development and is the site of new softwood processing as well as of hydro-electric power installations.

tracts of the continent. The contorted trees of its primeval Lappish forests with their aboriginal fauna and unpeopled wastes, stand in pronounced contrast to the intensely humanised landscape of Åboland. North-east Finland displays an ecological climax; south-west Finland, a cultural climax. The climax, in each case, spells maturity. The maturity in the north-east is seen in the delicacy of adjustment of bird and animal to plant life. That of the south-west is reflected in the rough-hewn medieval granite churches, with their semi-barbaric wall paintings, juxtaposed by some of the most progressive architectural structures in the world, decorated with the most sophisticated products of the applied arts. In the face of the physical challenge of high latitude and the political challenge of a marchland location, the Finns have succeeded in creating a viable economy and a resilient state.

FURTHER READING   *Atlas of Finland*, 1960.

Guide Book to Finland, I.G.U. Congress, 1960, *Fennia*, 84, 1960.

Fennia is the title of the geographical publication of the Finnish Geographical Society. Most of its contributions have English summaries.

The relevant chapters on Finland in (Ed.) A. Sømme, *The Geography of Norden*, Oslo, 1960; W. R. Mead, *An Economic Geography of the Scandinavian States and Finland*, 1958; R. Millward, *The Scandinavian Countries*, 1965; A. C. O'Dell, *The Scandinavian World*, 1957.

W. R. Mead, *Farming in Finland*, 1953.

W. R. Mead, *Finland (How People Live Series)*, 1965.

W. R. Mead (with H. Smeds), *Finland in Winter*, 1966.

H. Smeds, 'Post War Land Clearance and Pioneering Activities in Finland', *Fennia*, 83, 1960.

R. Platt, *Finland and its Geography*, New York, 1957.

Suomi, A general Handbook on the Geography of Finland, Helsinki, 1952.

A catalogue of maps published in Finland may be obtained from the Finnish survey office—Maanmittaushallitus, Helsinki.

CHAPTER FIVE   *By W. R. Mead*

Sweden

Sweden (in Swedish, *Sverige*) is the largest of the Scandinavian countries, with an area of 169,000 sq. m. (440,000 sq. km.). It is also the most centrally placed. It is a long land, stretching through nearly fourteen degrees of latitude. In the broader European context, it has overtones of central Europe (for Stockholm belongs to the same longitude as Berlin and Vienna), as Finland has overtones of eastern Europe. Sweden has the largest population of any of the countries of Norden, though the density is lower than that of Denmark. Historically, it has been Norden's most powerful state; economically, it is the richest.

In shape, Sweden is rhomboidal. Its geographical boundaries are relatively clear-cut; for most of their length they are maritime. In the north-east, Sweden shares a common boundary with Finland. To the west is Norway, its 'Siamese twin', with whom it shares a mountainous boundary in the ranges of the Scandes. The Norwegian boundary, plotted cartographically and astronomically over two hundred years ago, has been one of the most stable in Europe.

Sweden has no overseas possessions. But the island of Gotland, its most detached constituent, lies over seventy miles away in the central Baltic. Formerly, Sweden supported an extensive Baltic empire as well as North American colonies on the Delaware. The largest component of the Baltic realm was Finland, the historic eastern wing of Sweden from the thirteenth century until it was lost to Russia in 1809. In 1921, Sweden disputed the possession of the Åland Islands with Finland; but the Hague Court upheld Finnish Sovereignty. From 1815–1905, Norway was joined to Sweden under a dual monarchy.

GEOLOGY AND RELIEF

The morphology of Sweden is written in relatively simple terms. Sweden is primarily an Archaean land, sharing with Finland the western part of the Fennoscandian Shield. The Bothnian Sea is a submarine depression of the shield. Like Finland, Sweden is very much a land of granites. Its bedrocks are widely exposed—polished by the ice, scratched by the striae that indicate its direction of retreat, smoothed by summer sea and winter ice along the emerging Baltic shores, chafed by the stronger salt waves in the bald west coast archipelagoes, coursed over in the cataracts and rapids of many rivers, and shattered by powerful frosts along the hard skylines of the fells.

The surface of the Archaean Shield takes both upland and lowland forms. To the west of the low-lying Bothnian plains, it is elevated into an undulating upland commonly known to Swedes as the Norrland terrain. In south-central Sweden, along the lowland axis between the Stockholm archipelago and the Skagerak, the shield is heavily fractured. The fractured zone contains some of Sweden's largest lakes—Vänern, Vättern, Hjälmaren and Mälaren.

Folded on to the north-western edge of the shield are the nappes of the Caledonian mountains that form the Keel Ridge of the Scandes. Northern Sweden has a distinct piedmont zone, which anticipates the upstanding peaks of gabbro, gneiss and quartzite of the fold mountains. The highest peaks of the Scandes are found in Lapland, where Kebnekaise, Sarekjakko and Kaskasatjakko all exceed 6,000 ft.

The geological succession of Sweden is dominated by the Palaeozoic; but there are limited areas of both older and younger sedimentary rocks. Silurian relics (which Roderick Murchison saw himself) account for some of the most distinctive landscapes of Sweden. The Storsjön depression is contained in the most extensive of them, but the Siljan district of Dalarne and the islands of Gotland and Öland announce their limestone backgrounds more clearly. Earlier settlers were conscious of their opportunities for cultivation; contemporary tourists are sensitive to their scenic appeal. Limestone is laid bare in quarries from which blocks have been hewn for churches and chiselled into memorials. Fossils as long as sabres lie polished and imprisoned in the stone. Along Gotland's coast, the limestone reefs are eroded into residuals or *raukar*, of which the 150 feet high Jungfru and the Sphinx are most prominent. Its countryside conceals underground caverns, such as Lummelund grotto, ornate with diminutive stalactites and stalagmites.

Younger sedimentaries also overlap the southern edge of the shield, to crowd into the little province of Skåne some of the most diversified geology encountered in the whole of Norden. Gneiss, Cambro-Silurian, Rhaetic-Liassic formations, Cretaceous and Quaternary deposits, each with its differing scenic expression, succeeded each other swiftly.

The bedrocks of Sweden are heavily masked with superficial deposits, which have their origins in the meltwaters of the Quaternary ice sheet and in post-glacial land upheaval. As with Finland, Sweden is caught in a great mesh of glacial debris, the details of which reflect both the process and direction of ice retreat. The major morainic features which litter the northern part of the 'Great Lakes' depression are related to Finland's Salpausselkä and Norway's Ra moraine. The esker 'trains' which streak the face of the country are known by the Swedish word *ås* (plural, *åsar*). The investigation of glacio-fluvial features has been a primary concern of Sweden's physical geographers. Varve analysis, as a method of counting post-glacial time, was conceived and developed in Sweden by Gerard de Geer. Varves are the thin layers of clay deposited annually in shallow waters around the melting edge of the ice.

The shape of the land that is now Sweden has changed greatly in the last

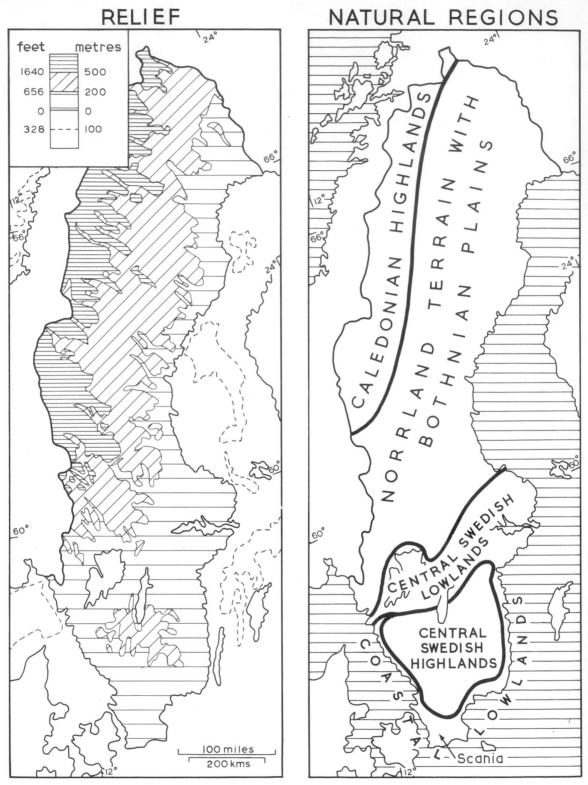

RELIEF

feet	metres
1640	500
656	200
0	0
328	100

100 miles
200 kms

NATURAL REGIONS

CALEDONIAN HIGHLANDS

NORRLAND TERRAIN WITH BOTHNIAN PLAINS

CENTRAL SWEDISH LOWLANDS

CENTRAL SWEDISH HIGHLANDS

COASTAL LOWLANDS

Scania

Fig 12   Four maps of features essential to the appreciation of the geography of Sweden

ARABLE AREA

■	over ⅓
▨	under ⅓
☐	none

POPULATION

per sq mile	per sq km
over 125	over 50
50 – 125	20 – 50
25 – 50	10 – 20
3 – 25	1 – 10
under 3	under 1

(Based on the *Atlas of Sweden* and the *Geography of Norden*)

10,000 years. In general, post-glacial submergence has been succeeded by a period of land emergence, but development has not been uniform throughout the area. The successive phases of evolution have been identified by the presence of the remains of fresh and saltwater molluscs.

For the layman, causes of changing sea level are perhaps less important than consequences. The principal consequences are the physical differences (especially in soil and vegetation) between the areas that remained above sea level and those which were submerged. Any consideration of Sweden's pedology looks to this fact as well as to the climate, which has played a rôle both in the widespread podsolisation and in the widespread development of peatland. The degree of land emergence has varied greatly—from a few inches in south Sweden to nearly 1,000 feet in the province of Ångermanland. Upheaval continues at the rate of 12–15 inches a century in the Stockholm area and a maximum of a yard a century around Quarken.

Land upheaval has given birth to the broad coastal plains of Norrland and the correspondingly shallow offshore waters of the tideless Bothnian Sea. It has hastened the down-cutting of the rivers draining to the inner reaches of the Baltic. It has converted and continues to convert bays into lakes, lakes into swamps, and swamps into dry land. The speed of conversion is sufficient for abundant cartographic testimony to have accumulated. Human consequences are everywhere apparent. It may be seen in the detail of coastal marsh as it is transformed into firm land for the farmer. It may be pondered by the weirs of Stockholm's watergates. In response to the shallowing waters, the administrative focus of medieval Sweden shifted from the shallowing Fyris River above Uppsala first to Sigtuna and then to the stockaded island that was to be the Old Town (*Gamla staden*) of Stockholm.

DRAINAGE   Sweden, like Finland, is a land of lakes and rivers. Although Lakes Vänern and Vättern differ from those of Finland, Mälaren and Hjälmaren bear a close resemblance. The elongated piedmont lakes in the upper collecting basins of Norrland's rivers generally occupy ice-hollowed basins with rock-dammed eastern outlets.

Sweden's rivers are longer and more well-defined than those of Finland and Norway. Klara älven, the longest, rises in Norway and debouches into Lake Vänern, near Karlstad. The Göta river drains Lake Vänern, by way of impressive falls, into the Kattegat-Skagerak. North Sweden is characterised by a drainage pattern strongly oriented from north-west to south-east, for a series of major rivers drains across the piedmont from the high fell to the emergent coastal plains of Bothnia. In keeping with their high latitude, they have a pronounced seasonal rhythm in their flow.

CLIMATE   Sweden has a considerable variety of climates. These are a reflection of its longitudinal extent and consequently differ from the climatic range of Norway, which is closely related to variations in relief. The regional differences in Sweden's climate are also closely linked with the degree of exposure to maritime and cyclonic influences. The modifying effect of the westerly air stream is seriously reduced for the northern two-thirds of Sweden by the obstruction of the Scandes. As a result, seasonal contrasts of temperature are greater, precipitation is lower, cloudiness is less, and sunshine totals are higher than for corresponding latitudes in Norway.

Most of Sweden is characterised by an element of continentality in its climate. This feature reaches its greatest intensity in north-eastern Sweden. In winter, a minor pole of cold lies over Swedish Norrland and adjacent Finland. Other results of continentality are the convectional rainstorms leading to a summer maximum of precipitation.

Temperature contrasts between north and south are less in summer than in winter. January temperatures in Gothenburg have a mean value of 0°C (32°F); in Stockholm, −2·5°C (27·5°F); in Östersund, −7·9°C (17·6°F) and in Haparanda, −10·3°C (13·5°F). July mean averages are respectively 17·1; 19·9; 14·2 and 15·5°C (62·9; 67·9; 57·5 and 60·0°F). As in Norway and Finland, these facts cannot be separated from the seasonal variations in daylight and darkness. Stockholm, for example, enjoys 22 hours of daylight (including dawn and dusk) at midsummer; but it has only $7\frac{3}{4}$ hours at midwinter. The northern quarter of Sweden has only about five hours of twilight at midwinter; but a full 24 hours of daylight at midsummer.

Independently of temperature, the seasonal contrasts in daylight and radiation affect growth conditions. Sweden has wide variations in its growing period. Around Gothenburg it extends from the end of March to the end of November; in the Stockholm area from mid-April to early November; around Östersund from late-April to mid-October; around Karesuando from mid-May until late-September. Duration of growth cannot be considered independently of speed of growth which is forced on by the accumulated temperatures resulting from the long days of higher latitudes.

Precipitation is relatively small over most of Sweden—25–28 inches (600–700 mm.) along the west coast; 18 inches or less (300–400 mm.) in the east of the country. The greater part of Sweden experiences a continuous winter snow cover. In Uppland it is persistent from mid-December until the end of March; but in southern Norrland it may establish itself in early November and remain well into April. Snow cover in Skåne and along the coast of Halland is intermittent. Interior waterways freeze almost everywhere; though the great lakes of the south only support a continuous cover of ice in harder winters. Severe winters produce ice over most of the Baltic Sea; but under average conditions, only the skerry zone is likely to have firm ice. Ice and snow forecasting are important tasks of the Swedish meteorological service. Bothnian harbours will be affected by icing, though their accessibility will depend upon wind direction and strength, as well as upon the severity of the frost. North-easterly winds, for example, will cause pack ice to drift and pile up along the coast of Sweden. Gävle and Sundsvall are not usually closed for more than about a month; but Luleå may be inaccessible, under average conditions, from mid-December until mid-May.

Sweden is a country of coniferous woodland—*barrskog*, as it is called. Roughly 54% of the country is covered with timber and it consists mostly of spruce and pine. This represents 17% of the forestland of Europe west of the U.S.S.R. In broad outline, the pine stretches farther north and into higher altitudes than the spruce: it is also associated with the drier land. Birch is ubiquitous; alder and willow are widespread. Softwood stands usually consist of fairly homogeneous groups of trees.

To the north, and at higher altitudes, dwarf birch and willow take over before vegetation assumes more restricted forms on the rock-shattered high fells—the tundra zone proper. The timberline stands at 1,300 feet in the north; 2,600 feet in Dalarna. To the south, between Uppland and the south Norwegian border, there is a zone of transition from northern coniferous forest to mixed deciduous woodland. This is closely related to the more tolerant climate. Oaks make their entrance. Widespread destruction has been succeeded by careful protection and planting during the last 200 years. The *barrskog* resumes control in the Småland massif; but around its southern edges Knut Hagberg records woodlands reminiscent of 'Shakespearian Ardens' in which the 'coolness of the north and the luxuriance of central Europe' mingle. Over parts of Skåne, beechwoods are absolutely dominant, as in adjacent Sealand. The walnut ripens, the sweet chestnut and almond tree will grow.

In forested Sweden, swampland is also widespread and the proportion increases northwards. Around the margins of Sweden vegetation assumes distinctive forms. The windswept skerry zone of Bohuslän is largely treeless, but has a rich local flora of salt-loving species. It contrasts to the opulence of the *lövängar* or coastal meadows of Gotland, of which Linnaeus wrote, 'only English lords and Gotland *bönder* can have parks of equal quality'.

It is impossible to consider the plant geography of Sweden without recalling the name of Carl Linnaeus (1707–1778) who did much to bring the attention of the Swedes to the flora of their homeland, as well as creating his great system of plant classification. He also published a series of topographical studies rich in local botanical observations, and which contain much practical advice on the condition and possibilities for improvement of Sweden's vegetation. Linnaeus was among the active progenitors of conservation.

Sweden is celebrated for mosses and lichens, for mushrooms and toadstools, and (in the north above all) for mosquitoes and midges. It enjoys a rich spring flora, with the blue anemone coming as a harbinger before the snow has disappeared, to anticipate the breaking of the birch buds and the scent of the widespread lily-of-the-valley. There is also a rich harvest of berries, from the proverbial wild strawberries of July through blueberries and cowberries to the dark cranberries that may still be gathered beneath the winter snow.

Fauna is limited in variety. The larger animals have experienced considerable changes in numbers and distribution during the last century. Predators have almost completely disappeared; but larger herbivores (usually protected from hunting) are still widely distributed. The elk is not uncommon—even in the suburbs of Stockholm. Wild reindeer and roedeer are abundant in the northern third of Sweden. Bird life has wide seasonal and regional variations. Some, such as the capercaillies and ptarmigans are able to withstand the northern winter; some, such as the finches, blackbirds and fieldfares, migrate to western Europe; some, such as the swallows and cranes, fly a thousand or more miles south; the seabirds move from the frozen to the open waters.

Sweden has a varied range of fishes—though they may be less abundant than those in and around Norway. In the Skagerak waters, it shares the familiar North Sea species, with herring the dominant catch, but its rocky shores are a haunt of crustaceans. The offshore harvest has displayed substantial historical variations. The inland lakes have trout and pike; while the great rivers of the north retain a fair store of salmon, salmon trout and lavaret. Summer wanes as the crayfish is netted, to be boiled red for the parties that anticipate the fall of the year.

Population and Ethnography

Sweden is a country which has kept detailed records of its population for over 200 years and the facilities for tracing the evolution of its present distributional pattern, changing age structure and conditions of mortality are unique.

Sweden has $7\frac{1}{2}$ million inhabitants. The birth rate is 14 per thousand; the death rate, 10 per thousand. The mean expectation of life is 71 for males; 75 for females. Its people—by comparison with most, long in limb as well as long in life—are among the most ethnographically homogeneous of any in Europe. There is a minority of 10,000 Lapps (in Lappish, *Samer*).

Settlement has been oriented to water—first and foremost to coastal sites; thereafter, to lake and riverside. Abundant prehistoric artifacts occur on the well-identified raised beaches, shorelines and river terraces of earlier times. Sweden has a long tradition of curiosity concerning prehistoric antiquities. In addition to its Stone Age (*c.* 4,000–1,500 B.C.), Bronze Age (1,500 B.C.–A.D. 400), and Iron Age (A.D. 400–1,050) burial mounds and settlement sites, it has a rich legacy of more than 3,000 runic stones of the Viking period. Some of these recall expeditions by Swedes to the east, where, as Varangians, they did much to bring about the early crystallisation of Russia.

Swedish population distribution resembles that of the other countries of Norden. First, coastal concentration reaches its fullest expression in the capital city—Stockholm, in an historically strategic location. Secondly, the capital city has no serious provincial rival; though Gothenburg (Göteborg, in Swedish) is nearly as large as Oslo and Helsinki. Thirdly, as with Norway and Finland, population is increasingly concentrated in the southern third of the country. Fourthly, population is increasingly urban, with rural-urban migration continuing apace. Population increases by the annual addition of about 25,000 immigrants, mostly Finns. There is still a little 'blood letting' through emigration, about 14,000 a year, but Swedish emigration reached a climax in the last quarter of the nineteenth century.

Sweden has a healthy academic respect for its ethnographic antecedents. In few parts of the world have ethnographers gone through the relics, folkways and customs of the countryside with a finer-toothed comb. The Historical Museum in Stockholm has thorough records of the house forms, equipment, implements and land ownership conditions that prevailed in Sweden before its industrial and agricultural revolutions. In common with the rest of the countries of Norden, Sweden also maintains living folk museums, of which Skansen in Stockholm is the largest. Contrasting with the bygones of a peasant culture, are the Renaissance, Baroque and Rococo monuments from Sweden's more 'spacious days'. They reflect international contact. Even before the Vasa dynasty which, in the sixteenth and seventeenth centuries, transformed the Baltic into a Swedish lake and carried the Protestant cause deep into central Europe, Sweden had lively contact with distant places. In the Dark Ages, there was Mälaren's island of Birka, the black earth of which has yielded treasure from the Levant and the classical world. There was also the medieval walled town of Visby.

Economic Development

AGRICULTURE

Swedish agriculture has a forest setting. As with Finland, so much of the farmed land is land which has been born of water and cleared of wood. Most of the cultivated area is restricted to land of gentle slope and to depositional soils. The most extensive areas of improved land lie in the southern third of Sweden. Exceptional for Sweden and comparable with Denmark are the plainlands of Skåne, where brown forest soils overlie chalky marls and the fields are pock-marked with marl pits used for generations as a source of fertiliser. Outside these areas, discontinuity rather than continuity of cultivated area typifies the landscape. Farmed land is broken by forests, interrupted by water, and intruded upon by rock outcrops. Cultivated land is found everywhere in Sweden; but its returns are marginal in the northernmost communes.

Land clearance for farming continues locally today, though it is complemented by regional withdrawals of the frontiers of cultivation. Land clearance has been spurred in successive centuries by different motives. In the sixteenth century, land breakers from eastern Finland were encouraged to open up the Swedish backwoods. They colonised much of the interior of Värmland and Dalarna, leaving a legacy of Finnish place names as a record of their enterprise. Colonisation of the northern third of Sweden was spurred in the eighteenth and nineteenth centuries. It was essentially a valleyward development, inland from the estuaries of the great rivers that drain Norrland to the Bothnian Sea.

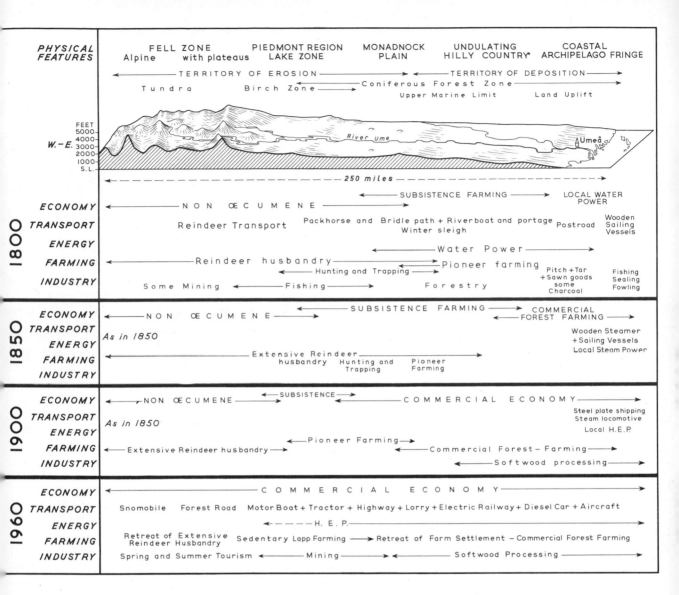

Fig 13 A transect diagram of Swedish Norrland, indicating aspects of historical evolution

The earlier occupation of the northern half of Sweden was marked by an extensive use of the land. The home farm was complemented by widespread woodlands and outland grazings. The land north of a boundary from South Gästrikland through to north Bohuslän also witnessed regular summer migration of domestic animals to the *fäbodar* or summer pastures. Expansion of rural settlement frequently developed through the intermediacy of summer sheilings. Retreat of rural settlement was first evident from the decline of their use. As Sweden's agricultural area is employed more intensively, production is concentrated in the most favoured areas. Rationalisation of Sweden's farming implies retreat of the frontier of

Plate 6   The Ångermanland near Forsmo, Sweden.
Ångermanälven is one of the principal rivers draining north-central Sweden to
the Bothnian Sea. It has helped to develop softwood lumbering country, and
river terrace farming focuses on animal husbandry.

cultivation—especially in Norrland. Reduction in the area of cultivated
land and reduction in the number of holdings proceed side by side. It is
estimated that the extent of cultivated land will be 1,840,000 acres (800,000
hectares) less in 1970 than it was in 1960. Most of the area going out of
cultivation is being restored to woodland.

Three-quarters of Sweden's farmers are owner-farmers. Many of their
holdings are relatively small in arable area; but most have a substantial
area of woodland. Half of Sweden's woodlands are owned by farmers and
landed proprietors. Agricultural statistics suggest that half of the holdings
have less than 50 acres (20 hectares) of cultivated land. A consequence of
this is that many are uneconomic. Operators of smaller farms engage in
supplementary activities, frequently leaving their wives to manage the
livestock. They may spend the winter season lumbering in state or company
forests. On the west coast, especially, fishing and small holdings are
combined (there are 10,000 occupied in the Bohuslän fisheries). Many
part-time farmers are also part-time factory workers.

Farming in Sweden is sensitive to the seasons. Because of its longitudinal extent, the range of agricultural opportunities is very variable. The relatively short growing season and the incidence of winter are the two basic physical circumstances to which farmers must adjust. Plant breeding has produced seeds more suitable for Swedish conditions. At the same time it has guaranteed the ample supplies of fodder necessary to feed farm animals during the 5–7 months that they are indoors. In winter, little work can be done in the fields, but the seasonal rhythm of labour has less pronounced troughs and crests than formerly because of the changing nature of animal husbandry.

Summer remains the climax of activity, not only because of field husbandry and harvesting, but also because essential improvements such as draining and stoning can only be done when the ground is free of frost and snow. Draining has become progressively more important as farmers have incorporated the peatlands in their arable area. Much of Sweden's mineral soils are under-drained; but most of the cultivated peatlands are still open-ditched.

The progress from subsistence to commercial agriculture has been accompanied by improved crops, stock and farm methods. These changes are inseparable from the farming societies, which for nearly two hundred years have worked towards farm improvement, and from the cooperative societies. While the central government initiated a reorganisation of land holdings comparable to and at the same period as British Parliamentary Enclosure, the local organisations have concentrated on new rotations, fertilisers, breeding schemes and cooperative marketing and purchase.

Animal husbandry dominates, and dairy cattle dominate Sweden's animal husbandry, though numbers are less than in Denmark and Finland. Pedigree Swedish stock, regionally varied, take precedence; though both Ayrshire and Friesian herds are widely seen. Pigs are complementary and Swedes have produced their own hybrid *Landras*, which is valued as an export stock in its own right. Horses play a diminishing role in farm operations and numbers decline accordingly. Gotland still has its wild ponies—the *Russ*, a 1,500 year old breed. Sheep are unevenly distributed—most are on the dry limestone plains of Öland, in Gotland and in southeast Sweden.

The principal crop grown in Sweden is temporary grass—a general mixture of timothy, rye grass and clover. Most of it is converted to hay—the old-fashioned hay frame and hay pike are seen no less than the latest hay-baling equipment. Ensilage is made on most farms. Potatoes are grown throughout the country. Fodder beet belong to the southern third; sugar beet are largely concentrated in Skåne, with refined sugar virtually adequate to meet Sweden's needs. The grain picture has changed substantially in the twentieth century. Oats and barley are the two chief crops. Rye acreage has steadily diminished, while the wheat area has increased. Most wheat is spring-sown; the frontiers of spring wheat cultivation have been carried north to the Arctic Circle, but the quantity harvested in north Sweden amounts to very little. There are limited areas of orchard, principally apples, in Skåne. Vegetables are also widely grown in Skåne for the canneries.

Manufacturing industry is Sweden's principal source of wealth and it employs nearly a quarter of the economically active labour force of 3,100,000. Those in agriculture number 630,000. In Norden, Sweden is the industrial giant, for its output is not far short of the total output of manufactured products from the other four countries.

Basic to Sweden's industrial wealth are the raw materials of forest, farm and mine. These do not have a constant value in time but experience considerable variations in demand as well as opportunities for supply. The variations are a reflection of technical circumstance. Until a century ago, Sweden was primarily a source of raw materials which other nations processed. Today, Sweden's sales of raw materials decline proportionately to its export of finished manufactures. At the same time, the range of its manufactures grows rapidly, partly because new ways of using old materials have been devised, partly because new raw materials have been discovered to use beside the old.

Swedish industry dates back to the Middle Ages, when metallurgical and wood-working industries first harnessed running water as a source of power. Abundant charcoal was available for smelting ores, of which copper and iron dominated. From the sixteenth century onwards, Sweden was alive to the significance of foreign skills and encouraged the immigration of technicians. In the two following centuries, the country became one of Europe's principal sources of bar iron.

Sweden lacks combustible fuels save for limited supplies of poor quality coal and a little oil shale. As a result, it was largely bypassed in the first stage of Europe's industrial revolution. Its eighteenth century decline in international political stature was therefore followed by a decline in international economic status. With the transformation in the value of softwood timber in the middle nineteenth century, Sweden began to import return cargoes of steam coal for saw milling. In this way the rebirth of its industry began on the estuaries of lower Norrland's rivers.

By the time saw-milling reached its zenith, about 1900, Sweden's exploitation of its rich water power resources for electrical energy was getting under way. In general, power sites in the south were developed first, and schemes have increased in size and remoteness as new methods of construction and new means of transmission have become available. Most of Sweden's hydro-electric power sites are far from the centres of demand but only the most northerly rivers still await development. A limited number of plants have been installed across the Norwegian border. Most of Sweden's electrical energy is integrated through a grid system. Even the island of Gotland, seventy miles from the Swedish mainland, is linked with one of the world's longest underwater transmission lines. In spite of its wealth of water power, three-quarters of Sweden's energy derives from imported fuels; oil is outstanding among these. As in Norway and Finland, demand for energy is greatest when supply is lowest; thermo-electric installations are consequently necessary supplements. Oil imports are twice as great as those of solid fuel. Oil refining is a significant industry in its own right, with the principal refineries on the west coast. Sweden has experimented actively with nuclear power, but there is little immediate prospect that it will be a supplement of any consequence in the domestic supply scene. However, a nuclear reactor heats the south Stockholm suburb of Farsta.

The siting of Swedish industry has been given growing flexibility with the improvement of electrical transmission. This has been especially important for the softwood industries. Although these continue to provide a limited volume of bulky, low value goods, the contemporary accent is on paper, pulp, processed boards and joinery products. Sweden is a leading world exporter of paper and pulp. The integrated softwood mills such as those in the provinces of Dalarna and Värmland have developed an enormous range of products and by-products. Matches and plywood still mean something in Sweden's export structure, but furniture and prefabricated housing units are significant rivals.

Mining activities are located in three principal areas. The oldest mining enterprises are in Bergslagen in south-central Sweden. Extraction of non-phosphoric ores continues at such sites as Grängesberg and Idkerberg; though output is not to be compared with that of the new mines of the north. Bergslagen contains an immense variety of metallurgical plants, strung along its winding river valleys and buried deeply in its wooded hills. Centres such as Fagersta, Surahammer and Avesta enjoy rural amenity, industrial modernity, and even the occasional element of the picturesque. A second area of mineral production (copper, gold, silver, zinc, lead, bismuth) lies along the Skellefte river in Västerbotten with

Plate 7   Kiirunavaara in northern Sweden.
The iron ores of northern Sweden are most important in the twin ranges of Kiirunavaara-Luossavaara. The settlement of Kiruna is located in a tundra environment and provides a rare example of a successful experiment in living in an arctic setting.

Kristineberg, Boliden and Rönnskär as the centres of operation. Thirdly, there are the so-called Lapland ore fields of Upper Norrland—known for several hundreds of years but developed only during the last three generations. Most of Lapland's ores, though having an ore content of 60–70%, are phosphoric. Their satisfactory employment awaited the Gilchrist-Thomas process in the late 1870's. From the mines of Kiirunavaara, Luossavaara, Malmberget and Svappavaraa, Sweden derives nearly three-quarters of its iron ore.

Some 15 million tons of ore are exported annually from the Lapland ore fields. Movement is mostly through Norwegian Narvik; about one-third is shipped via Swedish Luleå, which also has a state-operated mill, approximating in capacity to the major steel mills of Domnarvet in Dalarna and Sandviken in south Norrland. By substituting electrical energy for thermal energy, and by adopting new smelting techniques, Sweden has contrived to become one of the few countries in the world that have a significant steel industry without a base of domestic coal. Sweden specialises in the production of very high quality alloy steels. It also smelts a variety of non-ferrous ores. Falun, with its now deserted copper mine, its memorable museum and its red ochre house paint, recalls a centuries'-old industry now carried on elsewhere.

Swedish manufacturing marries generations of past skills with contemporary practices. It has developed its mining, electrical and engineering experiences to produce a range of goods that have household names—from Electrolux (in Stockholm) to S.K.F. (the Swedish Ball-Bearing Works in Göteborg), from the arms and weapons of Bofors to the agricultural and dairy equipment of Alfa Laval, from the telephones of the Eriksson concern to the tableware of Eskilstuna.

Sweden, which has long produced its own rolling stock for the State Railways, has also developed new transport industries. Its aircraft production, largely oriented to the country's defence needs, claims some of the most elaborate and highly organised factories in the world. Its automobiles, bearing names such as Volvo and Saab (originating in Göteborg and Trollhättan respectively), have acquired a world prestige. The Göta river is also the heart of the ship-building industries, its three major yards employing the greater part of Sweden's ship-building labour and (together with those of Malmö and Uddevalla) giving to Sweden a world status in this industry.

Although there are giant industrial concerns with a variety of interests at home and abroad and the occasional factory employing a thousand or more employees, most Swedish industrial plants are relatively small. They are also widely scattered. Most manufacturing activity takes place in small towns and Sweden has few heavy industrial concentrations. It is free of the 'black country' associated with the rise of nineteenth century industrial communities, and of all the mental and social inhibitions that such an environment bred.

So much that is old in the industrial scene has experienced apotheosis. The experience is seen in single plants. Hultsbruk, near Norrköping, provides an example. It was founded in 1697 and used to produce a variety of smaller steel goods. Now it is a world specialist in the production of axe blades, with an output of 200,000 a year. Entire industries repeat the situation. The textile industries, originally domestically based but now looking to imported raw materials, have been transformed by their designers so that the textile industries of Norrköping and cottons of Borås-Göteborg have a world market for their products. The glass workshops of east Småland and the porcelain of Gustafsberg have gone through the same process. All of the leading Swedish industries now have their subsidiaries in most advanced countries. Swedish advisers are sought wherever modern mechanical equipment is employed, e.g. the initiation of high voltage transmission of power from mainland British Columbia to Vancouver Island. The world relevance of Swedish industry has been made manifest in less than half a century.

COMMUNICATIONS AND TRADE

The Swedes have always had close relations with the sea. Naval power was a natural adjunct of military strength during the imperial period. In the seventeenth century warship *Vasa* (the hulk of which has been lifted from Stockholm Bay and restored) an example can be seen of Sweden's former maritime prowess. Naval skills are still active in Karlskrona yards, which have been operating since 1679 and find their latest strategic contribution in motor torpedo boats. As its world trade and status have grown, Sweden has increasingly felt the necessity of building up its own mercantile marine, now of some 4 million tons. The most strategic constituent of the contemporary fleet is the oil tanker and about one-third of Sweden's tonnage consists of this type of vessel. A second highly-specialised group of vessels is the ore fleet, owned chiefly by the Grängesberg Company. Beside carrying ore exports from Sweden and Norway to overseas customers, the fleet also engages in international freighting, trading regularly with Liberia, the Caribbean, Persian Gulf ports, Latin America and the U.S.A. As with Finland, Sweden maintains an icebreaker fleet; while, among the countries of Norden, its fishing fleet is second only to that of Norway.

Sweden's railway network, principally state-owned, has a track length equal to the total of the other countries of Norden. Construction was first begun in the 1850's, nearly half of the track is electrified, and rationalisation has brought about considerable closure. Roads are used by well over a million automobiles (driving on the right since 1967), which gives to Sweden one of the highest ratios of cars to population in the world. As in Finland, forest roads multiply apace. Cabotage is important and inland waterways also play a continuing role in commodity movement. There are relic canals from the 'mania' at the end of the eighteenth century; but only the enlarged portion of the Göta Canal leading to Lake Vänern is of significance. The Södertälje Canal gives Baltic access to Lake Mälaren. Of quite a different character and order are the 22,000 miles (ca. 35,000 km.) of interior waterways organised for timber transport. Domestic distances have been reduced through air transport; while Norway, Sweden and Denmark operate a joint international air line (S.A.S.)

Because of its geographical location, most of Sweden's trade follows maritime routes. Exports are increasingly diversified, but raw materials and semi-raw materials predominate absolutely. The need for fuel oil and petroleum, coal and coke, alloy steels and other metals adds bulk to the import structure. Location also implies that Sweden experiences a large-scale passenger traffic. The principal ferry routes are between the Stockholm area and Finland; Göteborg and the Jutish ports; Malmö, Helsingborg, Elsinore, Copenhagen and now Travemunde.

Plate 8   Gamla Sta'n, the medieval core of Stockholm.
Gamla Sta'n (the old town) occupies an island site between Lake Mälaren in the background and the inner reaches of the Baltic Sea in the foreground.

Natural
Regions

A traverse made by August Strindberg and recorded in an essay entitled *Svensk Natur* summarises the varied physical and human landscapes between Skåne and Norrland. For Strindberg, Skåne was at once Sweden and not Sweden. In history, it might be regarded as 'Sweden's Peleponnesus' or 'Scandinavia's Hellas'; but it had 'a completely foreign landscape'. Its trees, dominated by the 'romantically theatrical beech' even included the exotic sweet chestnut; its chalk suggested northern France; its broad arable fields were 'a land of Canaan'; the smell of its sugar beet was alien; the conical spoil heaps by its thin scatter of coal mines were foreign.

It was almost a relief to encounter the abrupt change to the Småland terrain—a bit of north Sweden in the south, with 'humid woods, frosty peatlands, ponds, lakes and the hard bedrock as the primary *motif*'. In the provinces of Halland and Bleckinge, which were tributary to it, Småland gneiss and granite sank into the warmer, saltier Kattegat waters (with 'oysters, lobsters and shrimps; saithes, whiting, plaice and halibut') and the less lively Baltic, meagre in fish and where the *strömming* was a virtual apology for a herring.

The Central Lowlands displayed in Östergötland 'a summary of south and central Sweden' with 'rich plains, great woods, mineral-bearing rocks, a fine archipelago'; looking on the one hand to Lake Vättern, yielding on the other to the grey granite bosses and blocks of Bohuslän with its skerries rich in 'the effects of light and of wave'. To the north-east, Östergotland merged with Södermanland, a province with a more broken landscape, lacking the spaciousness of its eastern neighbour, with plenty of estates but too many unsatisfactory small holdings. The red-painted wooden homestead made its appearance in Södermanland. Indeed, the red of oxidised iron and the green of the forest were Sweden's colours—in

Plate 9   Västergötland's plains in south-central Sweden.
This view, looking out from the forested heights of Mösseberg, is representative of the richer farming areas that surround the great lakes of south-central Sweden.

Strindberg's opinion much more appropriate for Sweden's flag than blue and gold.

Around Lake Mälaren 'which lacks any counterpart in Sweden, or even in Europe', the Swedish state was born. The many channels of Lake Mälaren opened routes to the most favoured parts of central Sweden, and at its estuary, where saltwater and freshwater mingled, was Stockholm. Uppland's plain lay to its north, 'dark with ice age clays', but still there were no bounding mountains on the horizon, 'only attentuated hills with modest sprucewoods'. Dalälven and Gävle, on the northern limits of many southern plants, lay beyond. Asian plants found a foothold among the granites and gneisses (from the White Sea basin as well as the Baltic), porphyries, limestones and sandstones that formed the boulders of Gävle Bay. These 'veritable botanical gardens' by the flat seashore were the ideal collecting grounds for 'a schoolchild's herbarium'.

The grey alder and the lofty northern birches began to assert themselves in Dalarna. Here was the gateway to what Strindberg called *Stor-Sverige* (perhaps best translated as 'greater Sweden'). At the frontier of this untutored landscape lay Lake Siljan, 'reminiscent of Lake Zürich', with its shaly shores; with suggestions of the Tyrol in its local architecture; with shaggy hay frames, relics of *saeters* and *saeter* life, and with the syringa bushes and feathery spireas of Mora market town.

Where the Norrland characteristic took over, everything was sketched on a larger canvas—'hills are higher, woodlands more widespread, rivers broader'. Altitudinally, the dark green of the coniferous woodland yielded to deciduous scrub ('pistachio green in early summer'), to lichens (grey, olive green, scabrous yellow and coral pink), and finally to the rock-shattered pyramidal peaks.

Suecia omnis divisa est in partes duo. In Strindberg's view, the northland stood in ultimate antithesis to the south. Civilised Sweden, with its time-worn barrows, mellowed manors, castles and cathedrals balanced a primeval world where nature still prevailed.

A Well-Ordered Land

Sweden is a country which has come to terms effectively with the twentieth century. Technical developments may have favoured this, but without the climate of opinion bred of an old-established scientific tradition, their adoption and adaptation would have been less easy. Already by the eighteenth century Sweden was renowned among Europe's natural scientists and had a lively concern with the industrial techniques of other lands. The connections between Britain's Royal Society and the Royal Swedish Academy of Science had an interesting complement in the movement of 'industrial spies'. To the organisation of its economy (and the school of 'Swedish' economists has made its philosophy felt) has been added a conscientious attempt to organise its society, so that in the field of social relations no less than that of economic relations, the Swedish example has been the object of studious attention. It has been a balanced attempt in which neither the present has been ruthlessly discounted for the future nor the individual for the community.

Planning and control are basic to the operation. If the long-term project of urban renewal in central Stockholm is North American in its conception, the re-afforestation of Norrland's uneconomic farmland is almost Russian in its zeal. At the international level, no less than at the national, Sweden is concerned with order and integration. It makes a steady contribution to the cadre of international administrators. It is also central to many of the schemes of social and economic organisation that tie the countries of Norden together. In their common labour market, Sweden absorbs the largest share of the migratory labour. Among the international power groups, it pursues a policy of non-alignment. Its economic association with E.F.T.A. is not complemented by membership of N.A.T.O. For the politico-geographical frontier of western Europe passes through Sweden, and Sweden is infinitely concerned with preserving a situation in which the policies of Norway and Denmark shall not disturb the status quo of Finland. Sweden is a well-ordered country from which many have much to learn.

FURTHER READING   *Atlas of Sweden*, 1953 to date.

Guide Books to Sweden, I.G.U. Congress, Stockholm, 1960.

Sweden's principal periodical publications are *Geografiska Annaler, Lund Studies in Geography* and *Ymer*. All publish a substantial amount in English.

The relevant chapters on Sweden in (Ed.) A. Sømme, *The Geography of Norden*, Oslo, 1960; W. R. Mead, *An Economic Geography of the Scandinavian States and Finland*, 1958; R. Millward, *The Scandinavian Countries*, 1965; A. O'Dell, *The Scandinavian World*, 1957.

G. Ahlberg, *Population Trends and Urbanisation in Sweden, 1911–50*, Lund, 1956.

(Ed.) D. Hannerberg, T. Hägerstrand and B. Odeving, *Migration in Sweden*, Lund, 1957.

B. Collinder, *The Lapps*, Princeton, 1959.

Catalogues of maps published in Sweden may be obtained from the Swedish survey office—Generalstabens Litografiska Anstalt, Kartografiska Institutet, Stockholm.

Norway

Norway (*Norge*, to Norwegians) has a strong geographical personality. A number of features of its personality are readily observable from the map. First, it is one of the most longitudinally extended countries in Europe, stretching through more than 13 degrees of latitude. Place one point of the calipers upon Oslo and the other upon Kirkenes in north Norway, inscribe an arc with the point on Oslo and the circumference will touch Rome. Secondly, Norway is a high latitude land, a full third of which lies north of the Arctic Circle. Thirdly, Norway is one of the loftiest countries in Europe and more than half of its area is over 1,600 ft. (ca. 500 m.) in altitude—'Switzerland by the sea' as Honoré de Balzac called it. The high *vidda* or plateau also supports one of Europe's largest glaciers—Jostedalsbre. Fourthly, Norway is a remarkably dissected country, with a mainland coast estimated at 12,500 miles (20,000 km.) in length. All of these facts impose isolation upon Norway and the Norwegians, so that its personality contains a problem in communication. But the coast implies that Norway is a maritime country, where movement by sea has been easier than movement by land. It is, moreover, a special kind of coast, because for such latitudes it is washed by some of the warmest waters in the world. Partly as a result of the North Atlantic Drift, partly as a result of the prevailing westerly winds, Norway's Lofoten Islands experience the highest temperature anomalies (24°C; 75·2°F) of any country in the world. These factors help to ease transport. Nevertheless, and this is a sixth feature of its personality, it remains one of the most thinly peopled countries in the world. Three and a half million inhabitants give to it a density of 28 per square mile (11 per sq. km.). Norway, a part of Denmark from 1380 until 1814, then of Sweden until 1905, was the first of the younger countries of Norden to acquire independence. As a land of superlatives and a country of curiosities (from maelström to midnight sun and lemming to Lapp) Norway is a textbook writer's paradise. It raises corresponding problems of balance and perspective.

The Physical Environment
GEOLOGY AND RELIEF

Norway, 125,000 sq. m. (324,000 sq. km.), occupies the western half of the Scandinavian Peninsula. Its background consists principally of a major series of mountains of Caledonian age folded on to the western flanks of the Fennoscandian Shield. The complicated series of overthrusts, with major and minor nappes, are frequently exposed in the bare surface of the mountain sides to provide clear evidence of the degree of disturbance. Some of the most pronounced areas of overthrust are found along the Swedish border. Here, the mountains, historically known as the Keel (Kjølen), are now called the Scandes. Pre-Cambrian elements, which account for about 30% of the surface of Norway, are consequently found at a variety of levels. Cambrian, Ordovician and Silurian deposits cover the greatest area. They display widely-ranging degrees of resistance to erosion according to their structure and chemical composition. The Ordovician deposits take the form of slates over a great variety of areas in south-central Norway. Metamorphism has much changed the character of many of the pre-Caledonian rocks and volcanic intrusion has left local legacies. The mountain-building epoch was succeeded by major erosion during the Devonian period. This yielded limited beds of conglomerates and sandstones. The Permian period is represented in the Oslo area, but the Mesozoic is barely encountered. Norway, like Finland, is very much a country in which old rocks are juxtaposed with recent deposits. As a result of the work of the Quaternary ice cap, it is also a country where the evidence of erosion is more pronounced than are the signs of deposition.

The advance of the Quaternary ice sheet, presumed to have been preceded by Alpine type glaciation, deepened existing depressions and eroded powerfully along lines of structural weakness. There is debate whether *nunataks* stood out above its surface. As it retreated to the high fells, it revealed evidence of pronounced cirque features—at sea level in the Lofoten peaks. It deposited a widespread, but unevenly distributed legacy of morainic materials. The south-east received the heaviest load. The infill of the major river valleys tributary to Oslofjord reflect its volume. Their hummocky moraines, dead ice fields and drumlin fields are frequently much water-worn. An extended terminal rampart, known as the Ra moraine, stretches from the Swedish border around Oslofjord and along a part of the south coast. As with most of the morainic features of lowland Norway, it has been much modified by marine agencies, for a significant rise in sea level followed the retreat of the ice. Subsequently, the land mass adjusted itself isostatically, so that the lower slopes of the plateau display suites of terraces. These may occur up to 650 ft (ca. 200 m.) above present sea level. Much work remains to be done in piecing together the history of Norway's Quaternary period. Not surprisingly, one of the first natural historians to seek for field evidence of an ice age in the features of deposition was a Norwegian, Jens Esmark. His work was undertaken in the 1830's.

As a result of its physical evolution, Norway is one of the most dissected lands in the world. Chile is its only rival. The highest peaks, which rise from high plateau surfaces, are not much over 6,200 ft (ca. 2,000 m.). Nevertheless, the clustered peaks of the Jotunheim, from pyramidal Galdhøpiggen to the perfectly cirqued Sognefjell, the dark exfoliation domes of Fjaerlandfiord or the white rock of Sukkertoppen at Stalheim, provide fine mountain scenery. The upstanding gabbro peaks of the Lofoten in the north are among the most striking landforms of Norway,

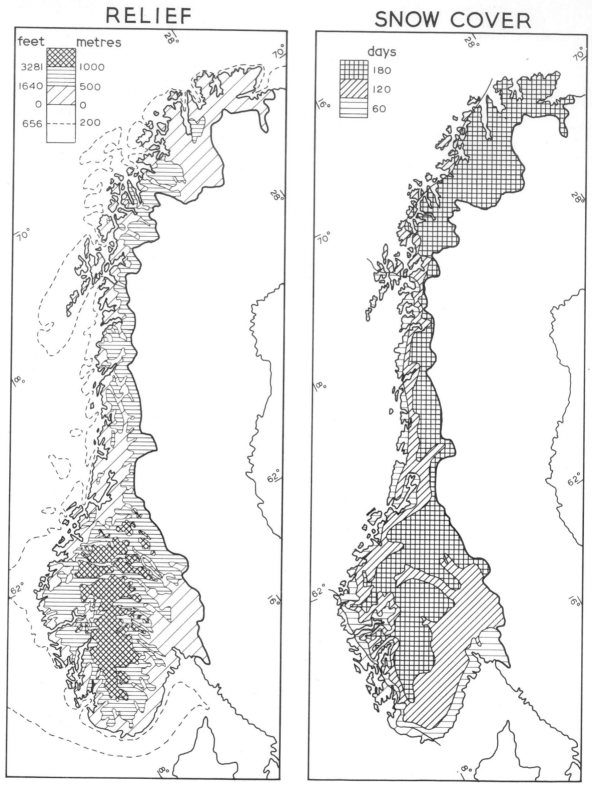

RELIEF

feet	metres
3281	1000
1640	500
0	0
656	200

SNOW COVER

days
180
120
60

Fig 14   Four maps of features essential to the appreciation of the geography of Norway

NATURAL REGIONS

POPULATION

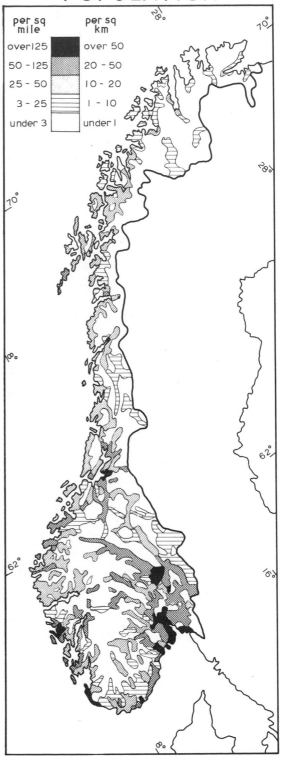

100 miles
100 kms

F I O R D S   A N D   A R C H I P E L I G O E S

A N D   M O U N T A I N S

P L A T E A U S

D A L E S

SOUTH EAST LOWLANDS

per sq mile | per sq km
over 125 | over 50
50 - 125 | 20 - 50
25 - 50 | 10 - 20
3 - 25 | 1 - 10
under 3 | under 1

(Based partly on the *Geography of Norden*)

because their *tindr* or peaks and horns rise precipitously from the low-lying *strandflat*. Dissection is most elaborate around the margins of the plateau where, as Balzac wrote, the 'tumultuous precipices . . . defy the bizarre terminology of geometry'. Not less impressive are the 'inscrutable depths' of the adjacent fiords (as a sixteenth century divine called them). In fact, the deepest parts, e.g. at Vik in Sogne, could submerge the highest peaks of England and Wales. The Sognefjord and Hardangerfjord are the longest inlets; their innermost recesses feel the pulse of the tide and are sufficiently salt for seaweeds to thrive over sixty miles (100 km.) from open water. Inland, the dales complement the fiords. Each has its own distinctive features and is physically isolated from its neighbours. Österdal and Gudbrandsdal are the two great eastern dales; while into the western plateau are carved dales such as Hallingdal, Numedal, Ottadal and Setesdal. In addition to the lowland tracts around Oslofjord, there are also coastal plains around Trondheimfjord.

Norway's coast, one of the most intricate in the world, is also one of the most richly islanded. The island zone varies in breadth and complexity. Along the south coast, islands are low-lying and limited in number; off the west coast, they proliferate—from skerries submerged at high tide to massive outlying remnants of the mainland plateau. They form a great breakwater almost all the way from the south-western Cape Lindesnes to North Cape. In their lee is the protected channel known as the Lead. The largest islands are found in the Lofoten and Vesterålen groups. The Arctic coast is the least islanded. Much of western Norway's island zone belongs to the denudation surface known as the *strandflat*. The origins of this feature, which Fritjof Nansen debated academically seventy years ago, are still disputed. Beyond the *strandflat* is the broad continental shelf, breached by the deep channel of *Norske Renne*, which leads into the Skagerak.

Given such pronounced variations in altitude and an extended coast facing the long fetch of the sea and ocean, it is not surprising that Norway experiences exaggerated forces of erosion. With valley hanging in valley, rivers leap in cataracts and waterfalls. With immature drainage, torrents are everywhere more likely than calms—save where moraine dammed lakes halt the rivers in their descent to the sea. Instability of slope gives rise to widespread rock-fall, scree-slip, avalanche and mud slide. The severe winter conditions that prevail over much of plateau Norway are in themselves forceful agents of erosion, as are the heavy rains of the west. In Norway, it is rare not to hear the processes of weathering at work. Because Norway is alive with physical hazards, it has been felt necessary to set up a commission to identify 'dangerous places' and to prevent or remove settlement in their locality. Such places as Ramnefjell, near Loen, and the Namsen river in north Trøndelag, are synonyms for catastrophe.

DRAINAGE   The manifold intricacies of Norway's drainage system spring from relief, recency of retreat of the ice sheet, and the pronounced variations in distribution and type of precipitation. The drainage structure is immature and displays widespread evidence of rejuvenation. At all levels, drainage is interrupted by rock structure and moraine. As a result, there is a generous distribution of lakes. Some are extensive and in the dales the lakes are strung out like beads on a string. Along the coast, lakes frequently repeat in fresh water the features of the adjacent saltwater fiords from which they are separated by narrow isthmuses. The chains of lakes recur at all altitudes to provide a series of natural reservoirs. Water rarely moves in a leisurely meandering manner and river profiles are notched with torrents, rapids, waterfalls and cataracts.

Norway's waterways are seasonally irregular in flow; the peak occurs in late spring and early summer, and is sustained by the prolonged snow melt. The flow is least in midwinter.

CLIMATE   Norway has a maritime climate and changeable weather conditions which spring from its location in the track of westerly cyclones. It has an immense range of local climates as a result of its longitudinal extent and variations in relief. The entire country enjoys a positive thermal anomaly, which is relatively greater in higher latitudes. Because of its high-latitude location, Norway also experiences exaggerated seasonal rhythms of day-

Plate 10   Winter scene near the Ski Hut at Trondheim, western Norway.
Snow plays a major rôle in the economics of Norwegian land use. In east Norway, it is of primary concern for forestry and lumbering. It is also important for the winter tourist industry.

light and darkness. One-third of the country lies north of the Arctic Circle and this implies a summer period of uninterrupted daylight, balanced by a midwinter period of darkness relieved only by several hours of twilight. Summer in Norway has been described as a time when no stars are seen. Describing Nordland, the Norwegian novelist Knut Hamsun measured the advance of autumn by the nightly appearance of new stars. The high north also experiences brilliant displays of the Aurora Borealis. Norway's interest in and concern over its weather has given rise to a great variety of recording stations, including automatic stations on remote Jan Mayen Island and lofty Fanaråkken. It has also bred a school of meteorologists of world renown. Tromsø is an established centre for the investigation of the aurora and other magnetic phenomena.

Norway's climate is commonly characterised by raininess, cloudiness and windiness. Yet, there are plenty of places in Norway which do not accord with this description. Precipitation varies from 150 inches (4,000 mm.) annually on the Western flanks of Nordland and Sogne with Fjordane counties. Yet it can fall to less than a tenth of that amount in Lom and Otta valleys, where irrigation sprays are regular summer features. Rainfall is generally lower in the north than in the south. A substantial part of the precipitation takes the form of snow, which may even fall in summer on the higher parts of the *vidder* and permanent icefields. Snow drifts are measured in many feet in exposed places. They are partly a reflection of windiness.

A measure of the mildness is found in the duration of the growing season. In the extreme south-west, plant growth may continue from the end of March until the beginning of December. By contrast, the interior uplands of Finnmark and Troms, with the mean temperatures of the warmest month hovering about 10°C (50°F), have a growing season of only nine or ten weeks. In turn, the tundra conditions of Norwegian Lapland contrast with the virtually continental climate of the Oslo area. Oslo may have a temperature range exceeding 50°F; but it also enjoys one of the highest July mean temperatures of any part of Scandinavia (22·4°C; 72·4°F), and higher sunshine figures than Copenhagen.

Norway has been sensitive to longer period climatic changes, no less than other high latitude lands. 'Iron nights' (frost nights) are a part of its summer vocabulary and their numbers increase in cooler years. More dramatic is the behaviour of glaciers during colder periods. There is photographic evidence to substantiate ice edge retreat in the last century, and documentary evidence from 200 years ago attesting to its advance.

VEGETATION   The distribution of vegetation in Norway differs greatly from that in the other countries of Norden. Most of Norway lacks timber cover, for reasons of altitude rather than latitude. The timber line rises highest in the south-east, to 1,200 ft (600–800 m.). Over most of Vestlandet and Sørlandet, there are few productive forests above 1,000 ft. (*c.* 600 m.); while on the westward-facing slopes, exposure and excessive rainfall

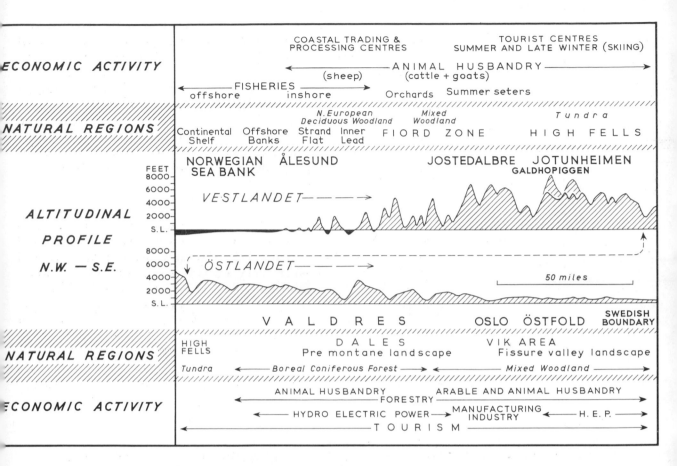

Fig 15 A transect diagram of southern Norway

force down the line to several hundred feet. Most of Norway falls into the boreal coniferous forest zone. Scots pine and Norway spruce are the chief trees, with the pine thriving in the warmer summers of the drier east (though it is a native of Vestlandet). In the great valleys of Finnmark and Troms, conifers yield to the scrub willow, dwarf birch, aromatic herbs and succulent berries of the tundra zone. In Norway, the sub-Arctic flora penetrates farther south than in any other part of Norden.

The North European mixed forest zone, which embraces the greater part of the Trøndelag lowlands, also pushes to its northernmost limits in Norway. The most northerly specimens of many of Europe's familiar trees are found along coastal Norway. Oak and ash, for example, reach 64°N. South Norway has residual beech woods as well as oak stands. Among more sensitive west European trees that occur in south-west Norway are the yew and the holly, while the rhododendron has been successfully introduced. Forest clearance for settlement, construction and heating, independently of destruction through open-range grazing, have much altered Norway's original woodlands. There are *Calluna* heaths, which have been man-induced, though they are less extensive than in Denmark. In the sheltered fiords, especially where the weathered Silurian shales yield locally rich soils, the flora has the familiar purple, blue and yellow opulence of the limestone lands of England or France. And the juniper stands erect around the farmsteads—though it crouches in cushions at higher altitudes. There are extensive and widely distributed bogs—sometimes fluttering with bog cotton, sometimes cushioned with cloudberries, sometimes edged with butterwort and liverwort. There is a rich aquatic vegetation, and the relatively warm coastal waters encourage a profusion of seaweeds and favour the formation of feathery corals.

The Regions of Norway

Although the map of Norway cannot be readily divided into morphological regions, Norwegians have a well-established image of the principal areas into which their country falls. Five areas are identified—four of them by the compass point. They are Östlandet (East Norway), which looks to Oslofjord; Vestlandet (West Norway), the tourist's Norway of fiord and fell; Sörlandet (South Norway), which is a wedge of country between them and commonly tied to the *fylker* or provinces of Aust Agder and Vest Agder; Trøndelag, which centres on Trondheimfjord; and Nord Norge (North Norway), which consists of the provinces of Nordland, Troms and Finnmark. These are not well-defined physical units; but each has a sufficiency of distinguishing features and problems to give meaning to the division.

Population Distribution

Norway has diversity of opportunity in a large number of extremely restricted areas. These are mostly coastal and population distribution reflects this fact; most of its $3\frac{1}{2}$ million inhabitants live in sight of the sea, including the 1,200–1,300 who stay over winter in Spitsbergen. All occupiable coastal sites seem to have been settled by Viking times and place-name evidence provides grounds for speculation on the chronology of their occupation. Settlement began to penetrate into the interior dales in the post-Viking period, when a great epoch of land clearance is recalled by the place-names terminating in *rud*, especially in Gudbrandsdal and Österdal. Oslo, Bergen and Trondheim have always been the principal centres of population. Stavanger is a rapidly increasing rival. One-third of the population of Norway is concentrated around Oslofiord. Coastal concentration of population has resulted in a peculiar vulnerability, as is evidenced by the ease with which the medieval Hanseatic League acquired and maintained control of Norway's ports, and by German seizure of similar critical points in the invasion of 1941.

Population distribution has changed considerably in the last generation. The direction of change can be investigated in detail from the population registers kept in each commune. There are several reasons for the mobility. First, rural-urban migration has resulted from the swift rise of industry.

Since the Second World War there has been a pronounced decline of dispersed population; though in all regions save Östlandet, at least half of the settlement is still classified as dispersed. Secondly, there has been a distinct drift to the south—especially to the south-east. Thirdly, the war years prompted redistribution both at large and in detail. In particular, the obliteration of many settlements in the northernmost provinces of Troms and Finnmark, encouraged the regrouping of population. Efforts to arrest the drift to the south have taken varied forms, from direct subsidy to indirect attempts to increase employment opportunities by encouraging industrial development.

Ethnographically, the Norwegians are homogeneous people. There are linguistic divergences which result from the romantic literary revival of the mid-nineteenth century. As a result, the official language of the government (*riksmaal*) is challenged by the revived language of the countryfolk (*landsmaal*). Both forms of the language are learnt in school; but it is difficult to generalise about the differences in distribution. In the northern third of Norway, there are 20,000 Lapps.

Norway has a tradition of emigration. Movement away from the country reached its peak at the end of the nineteenth century, though the first official emigrants left on the little sloop *Restaurationen* for North America in 1825. In its earlier stages, emigration was a positive feature, for given the technical situation in the nineteenth century Norway was probably over-populated. Most Norwegian movement was to the northern part of the Middle West and the Dakotas. Ole Rölvaag, son of an emigrant and professor of history at St. Olaf's College, Minnesota, has written of Norwegian experiences in land-breaking in his novel *Giants in the Earth*.

Economic Development
AGRICULTURE AND FORESTRY

Norwegian farmland is found largely in the interstices between fell, forest and waterfront. Only 3% of the surface area is cultivated. It is the infield, in contrast to the extensive grazings of the outfield. Most of the infield, the sites and slopes of which usually announce a marine, riverine or lacustrine origin, skirts the rocky core of Norway. The infield stands out clearly in the midst of the extensive wasteland—especially along the coast of Vestlandet and northern Norway, where there is no tree cover to conceal it, or to soften the hard outlines of the landscape. The most extensive areas of arable land are found in eastern Norway, around the Oslofjord and in the valleys tributary to it. Broad lowlands are also spread around Trondheimsfjord: more restricted flat country occurs around Stavanger.

Forest and fell, river, lake and sea are brought into the farmer's work calendar. Most Norwegian farmers are either forest-farmers or fisher-farmers (the term farmer-fisher is used in the employment statistics if returns from the land exceed those from the water). Supplementary pursuits are accordingly added to those associated with the infield. In Norwegian, the outfield is usually called the *saeter*. Its image is most

Plate 11 The Head of Geirangerfiord in western Norway.

The narrow farming zone between the mountains and the sea has been intensively occupied since before the Viking period. It is grassland country first and foremost—with the problems of haymaking indicated on the haylines in the foreground.

commonly derived from the *saeters* of Vestlandet, though it is a feature which varies greatly in character. Summer transhumance of animals and a part of the farm community continue, if less actively than formerly. Many farms (such as that in Figure 16) have several *saeters*, which may be used rotationally or successively throughout the grazing season.

The infields, centred on the *tun* or historic site of the homestead, are limited in size. Farming is accordingly small scale. The fact is underlined by the land-use statistics, which use the *decare* (one-tenth of a *hectare*) as their unit of reference. Holdings tend to be larger where the area of flatter land is more extended, e.g. in Östfold. Only 15% of Norway's farms have more than ten hectares of arable land. To an even greater extent than in the other countries of Norden, the Norwegian farmers are owner-operators. Most of the holdings are old-established and the farm name and family name are frequently identical.

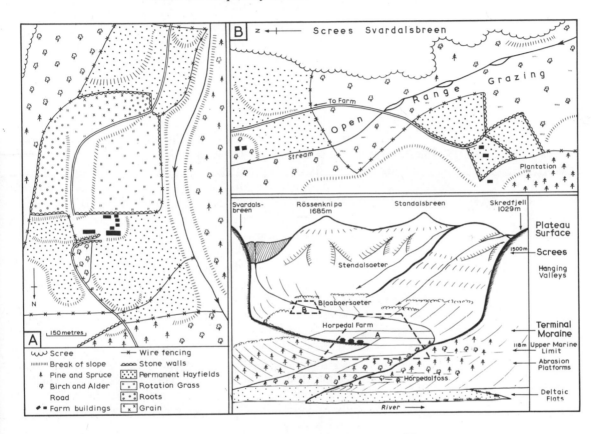

Fig 16 Horpedal, a farm in Fjaerlandfiord, western Norway

Norwegian agriculture has gone through a large number of technical and organisational changes in a relatively short time. In the third quarter of the nineteenth century, the break-up of the traditional farming structure began. Already, reorganisation of the fragmented land holdings had been set in motion and unitary holdings were succeeding to fragmented properties. More important, self-sufficiency began to yield to the pressures of the commercial economy. The self-sufficiency of local communities was frequently and seasonally more correctly described as deficiency. 'As the days lengthen, the belt must be tightened' runs an old proverb. The fiord and dale farmsteads slowly and sometimes painfully lost their bloom. Their clusters of ornate barns, storehouses and outhouses, turf-roofed over birchbark, their immense wooden dwelling houses regionally distinguished by elaborate architecture, were out of joint with a changing world.

To self-sufficiency succeeded the essentials of the present-day pattern of mixed farming—the mixture varying regionally. Norway's agriculture focuses upon animal husbandry, which, in turn calls for fodder cropping. Rotation grass thrives in maritime Norway, but for climatic reasons it is not easily converted into hay. The long hay frames that worm their way across the infields in July reflect much arduous labour, while hay hanging for several weeks before it is dry enough to take to the barn suffers deterioration in quality. Ensilage has greatly assisted fodder conservation. Kale, fodder beet and potatoes are valuable constituents in a husbandry that may be faced with adverse weather conditions. Six or seven year rotations characterise most of the country.

Food crops rival fodder crops only on farmlands around Oslofjord, Norway's granary. Here, the drier, warmer climate permits grain to ripen; but Norway is not self-sufficient in bread grains.

Among animal stocks, dairy cattle take precedence. Hybrid regional stock have been developed from Norwegian native breeds; imported stock are everywhere subordinate. Centralised cooperative dairies process the milk which was formerly treated on the farm. They have promoted a redistribution of milk cows; for they can only serve saeters and farms that are accessible to the routes of milk lorries and milk boats. Vestlandet has specialised goat herds, the milk of which is used for cheese production. Sheep are widely kept in the southern half of Norway, but the largest flocks occur in the extreme south-west where there are especially elaborate transhumant routes between the peninsula of Jaeran and the upland grazings. Pigs are complementary to dairying, but their management is less specialised than in Denmark. Poultry farming is more common in Östlandet. Fruit orchards, probably introduced by the Cistercians, thrive along the Hardangerfjord, Sognefjord and Nordfjord. Apples, cherries, plums, raspberries, strawberries and other small fruits have become a regional speciality of Vestlandet. In former times, Norway also bred and exported horses for both transport and farm work. Vestlandet had its own special breed, the *fjording*, an all-purpose animal which is still widely used despite the competition of tractors.

Structural problems afflict Norway's agriculture in general and in detail. The small size of holdings is the greatest problem, while their dispersion poses problems of integration. Not surprisingly, there is a retreat of the frontiers of farming, especially in higher altitudes and higher latitudes. In addition to farm abandonment, an increasing number of small farms, even in favourable farming areas, cease to operate as independent entities. Between 1959–64, farm numbers declined by 18,000. Sometimes, this represents failure at the individual level; but, equally, it may be said to represent farm rationalisation at the national level. The phenomenon is partly explained by the flight from the land of the younger generation, because in 40% of the cases the farmers who gave up their holdings were over sixty years old. It is ironical that, while farm abandonment takes place in some areas, elsewhere land reclamation (with state support) proceeds actively. There are other forms of financial assistance to farmers as well as the widespread provision of services where distance imposes such a heavy tax.

Mechanisation has been widely introduced to transform many farm operations, from drainage to stone clearance, milking to harvesting. The provision of small-scale equipment to meet the needs of small holdings and small budgets has been important. In fiordland especially, field size and slope conditions restrict the effective employment of most equipment.

By comparison with those of Sweden and Finland, Norway's forest resources are modest, yet they are of considerable value to a full 100,000 of Norway's farmers. Timber stands occur mostly in Östlandet, 40% of which is forested. Three-quarters of Norway's lumber output derives from this area. Most of the forests are privately-owned, with farmers as the largest group of owners. Less than one-fifth belong to the state. Norway's foresters are closely linked with those in the other countries of Norden, so that experiences in forest improvement are pooled. Drainage and afforestation are the two principal methods of improvement. Afforestation is especially active in west, south-west and north Norway. Experimental forest plots in Vestlandet have had considerable success with exotic species, especially from Alaska and British Columbia.

NAVIGARE
NECESSE EST

Norway has a long and strong maritime tradition. There are two reasons for this and a variety of consequences. The first reason is that the sea offers more food than the land—as well as oil and skins. The second reason is that movement by sea has been easier than movement by land. Norwegians have been kept apart by the land, but the sheltered coasts have offered easy routes. There are many communities in Norway which are still only accessible by way of the sea. Ship building was an immediate consequence of the maritime tradition. The earliest records of ships were chiselled out in rock drawings as long as 10,000 years ago.

Sea going made its first great impact over a thousand years ago during the Viking period. Viking movements, partly related to the restricted resources at home, consisted of both summer raiding parties and permanent emigrants. The latter went to the Scottish Isles, western Britain and the Irish Sea coastlands, heaping up their distinctive burial mounds and bequeathing a rich legacy of Norse place-names and dialect words. They also peopled the Faeroes, Iceland and the south-west coast of Greenland, as well as setting encampments upon the mainland of North America. As a result of ship burials, some idea may be gleaned of their vessels from museum specimens. After they had accepted Christianity the Norwegians became active in peaceful trading. Medieval east coast customs records attest to their commercial activity with England. The intensive use of the sea for fishing, transport and exploration are continuous themes in Norwegian national life.

Commercial fishing and hunting have medieval roots in Norway. Dried

E*

fish, sealskins, walrus hides and ivory, figure in some of the earliest references to Norwegian trade. A great range of vessels—from owner-operated, open-decked boats with two-stroke engines, to cooperatively-owned, decked, diesel-driven vessels with a crew of 6 or 7—now engage in the fisheries. The motor boat, introduced in the early years of the century, has transformed fishing and local communication. Radio has greatly eased adjustment to weather hazards; echo-sounding apparatus has facilitated the search for fish; while a host of ingenious minor innovations (from tin bait for mackerel to rubber worms for saithe) reflect the attention paid to detail.

The fisheries have three different locations—inshore (usually within the shelter of the fiords and skerries); offshore (identified according to sixty named banks, northernmost of which is 'Drink-All Bank' in the

Plate 12   Henningsvaer in the Lofoten Islands, Norway.
Henningsvaer is one of the winter fishing ports established on the skerries around the edge of the Lofoten Islands. Since the Middle Ages it has engaged in the drying and export of fish.

Barents' Sea); and long-distance (Norwegian fishing vessels operate as far afield as Greenland waters). The principal fish caught are cod and herring. Two remarkable seasonal concentrations occur—the cod fisheries of the Lofotens, which reach their climax in the great Vestfjorden in February and March, and the herring fisheries off the coast of Sunnmøre, which reach a peak in April. Both attract thousands of vessels. Fishing is not uncommonly combined with other activities, usually farming. Because of the dependence of small-scale operators upon the industry, Norwegians have been especially jealous of their territorial waters. They extend to 12 miles from base lines along the highly-fragmented coast, and are carefully patrolled against foreign intruders by fishery protection vessels. Among hunting operations, whaling has largely disappeared in northern waters and has declined sharply in the Antarctic. Sealing, off the coast of Greenland, takes the form of annual expeditions in the late winter.

Norway's world shipping status has its roots in domestic communication and local fishing. The Norwegian mercantile marine ranks third of any country with the highest per capita tonnage in the world. The progress from sail to steam was slow, but twentieth century advance from steam to diesel, and from general tramping to highly specialised cargo vessels has been swift. The very size of Norway's merchant marine means that most of its fleet continues to be built abroad, but it has also developed its own impressive ship-building industry. The first Bergen-owned steamship was bought in 1827, and from it has evolved the great fleet of coastal vessels that operate Norway's express coastal route. Norway's services as a carrier were first employed extensively by Britain and France during the Crimean War. As a specialist freighter, Norwegians dealt in the 1840's in Chilean guano, and in the 1880's with banana transport from Central America; today, half of the merchant fleet consists of oil tankers. During the last three generations, Norway's increasingly vigorous tourist trade has also been largely accommodated in domestic vessels.

It was the 'Northern Way' along the 'Lead' which directed attention to the Arctic. Norway's interest in the Arctic, prompted by a spirit of scientific enquiry and love of adventure, has had a number of consequences. Nansen was the first man to organise a crossing of Greenland—on skis. His feat, together with the activities of the Norwegian seal hunters on the east coast ice packs, aroused much interest in Greenland, but the territory was formally made over to Denmark in 1920. Nansen's subsequent journey in his ship *Fram* enlivened Norwegian interests in the Arctic Ocean, especially Spitzbergen (Svalbard) which was given Norwegian sovereignty by a Hague decision in 1921. Nansen was no less enthusiastic about Antarctic exploration. Roald Amundsen was the first man to reach the South Pole. His original map from the 1911 journey, in Bergen's maritime museum, is an appropriate complement to Captain Scott's diary in the British Museum. In the Great White South Norway has the territorial dependencies of Queen Maud Land, Peter I Island and Bouvet Island. These and the Polar Dependencies have encouraged continuing high latitude research, evidenced in H. U. Sverdrup's investigations between Alaska and the New Siberian Islands in his ship *Maud* (1922–5); the exploits of *Norge* which was the first airship to cross the North Pole; Norwegian ambitions to extend telemetric investigations to Svalbard; and the world's northernmost oil drilling at Blåhuken on Spitzbergen.

MINING
AND INDUSTRY While mining is old-established in Norway, manufacturing industry has made a significant impact only in the twentieth century. In the seventeenth century, the royal mines at Kongsberg in southern Norway produced a substantial output of silver. Kongsberg church recalls the former wealth of the community, a local small arms factory reflects the continuing skill in metal working, and the four-figure prices fetched by Norwegian silver tankards measure international appreciation of their workmanship. Another relict landscape that recalls earlier metal processing is found around Röros; this has a distinct personality, for the diminutive cottages of the artisans contrast with the impressive homes of the copper masters. There are conical tailing heaps, the ruins of smelteries, and a motif of pick and shovel on the church's weather vane that are painted by artists but forgotten by industry. Nineteenth century Norway had a scatter of mining and smelting centres, some brought into being by British engineers and entrepreneurs. They were mostly coastal in setting. There were also coastal saw mills—especially around Oslofjord. Oslo itself supported a string of workshops and small factories tributary to the water power of the little river Aker. Its deeply entrenched valley still has a variety of factories which frequently occupy their original century-old sites. In addition to water power, Norway employed timber, charcoal and (later) imported coal as fuel. Only a modest amount of its requirements of coal can be met from its own resources, which are 300 miles beyond the north coast of Norway in Svalbard, where production is difficult and winter interferes with shipment.

Industry grew in scale and significance as a result of several technological changes. Political independence in 1905 gave an additional spur to action, while the growth of a mercantile marine provided external earnings for capital accumulation. The softwood industries first sensed the changing techniques—in the same degree if not to the same extent as in Sweden. The main processing plants established themselves around Oslofjord, the area of greatest timber assembly. Sometimes, they grew up side by side with old-established sawmills, as in Sarpsborg and Drammen. The new paper and pulp plants first employed local hydro-electric power; but, as in the rest of Scandinavia, Norwegian industry was given a new flexibility in siting when long-distance transmission released industry from the need to locate at the site of energy production. At the same time, timber processing blossomed with a vast new range of products—from chipboard to laminated plywoods, chemicals to plastics. The interplay of technique and location are equally well illustrated in the group of plants born of the chemical concern, *Norsk Hydro*. Founded in 1905 in interior Notodden, exploiting the energy of fell-edge Rjukan and developing new factories in coastal Heröya, this was the first great Norwegian industrial plant to make an international impact. Its bulk exports of chemical fertilisers are measured in millions of tons.

The wide range of products emerging from the electro-chemical industry is repeated in electro-metallurgy. Most of Norway's electro-metallurgical plants originally arose in response to 'cheap' power; though hydro-electric power is no longer so cheap. Among them are the aluminium processing plants at Høyanger and Årdal in Sognefjord, and near Odda in Hardangerfjord. A new integrated plant at Karmöy illustrates the continued expansion, yet the bauxite is derived principally from the Caribbean. After Canada, Norway is the principal exporter of virgin metal. A diversity of aluminium goods is manufactured in the Oslo area. Magnesium production at Heröya is another light-weight electro-metal. Ferro-chrome and ferro-silicon are also produced with electric energy.

Plate 13 Sunndalsøra, a view from Kalken.
The fiord-side aluminium plant, typical of several in coastal Norway, suffers from a problem of siting and expansion owing to the very restricted flat land available at sea level.

Heavier industry is a more recent development. It is illustrated especially in the state-owned iron and steel plant at Mo i Rana in Nordland. This owes its existence to political decisions as well as to economic facts. In 1964, output totalled 255,000 tons of pig iron, 240,000 tons of steel and 195,000 tons of electric-steel. Hydro-electric power at Rössåga favoured the siting of the plant. Although there are iron ores in the hinterland of Dunderlandsdal, iron is drawn mostly from Narvik and Sör Varanger. Sör Varanger, in Finnmark, has a large deposit of low-grade iron ore which is partly refined before export. Its capacity is 2.4 million tons p.a. The mining is open cast and the operation state-sponsored. Coke needed for Mo i Rana is drawn from overseas, but a coking plant (with chemical by-products for export to Heröya) is projected. Spitzbergen coal mines yield about 500,000 tons p.a., but it is unsuitable for coking purposes.

A major product of the iron and steel industry is ships' plate, much in demand by Norway's expanding shipbuilding industry. The largest yard, in Norway's largest port of Oslo, employs 5,000. Norway is a great experimenter in specialist ship-building—from car ferries to catamaran ferries, from oil tankers to blown bitumen carriers.

Increasing diversification of industry characterises all parts of Norway, though it takes different forms in different areas. First, the rise of a considerable export industry has encouraged the larger-scale production of consumer goods. Thus, Norwegian culinary ware, oven ware, table ware, textiles, furnishing, glass and pewter have been revitalised. Secondly, new variations on old processing themes have transformed several branches of manufacturing. In fish processing, north Norwegian harbours have bypassed the canning stage which has meant so much for Stavanger, and have leapt forward from the production of wind-dried *stokkfisk* and *klipfisk* to the manufacture and packing of deep-frozen fillets for export. Thirdly, there have been attempts to bring many workshop industries to the skerries and archipelagoes, in order to provide alternate employment in slack seasons. The islands outside Bergen, itself a city of highly diversified manufacturing, produce goods as natural to the locality as nylon fishnets and as unexpected as clocks, watches and safes. The occupational structures of the south Norwegian towns are invariably more balanced than those of the north. They often manifest a surprising diversity. Flekkefjord, for example, a small south coast port, has leather tanneries (based upon Argentinian hides), footwear and glove manufacture; furniture manufacture and yacht-building; clothing and corsetry.

Range, scale and international connections springing from its shipping services, have enabled Norwegian industrialists to look to increasingly distant markets. As with the other Scandinavian countries, Norway exports integrated plants to countries as distant as India and Peru, Colombia and Kuwait. It has a number of large-scale consulting services (for dams, underground power plants and bridges), and standardised insurance services, and provides expertise for undeveloped countries from Africa to India.

There is another industry which the Norwegians have developed to the full—tourism. The tourist trade began with the handful of mid-nineteenth century fishermen and hunters who established the legend of the English 'lords', proceeded through late nineteenth century climbers and less energetic travellers who sought the verandahs of villas and hotels 'Victoria', to a contemporary trade in three million visitors a year. The tourist trade is also partly a winter enterprise. The word *ski* is Norwegian, and Norway initiated skiing as a sport. Oslo's Holmenkollen, where ski jumping competitions began, remains a European show place. Norway has come into its own as the continent's 'northern playground', an epithet given to it by W. C. Slingsby, a legendary climber who has literally left his name upon the map of Vestlandet.

TRADE, TRANSPORT AND INTEGRATION

Trading is vital to Norwegian independence. Norway is self-sufficient in relatively few of the modern necessities of life; while its contemporary industrial structure requires raw material imports no less than it needs an overseas market for most finished products. Although Norway's population is small, it is unable to produce all of its essential foodstuffs. Fuel is an equally strategic deficiency. Formerly, Norway relied heavily upon imported coal; today, it has a very great dependence upon oil. Oil touches Norwegians at a personal as well as a national level. It is the fuel which keeps in motion the fisherman's motor boat and the farmer's tractor. Oil

Plate 14   Oslo Harbour.
The view is taken along the deck of one of the massive new tankers constructed in Norway. The vessel is juxtaposed with a windjammer. Shipbuilding still takes place adjacent to the City Hall, the towers of which stand out in the photograph.

grows increasingly important as a complement to electricity, because Norway lacks a national power grid and supplementary thermal energy is locally and regionally vital in time of shortage (especially seasonal shortage). The growing consumption of oil has led to the establishment of large refineries on Oslofiord, and at Risavika, near Stavanger. Because of an industrial structure in which most units of production are of modest size, Norway must also import capital goods for factory plants. The network of Norway's overseas trading is spread especially wide because of its peculiar relationship to the sea. Europe, especially North-West Europe, dominates Norway's trade relations. The United Kingdom is the largest single trading partner.

Integration within has been and remains a primary problem for Norway. The configuration of the land imposes major obstacles. Settlements have been more easily linked by sea than overland. Not surprisingly, there are more generous grants for the preparation of coastal charts than topographical maps.

Although Norway's State Railways opened their first line between Oslo and Eidsvoll in 1856, their expansion was slow for both physical and financial reasons. Some idea of the primitive rural communications which prevailed may be obtained from the older guide books of Thomas Cook or Baedeker. Indeed, a century ago, Norway was described as only suitable for ladies of daring. Norway's arterial railway lines bear regional names. Among them, Bergensban is the best known; as a feat of engineering it has a European stature. Its progress over the high *vidder* between Gol and Voss remains a miracle of maintenance as well as of construction. The recently completed Sörlandsban, linking Stavanger with the capital, is less spectacular; but it has a greater length and frequency of tunnels than any of the other rail routes. Nordlandsban, partly built with conscript labour during the war years, has its terminal at Bodö. Bergensban was the first main line to be completely electrified; elsewhere diesel locomotives are usually employed.

For both rail and road, the degree of slope, the frequency of change of slope, the nature of the climate and the frequency of change in weather conditions, raise primary difficulties. Improved road building equipment, together with the introduction of cheaper and more efficient explosives and drills, have facilitated the conquest of the bed rock. Today, Norway may claim highways that are among the most exciting (and at the same time the most efficient) in Europe. The giddy route up the valley of Rjukanfoss provides an example. Tunnels and snowsheds, to protect against snowdrift, avalanche and rockfall, are a necessary additional expense. In general, roads are unsurfaced, though the trunk roads of the south are asphalted. A State Railway bus network complements the railroad. Beyond Bodö and Lönsdal, the bus takes over absolutely; though there is a short stretch of line, bearing the heaviest traffic of any in Norway, which joins Narvik with the Swedish iron ore ranges.

Norway's communications experience serious interruption during the winter. Snowfall in the west is usually so great as to defy the snow-plough. Most of the high fell roads linking Östlandet to the west coast are closed for six months of the year, though the railways are kept open. Frost heaving in springtime calls for widespread and expensive repairs to road surfaces; while the occasional land slide and land slip raise hazards of a different order.

Domestic airways lift a limited amount of passenger and goods traffic above the impediments of the land, though for reasons of climate Norway is not good flying country. The construction of airports, when only limited areas of well drained flat land exist, has called for considerable ingenuity as well as capital outlay.

Electricity and telephone communications also suffer from topographical and climatic obstacles. In planning their routes, the aid of a wide range of experts is solicited—the metallurgist (whose lighter aluminium wires lengthen the span between pylons), the electrician (who must devise means of preventing the accumulation of ice on wires), the engineer, the geologist and even the botanist (who from the ecology of different locations can assess the conditions of snow accumulation and duration). Topography also interferes with the distribution of television facilities.

Individuality and Individualism

Norway is, in many respects, the most individual of the countries of Norden: it is at the same time a nation of individualists. Individuality is largely an expression of the physical character of the country and individualism springs from a not-unrelated mental quality in the people. Norwegians live precariously between a wasteland of unoccupied territory, and a fecund but hazardous sea. All, at some time or another, are thrown upon their own resources. Accordingly, children are taught to live off the land, to respect the woodlands and fells, to handle boats, to use the snow on skis. There is plenty of sophistication and regulation in the urban dwelling unit that is planned with such care; its antithesis is the primitive summer holiday hut. Happily, a summer home is financially possible for most Norwegians, for there is in most of them the urge which moved Jo Gende to have inscribed upon his epitaph in the graveyard of Våga church: 'As is well known I am a man of the fells and so I go there as often as I can'. The contrast between the urge for urban amenity and the escape to rural simplicity is repeated in a nation which has sailed the seven seas since the dawn of history and yet can retain what Balzac identified as a 'half monastic' attitude to life; in people like Per Gynt who can accept the extremes of rationalism but yet harbour a belief in the supernatural. Geographers used to seek environmental explanations of mental attitudes. Such explanations are out of fashion. Yet until a better and more scientific understanding can be achieved, Norway and the Norwegians still provide plenty of confirmation that the effects of physical environment upon the minds of men cannot be lightly dismissed.

FURTHER READING

Norway's principal geographical journal is *Norsk Geografisk Tidsskrift.* Most of its articles are in English or with English summaries.

Guidebook to Norway, I.G.U. Congress, 1960, *Norsk Geografisk Tidsskrift*, 17, 1959–60.

T. Sund and A. Sømme, *Norway in Maps*, Bergen, 1947.

A. Sømme, *Geography of Norwegian Agriculture*, Bergen, 1954.

A. Sømme, (Ed.) *Vestlandet, Geographical Studies*, Bergen, 1960.

O. Holtedahl, *Geology of Norway*, Oslo, 1960.

W. R. Mead, *Norway, How People Live Series*, 1959.

There are farm studies of Norway in *Scottish Geographical Magazine*, 1954, pp. 106–23; *Economic Geography*, 1947, pp. 155–66; *Geography*, 1954, pp. 272–82; 1950, pp. 141–54 and 215–27.

The relevant chapters on Norway in (Ed.) A. Sømme, *The Geography of Norden*, Oslo, 1960; W. R. Mead, *An Economic Geography of the Scandinavian States and Finland*, 1958; R. Millward, *The Scandinavian Countries*, 1965; A. C. O'Dell, *The Scandinavian World*, 1957.

Catalogues of Norway's official map series may be obtained from the Geodetic Institute, Oslo.

Iceland

Iceland is exceptional among the countries of North-West Europe; it is the most detached part of the Old World and the nearest European country to North America. Iceland lies 660 miles (1,050 km.) from the Norwegian mainland: 530 (850 km.) from Scotland; less than 220 (350 km.) from Greenland. The area is 39,709 square miles (just over 100,000 sq. km.); after Great Britain, Iceland is Europe's largest island. It is the least populous country in Europe, having only 180,000 inhabitants. Few countries have such a remarkable record of their settlement and history.

As a land of catastrophe on the edge of the inhabited world, Iceland was cultivated by cartographers for the sake of Hekla and popularised by writers as a metaphor. Elizabethans had its geography concentrated for them in a madrigal by Thomas Weelkes, dated 1587:

> Thule, the period of cosmography, doth vaunt of Hekla,
> Whose sulphureous fire doth melt the frozen clime and
> thaw the sky.

Jules Verne, who did his geographical homework as thoroughly as any contemporary writers of science fiction, sought entrance through the crater of Snaefjell for his heroes on their journey to the centre of the earth. In the twentieth century, the image of Iceland's frost and snow yields to that of its storm and cloud. For the meteorologist, Iceland is the breeding ground of depressions and the adjective 'Icelandic' is almost inseparable from the noun 'low'.

Iceland was first settled about A.D. 874. It became an independent and sovereign state in December 1918, but remained in personal union with Denmark until 1943. Since that time, it has balanced political independence against economic and strategic dependence. Economically, it can exist only by vigorous trading in its limited products—and its principal market is Britain, which is at the same time its biggest rival in the North Atlantic fisheries. Strategically, it is a natural *point d'appui* on the Great Circle air route between the U.S.A. and the U.S.S.R. As a result, the Icelanders are usually less concerned with problems of barometric instability, to which they are born and bred, than with those of international political pressures to which they have fallen heir.

THE PHYSICAL BACKGROUND   No country in the world has been fashioned by fire so thoroughly as Iceland. Almost all of its bedrocks are igneous in origin and almost all

RELIEF AND ICE SHEETS

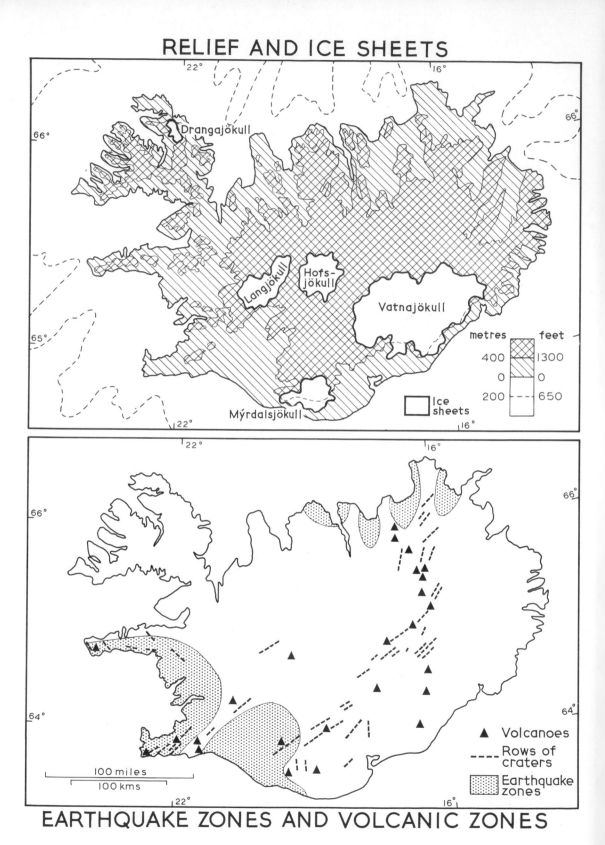

EARTHQUAKE ZONES AND VOLCANIC ZONES

Fig 17. Four maps of features essential to the appreciation of the geography of Iceland

SNOW COVER

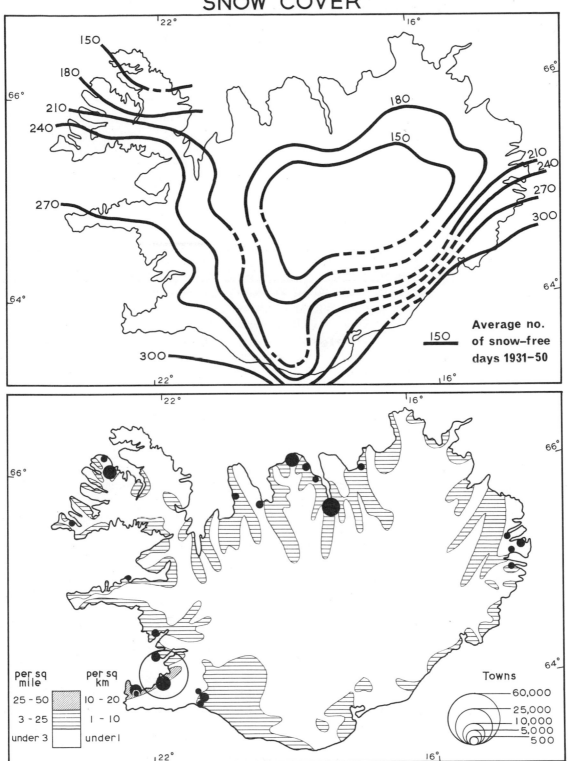

POPULATION

(Based on the *Geography of Norden* and V. Malmström, *A Regional Geography of Iceland*, Washington)

are youthful. The story of its geology begins where that of Scandinavia proper leaves off, for Iceland is dominated by basalts of Eocene age and by tuffs associated with the renewed vulcanicity of the Pleistocene era. The basalts belong to the same series as those which form the Faeroe Islands, and which occur in the Scottish islands, northern Ireland and eastern Greenland. The surface of Iceland has been affected by four principal processes—the extensive erosion of the Oligocene and Miocene periods, the faulting and fracturing associated with the late Pliocene, the renewed vulcanicity of the Pleistocene, and the advance and retreat of the Quaternary Ice Sheet.

Basalts account for about half of the surface area of Iceland and are absolutely dominant in the north-west and in the east (*cf.* Fig. 18). In each area, there is block faulting coupled with a general dip from the seaward face to the interior. The basalt zones are interrupted by sills and dikes of granite and gabbro. The rocks of central Iceland, originally an area of Pliocene subsidence, are of Pleistocene age. They are the combined product of ice and fire which have converted the great mass of depositional materials into tuffs and tuff-breccias.

The result is Iceland's broad central plateau, elevated to heights of 1500–2500 feet above sea level, its irregular surface further diversified by the cones of recently active volcanoes and the necks and stumps of extinct ones. The highest peaks of central Iceland have permanent snow and are generally surrounded by glaciers. The fragmented and fiorded peninsulas in the north-west have been sculptured by ice to form cirques and horned peaks. Their basalts, gunmetal grey and gunpowder black where exposed, show clear evidence of the bedding of lava. Most of Iceland's lower land is found in the south-west, around the margins of Faxaflói (Faxa Bay), in the peninsula of Reykjanes and to its south-east. Even here, the basalt cliffs frown down, rising to tabular mountains such as Esja which overlooks Reykjavik.

Iceland is a paradise for vulcanists and its curiosities have attracted natural historians for several centuries. Volcanoes are its most striking natural phenomena. On an average, an eruption occurs every fifth year and during the last thousand years about thirty volcanoes have been active. There are records of more than twenty eruptions by Hekla, best known of them. The biggest eruption in historical times took placc in 1783 and was the result of a linear crater which developed to the south-west of Vatnajökull. Eruptions may also take place beneath icefields, as instanced by Katla beneath Myrdaljökull. Such an event may give rise to a *jökullhlaup*, or glacial burst. The most recent eruption, in 1963, was submarine in location and poured out half a million tons of lava an hour to give birth to the new island of Surtsey. Surtsey is nearly fifty miles from the Westman Islands (Vestmannaeyjar), the morphological characteristics of which suggest that they may have had a similar origin. Volcanoes have given rise to extensive lava fields—called *hraun* (pl. *hraunur*) in Icelandic and a common place-name element. Odadhahraun is the largest of Iceland's lava fields. Eruptions have also resulted in the widespread distribution of volcanic ash.

Plate 15 Sulphur springs near Kröblu in central Iceland.
Among volcanic features the solfataras of Iceland are some of the most distinctive.
The barrenness of the landscape around them is inseparable from the chemical
constituents which they contribute to the locality and to the air above it.

The widespread thermal activity associated with vulcanicity accounts
for Iceland's 1500 hot springs and thirteen major natural steam fields (or
solfataras). Iceland gave the word *geysir* to the world and its own spouting
spring is the type feature. Earthquake zones are also linked with vulcanicity.

Over a tenth of Iceland is covered with glaciers. The Icelandic word
for glacier, *jökull*, is common on the topographical map. There are five

principal and many lesser ice sheets. The largest is Vatnajökull, which is
the most extensive in Europe. Soundings give a thickness exceeding
3,000 ft. to the main body of the ice sheet. Its associated south coast
outwash plains, defined as *sandur* on Icelandic topographical maps, are
up to 25 miles (40 km.) wide. They comprise a zone of shallow shifting
streams, lakes and lagoons, forbidding in appearance in bad weather but
transformed by the sun into sparkling water and bright sand against the
distant dazzling white of the ice sheet.

Iceland's glaciers are sensitive indicators of climatic change. Sigurdur
Thorarinsson believes that they were about the same size at the time of the
Norse settlement as they are today; but in the intervening period they have
waxed and waned considerably. The retreat of the ice edge in the course of
the last century has left a legacy of classical morainic features, as well as

Plate 16   Breidamerkurjökull.
A representative view of the melting edge of one of Iceland's numerous glaciers.
Outwash features and meltwater deposits may be seen in the right-hand corner.

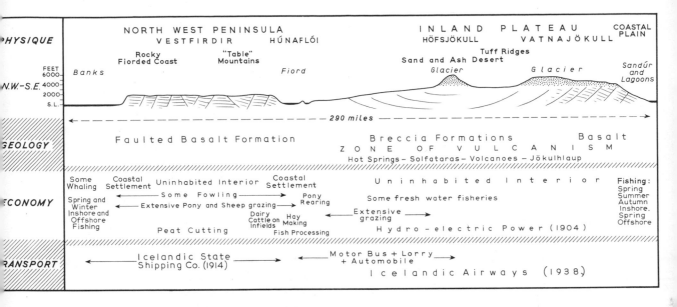

Fig 18 A transect diagram of Iceland

revealing the remains of medieval farms around the shrinking lobes of Myrdalsjökull.

Iceland is a well-watered land. In addition to generous rainfall, melt-water from the ice yields a diversity of lakes and water courses. The main watershed runs from the Snaefell peninsula in the west to Vatnajökull in the east. In keeping with the geomorphological evolution of Iceland, rivers and streams have youthful profiles. River terraces, abundant testimony to rejuvenation, complement the suites of marine terraces. Among the lakes, Thingvallavatn, in the south of the island, is the most famous: it is tectonic in origin. Myvatn, celebrated for its wild life, is dammed behind a lava flow. Waterfalls and rapids abound, though they are usually rather small in scale. As in Norway, the sound of running water is almost constantly in the ear. Given the climatic experience and physical circumstance of Iceland, it is not surprising that there are wide-spread swamplands. They stand in antithesis to the rather unexpected semi-arid desert areas of the north-eastern interior.

Iceland is surrounded by a marine shelf of varying width, with shallows and banks resembling those off the coast of Norway, and its indented coasts are subject to powerful wave and tidal action. The hard rock coasts of the north-west and north—fiorded, sometimes supporting a *skärgård* and relatively abundant in protected harbours—stand in contrast to the depositional shores of the south coast which, for several hundred miles, lacks harbours of consequence.

Eustatic and isostatic adjustment have also modified the shape of Iceland. During the maximum post-glacial submergence, the sea defined a shore line 330 ft. (110–120 m.) above its present level in northern Iceland and about 145 ft. (45 m.) above in south Iceland. Iceland is a lofty country, with an average height exceeding 1500 ft. above sea level. Only about a quarter of its surface area lies under 600 ft., so that the effects of submergence are limited; they are most evident in the soils of Iceland. As in Baltic Scandinavia, there are distinct edaphic differences above and below the upper marine limit.

Soils at large are those associated with a tundra environment. There are widespread organic soils (associated with the boglands), and soils of a loessal character which reflect the role played by wind. Most of the face of the land has been undisturbed by human action, so that the stone stripes and polygons associated with frost action in sub-Arctic soils trace their designs over extensive areas.

CLIMATE   Iceland's climate is principally a response to latitude and to maritime setting. Since most of the island has a mountainous topography, climate is also modified by altitude. Topography exerts a powerful influence upon local insolation. Iceland is located just to the south of the Arctic Circle; this implies exaggerated seasonal contrasts in daylight and darkness.

Maritime polar air masses prevail, but their effects are modified by the surrounding ocean currents. Principal of these are the North Atlantic Drift, which has a warming effect along the south and south-west coasts, and the East Greenland Current which has a contrasting effect upon the north-west and north shores. In both winter and summer, sea temperatures off the south-west coast are about 4–5°C (9°F) warmer than those off the north coast. Iceland is especially sensitive to any mechanism which modifies the behaviour of the Polar maritime air and the course of ocean currents. The East Greenland current is responsible for bringing pack ice to the north and north-west shores of the island. Pack ice has appeared with diminishing frequency in the course of the last fifty years.

For its latitude, the climate of the lower parts of Iceland is not conspicuously cold. In January, the coldest month, the 0°C (32°F) isotherm swings around the edge of the south coast, while about half of the island is enclosed in the −4°C (25·2°F) isotherm. July isotherms trace a more complicated pattern; though most of the island averages temperatures between 9° and 10°C (49°F).

Iceland experiences a high degree of humidity. Cloudiness is one expression of it. Amounts are greatest along the coastal areas of the south, west and north, where the sky is clouded for half of the days of the year. The figure rises to three-quarters in the north-west peninsulas. By contrast the number of clear days is extremely small—ten or twenty. Cloudiness is partly related to storminess. The extreme south-west of the country and the Westman Islands suffer storms on more than fifty days a year. The number of days with rain varies from more than 200 a year all along the west and south-west fringes to 125 days in the north-east. The southern third of Iceland averages 40 inches (1,000 mm.), with at least three times that amount on high ground; but the northern parts of the island, which lie in the lee of the height of land, have only 20 inches (500 mm.).

For its latitude, the number of days when Iceland is snow-covered is relatively few. Snow lies on the southern and south-western lowlands for up to sixty days a year; but over most of the highland and interior area, for well over 100 days. Frost and snow conditions are closely related. The number of days with frost varies from about ninety in the extreme south to well over 200 in the interior plateau.

Sunshine totals are small. The greater part of the island enjoys no more than a quarter of the possible. Vincent Malmström writes of sunshine in Iceland as a luxury product.

FLORA AND FAUNA Given this climatic regime, it is not surprising that Iceland has a meagre natural vegetation. The relative recency of retreat of ice and the isolation of the island also explain the poverty of plant species and the scantiness of their distribution.

The baldness of the Icelandic scene springs from the absence of timber trees. Although there is reference to 'forests' in saga literature, it is unlikely that the original colonists encountered trees other than birch scrub. As much as 5% of the surface area of Iceland is believed to have had a birch scrub cover. A little remains in the east (Hallormsstadaskogur) and in the north (Fjnoskadal). Mountain ash and willow also occur; though it is rare, even in Reykjavik, for the rowan to reach a height of more than several yards. There are a number of experimental forests in which conifers from Iceland's homoclimes are established. Mosses and lichens are rich in number. Sedges and cotton grass fringe the bogland margins; grass of varying quality covers the lower lands.

Isolation has also restricted Iceland's indigenous fauna. Most wild animals have been introduced—foxes, mink, reindeer. There are abundant seals and occasional polar bears. The poverty of wild animals is compensated by a rich bird life. At least sixty varieties of land and sea birds migrate to Iceland for the summer. Few species stay over winter; the ptarmigan, relatively abundant, is an exception. The falcon, now rare, used to be trapped for training and export and gives its name to Iceland's order of chivalry. Iceland has remarkable bird cliffs, e.g. the gannetries of the Westman Islands, and extensive nesting grounds which are similar to those of the Faeroes and Norway. The bird life is inseparable from the rich life of the surrounding waters—and the midges of summer.

Population and Settlement Iceland was first peopled by adventurers and refugees. Celtic divines, whose spiritual adventurings to the ultimate limits of maritime Europe may be recalled in a scatter of place-names, were probably the first to come. The second were Norsemen who sought escape from both physical and human restraints in their parent land. The record of Iceland's original landtakers is found in *Landnamabok*—not so elaborate as the better-known British Domesday Book; but a worthy prologue to the medieval literary contribution born of this 'desert in the ocean'.

Within a century of the arrival of the first Norse immigrants, the pattern of settlement had been established and most of the habitable land had been claimed. In A.D. 930 the first administrative assembly was summoned at Thingvellir; in A.D. 1000 Iceland adopted Christianity. The first bishopric was established at Skolholt, not far from Thingvellir.

To the same time belong the journeys of the Norsemen to Greenland and beyond. Iceland was the point of departure for the Greenland colonies—by Eric the Red in 982—and the Norse landfalls on the eastern seaboard of North America are inseparable from it. The details of daily life in medieval Iceland may be reconstructed more fully from its sagas than from archaeological remains. The National Museum in Reykjavik has limited finds from Viking age burial mounds, a few basalt tombstones (with runic script still employed after the introduction of the Latin alphabet), and a miscellany of domestic objects recovered from deserted medieval settlements. There are few historical monuments.

The climax in population and development attained in the thirteenth century was not to be repeated for over six hundred years. In 1262 Iceland's 'Commonwealth' ended and Iceland associated itself with the Norwegian monarchy in exchange for a guarantee of trading relations. In the fourteenth century, when Norway acquired a common monarch with Denmark, the centre of political gravity shifted to Denmark.

Iceland was born in insecurity. It was a land of deficiencies which could only maintain a satisfactory existence given regular communications and overseas exchange. In its medieval golden age, with a population of about 70,000, Iceland had established an economy looking to the grasslands as the basis of a pastoral husbandry and to the sea as a source of food. Sealing provided skins and fats: whaling yielded oil and bone. Farming assumed an extensive character. Its components were the homestead, with its sod-built turf-roofed buildings; the infield, turf or boulder-fenced; the common pastures, and the distant, usually privately-owned *saeters*. Settlements were relatively widely dispersed. A collecting economy supported and supplemented sheep, cattle and pigs (in that order). Mosses, lichens, reeds and roots; eggs, feathers and down; and driftwood were collected. Peat was dug for fuel; manure was also burned. Over-stocking and overgrazing were always a threat to existence. Grain crops were especially risky. The slightest changes in climate might have a critical effect on the length of the growing season. Ash and cinder, resulting from volcanic eruption, were additional hazards. The harvest of the sea was steadier, but it was also sensitive to changes in water temperatures.

The decline which afflicted Iceland at the end of the Middle Ages became progressive. Worsening of the climate, increased storminess at sea, exhaustion of the land, erosion of the soil, intermittent natural catastrophe (such as the overwhelming disaster of 1783 which caused the loss of more than half of Iceland's animal stocks) all had their weakening effect. Malnutrition, exaggerated by intermittent famines, reduced human resistance in the face of disease and sapped mental energy. The successive censuses taken during the Danish period indicate the decline of farmsteads. A measure of political neglect, the blockade of trade during the Napoleonic Wars, the final great wave of emigration (Iceland lost 15,000 emigrants to the U.S.A. and Canada between 1870–1900) brought the country to the edge of disaster. By contrast, the last eighty years have witnessed a renaissance. The reasons are partly physical (certainly climatic amelioration is evident), partly human. New techniques and the certainty bred of new communications have had a cumulative effect on Iceland's progress.

Contemporary Iceland has a high birth rate and a low death rate. Expectation of life is 70 years for females; 66, for males. These figures measure its escape from the years of decline. Within sixty years, population distribution has changed profoundly. Icelanders are town dwellers today—75% (as distinct from 13% in 1900). Most people live round the coast, with an increasingly disproportionate growth of population in the south-west. The capital Reykjavik has over 40% of Iceland's total population. The second town is Akureyri in north Iceland. The remaining

Plate 17   Akureyri in northern Iceland.
Akureyri is the principal settlement and fishing harbour of northern Iceland. The open water, unaffected by winter conditions, stands in contrast to the snow-covered fells.

thirteen towns are all ports—six are in the south-west. There are also nearly forty agglomerated settlements, each containing several hundred inhabitants. Among them is the hot spring and greenhouse centre of Hveragerdi.

Economic Development
AGRICULTURE AND FISHING

In the economies of most countries, fishing is subordinate to agriculture; in Iceland, it is the reverse. Iceland has always lived largely by fishing; the sea has provided opportunity and the land has imposed restraints. Indeed, the restraints imposed by physical circumstance upon Iceland's agriculture are more rigorous than those experienced by any other European country.

The basis of agriculture is livestock farming, which accounts for 90% of the farmer's income. Cattle and sheep are the two chief sources of wealth and in terms of value, the returns from dairy cattle dominate. About half of the 50,000 cattle are concentrated in the south and south-west near the principal market for liquid milk. Sheep are more evenly distributed round the island; but north Iceland has a full third of the flock of 750,000.

Iceland's agriculture has changed substantially since before the Second World War. Firstly, it has lost its position as the country's principal occupation. Less than one-fifth of Iceland's population looks to it for a living. The decline in the percentage of those employed in agriculture has been greatest in the south and south-west, but about half of the working population of north Iceland is still employed in farming. Secondly, agricultural operations have experienced pronounced changes in method. Rationalisation is inseparable from the transport revolution. This has promoted the rise of commercial farming in the place of the former semi-self-sufficient local husbandry. Thus, lorries carry most of Iceland's daily milk output direct to dairies for processing; while a full quarter of the farms have milking machines. Tractors are found on more than half of the holdings and the high per capita number of motor vehicles is closely related to farm ownership. Iceland still musters over 30,000 ponies, though they are used chiefly for purposes of pleasure.

Only 1% of the surface area of Iceland consists of improved farmland. Grass is the chief crop. Most of it is converted into hay, but ensilage is of growing interest. Oats are also grown as a green fodder crop. Potatoes, widely grown as a garden crop, are also grown as a field crop in the south and south-west. Most of the vegetable crop is concentrated in the same area; turnips, carrots and cabbage lead.

Iceland's most remarkable agricultural activity is based on the hot springs. Since 1924, when piped water from them was first employed for greenhouse cultivation, the activity has expanded steadily. Flowers, vegetables and fruit are produced. The climax is encountered in Hveragerdi, in the south-western county of Árnes, which in terms of value produces half of Iceland's greenhouse crops.

Farms combine infield and outfield husbandry. The intensively cul-

Plate 18   Storhamar i Eyjafirdi, Iceland.
This is a representative Icelandic farming tract, with settlements on the river terraces, strung together by dirt roads, in a countryside where distances are deceptive because of the absence of trees.

tivated and very restricted infield is complemented by the extensively employed outlands. These embrace nearly one fifth of the surface area of Iceland. Intakes from the waste have been made principally in the lowland areas of the south-west. They are generally old-established. Turfwalls, sometimes strengthened with boulders, formerly defined the infields, which today are protected from grazing animals by barbed wire. Mechanical equipment for ploughing, drainage and levelling has facilitated new intakes as well as improvements to existing arable area.

Most farms lack the 'cosiness' of those in mainland Scandinavia. Gardens are limited and there is rarely the protection of even a scrub growth of trees; but the bright green of their cultivated land contrasts with the dun colour of the unimproved outlands. The turf and corrugated iron byres, and the older wooden homesteads are yielding to cement and concrete structures—less picturesque, but more comfortable. For most holdings, the land beyond the homefields is a mixture of scree, swamp, ash desert, gravel, sandy outwash, slumped mud and lava. Steinahlidar, the south country farm of Halldor Laxness's novel *Paradise Reclaimed*, with rocks 'tumbling down as if the heartless cliff-trolls were shedding stone tears', is typical of those plagued by stonefalls.

The outlands are still widely employed for sheep. A considerable tradition still adheres to sheep rearing, with seasonal migrations and the tough ponies indispensable to shepherding. The outlands also yield their minor harvests of game, fish, eggs, berries, feathers and down. Fishing is the linchpin of Iceland's existence; though the number directly engaged in it declines steadily. It employs only about one-tenth of the working population.

Iceland is highly sensitive to its fisheries for two reasons. First, they are the principal source of its revenue. Secondly, they are a source of wealth deriving essentially from the waters surrounding the island. Considerably less than a tenth of the fish catch comes from distant waters—off Greenland, Bear Island and Labrador. Not surprisingly, Icelanders have been jealous of intrusion upon their domestic fishing grounds for centuries. Iceland's territorial waters have been extended until they are now internationally accepted as stretching 12 nautical miles from coastal base lines.

The cod is the chief catch. It occurs on all of the fishing banks, but is concentrated seasonally in the south and west. The cod fisheries are at their height between January and April—at the same time as those off Norway's Lofoten Islands. The herring fisheries are concentrated off the south and west coasts in March and April, and off the north coast from July to September. Yet the fish catch is far from stable. There are cyclical fluctuations, which may be attributable to natural or to human factors, which are the subject of continuing enquiry, and which cause considerable economic instability.

The Icelandic fishing fleet has changed its character substantially since the turn of the century. The first stage in the transformation was the adoption of the decked boat; the second, the introduction of motor power. Smaller motor boats predominate, but larger scale trawlers, cooperatively or municipally owned, number about fifty. The trawlers are highly efficient and the fishermen are specialists; part-time fishermen play no significant role in commercial fishing. Iceland's fish catch is large enough to give to it an international stature.

The fishermen are principally town dwellers and most of Iceland's urban settlements look first to fish as a source of livelihood. Their activities have been diversified as the products of the sea have been increasingly processed for export. The traditional export of dried fish has declined sharply; but salted fish is still in good demand. Refrigeration has enabled quick frozen cod fillets to become one of Iceland's most remunerative exports. Cod liver oil and meal factories are less important than those producing herring oil and herring meal.

The biggest ports for fish landings are Reykjavik, with its cluster of adjacent harbours, and Vestmannaejyar (all with cod dominant); Siglufjördur and Raunfarhavn, both in the north and both with herring dominant.

OTHER RESOURCES   Iceland has few raw materials for industrial processing; while manufacturing enterprise is restricted by the limited size of the home market and the distance from overseas markets. There are sulphur and pumice deposits; but they no longer merit commercial exploitation. Lignite occurs in a number of places. There are small occurrences of kaolin, of diatomaceous earth, titanium and calcite. The manufacture of cement and lime at Akranes, in the south-east of Faxa Bay, is based principally on underwater beds of sea shells. Other than fish-processing and agricultural-processing plants, the only other sizable manufacturing establishment in Iceland is a fertiliser factory near Reykjavik which produces ammonium nitrate.

Iceland is rich in energy potential, having running water, natural steam fields and hot springs. About three-quarters of the power generated derives from hydro-electric sources. Two principal rivers have been developed— the Sog, in the south-west, which was first harnessed in 1937 and has a multiple unit plant, and the Laxa in the north. The example of New Zealand indicates a possible method of using natural steam power for energy. The dispersal of population has added considerably to the costs of providing electricity supply, but over 90% of Iceland's homes are served.

INTEGRATION AND   In recent years, Iceland has been released from the major restraints
COMMERCE   imposed by geography upon its communications. The coming of the steel-hulled steamship made possible regular instead of intermittent communication with the outer world; it also enabled the introduction of a regular schedule of coastal services. Iceland has a small mercantile marine and scheduled services exist between Iceland and Scandinavian, British, German, Dutch, Belgian and American ports. Coastal shipping services, which are especially important for transporting goods that cannot easily be moved by overland routes, are uneconomic to operate, so a State Shipping Department (*Skipautgeid rikisins*) deals with the aid which is necessary to support them.

Iceland is a very air-minded country. It has two air lines of its own which link Reykjavik with a dozen North Atlantic cities, while foreign aircraft use nearby Keflavik airfield as a sub-Arctic staging point. Domestic air services have proliferated in the post-war years and they have overcome the many obstacles which afflict overland movement. The per capita number of air journeys made by Icelanders is one of the highest in the world.

Iceland never went through a railway age. It leapt straight from the packhorse on its trail to the combustion engine on its rough gravel road.

F

Icelandic ponies remain an indispensable aid to the sheep farmer, and the National Museum has a corner devoted to their culture. The jeep and the tractor both partly replace the pony.

Within living memory a road network exceeding 6,000 miles (10,000 km.) in length has been constructed. British and American forces in Iceland during the Second World War spurred road building. In addition to trunk roads across the island, the coastal settlements are linked by a ring road which is complete save for a stretch along the impassable glacial outwash of the south coast. The making and maintenance of roads, especially in winter, is a considerable tax on the small population. As much as a tenth of the national income may be spent on them annually. The construction of bridges is an extra toll in a countryside lively with river and stream. Distance and maintenance also make costly the widely distributed telephone and electricity services.

All of the countries of Norden are heavily dependent on external sources of supply and Iceland's dependence on foreign trade is the most critical of them. Its historical experiences emphasise the problems arising from the deficiency of most resources regarded as essential by the North Atlantic community. Technological advance may transform the life of Iceland; but it simultaneously intensifies dependence. External relations are concentrated in Reykjavik, which is also the centre of wholesale and retail trading. Fully 85% of Iceland's overseas trade passes through its port— the roadsteads of which are used as well as its harbour installations because of the relatively shallow approaches.

Iceland's exports consist almost entirely of the products of the sea— with fish absolutely dominant and the products of whaling and sealing making minor contributions. Animal husbandry contributes 2%, principally from the flocks of sheep. Iceland's exports have a traditional uniformity, but the phrase 'fish and fish products' conceals a growing diversity. Exports move to the markets of thirty different countries. Wet fish cargoes are shipped directly by trawlers to Britain and Germany. In order of importance, the chief markets are Britain, U.S.A., Sweden, West Germany and the U.S.S.R. The principal sources of supply are U.S.A., U.S.S.R., Britain, West Germany and the Netherlands. Iceland's import table reflects the absolute deficiency of fuel, timber, metals, cereals, foodstuffs and paper. Capital goods are critical—especially ships and vehicles, electrical equipment and implements.

The latest industry is tourism. Not less than 10,000 tourists visit Iceland annually. Many stop over on their Atlantic flights. The cultivation of tourists recalls an unexpected reference in Thomas Hardy's *Return of the Native*. Forecasting a change in the human appreciation of landscape, he looked to the time when 'the new Vale of Tempe may be a gaunt waste in Thule'. Some visit Iceland with this end in view, seeking escape from the twentieth century in Iceland's empty solitudes. Others (who are perhaps the logical successors to Prince Louis Napoleon's caravanserie or Lord Dufferin's nautical adventurings) avail themselves of tourist day-trips from Iceland to the *ultima Thule* of the Greenland ice-cap beyond.

A Physical and Human Laboratory

Iceland conveys a sense of isolation and of austerity. Its landscapes are hard and angular, in contrast to the rounded landforms that reflect geomorphological maturity, and bald, with only a meagre vegetational mantle. The impact of man on them is minimal. Despite the industry with which Icelanders have applied themselves, there is little visual evidence to suggest a millenia of occupation. As a laboratory for physical geographers, Iceland is renowned. Many processes which operated in other parts of Europe in former times may be seen there in operation today. Natural scientists make pilgrimage to it even more religiously today than Sweden's Uno von Troil in the eighteenth century or Paul Gaimard and his French colleagues of the Scientific Commission to Northern Scandinavia in 1838–40.

Plate 19   A canyon on the River Jökulsa, Iceland.
This canyon, north of Dettifoss, is typical of the fierce erosion which has eaten into the volcanic rocks of Iceland. It is surrounded by a landscape which has only a scanty cover of mosses, grasses and lichens.

Iceland has claimed less attention from the point of view of human geography. Yet there is an abundance of problems to explain. Paradoxes abound. Iceland thrives upon the individualism of its farmers and fishermen, yet witnesses the widespread migration of what Halldor Laxness calls 'progressive country boys' who no longer wish to 'chase sheep and haul cod'. Iceland's highly literate people have rationalised their enterprise in the most physically favoured south-western corner, but only at the expense of promoting an excessive concentration of wealth and population. Proportionate to the size of the population, Iceland has the world's largest capital city. Again, homogeneity of stock, language, religion and tradition contrast with pronounced local differences in outlook and behaviour. At the international level, a new-found dependence upon the outer world is balanced by a marked ambivalence towards it. And the explanation of the whole complex of attitudes becomes more perplexing when it is set in the stream of Icelandic history. The country knows a contemporary renaissance, separated from its medieval florescence by six centuries of scarcely relieved depression. Few have been moved to speculate upon the 'mainsprings of civilisation' which account for the course of such a story.

FURTHER READING

There is a series of research articles in English on Iceland in the Swedish geographical journal *Geografiska Annaler*, Volumes 19, 20, 21, 22, 25, 31, 33, 36 and 37. Volume 41, 1959, constitutes the *Guidebook to Iceland*, I.G.U. Congress, 1960.

The relevant chapters on Iceland in (Ed.) A. Sømme, *The Geography of Norden*, Oslo, 1960; W. R. Mead, *An Economic Geography of the Scandinavian States and Finland*, 1958; R. Millward, *The Scandinavian Countries*, 1965; A. O'Dell, *The Scandinavian World*, 1957.

V. H. Malmström, *A Regional Geography of Iceland*, National Academy of Science Publication 584, Washington, 1958.

S. Thorarinsson, *The Thousand Years' Struggle against Ice and Fire*, Reykjavik, 1956.

A good map coverage is provided by N. E. Nørlund, *Islands Kortlaegning*, Copenhagen, 1944.

Denmark

Denmark (*Danmark*, to the Danes) consists of the western peninsula of Jutland (Danish, *Jylland*) to the east of which is a complex of islands. It is the smallest of the states of Norden; but its modest size, 16,000 square miles (43,000 sq. km.), and status in the European scene represent a recent historical reduction. In the past, extended overseas territories were supported upon a broader home base. The Danish realm grew up around the Øresund, with Copenhagen (D. *København*) as its focus. The Swedish counties of Bohuslän, Halland, Bleckinge and Skåne remained Danish until the seventeenth century. From this base, Denmark expanded overseas.

To the west, King Canute imposed his Danelaw on south-eastern England; to the east, medieval Denmark held a part of Muscovy's Baltic forelands in fee; from 1429 to 1857, dues were collected at Elsinore (D. Helsingør) from all shipping passing through the Sound. Norway was joined in union with Denmark for over three centuries until 1814. The Duchies of Schleswig-Holstein were annexed by Prussia only in 1864. Iceland contracted out of the Danish realm with a declaration of independence in 1943. Although the parent state has shrunk, Denmark still has a vast overseas dependency in Greenland. The Faeroe islands have sought independence; but remain a 'self-governing community within the State of Denmark'.

Denmark is a natural bridge between the Scandinavian peninsula and mainland Europe. Visually, its landscape contrasts with those of the other countries of Norden. Its broad arable areas are enclosed neither by the wall of the fell as in Norway and Iceland nor by the line of the forest as in Sweden and Finland. From the point of view of land use, it is a mirror image of the four other countries. Nearly three-quarters of its surface area is cultivated.

As a result of the publicity given to its remarkable agrarian revolution and of the ubiquitous impact of the children's stories of H. C. Andersen, Denmark is often misrepresented as a rural, almost toy-town land. It may be a model agricultural state and the storybook image may be valuable advertisement for a remunerative tourist industry, but the truth is that industry is the chief source of Denmark's wealth, factories are the principal employees of its labour force, Danes are townsfolk rather than countryfolk and, in the capital of Copenhagen, they have Norden's largest city.

The Physical Environment

GEOLOGY AND RELIEF

Denmark is a geologically youthful country. Its solid geology is written in terms of the Tertiary; the only exception to this is the island of Bornholm. The oldest rock series encountered at the surface are the so-called Senonian and Danian chalks. The former comprises the basis of the Jutish peninsula north of the Limfiord and announces itself in low cliff features along both the North Sea Coast and the shores of the Limfiord. The cliffs of the island of Møn, recalling the Needles of the Isle of Wight in their upstanding stacks and pillars, are the counterpart in the south-eastern archipelago. Younger chalks form the basis of eastern Zealand and the easternmost lobes of Jutland. Central Jutland and Fyn have Tertiary clays and sands as their bedrock. The main mass of Jutland has a Miocene foundation, in which are encountered lignite seams. Bornholm is predominantly granite, but is partly overlain with Cambrian sandstones, Silurian shales and limestones, Rhaetic and Liassic clays. It has coal measures along its southern margins.

The landscape derives its present forms primarily from the last glaciation. It is a landscape of deposition, and depositional forms derive from two main stages in the retreat of the continental ice sheet. As a result, Denmark may be divided into the territories of the older and younger moraines. The older is associated with the Saale-Riss glaciation: the younger, with the Weichsel-Würm glaciation. The mature land forms of the former, weathered and considerably modified under sub-Arctic conditions, are restricted to south-eastern Jutland. Here, they commonly bear the name 'hill islands'. They rise to altitudes of several hundred feet above the level of the outwash plains, the flat sandy expanses of which dip gently westwards.

The younger morainic landscapes have their most continuous and prolonged expression in eastern Jutland, where they form a tumble of hills, sometimes extended into chains, sometimes assuming rampart forms, sometimes flattening into plateaus. The highest points are only about 550 feet (170 m.) high, but many lesser heights, bearing the impressive name *bjerg*, are Mont Blancs in the eyes of the local inhabitants. More circumscribed groups of morainic hills occur in the archipelago. In Fyn, they give rise to an appealing landscape which the Danish composer Carl Nielsen described as all 'little plains and plump hills'. The main island of Zealand has a number of distinctive esker as well as drumlin features. A different type of depositional landscape is encountered in north Jutland. North Jutland has experienced appreciable post-glacial uplift and marine sedimentation has produced some of the most extensive areas of flat land in a proverbially flat country. The most recently emerged beach ridges have developed little soil and form beach heaths.

Complementary to the features of deposition are those of erosion. Jutland's valleys for the most part contain streams which are but remnants of the meltwater rivers that carved out their valleys. The Gudenå, for example, follows meltwater valleys for part of its course. But the most striking erosional features of Denmark are the tunnel valleys. The tunnel valleys, attributed to sub-glacial rivers, cut their way deeply into the morainic hills of east Jutland parallel to the direction of ice movement. They are of varying width and their courses may be tortuous. Sometimes, they are a mile broad; sometimes, only a few hundred yards. Their steep sides, which often resemble the hangers of English chalkland coombes, have been subject to considerable erosion; although they are now stabilised by old-established deciduous woodland. To the east, the valleys are submerged and give rise to the series of broad, calm *föhrden* or fiords which characterise the Baltic flank of Jutland. These fiords bear no morphological resemblance to their Norwegian namesakes.

On a more limited scale, Denmark repeats the Scandinavian theme of an intricate relationship between land and water. This is evident both in the pattern of drainage and in the form of the coast. Denmark is a country of short rivers. The longest take their rise in the Jutland moraines and find their way to the North Sea coast. Others find their way into the melt-water channels and tunnel valleys where, by way of strings of lakes and swamps, they eventually drain into the föhrden. Denmark is a country with a variety of lakes. They are especially numerous in the eastern parts of Jutland. Dead ice fields, as in the hinterland of Copenhagen, are also characterised by a profusion of lakelets. Peat bogs are widely scattered, especially in Jutland, in the north of which are the largest in Denmark.

Because of its relatively low-lying and unconsolidated character, Denmark's coastline is subject to constant change. The changes have been liveliest along its western seaboard. Some have been large-scale, coinciding with the great invasion of the sea which formed the Zuider Zee and breached Frisia. These are seen in the root of Jutland, where a row of islands traces the outline of the former coast. Behind them lies the Wadden Sea, where tidal mudflats 11–13 miles (7–8 km.) wide yield landwards to saltmarshes. This marine foreland has polders and dikes and is the subject of active reclamation.

The interplay of wind as well as wave exerts a lively influence on coastal morphology. Western Jutland, an 'iron' or harbourless coast to mariners, has the longest sand beaches in Europe. They stretch for some 200 miles (320 km.). Landward, they are edged by a belt of dunes of varying width, which encloses lagoons. During the past two generations, much work has been done to stabilise the migratory dunes with marram grass and pines, but gales still give rise to impressive 'sandstorms'. The dunes reach their climax in northern Jutland—Grenen (the tip) to the Danes; the Skaw to the British. Here, in Raabjerg, they reach 130–160 feet (40–50 m.) in height and are still given free play. The sands trail away to the northern-most spits, 'just wide enough for a man to stand on and let the North Sea play over his left boot and the Kattegat over his right' as Hans Andersen saw it. But beyond the Skaw are countless shifting sandbanks, treacherous for shipping. They are a graveyard comparable to the Good-wins, where tell-tale masts and disintegrating hulls are present-day reminders of centuries of fatalities. *The Sandhills of Jutland* (the name of one of his stories) compose a landscape which made a great impact on Hans Andersen and which also attracted an artist colony at the turn of

GEOMORPHOLOGICAL FEATURES

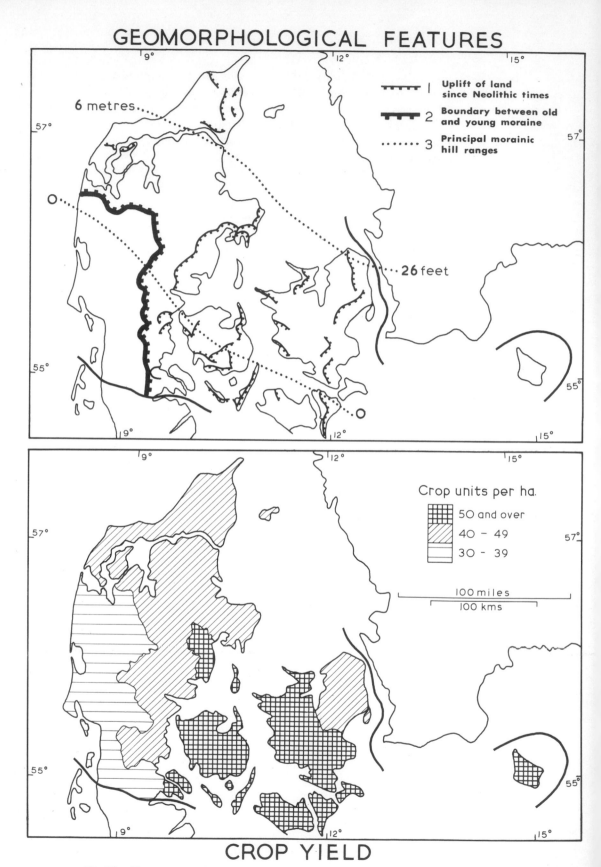

	1	Uplift of land since Neolithic times
	2	Boundary between old and young moraine
	3	Principal morainic hill ranges

6 metres

26 feet

Crop units per ha.

50 and over
40 – 49
30 – 39

100 miles
100 kms

CROP YIELD

Fig 19   Four maps of features essential to the appreciation of the geography of Denmark

GEOMORPHOLOGICAL REGIONS

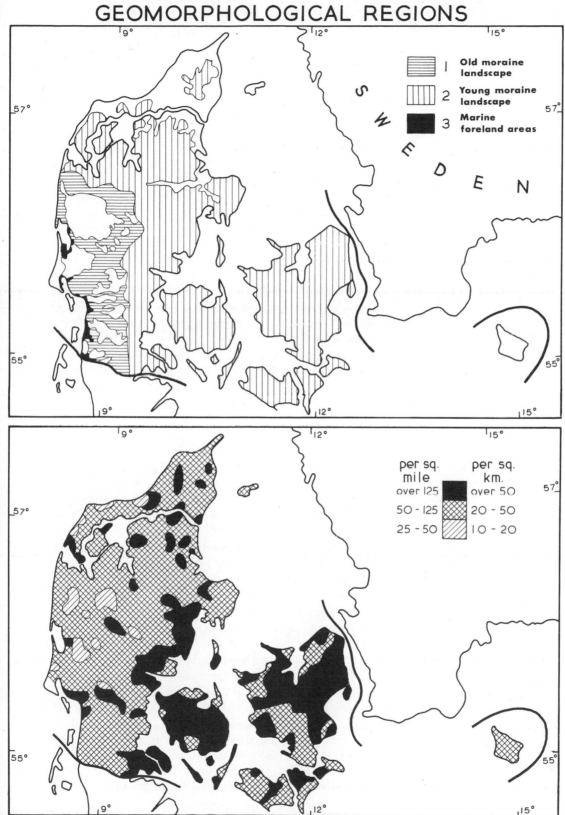

1 Old moraine landscape

2 Young moraine landscape

3 Marine foreland areas

SWEDEN

per sq. mile — per sq. km.

over 125 — over 50

50 - 125 — 20 - 50

25 - 50 — 10 - 20

POPULATION

(Based on the *Geography of Norden*, and the *Atlas of Denmark*)

the century to fix its landforms and life for posterity in the genre of the 'Skagen school'.

The coasts of the archipelagoes describe fantastic outlines with their reefs, spits, arcs and bays; but they are moulded by gentler waves and less vigorous winds than those of the North Sea coast. Their beaches are narrower, their storm ridges less pronounced. There are limited stretches of coastal marshes, e.g. in Lolland, but nothing comparable to western Slesvig.

As a landscape of deposition, which has been appreciably modified by marine, riverine and aeolian influences, Denmark is a country that has a variety of soils in relatively close juxtaposition. It is possible to generalise broadly and speak of eastern Denmark as predominantly clay country and western Denmark (i.e. western Jutland) as predominantly sand country. But there are many sandy areas in the clayland and some clay areas in the sandy lands. Generally speaking, however, the sandy soils have been subject to pronounced podsolisation; while the clays of the east rarely demonstrate it. Western Jutland had also extensive areas of peatland. Eastern Denmark's clay soils, which formerly supported deciduous woodland, are usually identified as brown forest soils. There are generous litters of flint where chalk nears the surface. Save for the more recently reclaimed areas of western Jutland, most Danish soils have been subject to tillage for many centuries. Their present structure and chemical content have been considerably altered by man.

CLIMATE Denmark's climate is controlled principally by powerfully maritime influences; but it is sufficiently continental in location to experience periodic extensions of continental high pressure which bring to it heat waves in summer and cold waves in winter. Weather conditions tend to be unstable, with considerable variations from the mean. Temperature variations are greater from west to east than from north to south. Precipitation variations follow the same tendency. Summer temperatures along the west coast of Jutland are about 15°C (59°F); winter temperatures average 0·5°C (33°F) in February, the coldest month. In Copenhagen the corresponding figures are 17°C (63°F) and −0·5°C (31°F). Annual rainfall diminishes from 32 inches (80 cms.) per annum in south-western Jutland to 16 inches along the Great Belt. The late summer and autumn tend to be the wettest times of the year. The interplay of maritime and continental forces implies that Denmark knows both mild, damp winters as well as cold winters with heavy snowfall. Under extreme conditions, such as the winters of 1939–42 (and also in 1963), the Sound and the Belts may become obstructed by ice. Much of Denmark has a six-month growing period; while temperatures above 10°C (50°F) for well over four months of the year favour the growth of both tree crops as well as farm crops. Danish weather can resemble British in its humidity and cloudiness. The windiness of Jutland makes its impact on most visitors. It is heard in what Hans Andersen defined as 'the roaring of the German Ocean' as if 'hundreds of wagons were driving over a hard tunnelled road'. It is seen in the crouching and wind-trimmed vegetation.

VEGETATION The original vegetation of Denmark was deciduous forest land. Great oak stumps are found deep in the Jutish peat bogs, but the beech appears to have been the climax tree over most of Denmark for at least the last 2,000 years. The distribution of woodlands has been much modified by man. About a tenth of contemporary Denmark is covered by woodland and almost all of it is man-made. The greatest single changes are the coniferous plantations which have spread over western Jutland, where extensive heathlands (also largely man-induced) predominated until the last century. Despite widespread reclamation, heather moors, dunes, peat bogs, saltmarshes, lakes and ponds still account for as extensive an area as woodland. Each supports a distinctive plant association. Hans Andersen has captured many of them in a phrase or two—the 'strand sand hills' softened around their edges by stiff, 'sharp-bladed, blue-green grasses', yielding to 'thorns and wild roses'; the heath beyond, where 'cypress-green juniper bushes and fresh-oak shoots seem like bouquets among the heather'; the pools, with 'yellow water lilies, brown feathered reeds and soft velvet-like bulrushes'. A correspondingly varied insect, small animal and bird life is associated with these plant associations, so that ecologically speaking, Denmark offers greater variety than most parts of Scandinavia. Increasingly intensive occupation of the land reduces the number of exotic migrants such as the much-esteemed stork; but a keen interest in conservation has resulted in nature reserves and bird sanctuaries. A beautiful vignette of the flora and fauna of a small part of Western Jutland is

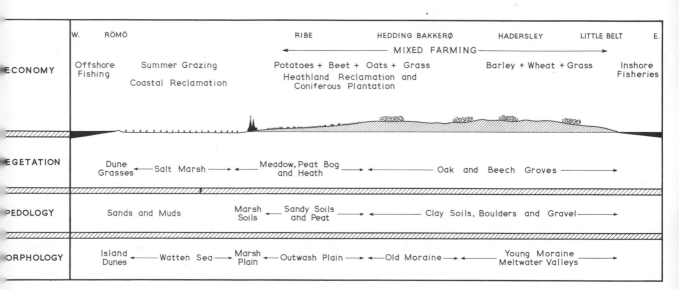

Fig 20 A transect diagram through south Jutland

given in the opening pages of *Birds around the Lighthouse*, a novel by Jacob Paludan.

Population Distribution

Denmark has a population of 4,600,000, giving a density of 277 per square mile (106 per sq. km.), which is the highest for any of the countries of Norden. More of Denmark has been occupied for a longer time than the rest of Norden. Earliest human relics date from a reindeer culture of about 10,000 years ago, when Denmark had a tundra climate near the edge of the retreating ice. The background to Denmark's earliest settlements has been vividly reconstructed by the novelist Johannes V. Jensen in his mythical saga *The Long Journey*. In primeval trade, the artifacts of reindeer bone and antler were succeeded by flint with which Denmark's chalk lands endowed Stone Age man. Settlement intensified as men began to use bronze and to work iron. Most of Denmark's low hills and eminences are crowned with the dolmens or rough grassed barrows of Bronze and Iron Age times. The most remarkable remains have been yielded by the peatbogs—Bronze Age inhabitants mummified in their oak coffins and wearing the gold ornaments of their day; the clutter of rusted military equipment recalling Iron Age battles. The widespread scatter of kitchen middens recalls periods kindly to population growth and expansion, in contrast to the great folk wanderings which suggest possible climatic worsening or overpopulation. The Dark Ages have left their fortifications and earthworks, especially Danevirken, the great rampart that traverses the root of Jutland (now a part of West Germany). In the twilight period between paganism and Christianity were added the runic stones, handsomely illustrated in Jutland's Jelling stone (from *c*. A.D. 940), which recalls Harald Bluetooth. These features of the human landscape are constant reminders that Denmark is long-occupied land. The features of the chemically-preserved head of the prehistoric Tolland man, which might fit upon the shoulders of so many contemporary Jutlanders, illustrates a corresponding continuity of human types.

In historic times, Denmark's population has shown an uneven distribution; it still does, though for different reasons. Varying agricultural opportunities, expressed chiefly in soil differences, originally accounted for the primary contrasts between occupied and unoccupied areas; now, the degree of occupation is equally likely to be a reflection of industrial opportunity. The position of Denmark in Europe gives to most Danish towns an initial industrial advantage over most Scandinavian towns; but there are also differing local advantages—and, no less important, accidents of local discovery or enterprise.

The expansion of settlement can be picked out partly from place-name evidence. For example, place names with the suffix *inge* and *sted* are usually ascribed to the period A.D. 300–700; *by* and *torp*, to A.D. 1000–1200. The density of medieval churches—often white-washed and crow-stepped on roof and tower—makes a distinct impact because of the openness of the landscape. Some of them were fortresses at the same time, as instanced

Plate 20   A prehistoric burial site in Jutland.
This burial site is in old established farming country between Nibe and Ålborg in Jutland. It points to the antiquity of settlement. The medieval church, surrounded by its hamlet, underlines the continuity of occupation.

by the solid round towers of Østerlars in Bornholm. There are cathedrals, too, adding to domestic brick the expensive imported stone; Ribe, on the edge of the south-west Jutish marshes, is a fine example. There are also monastic ruins, for example at Øm, Horsens and Odense, which reflect the impact of the Reformation upon Denmark. Castles, the other principal antiquity, tended to be either strategic bastions or royal residences. The former are illustrated by Kronborg on the narrows of the Sound at Elsinore, and Fredericia, a planned fortress town at the narrows of the Little Belt. Frederiksborg, in north-eastern Zealand, is the most elaborate of the moated royal residences. There are many other country strongholds and mansions which bear the name *slott* (castle) and which belong chiefly to the seventeenth century; they reflect a stronger legacy of the feudal in the Danish social structure than was common in most parts of Norden.

Church and castle were usually the centres of nucleated settlements. Formerly, most of Denmark's rural settlement was of a village or hamlet type—in strong contrast to the Icelandic and Norwegian experience. The growth of settlement is relatively well documented and the great land register of 1688 is a key document. Rural settlement was partly dispersed by the land reorganisation laws of the late eighteenth century.

As with the Parliamentary Enclosure Acts of England, these broke up the old system of open field husbandry. A no less powerful impetus to dispersal was given by the forces encouraging land reclamation in the later nineteenth century. Jutland, especially, is characterised by extensive areas where the isolated farmstead in the middle of its land holding is the keynote of the rural scene.

Statistics indicate that most Danes live in settlements of more than one thousand inhabitants. Copenhagen, residence of the Danish kings since 1416, but at least 150 years older, is the largest city, and Greater Copenhagen claims $1\frac{1}{4}$ millions. The capital, already disproportionate in size to the population of Denmark at large, is still expanding. Its extensive urbanised area contains within it the relics of former villages and estates: its outliers include dormitory suburbs and detached 'point block' housing.

The other principal cities are Aarhus, commonly regarded as the capital of

Plate 21   Central Copenhagen.
This is the core of Scandinavia's largest city. The view commands the inner section of the harbour, with the Bornholm ferry to the right. The principal administrative and financial areas lie adjacent to the waterways.

Jutland; Odense, principal city of the island of Fyn; the old city of Aalborg
in north Jutland, the young port of Esbjerg on south Jutland's North Sea
coast, and the older Jutish town of Randers.

As in the rest of Scandinavia, expectation of life is high. The population
is ethnographically homogeneous, but there are strong regional feelings
and pronounced regional dialects. A minority of Danes is found south of
the Danish-German border (revised in 1920) in formerly Danish Sønder-
jylland. Most are centred in the city of Flensburg. A smaller number of
Germans remain north of the border. As with the rest of Norden, Denmark
experienced a late nineteenth century flood of emigration, especially to the
U.S.A.

Economic Development
AGRICULTURE AND FISHING

Denmark is renowned as a land of farmers. Its inhabitants have practised tillage since at least the Iron Age, as the relics of early enclosures in
the Jutish heaths attest; but the character and structure of contemporary
farming have relatively shallow roots. They are, in part, an expression of
agricultural co-operation, for the success of Danish farming owes much to
organisation. The physical background to agriculture, while superior to
that of most of the Scandinavian world, is less favourable than that of
much of western Europe. Management has been immensely important
in the most effective combination of land, labour and limited capital.

The Danish agricultural scene is characterised by the intensity and
diversity of land use. Denmark is a country of small-holders who are at the
same time owner-farmers. The detached farmstead, surrounded by
25–75 acres (10–30 h.) of cultivated land is the typical unit; the larger
farms are generally associated with the poorer soils. Intensity of land use
is the result of scientific principles of agriculture applied to personally-
operated holdings. Rotational cropping diversifies the land use pattern on
each holding. Rotations are essentially arable, and commonly eight years
in length. Rotational grass, grains and root crops—their colours changing
seasonally—dominate the landscape with their homely patchwork.
Hedgerow and screens of conifers divide fields and properties in parts of
Jutland, but barbed wire and open field predominate.

Within living memory, Danish agriculture was a rather humble activity
in which there was an increasingly vain attempt to compete with New
World sources of grain and with the Old World's traditional methods of
stock-rearing. Land taxation records reflect the varying profitability of
grain crops in former times. The use of the military road from Viborg
south to Slesvig as an ox-way recalls an early specialisation in cattle.
Denmark was also a breeding ground of horses for military as well as
draught purposes. Sheep were traditionally associated with the heathlands,
from the impoverished wastes of which they grazed a scanty living. In
general, down to about a century ago, the better land was the best farmed
and tended to improve increasingly; while the poorer land was the worst-
farmed and tended to deteriorate still further.

Improvement gathered momentum slowly. It was inseparable from the structural changes in ownership, the example of publicly and privately sponsored heathland reclamation (particularly by the Danish Heath Society after 1866), the re-awakening of a national spirit after the German assault of 1864, and the associated rise of interest in education. Stock improvement, crop improvement, drainage schemes, fertiliser programmes, mechanisation and rationalisation of labour have gone forward side by side with the integration of the rural fabric through cooperative societies. The first society looked to the collection, processing and marketing of milk. To wholesale marketing was added wholesale purchasing, so that the small-holder is able to share the benefits of bulk-selling and bulk-buying. The management of his business affairs is conducted by his elected representatives who are mostly farm operators with similar backgrounds and problems to his own.

Plate 22 The farming scene around Mariager, Denmark.

The accent is on a low-lying landscape, with the windmill announcing windy Jutland and recalling a countryside where grain production was once more important than dairying.

Danish farming concentrates on the production of animals; though the relationship between different forms of stock has changed greatly in the last century. Dairy cattle and pigs are dominant. The Danish Reds and native Black and White breeds account for 85% of the dairy stock. Pigs, of a carefully selected cross between Danish breeds and Yorkshire Whites, are complementary to dairy cattle, skim milk and whey being significant food materials. Poultry are also widely bred. The numbers of sheep and of horses have declined sharply over the last generation, though Jutland horse fairs still attract an international clientèle.

More than four-fifths of the product of Danish farmland is consumed by animal stock. Grain crops occupy nearly one-half of the tilled area, with barley as chief among them. Pigs and poultry look to grain as a chief source of food. Grass crops account for about one-third of the total Danish cultivated area. Rootcrops cover about one-fifth. Cattle beet are more important than sugar beet; but sugar beet is widely grown and there is about enough sugar produced domestically to meet the home demand. Both yield better in the islands than in Jutland. Much of the sugar beet crop is consumed by cattle indirectly, if not directly. Potatoes are especially widely grown in central Jutland. Kohlrabi, which is both hardy and tolerant of poorer soils, is the leading root crop in Jutland.

The mechanisation of Danish farming was initially delayed by shortage of capital. More economic methods of producing farm equipment and the growing availability of capital have led to the widespread mechanisation of Danish husbandry in the last generation. Tractors and milking machines are ubiquitous; the horse-drawn plough, a rarity. Sowing, hay-making, ensiling and harvesting machines have changed the character of and need for much farm labour. Ditch-digging machines and bulldozers have eased the reclamation of marshland, as in the Tönder polders.

With the possible exception of the Netherlands, Danish agriculture is the most intensively developed in Europe. It reaches a peak of intensity in the market gardens around the capital, especially in the horticulture of Amager. It is a measure of its high organisation that Denmark's farm products are able to compete in the export market without government supports. It is one of the few countries in Europe whose agricultural geography is not seriously modified by subsidies and controls.

Danes fish as well as farm. They have a fleet of 8,000 fishing boats, the deep sea constituent of which operates principally in the North Sea. Most are based on Jutland's fishing ports. The North Sea ports, from Esbjerg (the largest) in the south to Hirtshals in the north, are twentieth century creations. Old-established Skagen and Frederikshavn have been so modernised that the romantic traditions and associations of the activity have largely disappeared. The North Sea grounds yield flat fish, herring, cod and haddock; but a variety of fish are caught all round the Danish coasts. Denmark has a fish culture that goes back to antiquity. Gastronomes seek Limfjord oysters (relished since Mesolithic times), smoked Bornholm herrings (which recall the remarkable medieval herring shoals of the Danish Sound), brown and rainbow trout (widely bred in hatcheries), Greenland prawns and smoked eels.

INDUSTRY The development of Danish industry, as with that of the rest of Norden, was delayed. Absence of domestic supplies of coal was a retarding fact at the time of western Europe's industrial revolution, though Denmark was in a more favourable situation to import coal from neighbouring producers than any of its Scandinavian neighbours. Denmark also lacked minerals and forests. So farm products provided the chief raw materials for its initial manufacturing activity. Their processing was first handled on a large scale by cooperative dairies, slaughteries and mills from the 1870's onwards. Contemporary processing is distinguished by the immense range of products.

In the first place, farming operations themselves encouraged the manufacture of agricultural equipment. Before the village smith yielded to imported equipment or established his own manufacturing workshop, farm implements were locally produced. Mechanisation of Danish agriculture has, in turn, given rise to an industry of world importance for Denmark. Its mechanical workshops have looked especially to the needs and pockets of the small scale operator. From milking machines which are within the reach of the farmer who keeps only half a dozen cows, through forage and beet harvesters to tractors and combine harvesters, equipment has been scaled down in size.

The refining of sugar-beet, grown by some 20,000 farmers, also ties together agriculture and industry. It takes place in some six centrally placed plants. The brewing industry, a substantial consumer of Danish barley, has developed an international reputation out of a local speciality. The first Carlsberg beer was already exported from Copenhagen over a century ago. The distillation of cherry brandy, begun at Dalby south of Copenhagen in 1818, and the production of *akvavit*, initiated in Aalborg in 1846, have also given rise to agriculturally-based industries that have a world market.

A second old-established group of agriculturally-based industries looks to imported raw materials. The vegetable oil industries, heavily concentrated in Aarhus and using tropical seeds and nuts, produce margarine, soaps, chemicals, lacquers and varnishes; while the large by-product of crushed seeds and fibres is converted into fodder concentrates. Tobacco manufacture (with cigars a speciality) is based on Copenhagen.

Norway, Sweden and Finland looked historically to wood as their principal building material, with stone for monumental purposes. Denmark's builders have had only boulders, clays, sands and chalk, with local hardwoods for the costlier half-timbered buildings, and willows with clay for the wattle-and-daub. Brick and tile manufacture, old-established and fairly widely distributed, has experienced major changes in the scale of production and has shown growing concentration in areas where demand is greatest e.g. in Zealand. A lively builder's hardware industry has sprung out of the building industry and contributes actively to exports. The cement industry, which began in 1873 on Mariagerfiord, has five primary areas of production and all are coastal in location. The industry rises to a climax on Limfjorden around Aalborg–Nørre Sundy. It has international implications for Denmark. It has added to the variety of Denmark's bulk exports and encouraged the production of special cements for particular purposes (e.g. rapid-hardening cements for cold environments). Over a thousand cement-processing plants have been exported to over seventy different countries and their assembly is a specialised Danish enterprise in its own right. The Danes have also been pioneers in pre-fabricated concrete buildings and now claim one of Europe's largest plants for the manufacture of prefabricated constituents.

Much of Denmark's contemporary industry has developed in response to a domestic need and then, by an ingenious turn of the screw, acquired an international market. Examples may be found in the textile and clothing industries. Jutland, the historical centre of the hosiery industry, has witnessed a striking transformation from farmhouse knitting to the concentration of mechanical workshops in and around Herning. Copenhagen, catering for the local clothing needs of a large city, has evolved a ready-made clothing industry of world consequence. Furniture manufacture repeats the experience. Carpenters, joiners and designers have transferred their attention from native oak and beech to the fashionable tropical hardwoods. As a result, furniture-manufacturing has expanded rapidly, and 40% of its output is sold abroad.

Ships are vital to Danish needs and there is a ship-building tradition which goes back to Bronze Age times. The most important yards are in Copenhagen, Elsinore, Nakskov, Aarhus and Aalborg. Diesel-engines for

Plate 23 Kronborg Castle and the Öresund.
Kronborg Castle commands the narrow straits at the northern end of the Danish Sound. It looks across to the Swedish port of Helsingborg. Adjacent to the castle is the old ferry port of Elsinore, with its shipyards.

ships are manufactured under licence. Ship-builders have tended to develop specialist skills, for example in the construction of ferries, refrigeration vessels, ice-strengthened ships for expeditions as well as trading and pleasure yachts. The manufacture of large-scale freezing plants is an industry which is related at once to ship-building and to the trade in perishable commodities. Freezing and air-conditioning plants are widely exported and installed by Danish engineers. The demand for metals for constructional purposes, for the transport, machine-tool and implement industries, has prompted the establishment of steel plants which use semi-refined and scrap materials as the basis of their production.

Contemporary Danish manufacturing industry is concentrated essentially in and around the capital; though there are interesting examples of dispersal, such as Danfoss with its 5,000 employees on the island of Als or the oil refinery of Kalundborg. In structure, the emphasis is on small concerns, with the 7,000 industrial firms mostly employing between 50 and 250 employees. The accent is principally on consumer goods, high in quality and frequently tailor-made in character. Denmark's success as an industrial state rests heavily upon its skill in handling a highly competitive market.

COMMUNICATIONS
AND TRADE

Denmark is a sea state. Its scattered islands lie mostly in the lee of the great 'mole' of Jutland; but communication between them nevertheless presents problems. Through the Great Belt, Little Belt and Sound, international shipping follows the shallow north-south routes. Denmark's greatest problem of integration is east-west. The Little Belt is spanned by a suspension bridge. The Great Belt is traversed by an armada of ferries, rail—(from Korsør to Nyborg) as well as car—(from Halskov to Knudshoved). The Sound has an even more elaborate shuttle of ferries, plying principally between Copenhagen and Malmö, Helsingborg and Elsinore. Imaginative schemes exist to bridge both the Great Belt and the Sound. To the south of the island of Zealand, Lolland and Falster are linked by some of Europe's longest bridges. A ferry ties Rødbyhavn on Falster to West Germany's Putgarden. To the north-west, ferries bind Aarhus with Copenhagen and Kalundborg. Aalborg is also linked with the capital by a shipping service. A hundred miles east of the chalky needles of the island of Møn is located the residual island of Denmark's Baltic Empire—Bornholm, with its lesser dependencies. As the need to maintain sea links has favoured the rise of ship-building, so the challenge of straits and sounds has encouraged a nation of bridge-builders.

On land, Denmark was the first country in Norden to introduce railways. State railways took precedence over private lines and what has proved to be a surfeit of lines came into being. The axial east-west line, which runs from Copenhagen to Esbjerg, carries more traffic than all the rest of Denmark's railways combined. Esbjerg, which grew up a hundred years ago in response to the demand for an express steamer link with Harwich, has a state-sponsored harbour. It has a large passenger traffic and busy repair yard as well as the traditional export of farm products.

Copenhagen, which is Scandinavia's most diversified port, has always been of more than national consequence. Its free port is a part of the Baltic setting, although the volume and nature of its entrepôt has changed much in the last twenty years. These changes have been related to alterations in the boundaries of mainland Europe.

Copenhagen responded to earlier adjustments in its hinterland after Germany opened the Kiel Canal in 1896. This continues to play a significant role in Danish transport relations, by shortening the distance between its most populous parts and the ports of West Germany, Britain and France. Local canals have played their own particular roles. In the days when Schleswig-Holstein was still Danish, there were schemes for

Plate 24   Great Belt Ferry.
Denmark is bound together by ferries, though there are constant proposals from engineers to replace them with major bridges and tunnels. The Great Belt has a rail ferry as well as the car and passenger ferry shown here.

linking the North Sea and the Baltic across Danish territory. Odense, principal city of Fyn, has a ship canal which gives the town access to the sea.

Denmark operates Scandinavian Air Services jointly with Norway and Sweden. The polar route to the Pacific has its European terminal in Copenhagen, where Kastrup airport is one of the busiest in Europe. Domestic air services are less intensive than in the other countries of Norden.

Copenhagen remains the point of departure for Danish shipping services to the Faeroes, Iceland and Greenland. In pre-war days, when icebreakers were less well organised, there was some debate about making Copenhagen a winter outport for Finland. In severe winters, communications in the Danish archipelago can present considerable problems.

All forms of transport employed by Denmark (the 3 million bicycles apart) rely heavily upon imported oil. In turn, this calls for adequate oil harbours. One of the problems is the relatively shallow coast around much of the country. The search for deep water harbours led to the establishment of oil ports in Copenhagen, Aarhus, Stigsnaes, Kalundborg and Fredericia. In general, for modern deep-draught tankers, the Great Belt coast of Zealand seems to offer the most favourable opportunities for future development.

It is not only transport which relies upon imported fuel. Domestic sources of supply are restricted to relatively poor quality lignites and peat. Historically, Denmark has looked to the north-east coalfields of Great Britain: contemporarily, it looks to West Germany and Poland for solid fuels. But most of Denmark's energy supply is derived from imported oil fuel and an uninterrupted flow of energy imports is more critical for Denmark than for any of the other countries of Norden.

Oil imports are the principal product that Denmark derives from outside Europe. More than 70% of its exports are to European markets, with Great Britain as the country's biggest single trading partner. The E.F.T.A. countries buy more than twice as much of Denmark's exports as the E.E.C. countries.

The Threshold of Scandinavia

Denmark is written on a smaller scale than the other Scandinavian countries. It does not lend itself to bold regional subdivision in quite the same manner as they do. Denmark falls logically into the peninsula in the west and the islands to its east. In turn, the peninsula may be roughly divided into the hilly moraines of the east and the flat country of the out-wash plains to the west. For essentially physical reasons, the west has been traditionally poorer than the east; but the contemporary provision of a uniform network of services and amenities has done much to reduce the inherent differences.

The countryside makes no great visual impact either in the forms of its physical landscape (which are gentle and quietly modulated) or in the features of its human landscape (which have an air of maturity and stability). The themes of its physical geography are those of the North European Plain (pp. 27, 156–8), while the human variations upon them are the product of an old-established independent realm which has drawn freely upon the ideas and devices of north-west Europe at large. The course of Danish history has fostered a people who retain an outward-looking mentality and who, for different motives but with no less energy than their ancestors, engage in enterprise beyond the seas. It has also bred in them a tolerant understanding of their domestic limitations. The trim and tidy landscape of Denmark appears to be the outward expression of a well-ordered land. In turn, the order seems to spring from a balance between organisation from below and planning from above. For this reason, Denmark is the object of emulation by other lands. As a transit land between the Scandinavian Peninsula and Central Europe, between the Baltic Sea and the North Sea, it claims an international importance disproportionate to its size.

FURTHER READING   (Ed.) N. Nielsen, *Atlas of Denmark*, Vol. I, 1949; Vol. II, 1961.

Guide Book to Denmark, I.G.U. Congress, 1960, *Geografisk Tidsskrift*, 59, 1960.

Geografisk Tidsskrift is the journal of the Danish Geographical Society and most of its contributions are either in English or have an English summary.

There is a research series *Folia geographica dannica*. Among works published in it is A. Schou, *Det marine Forland*, 1945, 4, with an English summary. There are also English summaries to the publications in the Royal Danish Geographical Society's series *Kulturgeografiske Skrifter*.

The relevant chapters on Denmark in (Ed.) A. Sømme, *The Geography of Norden*, Oslo, 1960; W. R. Mead, *An Economic Geography of the Scandinavian States and Finland*, 1958; R. Millward, *The Scandinavian Countries*, 1965; A. C. O'Dell, *The Scandinavian World*, 1957.

Denmark, A Publication by the Danish Ministry of Foreign Affairs (Various editions).

F. Skrubbleltrang, *Agricultural Development and Rural Reform in Denmark*, F.A.C., Rome, 1953.

The Danish map series is published by the Geodetic Institute in Copenhagen.

CHAPTER NINE   *By Peter Hall*

Germany

German geographers themselves have long argued about the definition of Germany. Unlike England or France, which have had a political existence and well-defined frontiers for centuries, Germany has possessed clear political unity only for a short period of history. The first German empire (*Erstes Reich*) was the Holy Roman Empire, established by Charlemagne in A.D. 800. Nominally it lasted one thousand years before Napoleon dissolved it in 1806, but it extended far beyond the German lands of Europe, across the Alps to Italy; and it soon lost all effective political unity. Throughout the Middle Ages Germany remained a bewildering mosaic of small states. By the early nineteenth century one of the eastern-most of these, Prussia, had acquired large territories in central and western Germany; after the fall of the Holy Roman Empire and then of Napoleon (1815), she rapidly gained ascendancy of Germany through the medium of a customs union (*Zollverein*), in which she was dominant partner.

In 1871, after victory in the war with France, Prussia established the second empire (*Zweites Reich*) under the Prussian Kaiser; this lasted until the Kaiser's abdication at the end of the First World War in 1918. At the Treaty of Versailles in 1919, though she remained a united country with a democratic republican government (Weimar Republic), she lost important territories: notably Alsace-Lorraine (acquired in 1871, returned to France), and part of Upper Silesia (acquired at the First Partition of Poland in 1772, returned to Poland). Adolf Hitler's third empire (*Drittes Reich*) was meant to last one thousand years, like Charlemagne's empire, but in fact collapsed in twelve (1933–45).

By the Potsdam Treaty of August 1945, concluded among the four allied powers, Germany was formally divided into four zones of military occupation (British in the north-west, Americans in the west, centre and south, French in the south-west, and Russians in the east). Thus a united Germany had survived only seventy-four years—1871–1945. Berlin, as former capital within the Russian zone, was divided into four sectors. Immediately at war's end, with Russian help, Poland assumed control of 44,000 square miles (114,000 sq. km.) of former German territory east of the rivers Oder and western Neisse, including southern East Prussia (the northern part passed to the Soviet Union), much of Pomerania, and the rich agricultural district of Silesia with its important regional capital of Breslau (Polish, Wrocław). Eight million Germans were expelled from this region and arrived as refugees in Germany. The Allied Powers agreed to the occupation of these territories pending the conclusion of a formal peace treaty; as this has never taken place, the frontiers of Germany remain under dispute.

Increasingly the four occupation zones aggregated into two blocks, the three western ones on one side, the Russian on the other; and after a dispute over currency reform and the consequent Russian blockade of West Berlin, in 1948, this received formal expression in the setting up of two German states in 1949. The Federal Germany Republic (*Bundesrepublik Deutschland* or BRD) represents the three western zones; it received full sovereignty from the western powers in 1955. The German Democratic Republic (*Deutsche Demokratische Republik* or DDR) represents the former Russian zone; it includes East Berlin, its capital. Neither the Federal Republic nor the western powers have recognised the Democratic Republic, and in the Federal Republic it is always referred to as the Soviet Zone of Occupation (*Sowjetbesatzungszone* or SBZ). In addition the Federal Republic does not legally recognise the loss of the German eastern territories to Poland, and all maps published there show Germany within her frontiers of 31st December 1937, i.e. before Hitler occupied Austria, the first of his territorial violations.

Nor do cultural criteria give the geographer much help in defining a distinctively German area. German-speaking peoples, who share a common literary tradition, have for centuries occupied a very wide zone of central Europe, including two areas which since the Middle Ages have been organised in nation-states distinct from Germany: Switzerland (where German speakers occupy the northern and eastern part of the country) and Austria. A German dialect is spoken in French Alsace-Lorraine and in the Grand Duchy of Luxembourg. Formerly, too, there were German enclaves extending far into eastern Europe, as far as the colony on the Volga in the USSR; but these disappeared as a result of the Second World War. Thus there is a well-defined German linguistic zone in central Europe, including the two Germanies, Austria, part of Switzerland, Luxembourg and French Alsace-Lorraine; but all these areas have separate governments, political systems, national lives and cultures. Nor does it seem likely that any political assimilation will occur in the near future, even between the two German republics, though a gradual easing of relationships between them may take place. Consequently, in this book Germany will be treated within her post-1945 frontiers; and after an introduction to establish common points of physical and historical evolution, the two states will be separately treated.

The Physical Environment

Common to the two Germanies, and indeed to all the Germanic lands of central Europe, is a striking threefold physical division: northern lowlands, central uplands and southern mountains. These three elements are very largely the products of different periods of earth history; different agents of earth-building and earth-destruction have worked on them at different periods for different lengths of time to produce very different and very distinctive landscapes. Each of these main physiographic elements has a parallel with elements in the British Isles; but the parallel may obscure important differences in the outward form of the landscape.

The oldest of the three divisions is the Central Uplands. More accurately these consist of a series of relic blocks, the remnants of fold mountains formed in the Hercynian mountain-building period, and of basins of sedimentary deposition laid down in the succeeding Mesozoic era. These two elements are closely associated, for the first helped to form the second. The Hercynian mountains were upraised in a series of earth convulsions at the end of the Carboniferous period and the beginning of the Permian, that is about 240 million years ago. Immediately, a process of denudation set in. Throughout the Permian period (200–240 million years ago), the Triassic (175–200), the Jurassic (140–175) and the Cretaceous (60–140), the mountains were worn down almost to peneplane surfaces, and the resulting materials were redeposited in a series of sedimentary layers in nearby basins. In turn differential denudation of these rocks, which ranged from resistant sandstones and limestones to softer clays, produced a distinctive scarp and vale topography. Finally, in the late Tertiary period, only about 30 million years ago, the outer ripples of the great Alpine earth disturbance caused the Hercynian relics to be re-uplifted into upland plateau blocks with distinctively flat top surfaces, the form they assume today.

The two most important Hercynian blocks are the Rhine Plateau or Rhenish Uplands in the west, boldly incised by the north-flowing Rhine, and the great diamond-shaped Bohemian block in the east, of which only the westernmost edges extend beyond the Czech boundary into Germany. Between them is a bewildering series of small relics lying almost as islands within the later sedimentary basins: Rhön, Vogelsberg, Spessart, Harz. In south-west Germany the Hercynian relics (Black Forest, Odenwald) form the eastern half of an arch whose centre has collapsed along fault lines to form the Rhine Rift Valley and whose western side forms the upland block of the Vosges in French Alsace (pp. 400–401).

The Hercynian relics compare in age and form with similar blocks (the Pennines, mid-Wales, Exmoor) in Britain. They consist of extensive upland surfaces formed during the long period of Mesozoic and early Tertiary denudation—some of the most important of them in intervals between the actual Tertiary uplifts. In height these surfaces range between about 500 ft. (150 m.) and a little over 2,000 ft. (600 m.); while higher points, the summits of the Central Uplands, are usually formed by residual bands of more resistant rock, e.g. Feldberg in the Black Forest 4,898 feet (1,493 m.), Grosse Feldberg in the Taunus 2,887 feet (880 m.), Brocken in the Harz 3,747 feet (1,142 m.). Their landscape is, however, very different from their British counterparts. Climate, though bleak, is distinguished by lower precipitation; settlement in consequence has been taken to much greater altitudes, and it is common to find large stretches of land cleared for open-field mixed agriculture, though with large residual patches of both coniferous and deciduous forest, at heights up to 2,000 feet (600 m.) and more. Settlement in such areas is commonly in irregular nucleated villages, which range in size from hamlets of a dozen farms on the upland borders of settlement, to large units of a thousand and more people wherever farming conditions are locally favourable. This open field and nucleated village landscape, with extensive stretches of dark coniferous forest on the higher ridges, is indeed characteristic of the Central Uplands.

The sedimentary basins on the other hand correspond to the scarpland landscapes of south-east England. Indeed the best-developed example, the scarplands of south Germany, presents a sequence of rocks similar to that in southern England, though with the younger members (late Jurassic and Cretaceous) much more weakly developed. But again obvious comparisons may mislead. The average altitude of the scarpland basins is much greater than that of their English counterparts, and relief differences are more marked: thus the Jurassic scarp, which in the English Cotswolds rises to a maximum of about 1,070 feet (330 m.) above sea level, behind a plain at about 150 feet (50 m.) rises in Germany to 2–3,000 feet (600–900 m.) behind a clay plain at about 1,000 feet (300 m.).

Again, in contrast to the hedged and enclosed landscape of midland and much of southern England, with its isolated farmsteads set in their own fields, the German scarpland basins present the rich mosaic of the open fields with their individual strips, once cultivated according to a common rotation but now a patchwork quilt of different crops. Again too the nucleated village has retained its dominance in the settlement pattern, and isolated farms are much rarer than in England save in the remotest districts. The cultural or man-made landscape is therefore of the same broad central German type as that of the Hercynian blocks; but in general it is richer, due to better farming opportunities. Yet local differences due to geology, climate and soils are marked. There is a sharp contrast between the intensively-farmed cornlands of the Kraichgau between Heidelberg, Karlsruhe and Stuttgart, based on extensive tracts of wind-blown loess deposited in the Quaternary ice age, with their very large nucleated villages and their almost complete absence of residual forest, and the extensive dark coniferous forests of the Keuper sandstone areas some 60 miles (100 km.) to the east, with their small hamlets set in clearings.

The Central Uplands are by far the largest landscape element of the area of the two postwar Germanies. By contrast the second element, the Alpine fold mountains, form merely a narrow and almost unpopulated strip at the southern frontier of the Federal Republic. These fold mountains represent merely the northernmost folds of the great 150-mile (240-km.) wide Alpine mass. The sediments which form them, laid down in a great structural depression in Mesozoic and early Tertiary times, are dominated by Jurassic limestones, with dolomitic limestone appearing in the lower hills flanking the main ranges to the north. They were upraised in Miocene times (12–26 million years ago) into fold mountains of sharp relief, which subsequent denudation has not had sufficient time to diminish much. In addition, glaciation during the Quaternary ice age further sharpened the relief, causing knife edge ridges and pyramidal peaks on the higher slopes, and deep U-shaped valleys lower down. Today the Bavarian Alps still present the highest and least penetrable mountains in Germany, e.g. the Zugspitze, 9,721 feet (2,963 m.) and their chief economic importance is as a tourist centre.

The third element (chronologically speaking) in the physiography of Germany consists of the landscapes of the Quaternary glaciation which began about six million years ago and ended a mere 10,000 years ago. The effects of glacial erosion are limited to the highlands and in particular to the Alps of Germany's southern borders; but the effects of deposition are widespread. In the north, continental ice sheets moving from Scandinavia deposited great masses of material over the Mesozoic and Tertiary rocks right across the extensive lowland area which stretches from the North and Baltic Sea coasts in the north to the edges of the Central Uplands in the south, a distance of between 70 and 150 miles (110–220 km.) and from the plain of Flanders beyond the western frontiers of Germany to the Urals in the east. Before Germany's territorial losses of 1945, this northern lowland was, indeed, the largest single landscape element in Germany. The landscapes thus formed include the familiar elements of ground moraine, terminal moraine, drumlins, lake basins, and outwash plains. But the simple sequence of glacial deposits is complicated by the fact that several glaciations took place, each with a number of stillstand periods, during which lines of terminal moraines were laid down. Further, the ice sheets blocked the obvious drainage routes to the

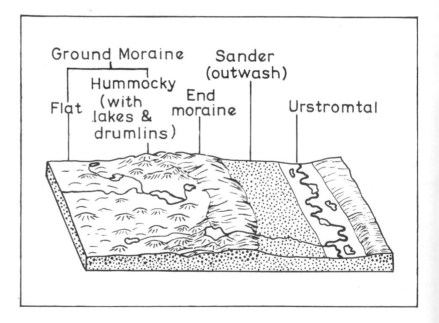

Fig 21   A typical lowland of glacial deposition

north and produced extensive diversions of the river system in a generally north-westerly direction. The valleys thus formed—old stream valleys, in German *Urstromtäler*—still form one of the most prominent features of the Northern Lowlands, and the modern rivers use them for parts of their courses, forming abrupt elbows with the direct north-south elements of the drainage system.

In general the Northern Lowlands form negative, sparsely populated lands. There are extensive areas of forest on the sandy ground moraine and terminal moraine zones, while impeded drainage in the Urstromtal zones and in the drumlin belts within the terminal moraine loops has created large areas of peat bog (German, *Moor*; not to be confused with the upland moors of Hercynian Britain). In addition, coastal changes along the North Sea coast in post-glacial times have led to the formation of large tracts of sea marsh, which have been reclaimed for settlement and cultivation only slowly and with difficulty. The moraine lands characteristically have extensive tracts of coniferous and birch forest, with small hamlets or isolated farms based on the cultivation of rye in large fields; the lower Moor lands and the coastal marshlands tend to have planned linear villages (in the Moor along canals, in the marshes along dikes) with individual strip holdings. To this generally unfavourable picture there is, however, one notable exception. A narrow belt of wind-blown loess, formed during interglacial and early post-glacial periods, extends along the margin of the Northern Lowlands and Central Uplands, widening out into extensive lowland basins which make deep incursions into the Hercynian blocks of the south: the Cologne Bay in the west, centred on the city of that name; and the Saxon Bay in the east, centred on the cities of Halle, Leipzig and Dresden. These contain some of the richest agricultural lands of Germany, intensively farmed in large open fields with almost no remnant of surviving woodland; the farmers live in big irregular nucleated villages. Like the better loess-covered areas of the southern scarplands, these are Germany's "corn chambers". In addition they both have a strong industrial base in chemicals and electric power production, and intense urbanisation.

The other area of extensive glacial deposition is found in the south, in the Alpine Foreland zone between the northernmost foothills of the Alps and the river Danube, a distance at most eighty miles from south to north. Most of this area (save the extreme west, which is in the province of Swabia) belongs to Bavaria, hence the common name "Bavarian Foreland". Here the Quaternary ice extruded itself from constricted valley glaciers as it left the mountains, forming well-marked terminal moraine loops, which enclose tongue-shaped basins marked by drumlins and often by residual lakes and alluvial lake plains.

As in the Northern Lowlands, different glaciations can be distinguished. The results of the older glaciation have been much more completely denuded than the still fresh moraines of the last ice advance (here called the Würm but equivalent to the Vistula glaciation of the north), which lie in great loops close to the Alpine foothills. In both older and newer glacial zones, a rather damp climate further encourages a regime of pastoralism. The resulting landscape is distinctive, and unlike any other in Germany: there are rolling hills with much impeded drainage and a multitude of lakes, small residual forest clumps, large fields of grass, and big isolated farmhouses built to accommodate stock during the often severe winter.

DRAINAGE   The Hercynian upland zone of middle Germany provides the key to the understanding of the major German river systems, because most of them rise here. The four major rivers of the north German plain—the Ems, Weser, Elbe and Oder—all have sources in Hercynian relic blocks and pursue courses northwards to the North and Baltic sea. The Ems actually rises on the slopes of the Weserfestung, a north-westerly projection of the uplands into the northern plain; the two main headwaters of the Weser, the Fulda and Werra, rise deep in the complex corridor zone between the eastern side of the Rhine Plateau and the relic block of the Thuringian forest; the Elbe begins life within the Bohemian Massif, and the Oder rises on the slopes of the Sudeten Mountains, which bound the Bohemian block on its north-east side. All these rivers, on escaping into the plain, have been heavily affected by the Quaternary glaciation; they leave their obvious and direct south-north courses to follow lines of least resistance formed by the Urstromtäler, causing abrupt elbow turns in their courses. An important effect is that three of the rivers flow into the North Sea, only one (Oder) into the enclosed Baltic.

The major river of south Germany, the Danube, also rises in an Hercynian relic block: the eastern slopes of the Black Forest. Thence it flows east-north-eastwards along a line of easy passage, where the back-slope of the major Jurassic scarp is overlain by later material, receiving right-bank tributaries from the Alps, as far as Regensburg. Here it turns through a pronounced angle to run east-south-eastwards, against the south-west margin of the Bohemian relic block, across the German-Austrian boundary towards Vienna, below which it escapes through a narrow gate between the Bohemian block on the north and the Alpine system on the south into the great Alfold Basin of Hungary. The boundary in south Germany between the Rhine and Danube systems is one of the great drainage divides in Europe, marking as it does the watershed between North Sea and Black Sea, and therefore indirectly between north European and south European systems.

To this rather simple pattern of drainage, Germany's major river presents an outstandingly anomalous exception. The Rhine rises in the Alps of Switzerland and is glacier-fed. It flows for many miles westwards through the Mittelland of Switzerland, a continuation of the Alpine Foreland of Bavaria, and then at Basle turns abruptly northwards into the great Rhine Rift Valley (pp. 206–7), where its original course was like that in the Northern Lowlands. One hundred miles (160 km.) below Basle it receives one major tributary, the Neckar, which has risen on the north-east slopes of the Black Forest; 50 miles (80 km.) after this, at Mainz, it receives the Main, another right bank tributary which has risen on the north-western edge of the Bohemian block and has flowed westwards through a series of great elbows, representing captures of streams which formerly flowed south towards the Danube. The Rhine then runs westwards for a few miles along the southern edge of the Rhine Plateau block before suddenly turning through a right angle (at Bingen) and plunging into the famous deep gorge by which it cuts completely across the block for fifty miles. In the middle of its course through the plateau, at Koblenz, it receives its only significant left bank tributary, the Moselle, which rises on the northern slope of the Vosges in France and which plunges anomalously into the plateau block through a deeply incised gorge.

The origin of the middle Rhine-Moselle drainage is the phenomenon of antecedence: the rivers were initiated when the old Hercynian mountains were worn down to peneplane surfaces, and as these remnants were upraised during the Alpine upheaval, downcutting by the rivers kept pace. But there was no time for lateral erosion, and so the characteristic gorge-like incision took shape. Below its escape into the Northern Lowlands (actually the Cologne embayment) at Bonn, the Rhine soon assumes a very different form. Due to the lack of gradient the river naturally flowed very sluggishly in great meanders within a wide floodplain, and it was only in the nineteenth century that artificial regulation has given the river a more direct course across the Dutch boundary to the North Sea at the Hook of Holland.

Basically, therefore, nearly all Germany is drained by three major systems of rivers. One consists of the roughly parallel rivers of the Northern Lowlands, draining to the North and Baltic Seas. A second consists of the Danube system, draining eastwards into the Alfold of Hungary and eventually into the Black Sea. A third consists of the Rhine, which drains a very large area of western Germany and extends its influence (via the Main) to the very borders of the Hercynian block. The importance of these systems lies in the fact that to a much greater extent than English rivers these are either naturally navigable or can be made so. Their potential development then depends on the sea routes to which they provide access; and here the Danube, with its long and tortuous course to an East European inland sea, labours under an obvious disadvantage compared with the systems which provide a link with the busy seas of northern Europe.

CLIMATE   In broad continental terms, the German lands nearly all fall within one major climatic division: that of the Short Cold Winter. Only a narrow strip along the North Sea coastlands is distinctive in joining the coastal Netherlands, western Norway and Britain as representative of the West Coast Marine type; while the Alpine strip in the extreme south falls into the special category of Mountain climate. Yet differences in climate, across a latitudinal extent of 800 miles (1,280 km.) and a longitudinal extent of 500 miles (800 km.), are greater than this simple division suggests. The German zones are essentially a zone of climatic transition, in which

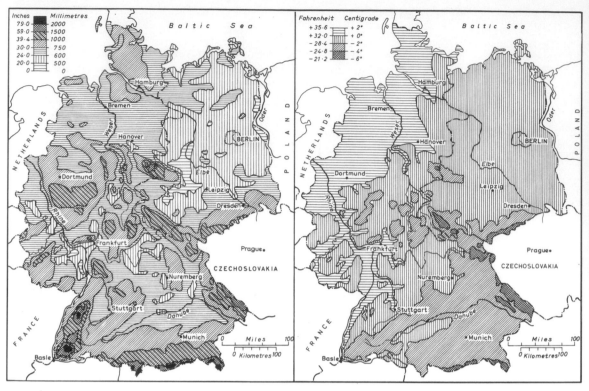

a   Rainfall

b   January isotherms

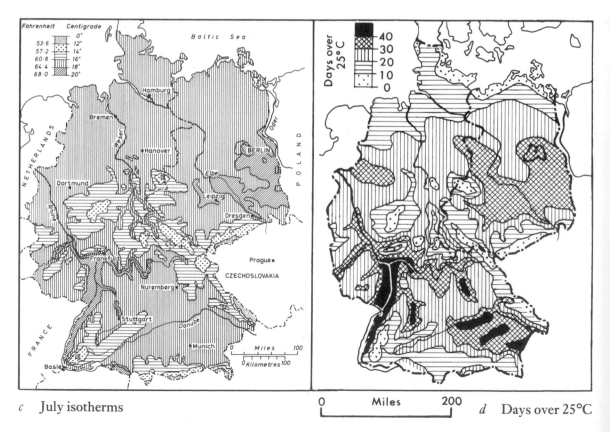

c   July isotherms

d   Days over 25°C

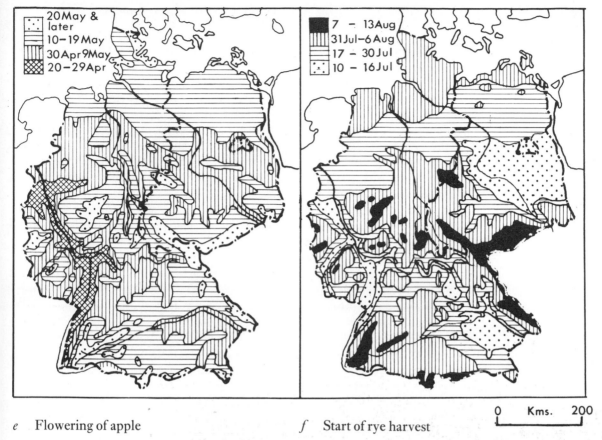

e Flowering of apple	*f* Start of rye harvest

Fig 22 Climate of the Germanies

maritime weather conditions from the Atlantic west struggle for ascendancy with continental conditions from the Siberian east; and the relative strength of these forces, over the year, produces a variation from a nearly pure oceanic climate in the extreme north-west to an almost purely continental regime in the east and parts of the south.

Three chief influences help to produce the internal variations in climate: latitude, continentality and altitude. Of these, latitude is the least important. It affects Germany very marginally in summer, when the July isotherms (corrected for altitude) take an east-west direction. But considering actual temperatures, though north Germany does have mean temperatures 1–2°C (2°–4°F) colder than the south, virtually all Germany below the 1,500-foot contour has July means between 16° and 18°C (61° and 64°F). And any effect here is much less pronounced than the winter effect of continentality. In January the sea-level isotherms have swung round in a pronounced north-south direction: the 0°C (32°F) January line, for instance, runs along the middle Elbe and the Saale from Magdeburg to Erfurt, and thence southwards again to Regensburg. And the actual recorded temperatures, too, show a notable gradient from oceanic west to continental east. Cologne and Koblenz both register January means of 2°C (36°F) while Frankfurt-on-Oder nearly 400 miles

(640 km.) to the east records —1°C (30°F). Since this influence begins to have effect on autumn and lasts well into spring, it exerts a certain control over the length of growing season for many crops. Frost days, for instance, rise from an average of 44 at Cologne to 78 at Magdeburg, 90 at Berlin and 96 at Frankfurt-on-Oder. Rainfall, too, decreases quite regularly from west to east across the Northern Lowlands, from an annual average of 27 inches (686 mm.) at Cologne to 23 inches (584 mm.) at Berlin, while at the same time the seasonal distribution and the origin of the rainfall changes, with a progressively higher proportion of summer convectional and storm rainfall as one moves eastward.

The most important single influence is altitude. A large part of the settled and cultivated area of Germany reaches considerable altitudes, which by British standards would be regarded as quite outside the range of normal human occupation; thus in areas like the Rhine Plateau or the Jurassic limestone belt of south Germany there are large settled tracts above 1,500 and even above 2,000 feet (450 and 600 m.) Both in summer and winter, altitudes like these have a substantial effect on climate. In January the high plateau areas of the Rhine Plateau are about 2°C (4°F) colder than the adjacent lowlands of the Cologne Bay, in July anything up to 3°C (6°F) colder. This has a notable effect on the number of freezing days per year, because it means that within a relatively short horizontal distance the marked oceanic amelioration of temperatures, so marked in north-west Germany in winter, can be largely nullified. Across the Hercynian middle belt of Germany, local differences in temperature are apt to be very pronounced: the sheltered Rhine rift valley and Rhine–Main Plain stand out in the sharpest contrast to the Hercynian uplands which border them. And farther south, the mean January temperature at Munich on the Alpine Foreland is more than 3°C (6°F) colder than at Freiburg in the Rhine Rift Valley. Even more pronounced is the effect of relief on precipitation, particularly where high uplands are exposed to rain-bearing winds during the passage of winter depressions. This is particularly marked in the case of the Rhine Plateau and Black Forest, and there are noticeable rain-shadow effects in bordering lowlands like the Rhine Rift Valley, which are among the driest areas in the western Germanic lands (see also p. 346–7). Basle in the valley, for instance, has an annual rainfall of 32 inches (820 mm.); the high surfaces of the adjacent Black Forest, only some twenty miles away, have as much as 80 inches (2,030 mm.). To a remarkable degree, indeed, the map of annual average rainfall proves to be a map of relief (Fig. 22a).

SOILS Although on a world-wide scale soils can be classified according to the climate in which they develop, local soil variations in a country like Germany usually prove to relate first to geological differences, secondly to local climatic conditions and thirdly to local differences in relief (in particular slope and aspect) which affect temperatures, rainfall and drainage. Thus in the Northern Lowlands the soils which develop on the sandy moraine lands tend to be very permeable and so are easily leached of their supplies of plant foods, while the lower-lying boglands suffer from impeded drainage and produce 'gleyed' soils which in their natural condition are also highly unattractive to the farmer. Farther south, though, the loess lands at the southern border of the plain produce a deep, rich, well-drained soil which in places is similar in character to the black earths of Russia; it is among the most fertile soils of middle Europe.

The plateaux of the Central Uplands produce a great variety of soils which however all show a common tendency to leaching in some degree. On the higher surfaces, if the land be flat and precipitation high, problems of impeded drainage may occur. The most valuable soils of the Hercynian lands are provided by isolated occurrences of limestone or basic volcanic rocks, where the character of the parent material helps to counteract the natural tendency towards leaching; these soils tend to form local pockets of much more intensive agriculture than is usual in the uplands.

Most varied of all are the soils of the scarpland basins of south Germany. These range from the highly fertile, intensively farmed soils of black earth type, developed on the loess lands; through heavy, reasonably fertile but rather intractable brown forest soils on the claylands; to thin dry soils on the limestone plateaux of the Jurassic region; and to hungry, highly-leached, infertile soils on the permeable Bunter or Keuper sandstones. In the Bavarian Foreland soils tend to be heavier and of better quality on average than in the glacial lands of the Northern Lowlands, but there are numerous areas of gleyed soils in the lower-lying basins within the terminal moraine loops. Some of these are, however, potentially fertile if they can be drained. The Alpine zone has either very thin and poorly structured mountain soils, of no significance for agriculture, or no soils at all.

INDUSTRIAL
RESOURCES

In the modern world the German lands have possessed one priceless advantage: they lie astride the major belt of bituminous coal in Europe, which extends along the border of the North European Lowlands and the Hercynian uplands in a series of discontinuous basins from the British Isles to the U.S.S.R. In Germany, as elsewhere, this discontinuous character gives contrasted coal resources in different areas. The greatest concentration of all is found in the west, in the Ruhr coal basin of Westphalia, which underlies the fertile loess soils just east of the Rhine. Here are found almost precisely one-third of all the bituminous coal resources (down to economic working levels) of continental Europe excluding the U.S.S.R., and some 90% of the resources of the two German states within their post-1945 boundaries. (An important coalfield, that of Silesia, was lost to Poland in 1945.) Almost the only other coalfield of any significance in post-1945 Germany is the Saar coalfield on the south-west corner of the Rhine plateau block; lost to France in 1945, it was restored to Germany in 1957, after a plebiscite of the inhabitants.

The Ruhr coalfield has helped to produce one of the greatest concentrations of industry and people in Europe. But the relative importance of bituminous coal in the German lands of Europe has never been quite as great as in Britain, because Germany also possesses considerable reserves of a type of coal almost unknown in Britain: brown coal, which was laid down in the tertiary era of geological time at shallow depths in the great lowland embayments of Cologne and Saxony. This coal is low-grade, it has little value for coking and hence for iron and steel production; but it can be compressed into briquettes for domestic purposes and it can also be used to produce electricity from power stations sited on or adjacent to the coalfields. Further, since it occurs in relatively undisturbed horizontal beds at relatively shallow depths, it can be mined open-cast very economically indeed. A particular economic advantage of the brown coal is that its main areas of occurrence are very near to existing concentrations of population with heavy demands for domestic fuel and for electricity. Much of the demand for these purposes is therefore met by the brown coal, leaving the Ruhr bituminous coal for coking, chemical production and gasification.

The German lands were not well endowed with the other great raw materials of nineteenth-century industrialisation, iron ore. Local deposits in the Rhenish uplands and the borders of the Bohemian block had provided the basis for small scale medieval iron industries, but after the growth of modern industry they could no longer meet demands. After the discovery in 1879 of the Gilchrist-Thomas process which permitted the use of phosphoric ores, the great reserves of Lorraine (which had passed to Germany from France in 1871) were rapidly brought into use. However, at the turn of the century, they were supplanted increasingly by ores from northern Sweden; after 1918, with the return of the Lorraine ores back to France, the dependence on Swedish ore became almost complete. The Nazi attempt to achieve a high degree of economic self-sufficiency during the 1930s, led to the attempt to exploit the low-grade ores of the Harz foreland zone of the North European Plain, around Salzgitter near Brunswick. Ironically, these attempts only bore fruit after 1945, and the north German deposits now supply a significant proportion of the Federal Republic's iron needs.

Germany's other great mineral resource is her deposits of chemical raw materials, in particular those of potash and associated salts, in the western part of the Saxon Bay around Halle, Magdeburg and Stassfurt. Latterly also increasing oil reserves have been discovered beneath the western part of the Northern Lowlands, in particular south of Emden, and there may well be rich resources in the section of the North Sea adjacent to the north west German coasts.

But no modern industrial nation, apart from giant powers like the United States or the U.S.S.R., can hope to produce most of its needs for industrial raw materials itself. It can be said therefore that one of Germany's most precious industrial resources is its magnificent system of natural waterways, which bring the low costs and high capacities of sea-borne transportation deep into the heart of the continent. Until the nineteenth century this advantage was only potential, because the rivers in their natural state offered all sorts of hazards to navigation. But once the waterways were deepened, straightened, and connected where necessary by canals built to accommodate substantial vessels, then bulky low-grade materials like iron ore, petroleum or chemical materials could be brought almost as cheaply to the Rhine or Saxony as to the ports of the North Sea coast. Further, the rivers and canals were the means of supplying the dense industrial populations of the Ruhr or Saxony with their needs in bulk foodstuffs, such as grain or meat, which had to be brought increasing distances either from the agricultural surplus area of the German east (much of which has been lost to Poland since 1945), or from the new lands of North and South America, Australasia or South Africa. Without this advantage it is difficult to see what challenge Germany could have offered to the industrial might of Britain, based as this was on the unique asset of her partly coastal coalfields.

The Process of Settlement

Against these variations in agricultural and industrial potential, we can begin to understand the pattern of settlement in the German lands. The basis of this pattern is still the rural settlement, which evolved slowly over many centuries, and which still explains the distribution of population in the very substantial areas where industry and urban life are weakly represented. The earliest people who inhabited the German countryside in prehistoric times, like those who settled England, were Celtic peoples who appear to have practised a shifting form of agriculture leaving few traces in the modern landscape. Germanic tribes therefore invaded Germany as (in the form of the Anglo-Saxons) they invaded England. The first records of them, about the first century A.D., show that they were then concentrated around the shores of the Baltic, in southern Sweden, Denmark and north Germany. At this time the Romans were occupying the western and south-western fringes of Germany, and as the Germans advanced southwards they met Romans coming northwards, defeating them decisively at the battle of the Teutoburg Forest (A.D. 98). From then on the Roman Empire was firmly bounded to the north-east by a line running from Cologne in the north to Regensburg in the south, while the Germanic peoples continued to pour southwards and westwards. The most important of these peoples, the Franks, split into two streams, one passing westwards through Flanders into the Paris Basin (and thence turning east again into the Rhine plateau), the other passing up the Rhine into Roman territory. After the disappearance of the Romans in the fifth century the Franks quickly overcame the other German groups and established their hegemony: they conquered the Alemanns in 496, the Thuringians in 531, the Bavarians about 550, the Frisians in the course of the sixth century, and finally the most important rival group, the Saxons, in 804.

At this point, for the first time, the western German lands were united into a single kingdom: that of Charlemagne. This kingdom extended westwards to include most of France, and southwards across the Alps into Italy. Its eastern boundary ran from the great elbow of the Danube at Regensburg, northwards to Erfurt in middle Germany, and thence northwards again along the Saale river to its confluence with the Elbe. The Elbe-Saale line remained the eastern boundary of the German peoples for three centuries, until after 1100, and so became one of the most important dividing lines in German geography. For during these three centuries German settlement thickened west of the line, taking forms characteristic of all the German settled lands of western Europe. As in the Paris Basin and southern England, the better lands were developed with the irregular nucleated village and big open common fields, while the poorer lands were adapted to a more extensive and pastorally based regime, with smaller villages or hamlets. To the east, however, Slav tribes practiced a different and simpler rural economy.

It was only after about 1150 that German tribes moved into the lands east of the Elbe; then, during two centuries, they moved swiftly across the Northern Lowlands as far as Silesia and East Prussia, producing a complex pattern of settlement in which German villages and towns alternated with Slav hamlets. As befitted a rapid movement of planned occupation, the landscape which resulted had a far more regular, geometrical character

Plate 25 A Rundling Village
The round Rundling village, with the houses facing inwards around a central place, is typical of the borderland between eastern and western Germany, where there was conflict between Germans and Slavs in early medieval times. This example is from the eastern Lüneburger Heide.

than the landscape of the older-settled western German lands. Later in history, during the seventeenth and eighteenth centuries, these eastern lands inherited a problem which the west was spared: much of the lands were occupied by a rich landlord (*Junker*) class, while the peasants were reduced to the status of landless labourers. In the west, on the other hand, a society of small peasant proprietors arose, as in France. After 1945, the problem was forcibly settled by the communist regime in the east, which expropriated the landowners and passed the land to the labourers, afterwards compelling them to regroup themselves on collective farms. Curiously but significantly, therefore, the historic Elbe-Saale line has reasserted its significance in the period since 1945; it is marked by the Iron Curtain which divides the two German states.

The pattern of urban settlement, which superimposes itself on this rural backcloth, also reflects long-active historical forces. In the Middle Ages, the revival of European trade about the time of the tenth century brought the development of several well-marked continental routeways, particularly those running north-south from the North Sea ports to the Alpine passes (and so to the Mediterranean ports); and those running east-west from the Slav lands to Flanders and the Paris Basin, along the line of easy movement marked by the loess belt at the southern edge of the Northern Lowlands. Where these routes met water, or where they crossed or were gathered together, major towns were bound to develop. Thus ports arose like Hamburg or Bremen on the North Sea, or Lübeck on the Baltic. Another line of towns developed where routes southwards from these ports intersected with the loess route, as at Magdeburg, Brunswick, Hanover and above all in Westphalia (Dortmund, Essen, Duisburg). Where the great loess route met the Rhine waterway, there grew Cologne, a Roman foundation and one of the great cities of medieval Europe. South of the Rhine Plateau, the concentration of routes in the Rhine-Main Plain established Frankfurt-on-Main as a trade and finance centre; while in south Germany, cities grew where important north-south routes to the Alpine passes intersected with water routes, as at Stuttgart on the Neckar, Würzburg on the Main and Nuremberg on the Pegnitz, a tributary of the Rednitz. Munich, the major city of southern Bavaria, grew where an important route from north-west to south-east, directed at the exit of the Inn Valley routeway into the foreland zone, met the north-flowing river Isar; the same route helped to develop Augsburg at the crossing of the Lech, and Ulm at the crossing of the Danube.

In the eastern lands, cities were less frequent. The biggest concentration was in the fertile Saxon basin, where the Elbe river provided an important breach through the uplands into the Bohemian Massif. Here Leipzig, Dresden and Halle developed. Farther north, the inhospitable moraine lands did not provide any obvious basis for urban growth. The routes which developed in this area ran from east to west and were gathered together in the low-lying belt where a number of old river valleys (Urstromtäler) ran together; here Berlin developed. The major cause of Berlin's rise to importance was, however, not her strategic position with

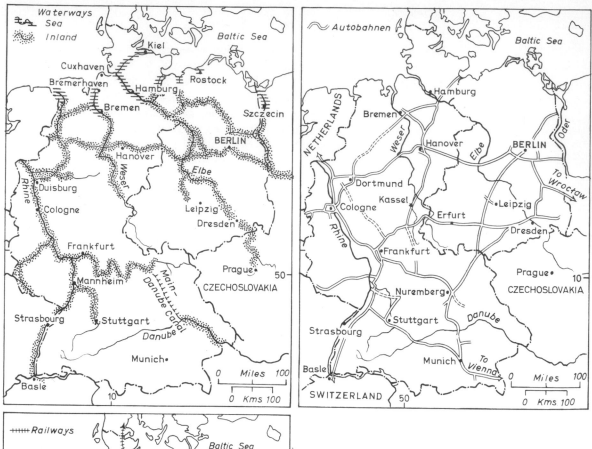

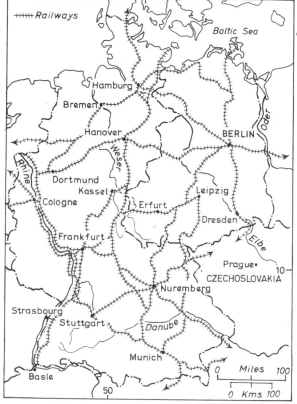

Fig 23 Major cities and routes

relation to trade routes or industrial resources, but the purely historical factor that the Prussian rulers chose it as their capital. Despite its eccentric position in relation to the centre of gravity of population in the Germanic lands, Berlin grew with Prussia's progressive ascendancy over Germany. It grew most rapidly of all as capital of a united Germany, between 1871 and 1945; since the Second World War, its position has been an anomalous and uncertain one.

For centuries between the end of the Middle Ages and the Industrial Revolution, the German cities stagnated; indeed, many of them were little bigger in 1850 than they had been in 1450. Then rapid growth took place. The Industrial Revolution came nearly a century later to Germany than to England; and this profoundly influenced its effect on German geography. In England, industry grew up on the coalfields, often far from the existing towns, which had mainly developed for trading purposes in the Middle Ages in the southern and midland counties. Consequently, towns rapidly grew up out of villages. But in Germany, when the Industrial Revolution arrived, the railways were already in existence, and soon afterwards electricity production became commercially feasible as a motive power for industry. The result was that industry was not attracted in the same degree to the coalfields. It went to the major centres of the new railways, which were also the best areas for the supply of labour; and these naturally enough were the old towns of the Middle Ages, whose importance as route centres now reasserted itself. As opposed to the English concentration of industry and people in a small axial belt between London and the major coalfields, Germany is characterised by a number of industrial agglomerations which have grown outwards from medieval cities, such as Hamburg, Bremen, Cologne, Frankfurt, Stuttgart, Nuremberg and Munich. Only the great Ruhr coalfield agglomeration, with its five million people, recalls the British pattern of industrialisation; and even there, many of the most important centres have medieval trading origins.

To a large degree, then, in the German lands the concentrations of urban population due to commercial or industrial development correspond to the concentrations of the farm population which arise from exceptionally fertile soils or favoured climates. Along the North Sea coast population densities are moderately high because of prosperous agriculture on the drained marshland and the presence of many small ports. There are two major urban concentrations on this coast: Bremen with over half a million people, and Hamburg with two million. Along the Baltic coast the distribution is more variable, with rather low densities towards the east. Behind the coastal belt the glacial lands of the Northern Lowlands are a negative zone. Areas like the Lüneburg Heath south of Hamburg or the Mecklenburg Lake Plateau north of Berlin form part of the largest zone of relatively sparse population (below 200 per square mile or 75 per square kilometre) in the whole of rural Germany. The great concentration in the Urstromtal zone around Berlin appears as an isolated island. A zone of dense urban and rural population marks the loess belt at the border of the central Hercynian Uplands, widening out into the giant concentrations of the Rhine-Ruhr region (ten million people) and the Saxon Bay (eight million).

The Upland belt itself is much more densely populated than might be expected, due to the local presence of specialised crops (wine along the Rhine and Moselle), and of small-scale home industries which have often turned over to a factory basis in modern times. In south Germany a belt of dense population follows the Rhine Rift Valley with an extension up the Neckar Valley into the Stuttgart concentration; more isolated patches of dense population are noticeable around Nuremberg and Munich. But the Keuper sandstones and the Jurassic limestones in the scarplands, and some of the sandstones and glacial materials of the Bavarian Foreland, are very sparsely populated. These tend to be zones with limited agricultural potential, which are also far from the main urban centres of population. Further, in the modern age they have tended progressively to lose population, particularly under the impact of the rationalisation of agriculture which has taken place in both German states since 1945. The major urban concentrations (save for Berlin) have on the other hand all tended to show rapid increases of population in the period since the Second World War. The German lands, like most of continental western Europe, are tending to show rapid urbanisation—a process that was almost complete in Britain by the end of the nineteenth century, when four in five of the population were already living in towns.

The German Federal Republic

In the postwar division of Germany, the Federal Republic of West Germany inherited over one-half of the former territory of the pre-1937 *Deutsches Reich*, or five-sevenths of the reduced territory of the two German states. And almost throughout the period since 1945, it has accounted for four-fifths of the combined population of the two Germanies: a reflection of her much better basis in agricultural and industrial resources than her communist neighbour, and of a large influx of refugee population. This population is however unequally distributed. Of the ten provinces or *Länder* into which the Federal Republic is divided (and which are responsible for many government functions run centrally in England), one province alone—North Rhine Westphalia (*Nordrhein Westfalen*) accounts for 30% of the total population of the Republic, living on only 14% of its area; while Bavaria, almost a state within a state with some 28% of the total area, has only 17% of the population. Such differences reflect variations in the economic potential. Already surveyed in outline in the previous section, these must now be analysed in more detail.

AGRICULTURE

With only 14% of its employed population in agriculture and forestry, Federal Germany is now almost as completely urbanised and industrialised as Britain. Furthermore, the traditional pattern of small-scale, unproductive and inefficient peasant agriculture has been much changed since

1955 by the operation of the government's 'Green Plan', which is designed to improve agricultural standards through consolidation of scattered holdings, to increase yields and improve quality, and to secure greater production with more economical use of labour. Nevertheless, as compared with Britain, the Federal Republic is more dependent on home food production; and in many areas the commercial farmer who is so typical of England is replaced by a peasant to whom farming is not so much a business as a traditional way of life. Holdings remain smaller than in Britain, labour is too plentifully and too wastefully used, and so is mechanical equipment when it exists at all. Cooperation, which has done so much to raise farming standards in other areas of Europe, is still a minority movement in much of the Federal Republic.

Most farming, as in Britain, is mixed farming. Of the total area of the country, 14% is withdrawn from agriculture or forestry, mainly for urban uses of various kinds. Nearly one-third is in forest, a higher proportion than in any other west European country; this reflects the poor quality of much of the morainic country of the Northern Lowlands, the higher Hercynian Plateaux and the sandstones of the Southern Scarplands. Of the remaining land—nearly 60% of the total—some 34% is in arable, and some 23% in all forms of meadow and pasture. The traditional emphasis then is on arable; and stock farming tends to be a by-product of the basic preoccupation with the cultivation of crops, being introduced perhaps to help maintain fertility, perhaps to make use of crop surpluses. Furthermore, there are few areas or even individual farms which do not grow some crops (even if only fodder crops), or keep some stock (even if only for the needs of the farm or the farmer's family).

There are, however, great variations in the proportions of arable and grassland from region to region, reflecting the potentialities of soil and climate. The proportion of arable rises highest of all on the fertile sheltered loess lands like the Cologne Bay, the Westphalian Börde between Soest and Paderborn, the Wetterau north-east of Frankfurt-on-Main, the Rhine-Main Plain and parts of the Upper Rhine Rift Valley, or the Kraichgau between Heidelberg, Karlsruhe and Stuttgart. In these areas the proportion of specialised crops tends to be high. Root crops are usually an important part of the basic arable rotation, with nearly as big an acreage as cereals (and in exceptional cases even bigger); wherever climatic conditions are appropriate they are joined by fruit, tobacco, hops, wine or intensively-cultivated vegetables. The cereal base to the farm economy tends to be wheat or barley. In such areas a third of the total farmland may be in roots, up to one-half in cereals. Virtually the whole of the land is given up to the farmer, and there is no residual forest land—almost always, in Germany, the critical sign of the high value of the soil.

In sharpest apparent contrast to this pattern are areas like the hedged landscapes of the Emsland coastal marshes of north-west Germany, or the great open green fields of the Allgäu area on the Bavarian Foreland, where the emphasis is all on dairy farming. Here as much as 70%, in special cases even more, of the total farm area is in grass and fodder crops.

The arable element of the farm economy here plays a subordinate and shifting role; a field area will be put down for two or three years to cereals, then left to 'recuperate' in grass for up to twenty years. These areas, disparate as they may seem at first sight, are united in having a high precipitation which makes them completely unsuitable for intensive arable cultivation. Because food production through animals takes much more space than through crops, these are areas of sparse rural population. It should not, however, be thought that they are negative or poor; quite the reverse, as the general lack of forest or waste and the prosperous condition of the big farmhouses will show.

The real contrast with either of these specialised farming areas is provided by the areas of marginal farming on the higher, bleaker plateau surfaces of the Hercynian plateau lands. Here, as in the Emsland or the Allgäu, 70% or more of the farm area will be in grass or fodder crops, and the rotations will be based on the 'rotation of fields' rather than the rotation of crops, with a short arable break generally for oats (the only crop which will bear the climatic conditions) followed by years in grass. The difference lies in the very large areas outside the farmlands, which still lie in forest or perhaps (in the highest and bleakest areas) in open wasteland. In consequence of the low proportion of total farmland and the very small part played by arable, the power of the land to support people is very weak; the population in these areas is invariably sparse and almost inevitably enjoys a rather low standard of living, which it does its best to supplement by forestry or by cottage industry. Such are the conditions in areas like the remoter parts of the Eifel or the Westerwald in the Rhine Plateau, the Vogelsberg or Rhön, or some of the Keuper sandstone areas of the Southern Scarplands.

In a category apart are the very limited zones of very specialised cultivation, sometimes amounting to monoculture, which arise from local peculiarities of position. The more obvious are those with special advantages of climate or aspect, which make them uniquely suitable for the cultivation of a particular crop; such are the vineyards of the Rhine, Moselle and Neckar or the hopfields of the Spalt area south of Nuremberg. The German vineyards are restricted almost completely to the near neighbourhood of the river valleys in the westernmost strip of the Federal Republic; but here they are locally very important, extending for instance in the Rhine Valley almost from Basle down to a few miles above Bonn. The wines best known in Britain come from a much more restricted section of the Middle Rhine, either from the favoured east-facing slopes on the left bank of the river between Worms and Bingen, or from the south-facing slope of the Rheingau on the right bank between Wiesbaden and Rüdesheim, at the entrance to the Rhine gorge. In these zones the vineyards extend almost continuously. But in the gorge sections of the Rhine and Moselle it is easy to see how the distribution of the vine is controlled almost completely by the accidents of slope and aspect. So poor and thin is the soil on these steep slopes that where the vine fails, all cultivation ceases.

Less obviously noticeable are the specialised market-gardening zones near the greatest zones of urban population concentration, as in the Elbe valley below Hamburg, the northern suburbs of Frankfurt-on-Main, and the so-called 'Garlic Land' (Knoblauchland) north-east of Nuremberg. These are often of considerable antiquity, and arose when the transportation of fresh vegetables to market was slower and more costly than it is today. They have kept their competitive position through the inherent fertility of their soil, which has been laboriously built up by fertiliser through centuries of cultivation, and through the skill and local marketing knowledge of their diligent peasant cultivators. Characteristically, even in these most intensive of all the farming areas of the Federal Republic, the proprietors usually insist on growing their own needs in cereals and roots, reserving their specialised cash cropping to an intensively cultivated section of their holdings.

MINING AND INDUSTRY

The industrial economy of the Federal Republic takes two distinctively different forms. On the one side is the pattern of heavy, capital-intensive, basic industry, using large amounts of bulky, rather low-value raw materials and often depending on coal as a fuel supply or raw material, producing goods which are then sold to a number of other industries where the later manufacturing processes are carried out. On the other is the whole diverse pattern of lighter finishing and assembly industry, using varied raw materials which may be either raw, semi-processed or fully manufactured but which are usually quite valuable in relation to their bulk, and working them up into highly processed goods which are often readily transportable. British people commonly associate the first pattern of industry with older coalfield industrial areas like Central Scotland or the North East, and the second with newer factories in the Midlands and Southern England, though this distinction is in part breaking down. In Federal Germany too the distinction is between coalfield or water-based industry, and south German industry.

Within the heavy industrial sector two basic industrial complexes can be traced, in which the distinctive feature is linkage of different productive processes. The first of these combines coal mining, the production of iron and steel, and the manufacture of heavy engineering products. The dominant locational factor is necessarily coal, for even though the amount of coal needed to smelt a ton of steel has progressively fallen, further coal may well be needed in the manufacture of the heavy engineering goods from the various steel products. In any case, all over the world such heavy industry tends to show considerable locational inertia after its original positioning on the coalfields during the early initial period of industrialisation. It is true that in certain cases, as in the United States or England, industry has moved away from the coalfields to the break of bulk point between land and water transport (the Great Lakes, where ore from Lake Superior or Labrador meets coal from the Appalachian fields; or Middlesbrough, where imported ore meets coal from Durham). But Federal Germany is extremely fortunate in that its major supply of coking coal, in the Ruhr field, was situated immediately next to the Rhine, a waterway which during the nineteenth century was made fully navigable for large motor barges. The Ruhr further consolidated its position by the completion of the Dortmund-Ems Canal (1899) which allowed it to reach the North Sea without passing through foreign territory, and then by the Rhine-Herne Canal (1914) which connected the Rhine with the Dortmund-Ems system. It has therefore kept its dominance over the years, with about two-fifths of the total steel production of continental western Europe and about four-fifths that of the total post-war Federal Republic. Much of the final engineering products indeed have a use within the area itself, for instance coal mining machinery, iron and steel furnaces, rolling mills, engines, turbines and stationary boilers.

Two possible rivals to the Ruhr exist, but neither accounts for more than a small minority of total Federal German steel or engineering production. One is the ironfield location, represented by the Salzgitter area near Hanover, which does not account for more than about one-tenth of total Federal steel production. The economies of production here rest on the low-grade character of the Salzgitter ore; it is economic to send out only part of the ore to the Ruhr, bringing Ruhr coal back on the return journey. The other location, reflecting modern developments, is the Klöckner tidewater plant at Bremen, which imports both ore and coal by sea at highly economic rates. But even then the cost advantage *vis à vis* the Ruhr is not decisive, and the plant might not flourish without an important local market in the shipbuilding and car industries.

The other basic complex, and a more sophisticated one, consists of the primary chemical industries. Here again there is a chain of industries and of operations, each process providing the material for the next stage, and thus linking together a whole range of stages of production and indeed of separate industrial plants at the same location. Here, however, both the basic products and the raw materials are much more varied. The basic chemical products include saltpetre, sulphuric acid, soda, nitrate and phosphate fertiliser, synthetic oil and petrol, synthetic rubber, cellulose, plastics, dyes and light metals; they go to make soap and detergents, pharmaceuticals, synthetic fibres and photographic materials. The raw materials, which tend to be locationally critical, are both home produced and imported. There is Ruhr coal, not merely as fuel and power, but also as a raw material (in the ammonia process for making nitrate fertiliser and coal-tar products); brown coal from the Cologne Bay (especially important in synthetic dyestuffs manufacture) and potash salts from the Werra and Fulda valleys; imported oil, increasingly important for a range of petro-chemical products; imported pyrites for sulphuric acid production brought from Spain, Norway and Cyprus; phosphate rock from North Africa; and many others.

Because of the complexity and also the great bulk of many of these materials, chemical production invariably seeks one or two possible locations. First, it may go to coal or to brown coal production; here the close juxtaposition of the bituminous coal of the Ruhr field, and the brown coal of the Ville ridge west of Cologne, has proved decisive for many plants like those of Leverkusen, north of Cologne, and Wesseling, south of Cologne. But secondly, it is notable that both these plants have direct access to navigable water for sea-borne ships to bring in imported raw materials; whilst another complex of chemical plants occurs round the confluence of the Rhine and its major tributary the Main, far from coal but with excellent water communications. The leading centres of chemical production in this area are Hoechst, west of Frankfurt, and Mannheim on the Rhine-Neckar confluence some forty miles above the entry of the Main.

Both the heavy basic industrial complexes therefore tend to seek water; in addition they may seek coal, either bituminous or brown. It is no surprise therefore that the Rhine-Ruhr confluence zone, extending eastwards across the Ruhr coalfield forty miles to Dortmund, and southwards up the Rhine forty miles nearly to Bonn, has become indisputably the major centre of heavy industry in the Federal Republic; or that the Rhine-Main triangle, formed by Frankfurt, Wiesbaden and Mannheim, has become the second. But in both cases, it is notable that here were dense concentrations of old-established towns, representing the juxtaposition of easy routeways in medieval times. Even here, therefore, industry tended to colonise long-established cities and towns.

The other type of industry—that which works up lighter materials into a range of highly-manufactured products—has altogether different locational requirements. Some of these industries may produce products which are difficult or relatively uneconomic to transport: bread, for instance, or beer. These goods tend to be produced locally, near to their immediate markets, though early stages of food production (flour milling, edible oil crushing, margarine production, coffee, tea, tobacco) tend to be tied to sources of imported materials at the ports, or to local agricultural supplies (sugar beet on the loess lands). Every village may have its baker; any town of any pretensions its brewer. Within any place, a substantial proportion of the industrial workforce may be engaged in such local factory industries. But since they are only there because the town is there, they do not require any complex theory of industrial location to account for them.

It is the remaining industries, then, that are of interest. They can be said in principle to be 'footloose' because they are not tied to any particular location, or to any one type of location, by transportation requirements. In fact all sorts of locational factors seem to come into play. For many of the engineering trades, catering for the rather specialised demands of a particular local market, it is important to be able to maintain close personal contact with the buyer and user. Thus agricultural machinery is made near service centres for rich agricultural districts, like Mannheim on the upper Rhine plain, Hildesheim and Essen in the northern loess lands; textile machinery making goes to textile centres like Aachen, Krefeld and Wuppertal; whilst ships clearly have to be built in seaports, principally Hamburg, Bremen and Kiel. In some cases, purely local skills persisted for centuries while the industry evolved from a handicraft

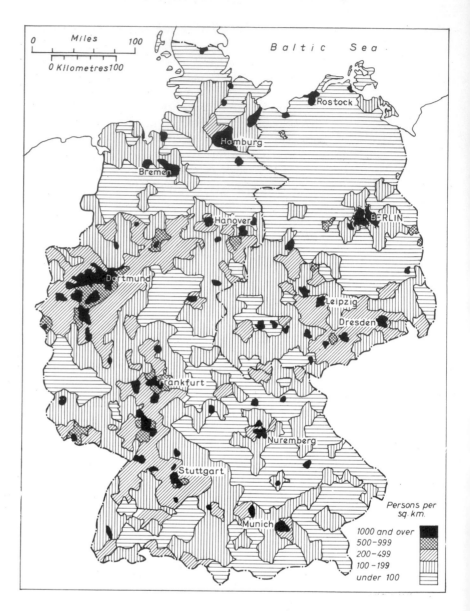

Fig 24   Population densities in the two Germanies

trade into a modern factory industry, as in the manufacture of cutlery at Solingen, or of locks and keys at Velbert in the bleak Bergisches Land south of the Ruhr, or the manufacture of optical equipment in the small towns of Württemberg in south Germany, where refugees from the east have settled since 1945. In some cases the location of a pioneer of the industry could be decisive, as in the motor car industry with the Daimler and Mercedes organisations in the Stuttgart district. Other locations of the car industry were due to deliberate planned choice, as with the great Volkswagen works at Wolfsburg east of Brunswick, chosen because of its excellent transport links (in the east-west belt of movement along the loess belt, with railway, canal and motorway) and its central position within prewar Germany; ironically, it is now only five miles from the Iron Curtain, so that all products have to go westwards. Yet other types of engineering industry seem to have arisen out of older industrial traditions within the climate of innovation characteristic of a metropolitan city: this is particularly true of the electrical engineering industry, where the giant complexes of Siemens and AEG still flourish in West Berlin. Outside Berlin too, the electrical industry tends to locate in the bigger regional capitals like Cologne, Frankfurt, Nuremberg and Stuttgart. Therefore in Federal Germany, as in Britain, the engineering industries flourish in a great variety of locations, some near coal—the Ruhr is a major centre, even for the lighter types of industry—some far from it. Perhaps the extreme case of a successful specialised engineering centre depending on locally traditional skills, but without any obvious locational *raison d'être*, is the small town of Schweinfurt on the Main valley in rural south Germany: it is the leading German centre for the production of ball bearings.

The textile industry of the Federal Republic, like some branches of the engineering industry, provides a case of an industry which was originally located next to local raw materials but which continued to flourish on the basis of traditional skills even when the raw materials had to be imported from great distances. Both in Württemberg and in the Wupper valley south of the Ruhr, textile production started on the basis of local wool. Now both wool and particularly cotton are brought in from outside the country, but these are substances which will easily bear transportation costs. A big pool of skilled labour—and particularly in the case of Württemberg, surplus female labour from an overpopulated countryside—is a critical factor at work. Two main areas of production can be distinguished: the Württemberg region, round Stuttgart, Reutlingen and Göppingen, and the Rhine-Ruhr region, round Duisburg, Cologne and Mönchengladbach. It is notable that the industry in Germany shows no clear sign of specialisation by area into cotton and woollen sections, as between Lancashire and Yorkshire in Britain. The manufacture of synthetic textiles is exceptionally well developed, and has tended to settle in existing textile centres, particularly the left bank of the lower Rhine round Krefeld and Mönchengladbach, in Wuppertal, and in the upper Rhine region. But it has gone also into leading chemical centres such as Mannheim. The clothing industry of Germany was traditionally located in Berlin, but since 1945 has been centred in a number of places in the Federal Republic, with special reference to the presence of female labour supplies: they include Frankfurt-on-Main, Aschaffenburg on the borders of the Spessart south-east of Frankfurt, Nuremberg and Stuttgart, as well as the traditional textile towns of Wuppertal and Mönchengladbach in the Rhine-Ruhr industrial region.

The general rule in this type of manufacture, then, is that the lighter and more valuable the product, the freer is the industry to seek special advantages like a skilled local labour market. This is true, for instance, of the optical glass industry, which is located in a number of towns both large and small in south Germany, including Oberkochen near Heidesheim (the home of the Zeiss works, part of which split away from its parent in the east in the post-war years), Göttingen, Wetzlar, Stuttgart and Er-langen. The manufacture of the finest porcelain, too, is concentrated in a number of former princely capitals like Munich (Nymphenburg); and in some cases the works are still partly State factories.

COMMUNICATIONS
AND TRADE

The pattern of inland transportation in the Federal Republic is excep-tionally dependent on navigable waterways. Measured in ton-miles, nearly one-third of goods traffic goes by inland waterway, compared with a negligible amount in Britain. For this there are two reasons. First, Germany was blessed with a number of exceptionally long rivers which are naturally or potentially navigable, including the Rhine, Ems, Weser, lower Elbe and Danube. These rivers were comprehensively improved during the late nineteenth century through widening, straightening and deepening. Secondly, the canal era came much later to Germany than to England, so that canals were built to carry motorised barges. The most important of these canals, like the Dortmund-Ems Canal, the Mittelland Canal and the Main-Danube Canal (under construction), link up the navigable rivers so as to form continuous waterways from one major industrial district to another, or between these districts and the sea. The waterways are particularly important in carrying the low-value, bulky raw materials of heavy industry like coal, oil, iron ore, stone, cement, and timber; and as already seen, they have had an important influence on the location of this type of industry. Overwhelmingly the most important navigable waterway in the Federal Republic is the Rhine, which has the two largest inland ports in Germany: Duisburg in the Ruhr, one of the greatest inland river ports of the world, and Mannheim which serves the intense concentration of heavy industry at the southern end of the Rhine-Main Plain.

Apart from the waterways, the pattern of transport in the Federal Republic is very like that in Britain: the numbers of private cars and road goods vehicles are rising, the roads and the railways compete to carry the industrial goods traffic, and in this contest the roads have been winning. However, the geographical pattern of both roads and railways in Germany is rather different from that in Britain. Although before the war Berlin was the most important railway junction, and an important road centre, it did not have the same significance as London to England or Paris to France; and since 1945, with the loss in Berlin's significance, the pattern in the Federal Republic has focused not on one centre but on a number of important urban agglomerations like Hamburg, Hanover, Rhine-Ruhr, Rhine-Main, Stuttgart and Munich. The basis of this pattern goes far back into history, for these were the major towns of the Middle Ages, where trade routes converged. In many cases, indeed, the modern road pattern of Germany proves to follow the lines of the old medieval roads, which were simply improved and rebuilt during the nineteenth century; and it was natural that when railways began to be built during the 1830s, they too should focus on the existing centres. Lastly, the motorway (*Autobahn*) network, which was started during the 1930s and is still being expanded, took a very similar form.

Since the dropping of the Iron Curtain on the eastern border of the Federal Republic, links to the east have been cut to a formal minimum: eight railway crossings, five roads, two navigable waterways and three air corridors. In consequence, the road and rail network of the Federal Republic has come to assume a pronounced north-south emphasis, with one important line connecting Hamburg, Hanover, Frankfurt and Basle, another linking the Ruhr, Cologne, Frankfurt, Stuttgart and Munich, with a branch from Frankfurt to Nuremberg. The crossing-point of these two lines is in the middle of the Rhine-Main plain, which can be regarded as the nodal point of the Federal Republic if one exists. Here at Frankfurt-on-Main is the greatest railway station of the Republic, and here also is its busiest international airport, next to the great junction at the crossing of the major motorways.

SEAWAYS AND TRADE

If the Federal Republic has a priceless asset in its network of natural and artificial inland waterways, it has a severe disadvantage as an industrial nation in its poor relation with the sea. The Republic, except in the extreme north, is a landlocked state; even its major river, the Rhine, enters the North Sea through the Netherlands. The sea-borne trade of the country therefore depends almost wholly on the 350-mile-long North Sea coast, with its treacherous mudflats and unpredictable weather. Fortunately, two major river estuaries and one less important one allow sea-going trade to penetrate far inland into the North German lowlands. It is logical then that no less than 60% of that part of the sea-going trade of the Federal Republic which goes through German ports should pass through Hamburg, 70 miles up from the mouth of the Elbe, with another 30% going through Bremen, a similar distance up the Weser, and its outport Bremerhaven. But despite the connections of these ports with the inland waterways of the Federal Republic, they are too eccentric to the main centres of industry to take more than a limited share of the total seaborne trade. In an important respect Rotterdam, with its unequalled position at the Rhine mouth, is Federal Germany's leading seaport. With the development of trading links within the European Economic Community, this is likely to become even truer in the years to come. It can be said, indeed, that since 1945 the Federal Republic has turned its economic face sharply westwards, with the result that Rotterdam has expanded its trade dramatically, becoming first port of the world in tonnage handled, while Hamburg, cut off from its obvious hinterland in Middle Germany by the Iron Curtain, has shown much more modest growth.

This change reflects itself in trade figures. To a greater extent than the

prewar united *Deutsches Reich*, the Federal Republic is a highly industrialised state which must depend on outside sources for many of its needs
in foodstuffs and industrial raw materials. Over four-fifths of the Federal
Republic's exports are manufactured products; but interestingly, over 50%
of her imports fall into this category too, marking the recent tendency for
the development of mutual west European trade in an increasing variety
of finished goods. About half of her import trade and about two-thirds
of her export trade is with western European trading partners. And close
on two-fifths of both import and export trade is with the Federal Republic's
five partners of the European Economic Community. In contrast, inter-
zonal trade with the communist eastern section of Germany is of negligible
importance. This alone would provide justification, at least for the
foreseeable future, for treating the Federal Republic as a separate economic
unit with a totally different pattern of economic life from the old united
Reich.

The Natural Regions of the Federal Republic

THE NORTH GERMAN LOWLANDS

The North German Lowlands form only part of one of the great physical
regions of Europe: the North European Plain, which extends from the
Paris Basin through Flanders and the Netherlands, North Germany
and Poland, to European Russia and to the Urals. This whole region has a
broad physical unity, in that its present-day form arises almost wholly
from events of relatively recent geological time: the Quaternary glaciation,
between 1,300,000 and 10,000 years ago, which deposited anything up to
600 feet of material on top of the original Mesozoic and Tertiary cover;
and post-glacial changes. So it may seem arbitrary to treat separately the
part that happens to fall within the Federal Republic.

Examined more closely, this is not so. This western section of the
coastlands was affected profoundly by certain events rather than others.
First, in contrast to the east German lowlands, it was influenced hardly
at all by the last of Vistula glaciation. (The one exception, within the
Federal Republic, is the small part that happens to lie east of the Elbe:
the eastern section of Schleswig-Holstein.) Instead, the physical landscape
is almost wholly the work of the earlier ice advances and, in particular,
of the last of these, the Riss glaciation. In Schleswig-Holstein, as in the
eastern lowlands, the landscape of the last glaciation has had little time to
be affected by subsequent denudation: it remains much as the ice left it,
with hummocky hills, sharp relief differences, and immature drainage
patterns with many small lakes trapped in internal basins.

Yet the central characteristic of the western lowlands is that there has
been time for later, sub-aerial erosion to modify the work of the ice; the
more spectacular features of the original landscape have been almost
stripped away, giving a much more horizontal, monotonous landscape.
Only in a few areas, as in parts of the Lüneburger Heide south of Hamburg,
do the terminal moraines of the Saale glaciation rise as high as 500 feet
(150 m.) and give some impression of the titanic work which the Scandina-

vian ice sheets originally performed. Elsewhere, the western lowlands are distinguished by extensive areas of quite flat ground-moraine remnants, known as *Geest* (from an old German word meaning 'waste') and of low-lying fen peat or bog known as *Moor*, many of which occupy the former water escape channels of glacial times, the Urstromtäler. In modern terminology, Geest is more commonly reserved for cultivated moraine land; for waste, the word *Heide* (heath) is used. At the southern edge of the glaciated lowlands, however, the fertile strip of loess—in German, the *Börde* lands—is common to both east and west.

The second major event which affected the western lowlands, but which affected the east not at all, is more recent and more localised in its effects. The western lowlands are bordered by the tidal and often storm-racked North Sea: the eastern lowlands by the weakly-tidal and more quiescent Baltic. Along sections of both coasts, there has been a tendency to subsidence since the end of glacial times; this has been a usual consequence

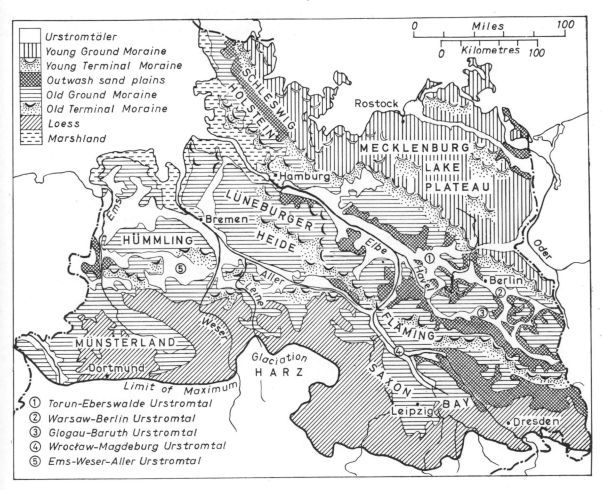

Fig 25   The North German Plain

of the melting of the ice all over northern Europe, but on the North Sea coastlands—not only in Germany but also in the neighbouring Netherlands and on the East Anglian coast of England—the effects have been particularly profound. In the 10,000 years since the final glaciation, the North Sea coastlands have experienced three major periods of sinking and only two periods of much weaker elevation; today, they lie some 70 feet lower than when the ice retreated. Particularly in the wet and stormy period at the end of the Middle Ages, they suffered grievously from storm floods; indeed, major features of today's coastline arise from incursions of the sea in those times, including the inlet of the Dollart at the mouth of the Ems in the thirteenth century, and the Bay of Jade farther east in 1511. In more recent centuries, these losses of land have been reversed by diking and reclamation. Over the past thousand years the net loss of land has been about 2,000 square miles in the German North Sea lands; reclamation has recovered only about one-half this amount.

These events establish the basic natural divisions of the western lowlands. First there are the coastlands, the lands of the *sea marshes* and *river marshes*. Then there are the glacial lands, the areas of Geest and Heath and Moor, together with the loess Börde lands. Finally, there are the great cities of the region; because these exist predominantly in response to outside forces, they need to be discussed separately.

The Marshlands. Basically the marshlands are a phenomenon of the coast; but along the major river estuaries like the Weser and Elbe, they may extend as much as 80–100 miles (128–160 km.) upstream (Fig. 25). And they are a joint product of river and sea: the marsh material consists of fine fertile particles washed down by the rivers from areas like the loess belt, but it is then enriched by the sea, which impounds it through tidal action and adds fertile organic material. Thus, in their constant battle against the storm floods, the people of the marshlands have a powerful incentive to reclamation.

This work has gone on constantly for centuries, so that the landscape today is almost wholly a man-made one. Even in the oldest-settled areas, dating from more than a thousand years ago before modern diking techniques were developed, there is an artificial element: settlements are concentrated on to circular mounds above general flood level (in Dutch *Terpen*, in German generally called *Wurten*), which had a natural basis but which were built up painstakingly by man over centuries. In these areas settlement is sometimes crowded in big circular villages, very distinctive on the modern map; in others, where the mounds were more freely available, they are scattered in the form of individual farms. Seawards, successive dikes tell the story of reclamation since the thirteenth century; here, the dwellings of the marsh dwellers themselves may be strung out along the dikes, in villages (*Marschhufendorf* type villages) as much as a mile long.

Finally, at the very coastal border, the work of reclamation still consistently goes on. Between the line of offshore dunes which forms the

Frisian Islands (North Frisian Islands, north of the Elbe along the Schleswig-Holstein coast; East Frisian Islands, west of the Elbe along the Lower Saxon coast) and the present day coastline, there extends a huge area of sand- and mud-flats, the so called *Watten*, which are exposed for many hours at low tide. The Watten can be reclaimed by cutting drainage ditches and finally by diking against the sea—a process which takes forty years before settlement can take place. West of the Elbe, as in Holland, such a reclaimed area is called a *polder*: north of the Elbe, in Schleswig-Holstein, a *Koog*.

The landscape of the marsh is distinctive and unmistakable. The surface of the ground is absolutely flat, broken only by the drainage ditches and dikes. This prevailing evenness is interrupted strikingly by the windmills, now being replaced by electric pumps, and by the great farmhouses, which combine all the functions of the farm economy—living, storage of crops, space for stock—under the same roof. Everywhere the strongly oceanic climate gives rich grass, so that despite its potential fertility for crop

Plate 26   A Wurten Settlement.
The North Sea coast of Germany has many examples of these ancient settlements on mounds, originally natural, but with artificial additions. Some carry villages, some (like this one from Schleswig-Holstein) isolated farms. The large farmhouse is typical of the northern coastal marshlands.

production the marsh is predominantly devoted to cattle-and-horse-rearing. The small market towns are marked by their big central market places where stock are brought for auction. Most importantly, the marshlands provide a valuable source of dairy products for the dense industrial populations to the south—especially in the Rhine-Ruhr belt.

Geest, Heath and Moor. In the great belt of glacial landscapes which stretches over 90 miles (144 km.) from the marshland edge in the north to the loess border in the south, three major physical elements need to be distinguished. Two of these are found on the low morainic platforms: they are the heath (Heide) lands, with the accompanying afforestation of recent decades, and the cultivated Geest lands. On the lower-lying lands, particularly in the great Urstromtal belt at the southern edge of the morainic platforms and at the marshland edge on the north, are the Moor areas.

The moraine platforms are defined by the major rivers of the western lowlands. One, the smaller, lies between the Ems on the west and the Weser on the east, and between the peat bogs of Oldenburg on the north side and the bogs of the Urstromtal zone on the south. Here, the more fertile, flatter ground moraine was early settled and cultivated by prehistoric man, to give classic Geest landscapes: the small loosely grouped hamlets, with their big fields cultivated permanently for rye by the aid of careful manuring, represent one of the oldest forms of settlement to be found in the Germanic lands, the so-called *Drubbel*. Only in very limited areas of poor uncompacted sand—the Hümmling on the north western corner, overlooking the peat bogs close to the Ems River, and the terminal moraine loops of the Riss glaciation on the southern edge, against the Urstromtal zone—does true heathland (Heide) appear.

Even in the other, much larger moraine tract—the Lüneburger Heide which covers an area of 3,000 square miles between the Weser on the west, the Elbe on the north and east and the Aller Urstromtal on the south—a true heathland, with its characteristic heather vegetation, is a small and declining element. It has been supplanted within the last century by extensive afforestation—covering nearly 300 square miles since the mid-1920s—and by the extension of Geest cultivation based on the extensive use of artificial fertiliser. Forests alone cover one-third of the Lüneburger Heide, and the heathlands tend to be restricted to the hillier terminal moraine areas where agriculture would be impossible on ground of relief. Only in such areas—notably in the protected Nature Park round the high point of the Wilseder Berg (570 feet, 169 m.) in the middle of the Heath—is it possible to recapture the romantic atmosphere which moved poets and writers a century ago.

The history of the Moor zones is similarly one of reclamation, which began with the introduction of Dutch colonists into the bogs of Oldenburg in the early seventeenth century. They brought a pattern of settlement which soon proved its worth and which became dominant in the Moor lands: the Fen colony, based on a system of canals which served the twin

Plate 27 Lüneburger Heide.
The sheep feeding on the heath represent the traditional face of the Lüneburger Heide. Now, much of the area is either reclaimed for agriculture or afforested. But some areas are being deliberately retained in their natural state.

purposes of draining the bog and shipping out the dried peat for sale as fuel. Many hundreds of square miles of formerly uninhabitable bog land have been reclaimed in this way. Yet much still remains to be conquered, notably in the Devil's Bog (*Teufelsmoor*) north-east of Bremen, in the Wietingsmoor south of the Ems-Weser Geest, in the Oldenburg bogs which border the heathlands of the Hümmling on their north-west edge, and above all in the great Bourtanger Moor along the lower Ems Valley.

The Loess Börde lands. In sharpest contrast to all the moraine and bog tracts of the lowlands is the narrow strip of loess along their southern edge, at the border of the Hercynian Uplands. Here, particularly between Dortmund and Paderborn in Westphalia, and again on the northern side of the projection of the Hercynian uplands into the plain (the so-called Weserfestung), from Hanover through Brunswick to the eastern frontier of the Federal Republic, are some of the most fertile and intensively farmed lands in western Germany. In these lands, there is no question of un-reclaimed heath or bog, or of afforestation; for centuries, these lands have been completely cleared to give rich crops of cereals and (increasingly in recent decades) root crops such as sugar beet. The characteristic form of settlement is the very big nucleated village of up to 2–3,000 people, which in the most fertile tracts may be only a mile from its next neighbour.

Since the 1930s the traditional face of the Börde has been substantially altered by industrialisation particularly in the easternmost section next to the zonal frontier, around Brunswick, Salzgitter and Wolfsburg. This development stems partly from the exploitation and processing of the low grade iron ore deposits of the Salzgitter area, partly from the extremely good east-west communications along the loess belt, which include rail and *Autobahn* (Ruhr-Berlin, open for traffic to West Berlin)

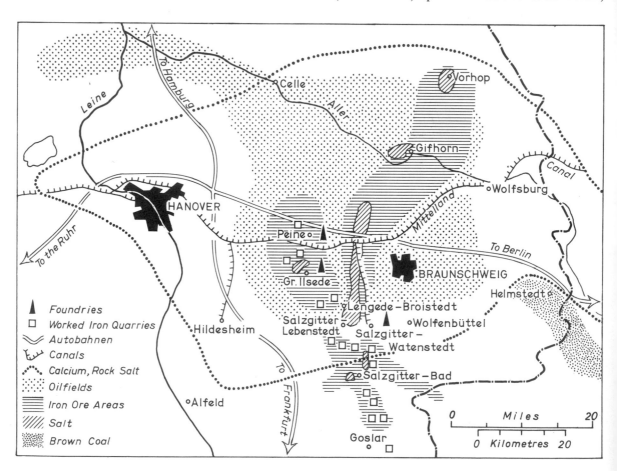

Fig 26   The Hanover-Salzgitter industrial area

Plate 28 Crossing of the Mittelland Canal over the River Weser at Minden.
Like the east-west Berlin-Ruhr Autobahn, the Mittelland Canal follows the border of northern plain and central upland. Just west of this point it is diverted by the projection north-westwards of the central upland known as the Weser-festung. The Weser has, however, cut through the barrier from the south to reach the northern plain at this point.

and the Mittelland Canal (open for goods traffic to West Berlin). Communications were of prime importance in the decision to locate the giant Volkswagen works at Wolfsburg, near Brunswick, in 1937; despite its wholesale destruction in the war and its position next to the frontier, it is the greatest car factory in Europe.

The Towns of the Lowlands. There is a sharp and obvious distinction within the lowlands between the hundreds of small market towns, which perform merely local service and supply functions for the often thinly-scattered farm populations round about, and the major towns which owe their *raison d'être* to the existence of inter-regional and even international trade routes. Among these latter, a few of the smaller examples are found in the heart of the lowlands, at local concentrations of routes: Lüneberg and Celle on either side of the Lüneburger Heide, for instance. But the really large cities are of two types: first, those which arose at the junction of Northern Lowland and Central Upland, most of them along the Börde tract; secondly the great ports on the coastal estuaries.

The two major cities of the lowland-upland border owe their existence to the crossing of the great east-west routeway with the north-south routes from the northern ports. The larger, Hanover (German, Hannover) has a peculiarly strategic position in that it stands just north-east of a major gateway, the *Porta Westfalica*, by which the loess route itself finds a route through the highland barrier of the projecting Weserfestung. It also stands at the north west corner of a funnel of routes which are concentrated gradually, along the line of the Weser and Leine rivers, into one of the great north-south passages through the Central Uplands. Brunswick (German, Braunschweig) stands at the north-east corner of this funnel, where southbound routes deviate westwards due to the barrier of the Harz Mountains, a particularly high and impenetrable section of the Central Uplands. Both cities have become major seats of industry: Brunswick as the centre of the Salzgitter-Wolfsburg industrial belt, with engineering, vehicle building, optical works and food processing; Hanover at a critical junction point between north-south (Hamburg-Frankfurt) and east-west (Berlin-Ruhr) motorways, with engineering, agricultural machinery, chemicals, paper, textiles, rubber and records.

The northern port cities also have clear resemblances to each other. Hamburg, founded in its present form in the twelfth century, owed its great development during the nineteenth century to the Atlantic traffic. Since 1945 it has suffered in competition with Rotterdam from two handicaps: the loss of much of its natural hinterland through the Iron Curtain only 30 miles (50 km.) to the south-east, and the fact that the Elbe channel cannot take the largest ocean-going ships. Both these handicaps are being overcome with difficulty, one by a new north-south canal link to the Mittelland Canal and so to other west German waterways, the other by deepening the Elbe channel and by a new outport near Cuxhaven. Despite the limitations the trade of Hamburg is greater, in absolute tonnage terms, than in pre-1939 days; now as then, this trade is predominantly in imported raw materials. The existence of the port has also given rise to the greatest concentration of industry in the Federal Republic, in which special importance naturally attaches to the shipbuilding and associated engineering industries, and to the processing of imported raw materials (oil, rubber, margarine, tobacco).

Lying 50 miles up the Weser from its mouth Bremen, like Hamburg, was a great Hanseatic port in the Middle Ages, but also owes its importance as the Federal Republic's second port to the development of the New World. Before 1939 she stood at a disadvantage in comparison with Hamburg, because she did not command a major waterway into the heart of the continent; now, with the Iron Curtain on the one hand and the improvement of the Weser's connections with the West German waterway network on the other, the positions are almost reversed. Bremen's industries occupy many miles of the Weser downstream from the city, marking their dependence on water-borne trade: like Hamburg's they are dominated by shipbuilding and by the processing of imported raw materials such as cotton, grain, oil seeds, coffee, chocolate and tobacco.

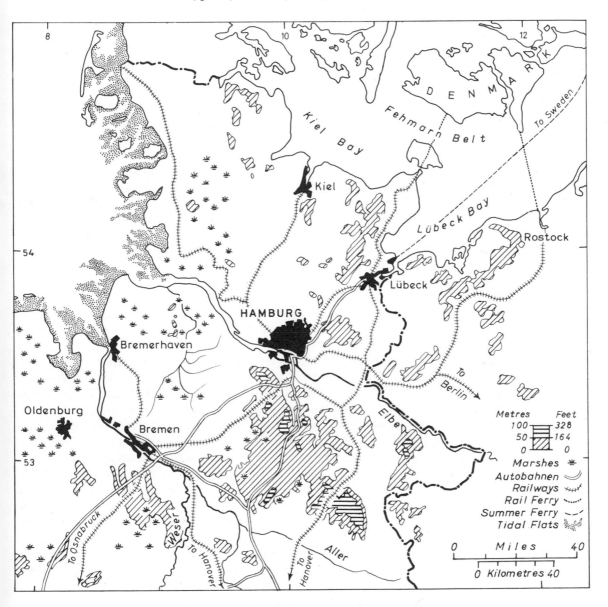

Fig 27   Hamburg and Bremen

RHINE-RUHR   The Rhine-Ruhr region, a small area of only some 2,500 square miles (6,500 sq. km.) based on the exit of the Rhine into the North European Lowlands and on the neighbouring Ruhr coalfield, is the greatest single concentration of population on the European continent, containing well over 10 million people. To a much greater degree than any other area of the Federal Republic, it offers the picture of a landscape largely created by man during the last hundred years. Yet urban development in this region goes back to the Romans; and to understand fully this unique region, it is necessary to consider the facts of economic, social and political history against the control exerted by the physical makeup.

This makeup has given the region four attributes of the greatest importance. First, though much of the eastern part of the region consists of the bleak Hercynian uplands of the Bergisches Land, which form a northerly extension of the great Rhine plateau block, large tracts in the west and north are part of the fertile loess-covered Börde zone at the junction of Central Uplands and Northern Plain. This early gave the region a dense agricultural population, whose demands for urban services would alone produce notable town development. Secondly, the line of easy movement along the loess belt from the west (Flanders and the Paris Basin) here meets the great Rhine route from the south (Rhine-Main Plain and south Germany) as well as the alternative route across the lower plateau lands to the east of the river; the west-east route is then diverted together with the south-north one for forty miles northwards by the projection of the Bergisches Land until it again finds the loess, east of Duisburg. This fact alone explains the two old-established main concentrations of town life in the region: that around Cologne, founded already in Roman times, and that marked by the line of medieval cities along the *Hellweg* (light way): Duisburg, Essen, Bochum, Dortmund. Already by the Middle Ages, therefore, the fertility of the land and the crossing of the routes had produced a concentration of major cities.

Thirdly, there is the high grade coal—especially the so-called *Fettkohle* (fat coal), the first-class Ruhr coking coal. Mined for centuries in galleries and shallow shafts along the Ruhr Valley, this coal was only fully exploitable with the advent of modern deep mining techniques (ventilation, pumping) after 1840; and this caused a northward extension of the worked coalfields to progressively greater depths, under the loess and eventually under the glacial deposits of the Münsterland to the north of the loess. Today, the deepest pit near Münster itself reaches a depth of 4,000 feet (1,220 m.).

Lastly, there is the great brown coal deposit which occurs in thick horizontal masses in the Ville ridge, stretching north-westwards from Bonn to north west of Cologne. This ridge, which approximately bisects the great Cologne embayment, represents the greatest brown coal deposit in the Federal Republic; it is intensively worked by big open-casts pits for domestic briquettes, and especially for electric power generation in the great power stations on the ridge itself.

Today, the location of the coking coal is still decisive in producing

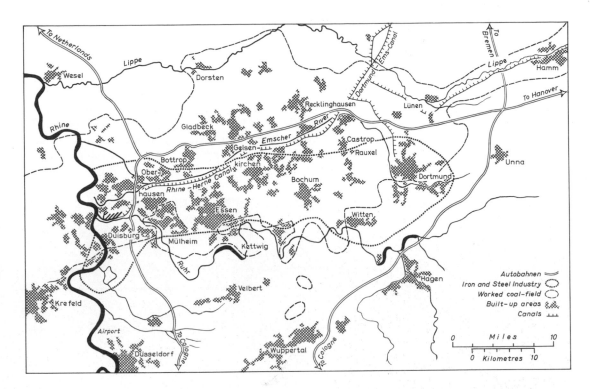

Fig 28 The Rhine-Ruhr region

a distinction between the major cities of the southern or Rhineland part of the region, which have a many-sided development based on a wide variety of regional or national service functions as well as a strong and well-diversified manufacturing base, and the Ruhr cities which depend more exclusively on manufacturing and mining. Even within the Ruhr, an important distinction is to be drawn between the better-balanced cities of the Hellweg zone in the south, and the coal-mining towns of the north.

In the southern or Rhine section, three cities dominate the scene. Bonn is sited at a strategic position where the Rhine finally emerges from the constriction of its gorge into the Cologne Bay. It was a Roman foundation, which afterwards became capital of a small principality and achieved some fame as Beethoven's birthplace; after the formation of the Federal Republic in 1949, it secured a new lease of life as Federal capital. Bonn however demonstrates the important point that a capital city for a nation of 50 million people, based on a political system which gives major powers to provincial government, does not necessarily achieve the scale of a city like London or Paris. It has remained a medium-sized town of about the same order as Bournemouth or Wolverhampton or Bolton, which to some extent justifies the German epithet of 'Federal village capital'.

Essentially, Bonn has continued to be overshadowed by its more successful rival since Roman times, Cologne, twenty miles downstream. Founded in A.D. 50 at the junction of the Rhine left bank route and the loess route from Flanders, and with an important route also from Trier to the south-west, Cologne flourished in the Middle Ages on the basis of the convergence of the great trade streams which flowed from the Netherlands and Flanders up the Rhine into south Germany and Italy, thus acquiring a position she never lost. Like other major German cities she stagnated between 1500 and 1850, but then expanded rapidly as a trading and industrial centre with the coming of the railways. Now, fully

Plate 29   Central Cologne.

This picture, looking north-west across the Rhine, centres upon the cathedral at the north-east corner of the original Roman settlement. The central business district of today occupies much of the semicircular area of the medieval town; a green belt (seen in middle background) runs just outside the line of the medieval wall. Industry tends to be outside this belt (background of picture) or in the right bank suburbs (right).

recovered from wartime destruction, Cologne is a major commercial, shopping and office centre, performing many functions that in other countries would be undertaken by a capital city; it has an important inland port, and a varied industrial development which ranges from heavy oil refining and petrochemical production on the Rhine front just outside the city limits, through varied engineering products, to an extensive range of light consumer goods stemming from medieval handwork traditions, including leather, chocolate and clothing.

Between Cologne and the third great centre, Düsseldorf, is a tremendous concentration of heavy chemical production, centred on the great Bayer plant at Leverkusen on the right bank of the river. Also on the right bank, Düsseldorf was not a major medieval city; it owes its importance to a small principality, which achieved some prominence in the seventeenth century and made its capital here. From this stems the elegance of its baroque quarters, notably the broad Königsallee, one of the most notable shopping streets in all Germany. Since the Second World War Düsseldorf has been capital of North Rhine Westphalia (*Nordrhein Westfalen*), richest and most populous of the ten provinces or Länder of the Federal Republic; and this administrative function has attracted many headquarters offices here. To perhaps an even greater degree than Cologne, therefore, Düsseldorf performs the functions of a metropolitan city. It also has a varied industrial base with a special emphasis on engineering of all kinds.

The Ruhr region itself is difficult to define, but there is an obvious and important distinction between inner and outer Ruhr. The inner Ruhr is easier to identify: it is the almost continuous concentration of industries, cities and towns, stretching from Duisburg in the west to Dortmund in the east (40 miles, 25 km.) and from the east-west *Autobahn* in the north to the Ruhr Valley in the south (on average, 15 miles). But then there is a much wider and vaguer fringe on the north, west (i.e. west of the Rhine) and south, where industries or cities form mere islands against a fundamentally rural backcloth.

The central Ruhr, numbering $3\frac{1}{2}$ million people, is the classic land of coal and steel: it produces some 90% of the Federal Republic's bituminous coal output (50% of the Common Market's) and 80% of its steel (30% of the Common Market's). It is indeed the greatest single producer of both on the European continent, outside the U.S.S.R. In general, the steel comes from the south, from the Hellweg towns; and the coal comes from the north, where the deeper and more economic pits are increasingly found. But the Hellweg cities are more than steel producers. In the first place, steel production itself is concentrated: blast furnaces and converters tend to locate next to sources of water-imported iron ore, so the industry is highly concentrated at either end of the coalfield, at Duisburg and at Dortmund. Duisburg alone, with its unique port facilities for the importation of raw materials in bulk, makes over one-fifth of the Federal Republic's pig iron and raw steel. The towns away from water—Mülheim, Essen and Bochum—are engaged principally in working up the products of this first stage of manufacture into engineering goods. And in the second place, the ancient medieval trading traditions of the Hellweg cities have provided a basis for the modern development of important central service functions for the whole Ruhr region, and even—in the case of the headquarters of coal and steel undertakings—for the whole Federal Republic.

Consequently, the Hellweg cities have a reasonably well-balanced economic structure, in which heavy metals are balanced by the rapidly-growing service industries. In contrast, the towns of the northern Ruhr—Bottrop, Castrop-Rauxel, Gelsenkirchen, Wanne-Eickel—are in fact little more than conglomerations of workers' housing estates, which happened to grow together during the late-nineteenth or early-twentieth centuries round a convenient nucleus such as a village green or a railway station. Corresponding to this lack of any normal urban form is a profoundly unbalanced urban economic base; for most of these towns depend to a dangerous degree on coal mining, which since 1958 has shown a serious decline in employment in the face of competition from oil and of economies in power stations and steel converters. The best hope for these towns lies in the further development of manufacturing industry, especially in the faster-growing categories such as chemicals manufacture, which finds excellent sites on the flat lands along the canalised Emscher and the Rhine-Herne Canal.

Outside the inner Ruhr the degree of urban development drops sharply. To the north, indeed, the newer coal mines tend to be accompanied by nothing more than an isolated miners' estate, set often in the midst of forest or heath; the small towns along the Lippe Valley, which marks the formal northern boundary of the extended Ruhr, have shown only modest growth in recent years. To the west, on the left bank of the Rhine, two notable urban concentrations of the west German textile industries are found: Krefeld, traditional German home of silk and velvet production, and Mönchengladbach-Rheydt, the so called Manchester of the lower Rhine, with its concentration of wool and cotton mills, clothing factories and textile machinery works.

The most interesting of the Ruhr fringes is that to the south, on the bleak plateaus and in the deeply incised valleys of the Bergisches Land. Here is still found evidence of the medieval origins of the Ruhr industry, origins based on the smelting and working-up of local iron ore deposits with the aid of charcoal from local forests. The natural resources have long since become uneconomic to work, and have been superseded by supplies of semi-manufactured material from the coalfield to the north; but the skill accumulated over centuries has permitted the development of highly-specialised industrial concentrations such as the cutlery manufacture of Solingen and Remscheid, on the middle Wupper, and the lock and key manufacture of Velbert, on the plateau south of the still idyllic Ruhr valley. The biggest urban concentration of the southern fringe, however, has little to do with metals; it is the old-established textile-producing complex of Wuppertal, formed out of the amalgamation of two separate towns which strung themselves out along the Wupper Valley in the old water-power days.

The existence of this vast concentration of population naturally gives rise to unique problems of urban organisation, not least those of local government, planning and water supply. Within the central Ruhr the urban areas are grouped into a limited number of major administrative cities, each separated by a remaining green area from the next. But for planning purposes even these major cities have found it necessary to surrender many of their rights to an overall regional planning organisation, the *Siedlungsverband Ruhrkohlenbezirk* or Ruhr Planning Authority, which since 1920 has tried to create a better urban structure for the region, re-shape the pattern of roads and other communications, preserve open space, and provide for the progressive planned development of the still-open areas of the north, west and south. For water supply purposes too the authorities have been forced to band together in order to meet their heavy domestic and industrial demands by the construction of distant reservoirs in the Rhine Plateau to the south.

RHINE PLATEAU   A distorted quadrilateral stretching roughly 160 miles (256 km.) from Trier in the south-west to Kassel in the north-east, 100 miles (160 km.) at its greatest extent from the river Ruhr in the north-west to Wiesbaden in the south-east, and continued westwards into the Ardennes of Belgium, Luxembourg and France, the Rhine Plateau is indisputably the greatest of the Hercynian relic massifs in all the German lands. The fundamental characteristic of this massif, as of all the Hercynian lands, is that it is negative for human settlement. Yet this is not an absolutely negative quality; the environment offers difficulties of varying degree, sometimes severe, sometimes (in extremely restricted lowland basins) hardly notice-able. It is this subtle transition within the area that makes it such an ideal region for geographical analysis.

The overall negative character stems from geology, reinforced by relief and climate. Most of the area is composed of sediments of Devonian age—schists, greywackes, slates, shales—intensely folded in Hercynian times, worn down to peneplane level, and uplifted in stages during the Alpine disturbances. The resulting landscape, as in Hercynian England, consists essentially of a series of upland plateaus at various levels, the highest at over 2,000 feet (600 m.), the lowest (consisting of terraces above the gorges of the Rhine and Moselle) as low as 700 feet (210 m.). The average altitude is thus high, and this coupled with the westerly position produces a raw climate, with high precipitation (much of it in the form of snow) and a short growing season, giving a damp cool summer climate. In turn the high precipitation, plus the character of the parent rocks, produce heavily-leached, infertile soils; the sole exceptions occur in isolated areas where base-rich soils outcrop, as in the limestone belt of the western Eifel or the basic volcanic rocks of the Westerwald. Deep dissection by the main rivers—Rhine, Moselle, Sieg, Lahn, Ahr—makes for difficulties in transport. Indeed the rivers divide the plateau up into four distinct units, with an extension of the fourth really making a fifth:

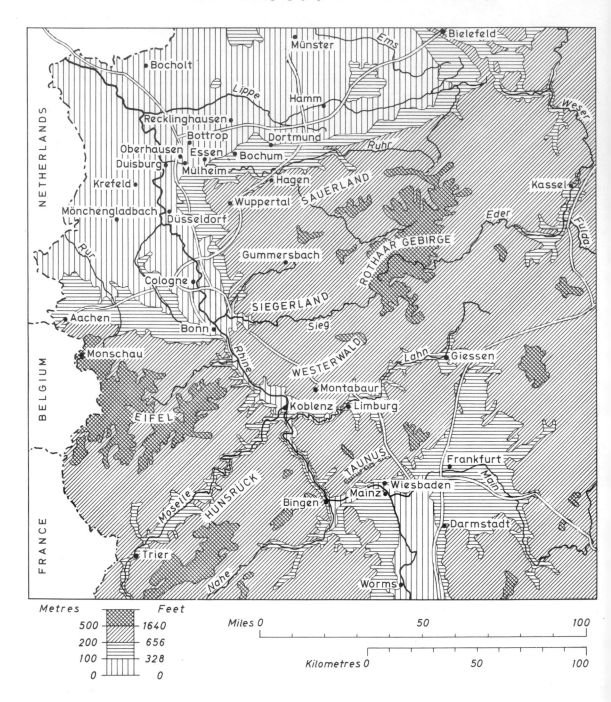

Fig 29 The Rhine Plateau

the Eifel, west of the Rhine and north of the Moselle; the Hunsrück, west of the Rhine and south of the Moselle; the Taunus, east of the Rhine and south of the Lahn; the Westerwald, east of the Rhine and north of the Lahn; and the Bergisches Land-Sauerland, an extension of the Westerwald northwards.

The force of these limitations, however, depends to a great degree on details of geology, slope and aspect. Most negative of all are the highland quartzite ridges which rise above even the highest plateau surfaces. Invariably above 2,000 feet (600 m.) in height, they rise to 2,900 feet (880 m.) in the main Taunus ridge (Grosse Feldberg), to 2,400 feet in the Rothaar Gebirge in the eastern Westerwald or the Hunsrück, to about 2,200 feet (675 m.) in the Schnee Eifel or Hohes Venn in the western part

Plate 30   The Eifel.
The part of the Rhenish Upland known as the Eifel is distinguished for its volcanic explosion craters, now lakes (Maare), of which a typical example, the Schalkenmehrener Maar, is seen here. Areas like this are cultivated to considerable altitudes—2,000 feet in places—but villages tend to be small.

of the Eifel. For the most part they remain under the original coniferous forest, though because of the bleakness of the climate even this may fail at the highest altitudes, to be replaced by a moorland type of vegetation. A similar effect is produced at a slightly lower level by the remnants of volcanic eruptions in Tertiary and Quaternary times, which dominate the landscape of the southern Eifel between Daun and Mayen in the form of conical wooded hills rising sharply above the general plateau surface.

The higher plateaux, at between 1,500 and 2,000 feet (450 and 600 m.), are usually distinguished without difficulty from the quartzite ridges or the volcanic remnants. They tend to be quite highly dissected and to have poor siliceous soils; large amounts of the natural beechwoods remain, and only the more favoured areas, in terms of soil or aspect, have been found worthwhile to cultivate. Here the characteristic settlement pattern will usually be the small village of at most a few hundred people, surrounded by open fields in which crops occupy only a small part of the total rotation, the land being put down afterwards to many years in grass. In the highest and remotest areas, indeed even the village and open field may be replaced by the completely isolated farm and by the block-shaped, enclosed field characteristic of isolated colonisation of the waste. However, even at these very high levels the right soil can produce a very different picture: at more than 2,000 feet the limestone belt of the western Eifel, round Blankenberg, has been completely cleared for cultivation since Neolithic times, and today has big villages more characteristic of the loess lands than an upland plateau.

Yet the main agricultural potentialities are on the lower plateau levels, the highest of which is the extensive Trog surface found in the Eifel and elsewhere at 1,300–1,500 feet (400–450 m.). Here the picture is very mixed, with extensive surviving woodlands in one place, large open fields and moderately big nucleated villages in the next; slight differences in soil and aspect are critical. In general the characteristic form of cultivation on the land nearer the village is the open-field system. Formerly this occurred with a fallow but now roots or cultivated grass have been introduced on to the land nearest the village. Farther away from the village, the extensive system based on short cultivation and long grass ley takes over. The settlement pattern is characteristically nucleated, as it is everywhere on the plateau save in the highest, remotest areas of all; the widespread isolated farm, so typical of north Germany, here finds little place.

Lastly, perhaps the most uniform lands of the plateau are the very limited tracts of more favoured land, such as the lowland basin around Trier, the much larger Middle Rhine basin at the confluence of Rhine and Moselle around Koblenz, and the middle Lahn basin around Limburg, together with the Rhine and Moselle terraces immediately above the Rhine and Moselle gorges. Here, on soils which are often akin to the fertile loess, and with a milder climate, the land tends to be completely cleared and intensively cultivated. The landscape characteristically

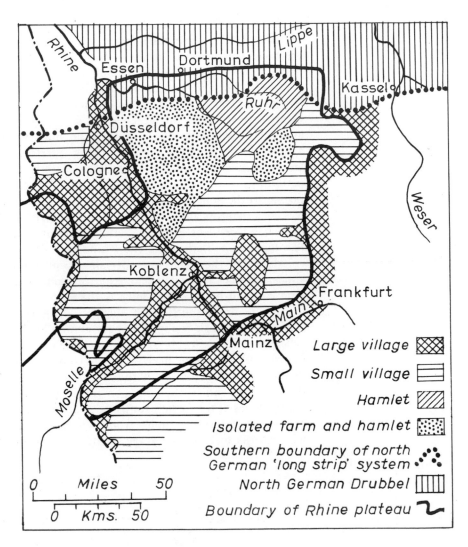

Fig 30 Rhine Plateau Settlement Patterns

consists of large open fields, which grow cereals and roots in rotation, perhaps with some specialised crops; there are no surviving woodland patches to be seen, and settlement is concentrated in very large nucleated villages with up to several thousand people.

Such differences have not been produced overnight; they have emerged slowly, in the course of over 2,000 years of settlement and cultivation by Germanic peoples. Evidence shows that the areas first settled were the lowland basins, which offered the most attractive settlement possibilities to early man and which were besides the most accessible from outside. As more people poured in, more intensive forms of agriculture were developed here, and the result finally was the system observable today:

intensive cultivation of roots and cereals in big fields around large nucleated villages. At the same time more and more people, particularly in the great clearance period between A.D. 500 and 1300, moved out of the more accessible regions to try to colonise the poorer, remoter areas. Naturally they did so less thoroughly, and as their agriculture became less intense and more dependent on stock keeping, so their form of settlement regressed from the larger to the smaller village or the small hamlet, and their farm from the familiar type built round a farmyard to the simpler single unit type with the living quarters built above the stables. In the Rhine Plateau today, therefore, subtle differences in settlement patterns give the clue to a long-continued historical adjustment of the people to the soil.

The agriculture and settlement of the main river valleys is a phenomenon almost independent of the patterns of life on the plateau a few hundred feet higher up. Both along the Rhine and along the Moselle, but particularly along the latter, the specialised cultivation of the vine is based almost completely on details of exposure to the sun, and even the poorest slate soil will be prized so long as the aspect is right. Basically, because the Rhine flows south-north through its gorge, the opportunities for finding good south-facing slopes are almost limited to the short tributary valleys which fall steeply to the level of the main river, and the production of wine in the gorge itself is small compared with that farther south in the rift valley zone. But the sharpest contrast is found just beyond the southern end of the gorge, in the Rheingau. Here, the great south-facing slopes of the main Taunus ridge are given over almost continuously to the vine for twenty miles from Wiesbaden to Rüdesheim, where the Rhine turns to enter the gorge itself. The almost unique exposure gives

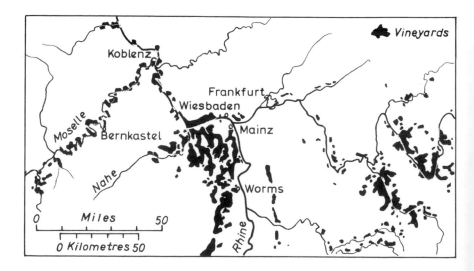

Fig 31   The Rhine and Moselle vineyards

Plate 31   The Rhine Gorge at St. Goarshausen.
This picture shows the sharp contrast in cultivation patterns between the gorge sides (vines on sunny slopes, otherwise scrub) and the arable fields of the plateau surfaces above, with their big nucleated villages. Road and rail follow both banks, and there is heavy river traffic as well. St. Goarshausen is a typical vintner's town.

fine, full wines which are among the finest products of the German vine-yards, and most of the villages have become internationally famous: Rüdesheim, Eltville, Oestrich and above all the great monastery above the village of Johannisberg. As befits its more northerly position, the middle Moselle produces wines famed for their great delicacy and lightness. In both areas, the intense nature of the cultivation produces a unique settle-ment form: the vintner's town, crowded together in the bottom of the valley, and composed of large and often ornate vintners' houses where the cellar is a prominent feature.

The frequency of these valley towns underlines the fact that on the plateau itself, urban development is thin and retarded. A number of small, widely-spaced market towns provides for the everyday needs of the

H*

scattered weekday population; they seldom reach populations of more than about 10,000. In a few cases, these towns also became historic seats of industry, as with the woollen manufacture in towns of the western Eifel such as Monschau and Münstereifel, or the notable pottery industry which based itself on local Tertiary clay in the southern Westerwald around the town of Montabaur, or the small iron-working towns of the Sauerland or Bergisches Land. But it is notable that major towns are restricted to the limited areas of fertile land, where they must originally have arisen to serve the needs of a local population but where they also flourished because of the concentration of major trading routes into the valleys. Such are the Roman foundations of Trier in the Moselle Valley, or Koblenz at the critical route focus formed by the confluence of the Rhine and Moselle, or the medieval town of Limburg in the Middle Lahn Basin. Even such towns, though they may serve very wide tributary populations for their more specialised occasional needs, do not rise above the status of medium-sized market towns with about 100,000 people. The major urban agglomerations are on the periphery of the region, but are more accessible from large parts of it than the interior towns themselves: they are Cologne in the Cologne Bay to the north, and Frankfurt-Mainz-Wiesbaden in the Rhine-Main Plain to the south.

RHINE-MAIN PLAIN

The Rhine-Main plain begins structurally to the Rhine Rift Valley, which in turn belongs to the complex of Hercynian relics and Mesozoic sediments known as the south German scarplands. The urban settlement in this region arises because of its position as a border area, a 'waiting-room' between north and south, east and west. The position of the great Hercynian barrier to the north, and of the river routes through the scarpland zone to the south, makes this inevitably the greatest junction of routeways in all the Germanic lands, now as in the Middle Ages. From the north-west, from Cologne, the Ruhr, Netherlands and Flanders, comes the Rhine gorge route followed by the railways, and also the plateau route first developed in the Middle Ages and now used by the modern *Autobahn*. From the north-east, from the northern plain through the corridor lands of Hesse and the fertile Wetterau, comes another route today followed by the Hamburg-Hanover-Frankfurt *Autobahn*. From the south-west comes the great upper Rhine Valley route, from Basle and so from the middle Alpine passes, as well as from Lyons via the Belfort Gap; and the route from the Paris Basin, via the Saar and the Kaiserslauten Corridor, which joins the Rhine route fifty miles above Mainz, at Mannheim. From the south comes the main route from Munich via Stuttgart, which today (in the form of the *Autobahn*) joins the Rhine Valley route at Karlsruhe. From the south-east comes the Main Valley route from Würzburg, which brings the traffic from Nuremberg and from the eastern Danube valley; today it is served by the railway which follows the valley, and by the modern *Autobahn* which cuts boldly across the Hercynian relic of the Spessart. All these routes meet in the heart of the Rhine-Main plain, at Frankfurt-on-Main. South of Frankfurt, in the heart of

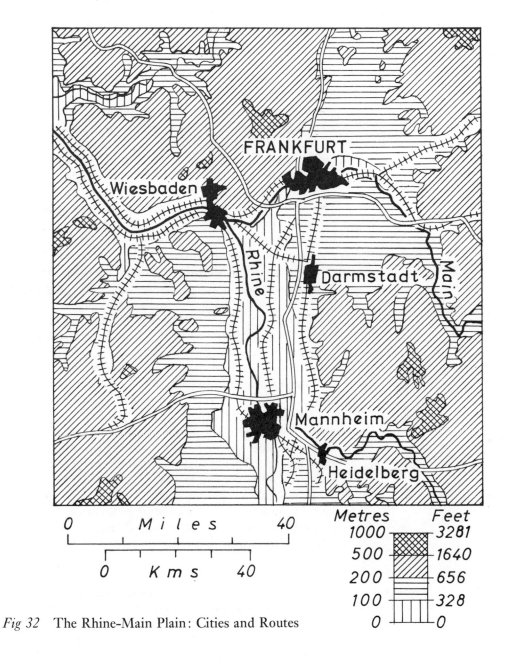

Fig 32 The Rhine-Main Plain: Cities and Routes

the coniferous forests that cover the infertile terrace gravels in the plain south of the river Main, the major motorways of Germany meet in the Frankfurter Kreuz (Frankfurt Cross). Immediately adjacent is the Rhine-Main International Airport, the busiest airport in all the German lands. The railway station in the heart of Frankfurt is the biggest in the Federal Republic, and the second (after Leipzig) in all of prewar Germany.

These advantages were equally evident in the Middle Ages. Frankfurt, the Franks' ford, was founded by them at the crossing point of the Main, some miles above the Roman town of Mainz at the Rhine confluence itself, at about the time they conquered the Alemannic tribes (A.D. 531). The town had a royal palace in the time of Charlemagne (*ca*. A.D. 800) and soon gained ascendancy over Mainz due to its more central position with regard to the routeways that enter the plain. With the opening-up of the great European trade routes from the tenth century, Frankfurt rapidly became middleman of Europe, acting as banker between the north and the south; its exchange became the main intermediary between Italy and the Netherlands. Like most German cities it stagnated between 1500 and the coming of the industrial revolution; then, its focal position in the German railway network guaranteed it a powerful accretion of modern factory industry especially engineering, electrical goods, chemicals and consumer goods. Today the town has grown far outside its medieval core in the form of suburbs extending into the fertile loess-covered farmlands which extend across the northern part of the plain to the wall of the High Taunus. Even the small spa towns (Königstein, Oberursel, Bad Homburg) at the foot of the Taunus itself, which developed originally because of the properties of the local mineral springs, are tending more and more to become outer suburbs of Frankfurt.

Frankfurt's continued growth has overshadowed its close neighbours in the northern part of the plain, Mainz at the confluence, and the spa town of Wiesbaden where the Taunus wall approaches the Rhine to mark the beginning of the Rheingau. But forty miles to the south, at the entry of the Neckar into the Rhine, another strong concentration of industry and urban life has developed in the twin Rhine towns of Mannheim-Ludwigshafen. Particularly important here is the heavy chemical industry, based on imported water-borne materials, and their working-up into products such as pharmaceuticals. Together with the great chemical concentration at Hoechst west of Frankfurt-on-Main, this makes the second greatest concentration of chemical industries (after the Rhine-Ruhr zone) in the Federal Republic.

THE SOUTH GERMAN SCARPLANDS

Bordered to the west by the Black Forest and Odenwald, to the north by the minor Hercynian uplands north of the river Main (Rhön, Vogelsberg), to the east by the Bohemian massif, and to the south by the Danube, the South German Scarplands occupy two ancient Germanic provinces: Schwaben in the south-west, now part of the Federal Land of Baden-Württemberg, and Franken in the north and east, forming the northern part of the great Land of Bavaria. Structurally, these lands are closely comparable with the scarp and vale landscapes of southern England; in the words of W. M. Davis they are 'younger rocks dipping off an oldland'. In both cases, the origin of the whole system is to be found in the ancient Hercynian relic blocks on the northern and western borders of the complex. Thus in Britain, the whole series of Mesozoic and Tertiary rocks dips down eastwards and south eastwards off the Dartmoor and Exmoor relics in the south-west, the Welsh Plateau in the west and the Pennines in the north. Similarly in Germany, the system dips off the Black Forest (Schwarzwald) in the south-west, the Odenwald and Spessart in the north-west, and the Rhön and Vogelsberg in the north. Like their English equivalents, these do not form a continuous highland barrier to north and west; lowland gaps between them perform an important function as routeways. In this respect the Kraichgau, between the northern end of the Black Forest and the southern tip of the Odenwald, can be compared closely with the Midland Gate between the Welsh Plateau and the southern end of the Pennines.

Thus far the comparison is a useful one. But at least three important differences need to be noted as between the English Scarplands and their German equivalents. In the first place, all such systems were by definition laid down in Mesozoic and Tertiary times in basins bordered on all sides by the Hercynian fold mountains, whose long-continued denudation supplied the sediment for the rock-building process. In England it can too easily be forgotten that there were Hercynian relics to east and south also. This is because the English scarplands are only part of a much larger

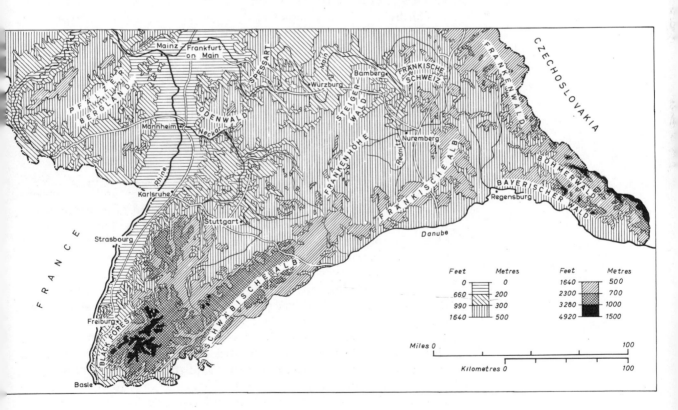

Fig. 33 The South German Scarplands

system embracing the Scarplands of the Paris basin on the other side of the Channel. The missing borders of the English system are the Ardennes and the Vosges on the east, and the Massif Central on the south. In Germany the eastern border is much more obvious: it is provided by the Bohemian Massif and more precisely by the folded relics at the western edge of that block, the Bavarian Forest (Bayrischer Wald) and Bohemian Forest (Böhmer Wald) on the south-east, the Upper Palatinate Forest (Oberpfälzer Wald) on the east and the Fichtelgebirge on the north-east.

In the second place, the pattern of deposition and of subsequent erosion has produced a rather different balance of deposits in Germany. Southern England has a representative selection of sediments ranging from the Permian Magnesian Limestone of Yorkshire and Nottinghamshire, or the Bunter Sandstone of Sherwood Forest, which were formed just at the end of the Hercynian mountain building period, right through to the Pliocene crag of the East Anglian coast, formed just before the Quaternary ice age. In the German scarplands the upper deposits in the series are much less well-developed: for all practical purposes, the range is only from the Permian and Bunter on the eastern slopes of the Black Forest and Odenwald, to the Jurassic of the Swabian and Franconian Alb, or the lower Cretaceous of the Naab valley immediately to the east of the Jurassic zone.

Thirdly, the whole complex of deposits starts from a higher base level, with much greater differences in relative relief than in the English Scarplands. There, the range is from sea level along the North Sea or Channel coasts, to 964 feet (294 m.) in Leith Hill or 1,070 feet (330 m.) in the Cotswolds behind Cheltenham in Gloucestershire. In Germany, the range is from about 280 feet (85 m.) at the northern end of the Rhine Rift Valley near the Main confluence, to over 3,100 feet (950 m.) in the Schwäbische Alb south-west of Tübingen.

At the same time these relief differences have by no means the same effects on climate, soils or vegetational response as in England. The scarplands lie firmly in the transitional zone of middle Europe which has moderately cool winters, moderately hot summers and a semi-continental rainfall regime. Whereas in England the limit of cultivation may be anything between 400 feet (120 m.) and 1,400 feet (430 m.), depending on aspect, and the upper tree line may be well below these limits, in south Germany cultivation extends well above 2,700 feet (820 m.) on the limestone surfaces of the Alb, and even where cultivation is excluded completely—on the acidic soils on the high Black Forest plateaux, for instance— there is still a luxuriant cover of coniferous forest at well above 3,000 feet (910 m.). As elsewhere in Germany, there is an almost complete absence of the bare moorlands which distinguish the negative areas of upland Britain; instead, it is the balance of forest cover against cultivated land which gives the measure of the value of the land. And almost everywhere in the scarplands, the key to this balance lies not so much in differences of altitude but in differences in rock type and thus in soil potential.

The natural starting-point in a study of the scarplands is the Rhine Rift Valley and its bordering uplands, the Vosges and Hardt on the west, the Black Forest and Odenwald to the east. The Black Forest and Vosges in particular form a classic case of twin massifs, once part of a continuous arch, between which the valley has sunk between parallel fault lines. As a whole the rift valley has the mildest climate of all the German lands, with the earliest appearance of spring blossom (and so the longest growing season, which allows the cultivation of specialised crops like tobacco and warm temperate fruit), hot summers and low rainfall. But variations in soil types are extreme, and largely control the degree to which this basic advantage can be exploited.

On both sides of the present regulated Rhine is the wide old flood plain (*Ried*), with damp meadowlands, old abandoned water-courses and much impeded drainage; this is negative land, whose best use is for pasture, industry and port installation. Just above this the wide flat lower terrace is composed of highly permeable gravel, giving a hungry soil which offers little potential to the farmer; most of it remains in forest. The real potentiality of the valley is seen in the loess-covered upper terraces which merge into the foothills of the fault scarps; here, away from the ground frosts which often trouble the valley floor in spring and winter, is one of the most intensive zones of specialised cultivation in all the German lands. Particularly notable are the Bergstrasse southwards from Darmstadt to Heidelberg on the east side of the valley, with its closely-spaced large villages growing vine, fruit and tobacco; the big wine villages on the slopes of the volcanic remnant of the Kaiserstuhl, close to Freiburg in Breisgau near the southern end of the valley; and on the north-west side, the great vineyards of the so-called German Wine Road, from Nierstein through Oppenheim to Worms. South of Karlsruhe, the Rhine itself forms the Franco-German boundary, so that the west bank terrace lands are in French Alsace; this area is described in Chapter 14.

The Hercynian relics of the east bank have a similar character. Their cores are composed of a mass of intensely folded and metamorphosed crystalline rocks, which have gone through many vicissitudes of geological history before their last upheaval in Tertiary times. Because of the long-continued denudation, this crystalline core often forms the lower, more easily settled parts of the Hercynian blocks, as in the so called pre-Spessart (Vorspessart) surface on the borders of the Rhine-Main plain, just east of Aschaffenburg, or the similar area of the western Odenwald, just east of the Bergstrasse. (In the Black Forest however it forms the highest peaks, such as the Feldberg which at 4,900 feet (1,493 m.) is the highest point in the German Hercynian uplands.)

The really dominant influence on the Hercynian relics is rather the great masses of Bunter Sandstone which cover the Hercynian cores on their eastern side, east of the Rhine, and west and north of the Vosges in France, making up the lowest of the series of sediments which form the scarplands proper. Here are found extensive high-level forests, predominantly coniferous, with isolated clearings where farmers eke out an existence by supplementing poor crops with rural handicrafts. In the Odenwald and Spessart some of these medieval colonisations have

Plate 32   The Black Forest.

This picture, taken in the heart of the Forest, shows the typical settlement pattern of an infertile Hercynian relic block, cleared for cultivation only late in the Middle Ages. The isolated unit farmhouses have the large roofs characteristic of the Black Forest house, though this type does not extend everywhere in the Forest. In the background is the Feldberg (4,900 feet), highest point of the German Hercynian lands.

produced a characteristic settlement form: the long, straggling forest-clearing village (*Waldhufendorf*) a mile or more long, where each farmer has a long strip holding which stretches back into the forest. But today these remote settlements no longer yield an attractive life in comparison with the towns, and areas like the Odenwald and Spessart have been losing population steadily for decades.

To the east, as the Bunter Sandstone dips under the Triassic Mussel Limestone (*Muschelkalk*), a dramatic change in landscape occurs. This limestone, named after a prominent fossil, has no equivalent in the Triassic rocks of the English Midlands. It is a hard, yellow limestone rather like the Oolitic Limestone of the English Jurassic series, and it forms low plateaux, which vary in average height from 700 to 1,500 feet (210 to 450 m.), covering very extensive tracts of the northern and western

Plate 33 The Main Valley
Between Würzburg and Aschaffenburg this is deeply incised into the Hercynian
relic block of the Spessart. At this point the river has eroded a wide and intensively
cultivated valley floor, which stands in sharp contrast to the forested slopes of the
Spessart. As the river barrage shows, this stretch of the Main is navigable.

scarplands. As a highly permeable limestone, this formation gives rise to
rather thin soils which have little to offer the farmer, and which often
remain in sheep walks or forest.

By a fortunate accident of the Quaternary ice age, large parts of the
Mussel Limestone plateaux have been covered by fertile loess deposits
blown out from the Alpine glaciers to the south. These alter completely
the character of the soil, and unite with the mild dry climate to produce
some of the most intensively-farmed areas in southern Germany, such as
the Kraichgau between the northern Black Forest and southern Odenwald,
or the Hohlenlohe Ebene north-east of the Kraichgau between Heilbronn
and Würzburg. Here the farmers combine the cultivation of basic cereals
such as wheat and barley, and of fodder crops, with specialised cash crops
such as sugar beet, soft fruit, hops, and the vine. Many farmers in areas

like these go to work in the factories of neighbouring towns, cultivating their fields part-time. On this double economic basis the large nucleated villages, set among the open fields where no trace of forest remains, may support population densities of up to 225 to the square mile (870 to the sq. km.). This type of completely-cleared, intensively-cultivated loess landscape is locally known in the western part of the scarplands by the collective name of *Gau* land. It continues eastwards on to the neighbouring Keuper claylands wherever a loess cover is present. So does the even more intensive and specialised cultivation of wine and fruit along the sheltered slopes of the Main Valley and its tributaries, both east and west of Würzburg, and of the Neckar Valley below Stuttgart.

Yet another sharp contrast is evident to east and to south, where the scarp of the Keuper Sandstones stands up prominently against the clay plain. Because of their massive character, these rocks have a much more pronounced effect on the landscape than their equivalents in the English Midlands. The scarp itself may rise 400 or 500 feet (120 or 150 m.), and the gently-dipping backslope behind it may be covered by dense coniferous forest for many miles. But the precise topographic effect is very much conditioned by local details of geology and geomorphological history. In the eastern lands, in Franken, the Steigerwald and Frankenhöhe have a deeply fretted scarp which gives almost the effect of giant geological battlements, while the back slope is dissected by wide valleys which have cut down to the underlying clays. In the south, in Schwaben, the whole sandstone formation is much more compressed; it forms a continuous and prominent scarp, occasionally eroded into basins like the one in which the city of Stuttgart lies, but the dip of the rocks is much sharper and the back slope is only four or five miles wide.

This brings out basic differences between the scarplands of Schwaben in the west and of Franken in the east, which is not restricted to the Keuper Sandstones alone, but which is increasingly evident in the disposition of the younger and uppermost outcrops of the Mesozoic series. The sediments of Schwaben were much more profoundly affected by the earth disturbances of Alpine times; they were laterally compressed, and the degree of compression progressively increases towards the southwest, so that at the extreme, in southern Baden just north of the Bodensee, a sequence which in Franken would stretch for many miles may be squashed into a few hundred yards. This difference is particularly evident immediately above the outcrop of the Keuper Sandstone, where the transition to the Liassic clay takes place. In the south, in Schwaben, the Lias outcrop forms a narrow but regular and well-marked lowland tract between the back slope of the sandstones and the massive scarp of the Jurassic Alb. The variations in relief due to the Jurassic foothills, and the lime downwash, make for an intensive mixed farming pattern in which stock rearing plays a prominent role on the heavier soils, and there is a sequence of closely-spaced industrial towns originally dependent upon water power, and now concentrating upon textile manufacture and engineering.

In Franken, where the formations spread more widely, this belt is marked by a feature without an equivalent elsewhere. The Rednitz, a tributary of the Main, and its tributary the Pegnitz have hollowed out a wide basin which became filled with infertile glacial sands during Quaternary times. This area is still among the most agriculturally negative in south Germany. The extensive tracts of coniferous forest are broken only once, but then spectacularly: north of Nuremberg, where an outcrop of well-drained upper Keuper Sandstone provides the basis for the Garlic Land (*Knoblauchland*), one of the most notable zones of intensive market gardening in all Germany. This arose in response to the exceptional concentration of urban population around Nuremberg and Fürth.

The Jurassic scarp is by far the most prominent single feature in all the South German scarplands, for it is visible for many miles across them from the north or west. Though nominally an equivalent of the Cotswold scarp, the comparison is misleading; for the German Jurassic, dominated in the lower levels by the massive Dogger Sandstone and higher up by other equally massive limestones, produces a scarp that in the Swabian section may rise in an almost sheer wall 1,500 feet (460 m.) above the Liassic plain in front of it. Equally surprising is the landscape of the backslope. Though the main limestone gives a thin soil, aided by a superficial cover this is still sufficient to support open-field arable farming at up to 3,000 feet (915 m.), with big nucleated villages which are stone-built and in-facing as protection against winter winds.

Only rarely does the porosity of the rock and the thinness of the soil give rise to real agricultural problems; most notably in the extensive zone of dolomitic limestone of the Fränkische Alb north of Nuremberg, where the boulder-strewn landscape fields and the deep gorge-like valleys with their fantastic rock sculptures have earned the area the name of the 'Frankish Switzerland'. This is a hard, remote, negative land which has lost population for many years, though in recent times the tourist industry has brought limited extra income to supplement the meagre returns from farming. Southwards, the wide backslope of the Schwäbische Alb dips directly and unconformably under the Tertiary rocks which form the northern part of the Alpine foreland, although the transition is masked by the recent deposits which occupy the wide floodplain of the Danube Valley. Only eastwards does the Jurassic backslope of the Fränkische Alb merge into a limited area of chalk and other Cretaceous deposits in the basin of the Naab, the left-bank tributary which joins the Danube at Regensburg.

Thus the South German scarplands provide an almost classical case of the variation of rural land use, rural settlement patterns and rural landscapes in accordance with changes in geology and hence with changes in soil and local climate. The smaller towns of the region, too, are part of this varied pattern of rural settlement; they are market towns located at frequent intervals in order to serve the local and most immediate needs of the agricultural populations around them.

In 1933 the German geographer Walter Christaller first developed for

Plate 34   Schwäbische Alb.

A typical scene in the scarp zone, with isolated outliers of Jurassic limestone in the Lias clay plain in front. There is a notable contrast between the grasslands on the clay, the forests on the slopes, and the sheep meadows on the higher slopes. The high level backslopes, rising to over 3,000 feet in places (not seen here), support mixed farming in open fields with big nucleated villages.

this region his theory of central places, in which towns can be classified in a hierarchy, the smallest serving the most local needs and occurring at intervals of as little as $2\frac{1}{2}$ miles (4 km.) apart, the largest serving very specialised needs and occurring as much as 116 miles (185 km.) apart. Characteristically, Christaller argued, the service areas of these towns would assume a hexagonal shape, and the smaller hexagons around the minor centres would nest inside the larger hexagons around the centres of a higher order. If the surface of the land were always everywhere the same, then towns of any order would always be the same distance apart. In fact, the potential of the land differs greatly from place to place, and so Christaller found in practice that the spacing of the towns varied widely in the scarplands, from a close network in the most fertile areas like the loess platform of the Kraichgau, to a relatively loose system in poorer areas like the Keuper Sandstone ridges or the backslope of the Jurassic Alb.

The largest cities of the scarplands fit well into the Christaller system. But their precise location and siting are only partly to be explained in terms of local needs; they arise also from the pattern of long-distance routes first established in the Middle Ages and little-changed since, and partly too from historical accident. Stuttgart, capital of Baden-Württemberg, occupies a site unique among German cities, in a great armchair-shaped hollow in the Keuper Sandstone ridge, which stands above the valley floor of the Neckar to the north. The location is a convenient one for crossing the sandstone ridge, but it was not the only possible location for a major city; the precise choice owes much to the accident that a local prince chose the site for his palace in the thirteenth century. Thereafter the city

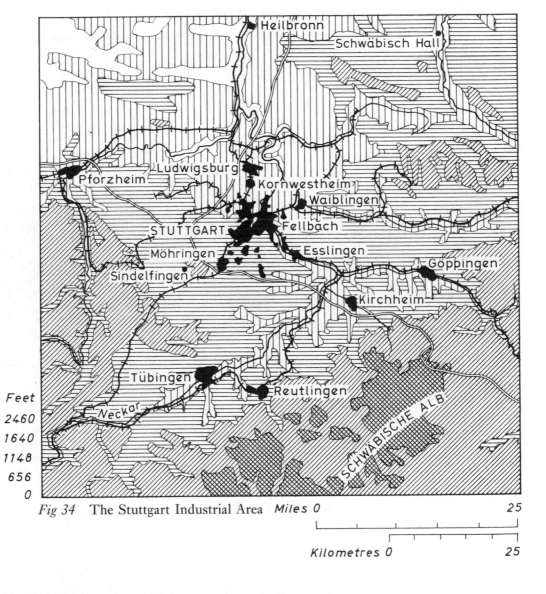

Fig 34   The Stuttgart Industrial Area

became a natural focus for trans-German and trans-Alpine routes, both in the Middle Ages and then, after a period of stagnation, after the coming of the railways in the nineteenth century. Stuttgart is the centre of the largest industrial area of south Germany, which extends southwards into the Liassic plain as far as the foot of the Alb, and northwards down the navigable Neckar Valley to Heilbronn. The older industrial tradition here is in textiles, developed in medieval times from local wool; but more important now is a wide range of engineering industries, including vehicle manufacture and precision instruments. Because the area is far from most raw materials it depends heavily on the assembly of light, valuable semi-finished components using much skilled labour. As agricultural reforms

Plate 35   Stuttgart.
The city occupies a notable site in an armchair-shaped hollow in the Keuper sandstone scarp, which is here very narrow. Owing its existence to a political decision in the Middle Ages, it derives its present importance from its role as a transport centre and as capital of the Land of Baden-Württemberg. It has a wide range of manufactures with special emphasis on engineering and vehicles.

on the peasant farms lead to greater labour savings, more and more farm workers are commuting from the surrounding villages into the factories of the Stuttgart area, and this great pool of labour is one of the area's greatest assets.

The other great city of the scarplands, Nuremberg, is something of a paradox, for it lies in the centre of the Rednitz Basin, one of the most infertile areas of all the scarplands. Thus it is to be explained hardly at all in terms of the demands of a local farm population, but almost wholly in terms of the crossing of long-distance routes from the Rhine-Main Plain to the Danube and Vienna, and from Berlin and Saxony to Munich and the Alpine passes. This was the source of its medieval fame and of its modern industrial growth after the arrival of the railways. Like Stuttgart its industrial pattern is dominated by processing industries, which range from the manufacture of the traditional Nuremberg cakes (*Lebkuchen*) to pencil-making, but which are dominated by engineering products. Nuremberg stands at the centre of an industrial area which embraces its twin town and rival, Fürth, ten miles to the west, and which extends even into the villages of the Keuper Sandstone area twenty and thirty miles to the west, where local crafts such as slipper-making have been developed to compensate for agricultural poverty.

THE ALPINE
FORELAND

The Alpine Foreland of south Germany, sometimes loosely called the Bavarian Foreland on the grounds that most of it falls within the *Land* of Bavaria, in fact extends westwards into the province of Schwaben (*Land* Baden-Württemberg) in the area north of Lake Constance (*Bodensee*). Structurally, indeed, it is continued farther westwards through central Switzerland. Essentially it is a southerly continuation of the scarplands region, for like the scarplands it is part of a great structural depression between the Alps to the south and the Hercynian relics on the west, north and east. However, the deposits are younger than in the scarplands; they are of Tertiary and Quaternary age. The area thus formed, bounded on the north by the Danube and on the south by the Alps, measures some 200 miles (320 km.) (within the borders of the Federal Republic) from west to east, and some 80 miles (128 km.) from north to south at its widest, between Regensburg on the Danube and Rosenheim on the River Inn.

Like the scarplands region, but in even greater degree, this is an area which on average is well above sea level, rising gradually from 1,200 feet (365 m.) on the Danube to 3,000 feet (915 m.) in the glaciated lands near the edge of the Alpine foothills. Its capital, Munich, is the highest major city of Germany (1,600 feet, 490 m.). The earlier, Tertiary, deposits form a solid basement to the whole of this region; but they are downwarped in the middle, and so outcrop only in the extreme north and south. In the latter, a narrow zone of sandstone and conglomerates marks the border of the Alpine Foothills; in the north, a much wider outcrop of sandstones and clays forms a series of plateaux south of the Danube. Here,

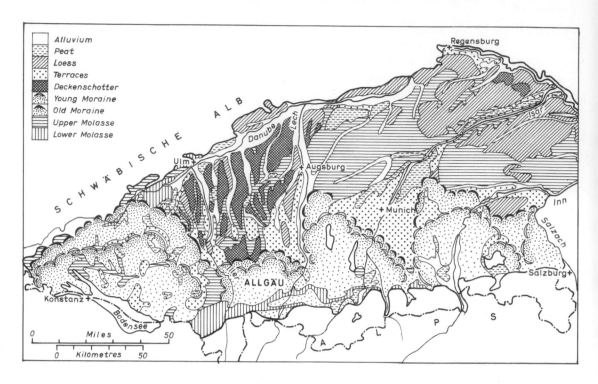

Fig 35   The Alpine Foreland

the plateaux in the western half of the foreland, west of the River Lech, have been covered by large areas of glacial outwash gravels (Deckenschotter), giving infertile soils which remain largely in forest. The Tertiary sandstone, or Molasse, is exposed to any large degree only east of the Lech, where it gives fertile soils under arable cultivation, with nucleated villages.

Both east and west of the Lech the right-bank tributaries of the Danube have cut wide, maturely-dissected, valleys in their northward courses, with much meadowland on the alluvial valley bottoms and with terrace gravels or Molasse outcrops giving good village sites and potentialities for arable cultivation just above the valley floors. Northwards, as they approach the Danube, the terrace zones of these valleys may widen into wide loess-covered platforms, such as the Lechfeld on the west side of the Lech Valley south of Augsburg; and these in turn merge into a narrow loess-covered terrace belt along the main stream. The floodplain of the Danube is distinguished by large areas of remaining undrained marsh, known in the west as *Ried* (*Donauried*, between Ulm and Donauworth) and in the east as *Moos* (*Donaumoos*, around Ingolstadt).

The glacial deposits of the foreland are broadly comparable with those of the North German Lowlands; but they take a different form. The most important deposits are those of the last glaciation, equivalent to the

Vistula Glaciation of the northern lowland but here known as the Würm
stage. Because these Würm deposits were laid down by glaciers escaping
from the constriction of the Alpine valleys, rather than by continental
sheet ice, large-scale ground moraine is conspicuously absent; and the
arc-shaped form of the terminal moraine loops is much more pronounced,
producing tongue-shaped basins. Each of the major right-bank tributaries
of the Danube—the Iller, the Lech, the Isar, the Inn and the Salzach—
created one such major basin; that of the Inn, the largest, extends over 700
square miles (1,810 sq. km.). But in the Swabian west, the Rhine-Rhône
glaciation created the greatest tongue-shaped lobe of all, extending northwards all the way to the upper Danube. In each of these basins, the land
inside the terminal moraine loop is characterised by groups of drumlins,
centring upon a moraine-dammed lake (the Chiemsee in the Inn glacier
basin, the Starnbergersee or Würmsee in the Iller glacier basin, Lake
Constance in the centre of the Rhine glacier basin). Often this central lake
has dried out in whole or in part, producing large central alluvial plains
at the heart of the tongue basin: thus the plain of Kempten on the Iller,
the plain of Rosenheim on the Inn, and the plain of Salzburg on the
Salzach.

In front of the terminal moraine loops of the Würm glaciation the older
ground moraine deposits extend to the north, towards the outcrop of the
Tertiary sandstones. Since they were laid down these older deposits have
suffered much erosion by the north-flowing tributaries of the Danube,
which have cut wide alluvium-filled valleys; and these rivers have carried
out large amounts of outwash gravels from the Würm glacial deposits,
depositing them on top of the older moraine remnants in the form of
terraces along the valley sides, and even as extensive high-level gravel
plains such as the great plain of Munich immediately south of that city.
Because of their permeability these outwash gravel plains are normally
dry and forest-covered. But at their northern edge, against the rising
ground of the Molasse platforms, the water-table may rise to the surface,
producing marshy areas like the Erdinger Moos and Dachauer Moos
north of Munich. Useless in their natural state, these areas have been
gradually reclaimed since the nineteenth century. The isolated farms, set
along the planned rectangular grid of roads, produce good crops of cereals
and roots, as well as market-garden products for the city of Munich.

The foreland is predominantly an agricultural land, and the pattern of
farming closely reflects differences in the potential of the soil. On the
northern Molasse platforms, so long as they remain free of the infertile
gravel cover, the rule is mixed farming with the arable mainly in cereals
and roots; the big farmsteads, built round courtyards, are grouped in
nucleated villages. But on the moraine lands to the south, above all on
the younger moraine, soil characteristics unite with higher precipitation
and shorter growing season to create one of the most strongly-marked
stock keeping regions in all Germany outside the North Sea Coastlands.
Here too the proportion of uncleared forest rises, to as much as one-half
the total area. Because of the large amount of negative land and the

essentially extensive character of dairying and stock rearing, population densities in this southern zone are low. As befits the pastoral economy, the population is scattered in isolated farms built in the characteristic Bavarian style, with all functions under the familiar flat-pitched roof.

The small market towns, which occur at regular intervals, provide local services and also act as collecting and processing centres for the dairy produce. This function is particularly important because away from the centres like Munich and Bavaria the economy of the area depends on rapid processing into butter or cheese. The region of south-western Bavaria known as the Allgäu, between the Lech and the Iller, is parti-

Plate 36   Allgäu.
The landscapes of the Alpine Foreland of Bavaria are characterised by frequent lakes, by a huge proportion of agricultural land in grass, and by the presence of isolated unit farmhouses which are well adapted to the prevailing pastoralism. The Allgäu is internationally renowned for its cheeses—a reflection of its distance from major consuming markets for fresh milk production.

cularly notable as a cheese producer and its products are found on many British grocers' counters.

As elsewhere, the larger cities of the Foreland are related less to local demands, and more to the pattern of long-distance trade routes. Ulm is the gateway to the Foreland for the main routes from Stuttgart and the upper Rhine plain, Regensburg performs the same function for the route from Nuremberg, Saxony and Berlin; both are at crossing places of the Danube where the treacherous marshy floodplain narrows almost to disappearing point. Augsburg, like Regensburg, is a Roman foundation; it stands at a critical point where the main north-west to south-east route, from the Neckar basin across Bavaria to the lower Danube and Inn valleys, crosses a north-south routeway from Würzburg, on the Main, to Füssen, at the foot of the Alps where a pass gives a direct route to Innsbruck. Since the coming of the railways Augsburg has become an important industrial centre with a variety of engineering and vehicle-building trades. As in the Middle Ages, however, she has been overshadowed by her near neighbour Munich, capital of Bavaria.

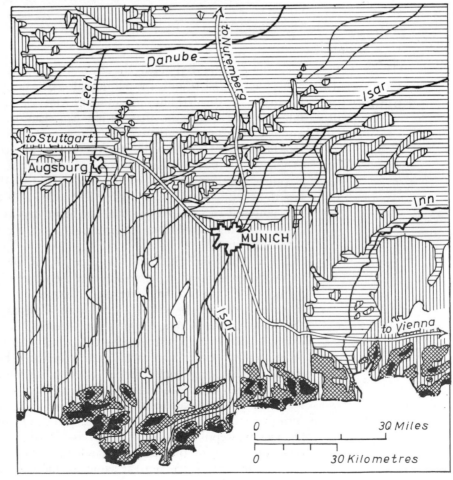

Fig 36 Munich

A latecomer among German cities, Munich was founded in 1158 on the site of a village and monastery; the German name, München, derives from *Mönchen*, 'monks'. The site, on a far from ideal crossing of the Isar floodplain, is not a particularly happy one; but once the city was established its prosperity was almost assured by its critical position with regard to major routes. From north-west to south-east came the major routeway from Stuttgart, Ulm and Augsburg to Salzburg and the Inn Valley; from the north came the route from Berlin, Saxony and Nuremberg. Between 1500 and 1900, while most German cities stagnated, Munich benefited from the location here of the Bavarian royal court. But its great rise into a modern industrial and service centre dates from the coming of the railways. Today, as capital of the largest Land of the Federal Republic, it performs many of the functions that a metropolitan city would perform in more centralised nation states; and it has a wide range of industries depending on its transport facilities and the demands of Bavaria's largest single market, including electrical engineering, machinery, vehicles, textiles, optical instruments and chemicals.

The German Democratic Republic and Berlin

Like the Federal Republic, the *Deutsche Demokratische Republik* is an almost accidental result of a political decision taken at war's end. When Germany was divided into four military zones of occupation in July 1945, few could have foreseen that within five years these zones would have grouped themselves into two separate and bitterly opposed states. Few too, taking any account of the facts of geography, could have been found to justify the precise form the exact division took. Because the Federal Republic was the bigger and more varied of the two, the anomalies mattered less to her. But for the Democratic Republic, with less than one-third of the combined area of the two states and about one-quarter of the combined population, they have mattered grievously, and have been overcome only with difficulty.

Though the landscapes and resources of the Democratic Republic are by no means uniform or homogeneous, the range of variation is less than in the west. This is a simple result of geography. The Federal Republic stretches from nearly 55°N. in Schleswig-Holstein to nearly 47°N. in the Alps; the Democratic Republic only from 55°N. in the Baltic island of Rügen to 50°N. in Thuringia. As compared with the Federal Republic, therefore, the eastern state is far more dominated by the Northern Lowlands, which occupy some three-quarters of its total territory. Instead of the Hercynian uplands splitting the country across the middle, as in the west, here they form the southern and south-western frontier. As compared with the rich and varied Mesozoic Scarplands of Southern Germany, the Democratic Republic has only the Triassic Basin of Thuringia. And there is no substitute for the Rhine; though the Elbe performs a useful navigational function, it has not the same significance for industry and urban life as the great river of the west. Bituminous coal too is almost lacking, so that the eastern area never developed a great concentration of population dependent upon coal and iron like the Ruhr. Apart from the concentration of population based on the brown coal and chemical deposits in the western part of the Saxon Bay, its great cities have tended to grow up either as trading centres at junctions of routeways, as in the case of the towns of Saxony, or as a combination of route centre and purely political capital, as in the unique case of Berlin.

In terms of agricultural resources, the Democratic Republic is a state of extremes. The Northern Lowlands here are no more fertile, on average, than in the west, but are more dominant. Well over a third of the country, extending well south of Berlin, is covered by the immaturely dissected deposits of the last, Vistula glaciation. Only in the extreme north, in the coastal lands of Mecklenburg, does this produce land of adequate agricultural quality. Elsewhere, as in the sandy lake-and-drumlin-strewn zone of the Mecklenburg Lake Plateau, in the sand dunes and swamps of the Urstromtal zone farther to the south, or again in the poor leached Geestlands of the Fläming to the south of that, the agricultural prospects are poor; to the earliest agricultural settlers they must often have appeared non-existent. Even now that reclamation techniques have won large areas of the Geest and the Urstromtäler for cultivation, few of these lands offer a prospect of easy cultivation or rich returns. In the extreme south, too, the wooded highlands on the edge of the Bohemian Massif are essentially negative lands.

In sharp contrast, the lowland embayments at the foot of the Southern Uplands can be counted among the most fertile zones of north central Europe. The sandstones and clays of the Thuringian Basin, or the vast tracts of rich black earth soils on the Saxon loess between Leipzig, Halle and Magdeburg, enjoy not only well-nigh perfect soil conditions for intensive arable farming, but an almost ideal climate. Rainfall, as elsewhere in the lowlands of the Democratic Republic, is low, a little over 20 inches a year, and the warm continental summers guarantee early ripening of the crops, which are harvested as early as in the sheltered upper Rhine Valley. As well as growing rich cereal crops, these areas have become especially notable in the last hundred years as sugar beet producers.

The agricultural pattern of the eastern lands has been influenced as powerfully by history as by physical potential or the lack of it. Almost the whole of the Democratic Republic lay east of that critical line where, from A.D. 800 to 1100, the Germans maintained their eastern frontier against the Slavs. The eastern territories were occupied in the great colonial movement of the Germans, the *Drang nach Osten*, in the period 1100–1350; so social organisation and settlement took quite different forms here compared with the older-settled west. The settlements of the east were consciously and carefully planned, and to this day the characteristic feature of the east German rural landscape is the planned street village (*Strassendorf*) or green village (*Angerdorf*), set in its great, regular open fields.

Between the sixteenth and the eighteenth centuries came the rise of the Junker landowners and the depression of the tenants to the status of landless labourers on the great estates. In the nineteenth century the eastern lands of Germany never became peasant proprietor societies like western Germany or France; instead the social problem of the big estates progressively grew more acute, though they conspicuously achieved greater efficiency and higher yields (despite the poverty of the soil) than the peasant system of the west. Finally, and ironically, it was left to the communist regime after 1945 to resolve this problem. It did so first by distributing the whole of the former Junker land into peasant holdings, save in the case of a few areas, where state farms were formed. Later, in the 1950s, the peasants were cajoled into forming collective farms, which often make profitable use of the central buildings of the old estate.

More serious for the Democratic Republic is the fact that it has a very ill-balanced assortment of industrial raw materials. Apart from a small field between Karl-Marx-Stadt (Chemnitz) and Zwickau, which is now rapidly approaching exhaustion, the state has no significant deposits of bituminous coal. Before the war, coal was brought from the Ruhr; now that trade connections with the west are virtually severed, the chief sources of supply are the Silesian coalfield, which passed to Poland in 1945, and the Donbas basin in the U.S.S.R. Under the stimulus of Stalinist ideas of 'national economic planning' in the early 1950s, the Democratic Republic made efforts to become independent of outside raw materials as far as possible. In particular this involved the replacement of bituminous coking coal by native supplies of brown coal from the great deposits in the Saxon Bay, which would be specially coked in new plants. In this way steel plants were established both in the Saxon Bay at Calbe near the confluence of Elbe and Saale, and at Eisenhüttenstadt (formerly Stalinstadt) not far from Frankfurt-on-Oder. Though these plants now produce significant amounts of iron and steel for the varied engineering industries of the Democratic Republic, the emphasis has shifted away from brown coal coking to importation of coking coal from other eastern block countries; and the giant 'Schwarze Pumpe' brown coal processing works in Lusatia, north of Karl-Marx-Stadt, will no longer produce coke as originally intended.

The ample supplies of brown coal have, however, much importance for other branches of industry. Brown coal underlies almost the whole of the Saxon Bay, with an important subsidiary field in Lusatia to the east. Nearly all of it can be won economically by open-cast mining. As in the Federal Republic, its most important uses are electricity generation, the manufacture of briquettes for domestic fuel, and chemical manufacture. Here the Democratic Republic has a unique advantage in the close juxtaposition of brown coal deposits and important resources of potash salt and common salt in the western part of the Saxon Bay around Halle. These are by far the greatest single source of potash fertiliser in the world, and they play a vital part in supplying other countries of the eastern block in their constant drive to raise agricultural yields; potash is the most important single export of the Democratic Republic.

While the new iron and steel complexes are an artificial result of the division of Germany, the great concentration of basic chemical plants and chemical processing works in the Saxon Bay is a natural consequence of the available raw materials. Before the Second World War, Saxony concentrated on the earlier stages of manufacture, sending large amounts of semi-processed basic chemicals westwards to manufacturing plants in the Rhine-Ruhr or Rhine Main regions. Now that this link has been broken, the Democratic Republic manufactures a much greater proportion of its basic chemicals itself. The most important single concentration of the industry are the Leuna works at Merseburg near Halle for fertilisers and petrol, the Buna works at Schkopau close by for synthetic rubber, the electro-technical complex at Bitterfeld north-east of Halle for light metals and synthetic fabrics, and the dye factory and east German Agfa photographic plant near Bitterfeld. But outside these major concentrations, many cities have their own important chemical plants.

Industry in the east German lands, just as in the west, therefore has an important heavy industrial base, tied to sources of raw material. But again as in the west, another significant element is provided by the relatively footloose industries, above all the many different branches of the engineering and electrical industries, which tend to locate in major cities where there are good transport facilities, an ample labour pool, and a fully developed range of specialised industrial services. In the west these industries are found both close to the raw material orientated heavy industry, e.g. in the Rhine-Ruhr region, and far away from it in south German cities like Stuttgart and Nuremberg. Here too they are found both near the heavy chemical plants of the Saxon Bay, and away from them in cities like Dresden, Karl-Marx-Stadt and above all East Berlin, which is still the most important single industrial centre in the Democratic Republic. Agricultural machinery is particularly important at Leipzig and Magdeburg, textile machinery at Plauen and Karl-Marx-Stadt, printing machinery at Berlin, Leipzig and Dresden, vehicle manufacture at Karl-Marx-Stadt, Plauen in the Southern Uplands, and Eisenach in Thuringia. The shipbuilding industry, never important in the Democratic Republic in prewar days, is being built up in the port of Rostock on the Baltic coast.

An important problem for industry is that many of the largest concerns, faced with nationalisation after 1945, migrated to the west taking many of their skilled workers with them. The Zeiss works for instance migrated from Jena to Oberkochen in Württemberg; the Jena glass plant went to Mainz and the world-famous Justus Perthes map-making firm moved to Darmstadt. But in each case a remaining nucleus reformed itself, so that in many cases there are today two firms bearing the same or similar names, one in the East and one in the West.

This migration of whole plants is, however, only one aspect of a wholesale migration of the active population out of the Democratic Republic into the West, a migration amounting to no less than $3\frac{1}{2}$ million in the years 1949–1965. Though political protest was no doubt one motive, it should not be forgotten that this was a continuation of a very old migratory trend in Germany, evident since the Industrial Revolution, from agrarian east to industrial west. Whatever the causes, the result was a serious problem of labour supply in the Democratic Republic; the sealing of the one remaining escape route, by the construction of the Berlin Wall in August 1961, put an end to the process.

Transport patterns in the Democratic Republic are guided by geographical conditions similar to those in the west. Before the war the most important east-west routes were two: one through the Urstromtal zone in the central part of the lowlands, from Frankfurt-on-Oder through Berlin to Magdeburg, with a branch north-eastwards from Berlin towards Hamburg; and another across the loess belt from Breslau (now Wrocław) via Karl-Marx-Stadt and Leipzig to Halle and so to the Ruhr. North-south routes splayed out from Berlin to the chief towns of the loess route, Dresden, Leipzig, Halle; connections north of Berlin were of minor significance because of the lack of major ports on the Baltic coast, with the sole exception of a route north eastwards to Stettin (since 1945 incorporated into Poland as Szczecin). After 1948, with the rapid descent of the Iron Curtain across Germany, the east-west routes declined in significance; the only one of importance today exists, in effect, outside the Democratic Republic, for it principally serves the traffic from West Berlin to the Federal Republic.

The Regions of the Democratic Republic and Berlin
THE NORTHERN LOWLANDS

In west and east alike, the North German Lowlands are the result of Quaternary ice sheets which moved southwards from Scandinavia, laying down great thicknesses of moraine and diverting drainage. But in the eastern lands represented by the Democratic Republic, the events of glacial and post-glacial time produced landscapes somewhat different from those already described in the west.

The first difference is that the major advance in the eastern lands was the last, or Vistula, glaciation—an advance which in the Federal Republic left its mark only in extreme eastern Schleswig Holstein. Here, however, the great Outer Baltic Ridge, the terminal moraine representing the first stage of retreat of the glaciation and therefore the approximate maximum limit of the advance, runs in a great arc through the sandy Geest areas of the Fläming and Lower Lusatia (Niederlausitz), respectively south-west and south-east of Berlin, and no less than 150 miles (240 km.) south of the Baltic coast. The effects of the glaciation however extend even farther southward than this, because great tracts of outwash material splay outwards from the end moraines—in the Fläming for instance—and mask the effects of the earlier glaciations.

The most spectacular effects of the Vistula glaciation are to be seen within 70 miles (112 km.) of the coast. Just behind the coast itself is a belt of ground moraine, between 20 miles (32 km.) and 50 miles (80 km.) wide, with heavy clay soils comparable with the very best soils which occasionally occur in the western Geest lands. The large planned villages here take various forms, some of them grouped in circular fashion (*Rundling* villages), some of them along streets, some on both sides of a village green. Most of them, up to 1945, were dominated by the big Junker manor house which may today stand as the headquarters of the collective farm. They are given over to prosperous mixed farming which combines the cultivation of rye, potatoes and vegetables with the keeping of sheep, cattle, horses and pigs. Southwards of this stands a very different area: the Mecklenburg Lake Plateau, a classic example of the landscape of recent glaciation. In contrast to the western glaciated lands, here later denudation has had little time to modify the work of the ice, and the terrain is dominated by high terminal moraine villages (the most prominent of which, the Inner Baltic Ridge on the south side of the plateau, attains a height of 550 feet, 167 m.), by swarms of drumlins, and by a host of lakes of all sizes which occupy pockets of impeded drainage, including the largest lake purely on German territory, the Müritz (43 sq. m., 111 sq. km.). Though the original coniferous and beech forest has largely been cleared from this area, except on the terminal moraine ridges, this remains one of the most negative and thinly-settled of all the Germanic lowlands. Small planned villages, on the street village or green village plan, eke out a poor existence from the cultivation of rye and the keeping of a few stock.

The second difference in the Northern Lowlands of the Democratic Republic is that to the south of the Mecklenburg Lake Plateau, the Urstromtal zone achieves much greater importance than in the west, extending over a zone some fifty miles wide, and incorporating no less than five major parallel Urstromtal lines, separated one from another by islands of upstanding Geest land. The Fläming south of Berlin, with its great Outer Baltic ridge, is indeed the largest of these Geest islands, separating the so-called Wrocław-Magdeburg Urstromtal to the south from the Baruth Depression (just south of Berlin) to the north. To the north again Berlin itself lies in the centre of the great Warsaw-Berlin Urstromtal; while some twenty miles to the north again is the Thorn-Eberswald Urstromtal, which is an important routeway.

The Urstromtal zone, which occupies the area historically known as the 'Middle Mark' of the province of Brandenburg, has a landscape rather different from its west German equivalents. There, extensive areas of bog or Moor land are characteristic; here, though there are important swamp areas (as along the Oder, or the Spree, reclaimed largely by Frederick the Great in the eighteenth century), the most important element is the great tract of valley sand, which has earned the area the name of 'Germany's sand box'. Frederick the Great of Prussia thought that few countries, save Libya, could contain so much sand as his. But by careful planned colonisation and the application of manure, he managed to reclaim thousands of acres for cultivation out of former heath and forest. In the nineteenth century the arrival of potash fertiliser from the plants of Saxony further helped this area achieve a significant advance in agricultural productivity. Where a special demand made intensive application

J

of fertiliser worthwhile, as in the market gardening zones around Berlin, very high yields might be obtained. As a result of the great wave of planned colonisation, both former swamp areas and former sand areas have characteristically regular settlement forms. The reclaimed swamps in particular are distinguished by linear Fen Colonies, modelled by Frederick the Great on the earlier examples in the western lowlands.

The third distinguishing feature of the eastern lowlands is their coast. Since the Baltic was weakly tidal, and affected to only a limited degree by storms, it could not effect the profound coastal changes which the North Sea achieved in the west. Instead of the landscape of marine incursion and slow reclamation, therefore, the Baltic coastlands are marked by a less spectacular terrain of long, irregular inlets (the so-called *Bodden*) produced by submergence as the sea level rose at the end of the ice age. In their outward form they resemble most closely the ria coastlines of Ireland or south-west England, though the mode of formation was different. They make potentially excellent harbours, but because the Baltic is an inland sea and routeways led naturally north-westwards along the Urstromtal towards North Sea ports like Hamburg, this potential was not exploited until after 1945. Since the severance of the links to the west, though, the

Plate 37   Rostock.

As a result of the division of Germany and the loss of Stettin (Szczecin) to Poland, the Democratic Republic lacked a first-class seaport. The port of Rostock is being deliberately built up to perform this function. As well as being the main source of seaborne trade for the Democratic Republic, it has passenger ferry services to Scandinavia.

authorities of the Democratic Republic have been building up one of the Mecklenburg ports, Rostock, into their major outlet. It is particularly important for the import of Swedish iron ore going to the blast furnaces and converters of the Saxon and Thuringian industrial region.

Most of the towns of the eastern lowlands exist to serve the needs of their local agricultural populations, and because these are so often sparse the towns remain small and scattered. Only in a few places do long-distance trade routes bring about the existence of major cities. The sea-ports of the Baltic—Rostock and its smaller neighbours Wismar and Stralsund—form one such obvious case. The cities of the Urstromtal zone, based on the concentration of rivers, railways or roads, provide another: Frankfurt-on-Oder stands at the most important crossing point (and, in the postwar period, the only recognised crossing point) between Germany and Poland; Potsdam lies at the point where the navigable Havel, which connects with the Elbe at Magdeburg, leads into the Havel-Spree Canal which gives direct access for bulky goods to Berlin.

But the urban pattern of the Urstromtal zone is distorted by the dominance of Berlin. The former capital of the united German Reich grew up in the centre of the Urstromtal zone, where small islands of sand gave an easy passage across the marshy lowlands and an easy crossing of the River Spree. Significant for the city's future growth was the fact that in terms of the old pre-1914 united Germany, this was the mid-point of the North German Lowlands, equidistant from the Baltic and from the Hercynian Uplands, from the Ems and from the Vistula. For this great zone of Middle Europe it was a natural route centre, at the crossing point of the great east-west line from Moscow to London and of the great north-south line from Scandinavia to the Mediterranean or Black Sea. This advantage could, however, probably have only been exploited through the medium of a united political entity. Berlin owed its rise into one of the world's great cities to the fact that it was capital of the state which progressively achieved hegemony over the German lands: known first as Brandenburg after 1450, this state became Prussia in 1701, and when Germany was united under Prussia in 1871, Berlin naturally became the centre of this great united realm. From then on, as the Industrial Revolution in Germany gained momentum, Berlin's progress was irresistible. It easily became the greatest single industrial centre of Germany, with a wide range of industries in which electrical engineering, clothing, food, printing and engineering were outstanding. The concentration of the bureaucracy of a highly centralised state also helped to swell its population; up to 1939 one-half of its workforce were employed in government and other service functions.

Since Berlin was the creation and expression of a united German state, it was tragic justice that the collapse of that state should find the city in ruins. Immediately after the capitulation of 1945 the city was divided into four military zones of occupation, and after the final break between east and west in 1948 the city was in effect split into two self-contained units—a process completed on 13th August 1961, when the

Plate 38   Berlin West and East.
The division of the city from 1948, and finally the wall of 1961, have created the paradox of two self-contained cities within a city. Because the wall passes close to what was the pre-war city centre, new centres have developed for west and east well away from the dividing line: for the west in the Kurfürstendamm, and for the east along the Frankfurter Strasse (Karl Marx Allee). With the abandonment of the Stalinist style in the east, the architecture of the two cities has become more similar; but the contrast in car ownership still gives a different appearance to the streets.

communist authorities of East Berlin built their wall across the city, severing the last remnants of any regular formal connection with the west. Since 1948, therefore, West Berlin has represented the most extraordinary urban anomaly in the world—an 'exclave' of the Federal Republic (though

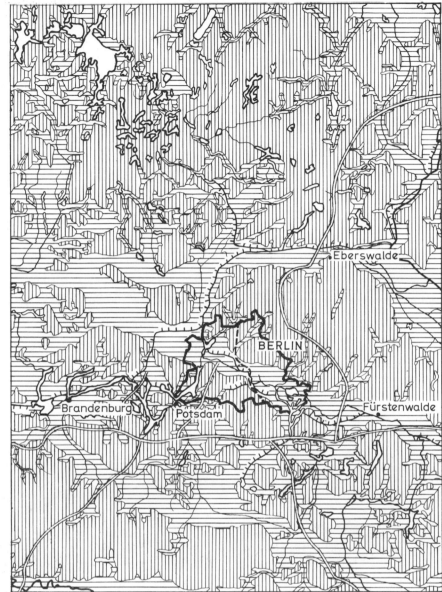

Fig 37   Berlin

not constitutionally part of it) separated by 110 miles of hostile communist territory. Not only has the western half of the city lost many of the functions that depended essentially on the role as a capital city—government, headquarters of banking and finance; it has been arbitrarily separated from the areas around it, which were its natural sources of many foodstuffs and raw materials, and also the natural markets for some of its produce. Today all West Berlin's supplies, and all its exports of finished goods, must pass along the two waterways, three air corridors, four road and six rail routes which connect it with the western world. By the mid-1960s

West Berlin had regained a good deal of the united city's former importance in electrical engineering and clothing industries, and its population was again close to pre-war levels for the equivalent area; but it was impossible to avoid the fact that this had been achieved only with special help and encouragement from the government of the Federal Republic and the Western Powers.

THE SOUTHERN BASINS AND UPLANDS

The southern borderlands of the Democratic Republic, making up about one-quarter of the total area of the country, stand in sharp contrast to the glacial monotony of the northern plain. They consist of a complex series of Hercynian relic blocks, folded originally along north-east–south-west or north-west–south-east lines, raised between faults during the Alpine disturbances, and enclosing lowland basins in which were deposited Mesozoic deposits eroded from the Hercynian fold mountains. In addition, these basins sometimes received an important loess cover during Quaternary times. The whole complex compares closely with the alternation of Hercynian uplands and lowland basins in the South German Scarplands.

The relic blocks have some common characteristics, though some stand as real mountain walls, some merely as upland plateaux. They tend to

Plate 39 Thüringer Wald
The Thüringian Forest forms part of the heavily fortified boundary between the Federal and Democratic Republics. The contrast between the sombre woodlands of the upper slopes, and the large open arable fields with their nucleated villages, is typical of the Hercynian lands of middle Germany.

reach 2,000–3,000 feet (600–900 m.) in height, they are largely negative for agriculture and they remain in heavy coniferous forest. The Harz on the north, the Frankenwald and Thuringian Forest on the south-west, and the Ore Mountains (*Erzgebirge*) on the south-east all owe what economic importance they have to the exploitation of mineral ores. The Thuringian Forest was colonised in the Middle Ages by iron miners, the Frankenwald by the opening of slate quarries, the Erzgebirge by mines of silver, iron, zinc, lead and other metals. Today, many of these old industries have grievously decayed, above all in the Ore Mountains. The remote forest clearance villages have turned instead to domestic manufacturing industries like the manufacture of toys, musical instruments, woollen goods, and precision instruments such as thermometers. As a result, remarkably high population densities may occur; the desolate Thuringian Forest, for instance, has more people to each square mile than the fertile Thuringian Basin to the north of it.

Although the Harz or the Thuringian Forest present sharp fault-scarp barriers to the lowland basin within them, the Ore Mountains slope gradually and imperceptibly down to the great Saxon embayment. Within this wide foreland zone, the tradition of home crafts established in the

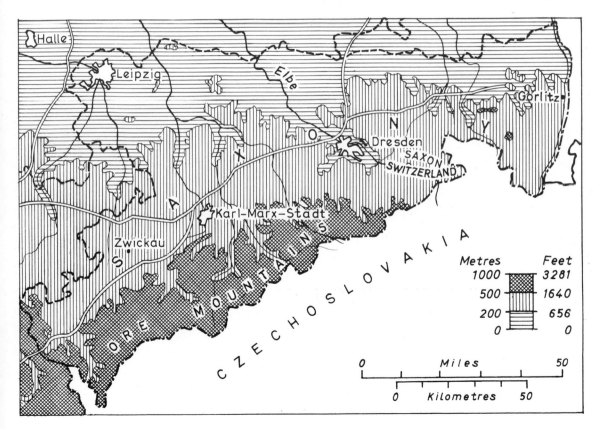

Fig 38   Saxony

highlands has become concentrated in a number of cities which today have the status of major industrial centres, such as Zwickau with its vehicles, engineering, metals and textiles, and Karl-Marx-Stadt, sometimes regarded as the 'Manchester of Saxony', with its strong traditions in the manufacture of cottons, linens and jute, as well as engineering, vehicle manufacture and chemicals.

Dresden, the greatest city of the foreland zone, owes its rise to more than pure industry. Where the Elbe has made its great breakthrough from the interior of the Bohemian Massif into the Saxon embayment, in the angle between the Ore Mountains and the highlands of Lusatia, it emerges from the spectacular Cretaceous sandstone landscapes of the 'Saxon Switzerland' into a wide fertile basin which gradually leads into the open land of the loess-covered Saxon Bay. Here the city of Dresden was capital of the former Saxon kingdom. Long after Saxony was merged into Prussia and then into the Reich, Dresden remained an important administrative

Plate 40 Saxon Switzerland.
Where the Elbe makes its great break through the wall of the Bohemian block towards the North German Lowland, the denudation of limestones and sandstones produces this spectacular tableland landscape. The Elbe is navigable and is intensively used by barge trains.

Plate 41 Dresden.

Subjected to some of the most severe aerial bombardments of any German city in the Second World War, Dresden had still not been completely rebuilt in 1966, as this picture shows. One reason is that Dresden, like most cities of the Democratic Republic, had less than its 1939 level of population in the mid-1960s.

centre; while its heritage of fine buildings and priceless art collections made it a tourist centre of the first order. Two weeks before the end of the Second World War an air raid destroyed much of the city. Since then it has been slowly rebuilt, and the art collections returned after a long disappearance in the U.S.S.R.; but much remains to be done. Dresden is again an important administrative centre, with large engineering, electrical and optical industries; but its population had not yet regained pre-war levels by the mid-1960's.

The two major lowland basins enclosed by the Hercynian relics merge into each other; the borderline is formed by the Saale, the most important left bank tributary of the Elbe. To the west the Thuringian Basin is almost completely enclosed on three sides by the Harz on the north, the

Thuringian Forest and Frankenwald on the west and south-west, and the Ore Mountains on the south; it looks eastwards across the Saale to Saxony. This is one of the greatest areas of Triassic deposition in all the German lands; most of the floor of the downfaulted basin is covered with Keuper clays and sandstones, and by Keuper Mussel Limestone (Muschelkalk), while Bunter Sandstone outcrops at the upland borders. The soils seem to have been naturally without forest cover, or at most lightly forest-covered, from earliest times; and the area was already settled in the pre-historic period. Parts are of outstanding fertility, notably the great 'corn chamber' of the Goldene Aue (Golden Meadow) in the north towards the margin of the Harz, and the basin of the middle River Unstrut in the centre, with its specialised cultivation of fruit and vegetables. The chief towns of the region, lacking important sources of raw materials, have a pattern of industry which is characteristic of the south German lands, depending on the skilled working-up of high-value products. Erfurt, the most important, specialises in engineering and electrical goods, and is famous throughout Germany for its nursery gardens; Eisenach has vehicles and engineering; Gotha is famous as the original home of the Justus Perthes cartographic firm, and Jena as a centre for optical glass.

To the east of the Saale, and extending eastwards to the Elbe below Dresden, the Saxon embayment has a more open character to north and to east, being enclosed only by the Ore Mountains on the south-east and the Harz on the north-west. Here the soils, developed on loess or on very fine glacial loam, include the most fertile arable land in all the Germanic lands, especially in the loess-covered Börde zone between Halle and Magdeburg. This is classic Börde landscape; the big villages, built in the period of late medieval German colonisation as street villages or green villages, occur at intervals of as little as a mile apart, and are set in their great planned, rectangular open fields; the whole landscape is cleared, with hardly a tree to be seen.

Increasingly since 1900, a new and foreign element has begun to affect this traditional landscape, especially along its western border. Cornfields disappear into vast open cast brown-coal quarries; power stations and chemical works, depending on the brown coal and on the salt deposits, appear around the older towns and even in the open countryside between them, especially along the Saale River south of Halle.

The major towns of the Saxon embayment, characteristically, are old medieval trading towns which have become transformed into modern industrial centres. Halle (the name is a Celtic word for salt) is a bridgepoint town on the Saale on the main east-west route across Saxony; it has become an important inland port. Its modern industrial importance stems from the nearby brown coal field and potash deposits, and it is the centre of a major chemical producing region, as well as having important engineering shops. Farther north Magdeburg occupies a similar crossing-point on the Elbe, at a strategic position on the border of the loess and Urstromtal zones; it is on the major routeway from Berlin to the west (an advantage with little significance since the division of Germany) and is an important centre for foodstuffs, engineering, vehicles and chemicals.

The major city of the Saxon Bay occupies rather a special position. Though at the geographical centre of the Bay, Leipzig is not at a crossing point of a major river. Its importance stems from its relationship to the great long-distance routes of central Europe: that from south-east to north-west (Prague-Dresden-Leipzig-Magdeburg-Brunswick) and that from south-west to north-east (Munich-Nuremberg-Leipzig-Berlin). This great crossing point of routes explains its 700-year-old importance as an international trading fair centre; and it could be argued too that its central position in the rich Saxon kingdom, subject to cultural currents from all over middle Europe, was basically responsible for its pre-war importance as the first book publishing and printing centre of the German lands. Today, with the division of Germany and the lack of cultural contact between the Democratic Republic and the German-speaking lands of the west, Leipzig printing and publishing is a shadow of its former self; many of the most important houses have migrated to the west. But it retains some importance in this, as in its historic fur trade; and it remains the second largest industrial city in the whole Democratic Republic after East Berlin.

Plate 42 Brown coal open-cast working near Halle.
Brown coal is the only large scale resource of indigenous fuel in the German Democratic Republic. Because of the low fuel value, cheap open-cast methods are essential. The coal from this pit goes chiefly to the giant Leuna chemical works, but also to a briquette factory and a power station.

Conclusion   Since 1945 the two German states have developed with different, bitterly opposed sets of political beliefs, different social and economic systems, and (increasingly) different man-made landscapes. In terms of the movements of people or goods, they are cut off from each other as fundamentally as any two states in the world. Yet it remains true that their geography cannot be fully understood except within a common physical and historical framework.

In the first place, the broad divisions of the physical environment are common to both states. Both show the extreme contrast between infertile glacial deposits in the northern lowlands, fertile loess at the border of lowlands and central uplands, bleak and intractable Hercynian massifs and rich scarpland basins. Both experience transitional middle European climatic regimes where micro-climatic differences due to local differences in relief are all-important. Both have concentrations of industrial raw materials in the borderland belt between Northern Lowland and Central (Hercynian) Upland. Both are landlocked states except on their northern sides; but both have navigable rivers which stretch far into their interiors.

In the second place, though Germany existed as a nation state only for a short period of modern history, both countries have shared centuries of common historical evolution. The western state was partly occupied by the Romans and was then progressively overrun by Teutonic tribes who flowed in from the northern coastlands. Centuries later, from 1150 to 1350, the eastern state was occupied by these same Germanic tribes in a great colonisation movement. Since then the areas have experienced a common political, social and economic history.

Germans occupied the land for the first time at different periods, and thus the results of their occupation exhibit different forms. But because these were peoples at a certain level of cultural evolution, with well developed techniques which were slow to change, the forms are variants of easily recognisable common types. The unplanned nucleated village of the west, and the planned nucleated village of the east, belong to the same family. In neither east nor west is the geographer long in doubt that here is a distinctively Germanic landscape.

For the geographer, then, it is singularly difficult to say whether Germany is one country or two. Traditionally geographers have sought to particularise and to differentiate areas from one another. If that is the object there is no difficulty in distinguishing two landscapes and patterns of development, one on each side of the Elbe-Saale line. If the geographer is more interested in definitions based on functional linkages, then here too there seems no doubt that since 1945 there are two distinct entities. The real truth perhaps is that there is no one all-embracing scheme of regional division, but rather a hierarchy of possible divisions at different levels. At one of these, each of the Germanies is divided internally; at another, each state is a separate entity; at yet another, they are to be considered together vis-à-vis the rest of Europe; and at a final level, Europe as a whole is to be considered a region in relation to the world.

FURTHER READING R. E. Dickinson, *Germany*, 2nd ed. 1961.

R. E. Dickinson, *The West European City*, 2nd ed. reprinted 1964, Chapter 6 (Cologne and Frankfurt-on-Main).

R. E. Dickinson, *City and Region*, 1964.

R. E. Dickinson, 'Rural Settlement in the German Lands', *Annals of the Association of American Geographers*, 1949, pp. 239–263.

R. E. Dickinson, 'The Development and Distribution of the Medieval German Town', *Geography*, 1942, pp. 9–21 and 47–53.

R. E. Dickinson, 'The Morphology of the Medieval German Town', *Geographical Review*, 1945, pp. 74–97.

R. E. Dickinson, 'The Braunschweig Industrial Area', *Economic Geography*, 1958, pp. 249–263.

T. H. Elkins, *Germany*, 1960.

T. H. Elkins, 'The Brown Coal Industry of Germany', *Geography*, 1953, pp. 18–29.

T. H. Elkins, 'The Central German Chemical Industry,' *Geography*, 1957, pp. 183–185.

T. H. Elkins, 'The Neuwied Basin', *Geography*, 1960, pp. 39–51.

T. H. Elkins, 'The Economic Background to Berlin', *Geography*, 1962, pp. 92–95.

T. H. Elkins and E. M. Yates, 'Lower Berg, a Distinctive Region between Rhine and Ruhr', *Geography*, 1958, pp. 104–113.

T. H. Elkins and E. M. Yates, 'The South German Scarplands in the vicinity of Tübingen', *Geography*, 1963, pp. 65–82.

A. F. A. Mutton, *Central Europe*, 1961.

A. F. A. Mutton, 'Place-names and the History of Settlement in South-west Germany', *Geography*, 1938, pp. 113–119.

A. F. A. Mutton and A. E. Adams, 'Land Forms, Settlement and Land Utilisation in the Southern Allgäu', *Economic Geography*, 1939, pp. 169–178.

H. Niehaus, 'Agricultural Conditions and Regions in Germany', *Geographical Review*, 1933, pp. 23–47.

N. J. G. Pounds, *Divided Germany and Berlin*, 1962.

N. J. G. Pounds, *The Ruhr*, 1952.

N. J. G. Pounds, *Coal and Steel in Western Europe*, 1957.

N. J. G. Pounds, 'Lorraine and the Ruhr', *Economic Geography*, 1952, pp. 283–294.

K. Sinnhuber, *Germany, its Geography and Growth*, 1961.

K. Sinnhuber, 'Central Europe—Europe Centrale—Mitteleuropa: An Analysis of a Geographical Term', *Transactions and Papers*, *Institute of British Geographers*, 1954, pp. 15–39.

E. M. Yates, 'Development of the Rhine', *Transactions and Papers*, *Institute of British Geographers*, 32, 1963, pp. 65–82.

Diercke Weltatlas (Braunschweig).

The standard German Federal Republic topographic series is the 1:50,000, while the much older 1:25,000 series has been revised. Formerly, the standard topographic series was the 1:100,000, but this has now been discontinued. Maps for the Democratic Republic are at present impossible to obtain; it is necessary to refer back to pre-war sheets of the 1:25,000 or the old 1:100,000 series.

Switzerland

Switzerland is a federal republic, with Berne as its capital. The federation originated with the formation of the 'Everlasting League' in 1291, when the cantons around the lake of Lucerne (known to the Swiss as the *Vierwaldstättersee* or the lake of the Four Forest cantons) united against the Holy Roman Empire. Hence Switzerland claims to be the oldest democracy in Europe. The twenty-two cantons (Fig. 39) are combined in the Helvetic Confederation (CH signifies *Confœderatio Helvetica*). The seat of the federal government is in Berne each canton having a large measure of self government, whereby men over the age of twenty may vote by the referendum system or, occasionally, as in the cantons of Glarus,

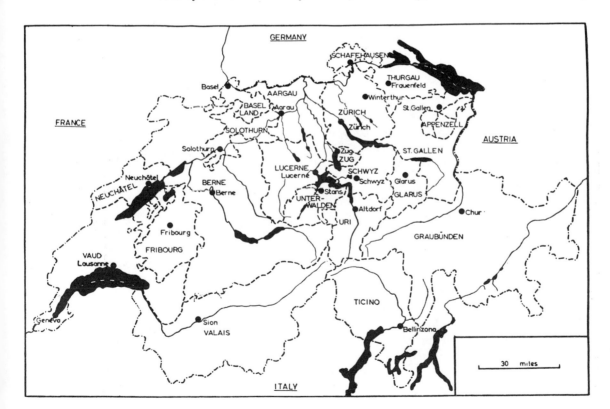

Fig 39 The Swiss cantons and canton capitals
(from the author's *Central Europe*, Longmans)

Appenzell and Unterwalden, by show of hands in the open air (the *Landsgemeinde*). The constitution dates from 1848, when Switzerland's neutrality was guaranteed by the other nation states of Europe. This condition of armed neutrality (every Swiss man over the age of twenty has the right to bear weapons) arises directly from the military importance of the state, located as it is on the cross roads of western Europe, controlling access to international road and railway routes over and through the central Alpine passes, particularly those of the St. Gotthard and Simplon. Communications between northern and central Europe focus on these historic highways leading southwards to Italy and the Mediterranean lands.

The fact that four official languages (German, French, Italian and Rhaeto-Romanic or Romontsch) are spoken in Switzerland is a reflection of the piecemeal growth of the federation, the Grisons (Graubünden) and Vaud not joining until 1803; Geneva, Valais and southern Ticino being added after the Treaty of Vienna in 1815. The application for membership of both Vorarlberg and Liechtenstein was refused after the First World War but the Duchy became part of the Swiss customs and postal union. The nucleus of the republic around the Lake of Lucerne is Catholic and German-speaking and Swiss German is spoken by all those cantons which were once part of Imperial Austria. These range from Basle in the north-west to Graubünden in the south-east, where the bishop of Chur was once a focal point of resistance to the Holy Roman Empire. Over 70% of the total population speaks a form of German dialect. In the west, as in the Geneva region, the southern Jura, the Neuchâtel district and the western part of Canton Valais, French prevails. On the southern slope of the Alps, in Canton Ticino, Italian is spoken. Rhaeto-Romanic, a Romance language derived from Italian, is preserved by the peasantry in the relatively remote valleys of Graubünden, where dual place names appear, notably in the Engadine.

The majority of the Swiss population belongs to the Swiss Reformed Church, a form of Protestantism which was adopted through the preaching of Calvin in Geneva and Zwingli in Zürich. The region around the lake of Lucerne is Roman Catholic and so are Ticino and most of Valais but Geneva and Neuchâtel are mostly Protestant. Many Protestant French refugees settled in the valleys of the Swiss Jura in the eighteenth century and others arrived from Alsace after Germany annexed that part of the Rhineland in 1871. The factory organization of both the Swiss watch and clock and the chemical industries owes a great deal to this stimulus.

Most well-educated Swiss speak at least two languages and some three or more, one of these often being English. As in the small countries of northern Europe, all with vital cultural and commercial contacts with the English-speaking world, this facility with languages other than the mother tongue is increasingly imperative. Switzerland has often been described as the 'playground of Europe' and the foreign tourist and winter sports industries are important sources of national revenue. By her constitution, Switzerland is prevented from being a member of the Common Market, with its political overtones, but she is one of the 'Outer Seven' or European Free Trade Association (EFTA).

Physical Environment

Switzerland has one of the hardest physical environments in western Europe, since the southern third lies in the central Alps and, in the north-west, the forested ranges of the Jura sever the Swiss Foreland from the Saône Basin and Rhine Rift Valley (Fig. 40). The average altitude of the Foreland is about 1,500 feet above sea level and, although a region of subdued relief compared with the long, parallel ranges of the Folded Jura and the dissected and glaciated massifs of the Alps, the Swiss Foreland is a region of broken surface features.

GEOLOGY AND STRUCTURE

The Helvetic Alps end eastwards along a line traceable from the Lake of Constance, following the upper Rhine to Chur and thence to the Septimer Pass on the Italian boundary. To the east of this line, the Alps of Graubünden are part of the Austrian Alpine structures. The Jura mountains are the outermost part of the Swiss alpine fold system. Between the two is the structural trough known as the Swiss Foreland where Tertiary

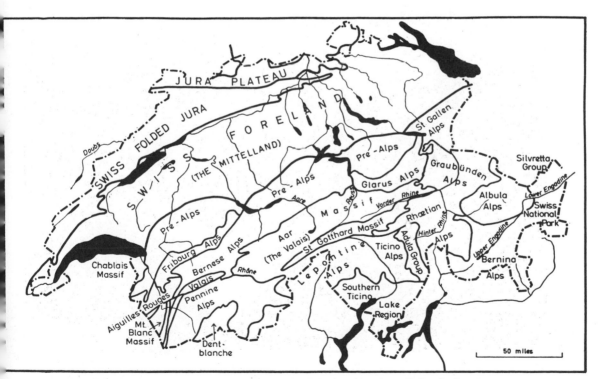

Fig 40 Chief structural regions of Switzerland and the Swiss Alps
(from the author's *Central Europe*, Longmans)

Molasse or sandstone and *Nagelfluh*, a conglomerate, occur but the surface features are mainly derived from glacial and post-glacial drift deposits, re-worked by river action.

The Swiss Alps are extremely complex. Geologically, the core of the mountain system consists of ancient crystalline massifs, such as that of the Aar and the St. Gotthard, though these do not coincide with the highest relief. Flanking these ranges to the north-west are the highly folded sedimentary rocks, known as the Helvetic *nappes*, where limestones are often exposed, as in the Toggenburg and the Calanda, opposite Chur (Plate 43). The outer or pre-Alps consist of highly folded Jurassic and Cretaceous rocks, as well as a Tertiary conglomerate known as *Flysch*. Along the Franco-Swiss-Italian boundaries a wide range of rocks is exposed, including metamorphic and crystalline formations in the Pennine and Bernina Alps. In the Swiss-Italian lake region younger Tertiary folds extend as east-west ranges which are part of the limestone Dinaric Alps.

In contrast with the resistant crystalline massifs against which the sedimentary rocks were intensely folded and overthrust, the Helvetic nappes have been piled up as a series of superincumbent beds. Since the Miocene-

Plate 43   Churfirsten and the Toggenburg in winter.
A panorama of eroded nappes in sedimentary rocks.

Oligocene folding, the resulting anticlines and monoclines have been fractured and heavily eroded and they form lines of rugged peaks, with the beds dipping steeply, as in the Säntis and the Churfirsten, the steep slopes of which rise from the northern shore of the Walensee. In contrast with the complexity of the Alpine folds, those of the Jura consist of simple alternations of anticlines and synclines, developed mainly on Jurassic and Cretaceous limestones. In the Foreland, Molasse is exposed in the dissected plateau of the Napf, between Berne and Lucerne, and also elsewhere, while the Nagelfluh forms conspicuous ridges on each side of the Lake of Zürich. Elsewhere, the Pleistocene and Recent drift mantle is complete.

SURFACE FEATURES The Alps show magnificent variety in their land forms. Not all peaks are horn-shaped, like the Matterhorn, or pyramidal, like the Jungfrau, but some are rounded, like Monte Rosa, while others are shaped like needles, as in the Engelhörner in the Bernese Oberland. The land forms have been accentuated by alpine glaciation. Vast snowfields and glaciers survive, as in the Aar massif, the Bernese Oberland and the Bernina Alps, but, with the milder winters of the present century, some valley glaciers, notably that of the Rhône and the lower Grindelwald, have retreated rapidly.

The youthfulness of the land forms derives largely from the effects of ice erosion, combined with frost shattering. Sharp ridges, known as *Gräte* or arêtes, strike off from mountain crests, as in the Gorner*grat* above Zermatt, and many summit ridges have been hollowed out below the *Gräte* to form glacial *cirques*. Some of these contain lakes, such as the Riffelsee below the Matterhorn. Many Alpine trenches, originally eroded after the Tertiary folding and uplift, were long occupied by valley glaciers and, above their level, lie the benches or shoulders in places covered by morainic debris, leaving a deep U-shaped valley form below. Subsequent erosion has led to the formation of spectacular ravines where side valleys join the main trench, as in the upper Rhône Valley, where the Val d'Anniviers enters. Waterfalls cascade over hanging valleys, like the Staubbach in the Lauterbrunnen Valley and the Giessbach Falls which tumble ceaselessly into the 'finger' lake of Brienz.

Alpine torrents bring down much débris, especially in spring, when they are swollen by melting snow and ice. Where the gradient suddenly changes, deltas have developed along lake shores, such as that of the Maggia at Locarno, the Lütschine, which divides the lakes of Thun and Brienz at Interlaken, and the Julier at Silvaplana in the Upper Engadine. Whereas the latest moraines may be seen alongside existing glaciers, the older moraines lie along and across many Alpine valleys, sometimes forming a bar across a lake, as across the Lake of Zürich at Rapperswil, and across that of Lugano between Melide and Bissone (Plate 44). Most Alpine valleys have an irregular and broken longitudinal profile, marking stages in the retreat of the piedmont glaciers. Long, straight stretches are interrupted by rock bars, where rapids or waterfalls may break the course of

Plate 44   Lake Lugano at Melide.
Here the road and railway follow the Würm moraine utilised by the causeway
spanning the lake.

the stream, as along the Aar at the Handeck Falls above Meiringen.

The relief reaches its maximum along the Italian boundary in the Pennine Alps, where Monte Rosa and the Matterhorn each exceeds 15,000 feet. The peaks of the Bernese Oberland, such as the Jungfrau, Mönch and Eiger, while lower (some 12,000 feet), are no less spectacular, with their permanent snow caps and glistening ice fields visible from Interlaken. The longest glacier, that of the Aletsch, extends from the ice desert of the Konkordiaplatz for over fifteen miles. Many smaller glaciers, such as those on the slopes of Piz Palü, like the Morteratsch and also the Rosegg near Pontresina, extend well below the summer snow line and are fringed by ridges of morainic débris. Their surfaces are riven by crevasses, covered in winter by snow.

The Jura ranges extend from south-west to north-east along the French border and rise to rather lower elevations than the pre-Alps. There is a marked accordance of erosion levels at about 4,000 feet and, because of the lower relief, glaciation was very restricted. Between the anticlinal limestone ridges, the synclinal longitudinal valleys have been eroded in a zig-zag pattern by streams which cut through the ridges by means of gorges, known as *cluses*. On the mountain sides, rounded valley heads have been eroded, known by the Celtic word *combes* (pp. 408–9 and Fig. 80).

The Swiss Foreland or Mittelland is 'plateau'-like only when compared with the bounding Alps and Jura ranges. Its dissected surface is derived from a wide variety of drift deposits rather than outcrops of solid rock, although these also occur over limited areas in the form of Nagelfluh and Molasse (p. 216). Long ridges are festooned across the Foreland as far as the foot of the Jura and these are the Riss and Würm terminal moraines. A number of former lake basins are floored by peat deposits, especially in the Neuchâtel and Biel regions. Streams have cut a series of river terraces into the fluvio-glacial gravels and deposits of loess occur locally.

DRAINAGE   The hydrography of the Alps focuses on the Aar-St. Gotthard massifs, from which streams drain northwards to the Aar, Reuss and Limmat (Linth) tributaries of the Rhine; eastwards to the Vorderrhein; southwards to the Ticino; and westwards to the upper Rhône, which rises in the Rhône glacier below the Furka Pass. The mid-Alpine furrow, formed by the upper trenches of the Rhône-Reuss-Rhine, is a striking feature of the relief map, as is the broad longitudinal valley of the upper Inn, with its chain of 'paternoster' lakes between the Maloja Pass and St. Moritz. Alpine rivers are torrential and their course is hardly less impressive across the Foreland, even though the piedmont lakes through which they flow serve as filters. Some of these streams, like the Aar and the Sarine, describe a series of incised meanders, providing the defensive sites of medieval Berne and Fribourg. At the foot of the Jura lie the long 'finger' lakes of Neuchâtel and Biel, but, apart from the Areuse, few major streams drain from these limestone ranges. Between the Lake of Constance and Basle, the swirling waters of the green-blue Rhine divide the Jura from the Black Forest, while the post-glacial diversion of the river is marked by the spectacular Rhine Falls at Schaffhausen, where the river is cutting back through Jurassic limestones.

CLIMATE   Switzerland has a central European continental type of climate, the winter cold being accentuated by the generally high altitude. It is therefore regarded as having a Mountain climate (Fig. 6). Precipitation varies widely, according to local factors; the observatory on the Säntis recording a mean maximum annual precipitation of 96 inches (2,400 mm.) but the upper Rhône Valley (Canton Valais), the Lake Neuchâtel region and the Lower Engadine, all 'rain-shadow' areas, receive an average of less than 25 inches (625 mm.) per annum. When the temperature falls below 0°C (32°F), precipitation occurs as snow (Fig. 41), blocking the high Alpine passes for several months and necessitating the use of snow ploughs to keep city streets and country roads open. Since high pressure prevails over the Alps during the winter, long sunny spells are usual, emphasizing the bright light and strong radiation experienced in the mountain resorts. In the Foreland and in some deep Alpine valleys, temperature inversion may occur, especially in the autumn when mist and fog may develop, especially where lake expanses have a chilling effect on

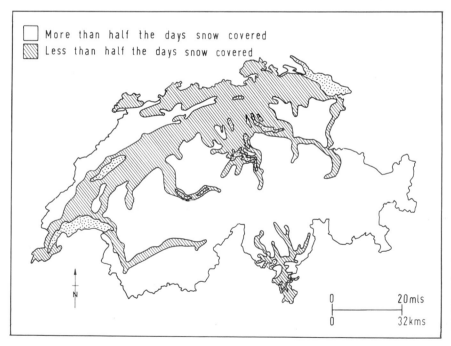

Fig 41   Average duration of snow cover January–March (1953–62).
(from the *Swiss National Atlas*)

the air above. In summer, temperatures in the *Mittelland* or Central Region are quite high (Zürich, 17·5°C, 63·5°F, July mean but, since this figure obscures the wide diurnal range, it must be noted that the day temperature is much higher). In the afternoon, storm clouds often pile up as masses of cumulus, so that thunderstorms may occur, giving sharp, heavy downpours of convectional rain. In general the relative humidity is lower than in Britain and fine, calm weather is much more common, making the winter cold more bearable.

In the mountains, temperatures fall with increase in altitude at the mean rate of 1°F for every 270 feet of ascent. Although winds are predominantly from the south-west or north-east, sudden changes of weather are associated with local winds, such as the warm, dry *Föhn*, heralded by cirrus clouds and frequently experienced in valleys trending north-south, which have a canalising effect on the wind, so that the Reuss Valley at Altdorf is particularly prone. The *Föhn* brings increased danger of avalanches in spring, through the sudden melting of snow, and it also increases the risk of fire in villages where the chalets are built largely of wood, for this katabatic wind has a desiccating effect. The *Maloja*, experienced in the upper Engadine, like the *Föhn* brings warm, dry air from the Mediterranean. In contrast, the *Bise* is a cold wind from the north, often experienced over lakes such as Geneva, bringing ice particles in its train in winter.

VEGETATION   In view of centuries of clearance of the original woodland for settlement and cultivation, very little 'natural' vegetation remains, except in the Swiss National Park in south-east Graubünden, where it is deliberately preserved. Today, about 25% of the total area is forested and the timber is systematically replanted when felled, though Switzerland is an importer, not only of hardwoods but also of cheaper softwood from Germany, Austria and Finland, including Christmas trees from thinnings in the Black Forest.

Whereas in the Mittelland fine stands of beech occur on the steep limestone and sandstone slopes (Napf Plateau), it is in the Jura where most reserves of mixed woodland are preserved, beech yielding to spruce and silver fir, intermingled with deciduous larch on the higher slopes. In southern Ticino, with its sheltered aspect and mild winters, the gentle slopes are mantled with splendid stands of walnut, beech and sweet chestnut.

In the High Alps, the zoning of vegetation according to increase in altitude is very pronounced. Above the valley floor, with its pattern of meadow and strip cultivation, the forest extends to about 5,000 feet (1,530 m.) on the northern slopes but rises higher on the south-facing ones. The finest stands of coniferous timber are on the northern aspects, longest in shadow, and such a slope is known as the *ubac* or *Schattenseite*; whereas that with the southern aspect is known as the *adret* or *Sonnenseite*; it is partly cleared for mountain pasture and terrace cultivation. The Lower Engadine and the Vorderrhein Valley, trending west-east, are clear examples. Above the tree-line are the alpine summer pastures or *Alpen*, forming unenclosed rough grazing covered by snow in winter. These grasslands contain a profusion of flowering perennials, including a variety of blue campanulas, Alpine pinks, gentians and, poisonous to cattle, the pale autumn crocus. This zone gives way to scree and bare rock before the permanent snow-line is reached. It is here that the Alpine flora are seen to perfection, especially the saxifrages, rock roses, arnica and the purple spring anemone; while the greyish-white edelweiss and the silver thistle are becoming increasingly rare. The dwarf Alpine rhododendron has a limited distribution, flourishing on acidic soils. Alpine flowers, along with mountain fauna, such as the mountain goat, the marmot and the wild deer, as well as the golden eagle, exist in their natural state in the Swiss National Park. In the Valais, the Alpine garden commemorating the Swedish botanist, Linnaeus, has been laid out at Bourg St. Pierre.

SOILS   A soil map of Switzerland shows a mosaic pattern on account of the wide range of parent rocks from which the local types are weathered, especially in the Alps and Jura, whereas, in the Mittelland, the soils are largely transported and derived from drift deposits. In the Alps, most are of the grey, leached, podsol type, best retained under forest, except where drift has filled in the valley floor. In the Jura, a rendzina type of dark brown soil is developed on the limestones and favours beechwood. In the Mittelland, rewarding soils are not widespread, since many are derived from cold, glacial clays and are poor in humus. Peat soils repay cultivation when drained but the best are those derived from fluvio-glacial gravels and from the few areas of loam soils associated with wind-borne loess. Many parts of the Alps consist of sheer rock faces with scree at the foot and here there is no soil development. The summit of the Flüela Pass, at 7,737 feet (2,809 m.), is such a region. In some Alpine valleys, where flat land is almost non-existent, artificial terraces have been laboriously built up to retain the soil. Many of these are no longer used for cultivation and have reverted to grass; they may be seen near the limit of crop cultivation (about 4,500 feet or 1,770 m.) in the Engadine near Samedan and also, at lower levels, in Canton Ticino, where they are used for viticulture.

Population
Distribution   A map showing the distribution of population (Fig. 42) sums up the response of man to the exacting Swiss environment. Out of a total population of five and a half million, three-quarters lives in the Mittelland, as it has always done, but the proportion is increasing, as is the number of people living in towns rather than in the rural areas, closely settled though these regions also are. The most prosperous and largest farms are in the Mittelland, as well as a number of small-scale industries, originally drawing on local labour for which work could not be found on the farms. Not only have people left the Alpine valleys and the Jura region for the more

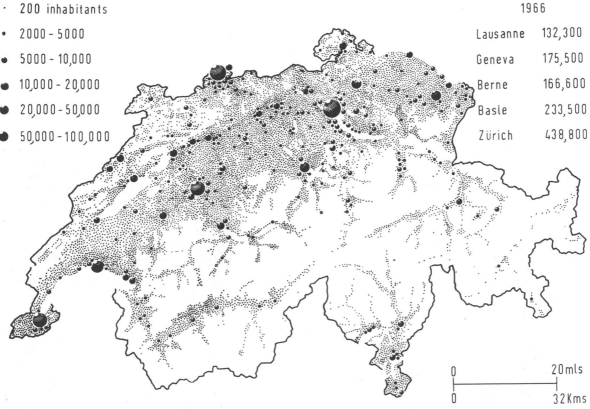

		1966
·	200 inhabitants	
•	2000 – 5000	Lausanne 132,300
◖	5000 – 10,000	Geneva 175,500
◖	10,000 – 20,000	Berne 166,600
●	20,000 – 50,000	Basle 233,500
●	50,000 – 100,000	Zürich 438,800

0
20 mls
0
32 Kms

Fig 42 Distribution of population
(from inset maps by H. Boesch, *Die Industrien der Schweiz*)

rewarding life of the Mittelland but an ever growing number of foreign workers have come to seek employment, usually as temporary immigrants, mainly from impoverished southern Italy and Sicily but also from other over-populated and underdeveloped Mediterranean lands. Switzerland has also had her quota of refugees who fled a generation ago from Germany, and more recently from communist eastern Europe.

Compared with the cities of heavily industrialized Britain, Belgium and the German Federal Republic, Swiss cities are small but picturesque and of great historic and architectural interest, for they have been spared the ravages of modern warfare and extensive demolition and re-building. The largest and most rapidly growing city is Zürich (Plate 45), the boundaries of which were fixed in 1934, so that the town itself has a declining population of under half a million. Greater Zürich, however, including the new towns which have grown up around original village nuclei such as Dübendorf, Kloten, and Kilchberg along the lake shore, now totals over half a million. Zürich is the commercial capital of Switzerland, with its stock exchange, its banks and insurance offices, and its wide range of small-scale manufacturing industry, luxury stores and shops, especially

Plate 45   The city of Zürich from the air.
The view is southwards over the forested ridges which hem Zürich in, the Limmat Valley and the Lake of Zürich towards the distant panorama of the Alps.

along the world-famous *Bahnhofstrasse*, as well as in the historic town or *Altstadt* and along the *Limmatquai*. Basle, at the present head of navigation on the Rhine and a frontier railway terminus, has long been the second city of Switzerland, with a total population of about a quarter of a million. Like Zürich, it is a major centre of commerce and transport, as well as of a number of light industries especially engineering, textiles and chemicals. The Bank for International Settlements is here.

The increasingly cosmopolitan city of Geneva, with about 175,000

Plate 46   The river port of Basle.
At the limit of barge navigation on the Rhine, the view shows harbour installations and storage facilities for oil, grain and coal.

inhabitants, has many functions. It is the largest city of French-speaking Switzerland, a business centre for the watch, jewellery and optical industries, as well as a centre of printing and publishing. Its international significance is derived from its frequent rôle as a world conference centre and as the European headquarters of the United Nations Organization, the International Red Cross Organization, the International Labour Office and the World Health Organization, with their palatial modern buildings set in parks along the lake shore.

Berne, with rather fewer inhabitants than Geneva, is one of the smallest but most attractive European capitals; its arcaded, medieval streets running the length of the peninsula encircled by the Aar. It has some industries in the newer part of the town, such as textiles, book printing and publishing. It is the headquarters of the World Postal Union and the International Telecommunications Union. Smaller towns are famous as centres of specialised industry, such as Neuchâtel, La Chaux-de-Fonds and Le Locle, with their clock and watch factories; while Yverdon has factories for the production of photographic equipment and for typewriters. Some Alpine centres have come to flourish as tourist resorts, ranging from medieval Lucerne, easily accessible to lake and mountain scenery, and Interlaken, both of which cater especially for English visitors, to Lugano and Locarno, with their sheltered southern aspect. At Zermatt, the centenary of the first and tragic ascent of the Matterhorn by Edward Whymper and his party was commemorated in 1966. International winter sports resorts, like St. Moritz with its Cresta run and luxury hotels, and Davos, with its annual ice-skating championships and its ski-lifts, attract the wealthy and athletic. Fortunately, the high mountain health resorts of which Davos is one together with Arosa, Leysin, and Sierre Montana

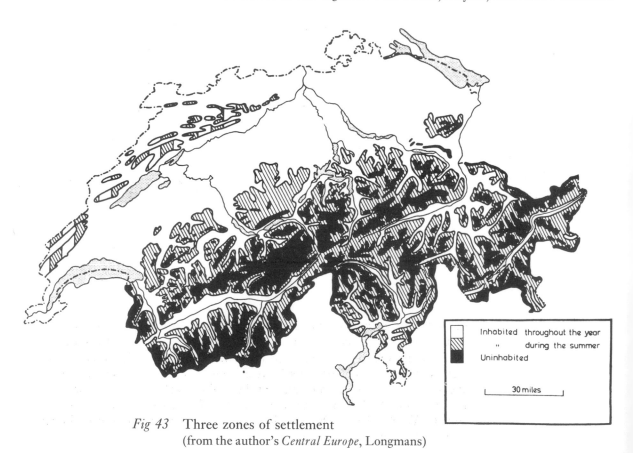

Fig 43 Three zones of settlement
(from the author's *Central Europe*, Longmans)

(Valais), need to cater decreasingly for sufferers from lung and chest complaints but the clear, pure air of the Alps remains an invigorating attraction to all comers.

Extreme winter cold, combined with prolonged snow-cover, prevents the high Alpine settlements from being occupied all the year (Fig. 43). In consequence, part of the peasant population, along with small herds of dairy cattle, store cattle and occasionally sheep and goats (as in the Engadine), migrate seasonally from the valley farm, where the stock are stall fed on hay all the winter, to the spring pastures or *Maiensäss* (mayen). At the height of summer, the alpine rough grazing is used, the herds following the retreating snowline, often along paths through the forest. In autumn, the reverse process takes place but it also involves the cutting and storage of the hay crop. This is gathered from incredibly steep slopes and stored in wooden huts or *mazots*, when not transported by horse-drawn cart or modern tractor to be stored in the hay loft under the roof of the chalet. This process is known as *transhumance* in French-speaking Switzerland and as the *Sömmerung* in the German part. There are, nevertheless, permanently inhabited villages and hamlets at the remarkable height of over 6,000 feet (1,970 m.) in various widely separated parts of the Alps, as at Juf–Avers near the Splügen Pass, where peat is dug and stored for winter fuel; Cresta, above St. Moritz; Findelen, above Zermatt, surrounded by patchwork fields of rye and potatoes, like Chandolin in the Val d'Anniviers (Plate 47). These high-level settlements enjoy high rates of insolation but life is very exacting and, in the Val d'Anniviers, some peasants augment their meagre income by migrating to the Rhône valley in early autumn for the grape harvest gathered in their vineyards around Sierre (Figs. 44 and 45).

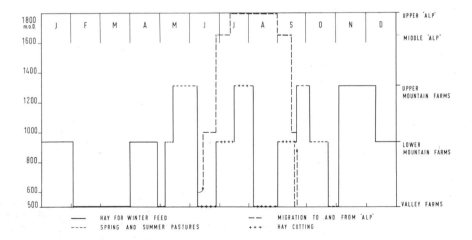

Fig. 44   Seasonal migration in the Valais Alps
(from E. Egli, *Die Schweiz*)

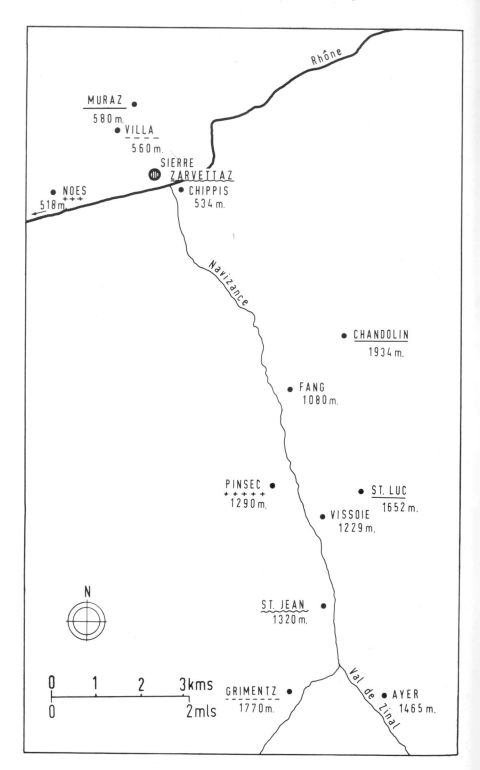

Plate 47 Chandolin, Val d'Anniviers (6,336 ft.), in winter.
This is one of the highest permanently occupied villages in the Alps.

Fig 45 Seasonal migration from Alpine villages in the Val d'Anniviers to 'vineyard'
villages of the Rhône Valley in canton Valais.
Seasonal migration is between villages shown with similar underlines.
(from E. Egli, *Die Schweiz*)

Economic Development

'The harder the environment, the greater the stimulus' to economic effort is a concept which is very appropriate to Switzerland. Nearly one quarter of the total area is unproductive and in the Alps and Jura mountains the steep slopes are frequently retained under forest. On account of the rather short growing season, the rainy summers and generally poor soils, together with the ability to import foodstuffs—especially bread cereals—pasture land predominates over arable to an increasing degree. High-value dairy produce, especially cheese, processed milk and chocolate, are major exports. Highly deficient in mineral ores, as well as in coal and oil, Switzerland has to import a wide range of raw materials for manufacture. The cheapest source of motive power, used by railways, most factories and by the domestic consumer, is hydro-electricity, generated first in the Alps, then in the Jura and along the upper Rhine between Basle and Eglisau. Yet Switzerland is increasingly short of electricity, especially in summer, when stream flow is reduced, and the state is constantly concerned with the development of new sites, especially in the Valais and Graubünden, and with capital investment in installations beyond the Swiss borders, as in the upper Adige Valley in Italy, and in the Austrian Alps (Vorarlberg especially).

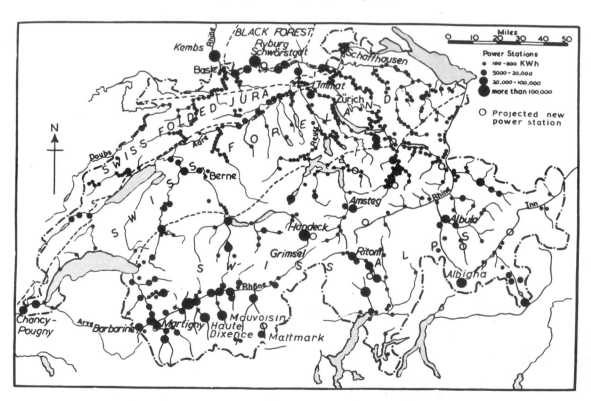

Fig. 46   Hydro-electric power development in Switzerland
(from the author's *Central Europe*, Longmans)

Plate 48 Albigna Barrage in the Bernina Alps.
It is situated near the Italian boundary above the Val Bregaglia.

AGRICULTURE
AND FORESTRY

A country of peasant farmers, Switzerland's average holdings are only about 14 acres (5½ h.) and, although stock farming predominates, the land is farmed very intensively. Traditional methods prevail in the mountain regions, where the difficulty of the terrain, lack of capital, and the tiny, uneconomic holdings, still often cultivated on the strip system, make mechanisation virtually impossible. Farms are usually worked as family units, and, with the growing exodus of young folk, some machinery is being introduced, especially for cutting the vital hay crop, a motor mower having been developed to replace the traditional scythe. Milk is sometimes sent by buried plastic pipe-line from the *Alp* to the creamery or cheese factory in the valley below.

In the Alps, the length of the growing season sets a limit to the range of

K

subsistence crops which may be successfully cultivated and these are mainly rye and potatoes, with maize and tobacco appearing in southern Ticino. In the upper Rhône Valley, where the summers are hot and dry, irrigation makes possible the cultivation of strawberries and tomatoes for city markets, as well as the apricot and the peach, all of which have to compete with cheaper produce from Italy. On the suntrap terraces which rib the northern shore of the Lake of Geneva and also the western shores of lakes Neuchâtel and Biel, vineyards reign supreme, and they also appear in southern Ticino.

In the Mittelland, stock farming predominates but here sown pastures are widespread. The lush meadows, with their wealth of flowers, are as much valued by the farmer as fields of wheat and it is forbidden to walk through them. In the Emmental, near Fribourg, and in the Sarine (Saane) Valley, near Gruyères, famous types of cheese are produced, partly for export. Much of the milk finds its daily market in the cities and resorts but some is processed and used in the manufacture of chocolate in all its rich variety, in such centres as Kilchberg near Zürich, Vevey, Neuchâtel and Berne.

In the Jura, horse rearing as well as cattle farming are important and there is some seasonal migration of dairy cattle to the upland pastures, a Gruyère type of cheese being produced. As in the Alps, one-quarter of the land area is forested and some land is taken up by lime quarries for the expanding cement industry. Soft-wood timber is the traditional building material of the Swiss chalet and wood is also still used as fuel in rural areas; neat stacks of sawn logs often being stored under the wooden balcony of the farm building.

MINING AND INDUSTRY

Apart from small local deposits of iron ore at Frick in the Jura and also at Gonzen, near Sargans, salt near the Rhine at Rheinfelden and at Bex (Canton Vaud), Switzerland depends on imported minerals, including coal, coke and oil, as well as bauxite for the aluminium industry. Basle handles most of these imports through the river docks on the Rhine but in future the pipe line linking the port of Marseilles (Lavéra refineries) with Strasbourg will also have a branch line to Basle and Olten. A second pipe line brings crude oil from the Italian port of Savona to the refinery at Aigle (Valais). Bauxite is brought by railway up the Rhône Valley from southern France (Var) to the reduction plant at Chippis (Sierre) in Canton Valais, where high voltage electricity is generated at the hydro-electric power station at the site. The resulting alumina is processed at Neuhausen, at the Rhine Falls, and there are finishing plants at Lausanne.

During the last hundred years, Switzerland has expanded her manufacturing production very considerably, so that she is now one of the most industrialized of the smaller countries of the world. What often began as domestic industries and as skilled crafts has expanded into small-scale factory production with plants dispersed through the Mittelland and Jura and occasionally located in Alpine valleys such as the Linthtal in Glarus, especially where directly dependent on hydro-electric power, as with the aluminium and electro-chemical industries. Since industry has never been geared to steam power, as on the coalfields of Britain and north-west Europe, it is not concentrated into large cities, except in Greater Zürich; there over 80,000 workers are employed in manufacturing out of a total population of over half a million.

Swiss industries are concerned mostly with the processing of raw materials, semi-manufactured steel and other metals, imported at high cost over long distances, usually by rail. Industries processing steel are mainly located in Zürich (Escher Wyss—turbo-generators, pumps, etc.), Winterthur (Sulzer—diesel motors, etc.), Baden (Brown Boveri—electric equipment), Schaffhausen (Fischer—machinery and equipment), Brugg (steel cables) and Biel (rolling stock). Light engineering is represented in Oerlikon, a suburb of Zürich, where machine tools and electric equipment are produced, and also in Basle (textile and other machinery). Neuhausen has a plant by the Rhine Falls now used for the rolling of

Plate 49 Baden, Swiss Jura.
This small town lies at the north-eastern foot of the forested Jura ranges, in the lower Limmat Valley, and has the important Brown Boveri electrical engineering plant.

aluminium sheets and no longer for the reduction of bauxite.

Textile manufacturing and textile machinery are typical of St. Gallen and the clothing industry of Berne. The long-established Bally shoe factory is outside Olten at Schönewerd and the firm of Hanro is on the outskirts of the ancient little town of Liestal, near Basle; here a large proportion of Italian women are employed.

The Swiss chemical industry is partly concerned with the electro-chemical production of artificial fertilizers, etc., but mainly with dye-stuffs, used in Basle in the finishing of nylon material and other synthetic fibres. Firms such as Geigy, Ciba, Sandoz and La Roche, all located in Basle, are known internationally for the production of a wide range of pharmaceutical products because of their world-wide export trade and they also have factories in south-east England.

The rise of the clock, watch and jewellery industry, as well as of photographic apparatus and equipment in the small towns of the Jura has already been noted (p. 252–3). Neuchâtel is one of the main business centres of these industries but production is carried out in a number of townships, originally accessible to water power and wood for clock cases, and also to semi-precious stones such as garnets. Le Locle is the factory town of Zénith, La Chaux-de-Fonds of Tissot, St. Imier of Longines; while, at Yverdon, Hermes typewriters are produced, as well as Bolex cameras and projectors by the firm of Paillard.

The production of foodstuffs, while widespread, is especially associated with centres of cheese processing (Fribourg) and chocolate production (Vevey, Neuchâtel, Berne and Kilchberg—near Zürich), as discussed on p. 258–9. These high priced commodities of little bulk are exported to a world market but, in return, cheaper Dutch cheese may appear in Swiss shops. The recent expansion of packaged and dehydrated foodstuffs is represented by the products of old-established firms such as Maggi, at Kempthal near Zürich, and by Knorr, near Schaffhausen.

TRADE AND TRANSPORT

Switzerland's high standard of living results largely from her extensive foreign trade in products of high quality and value, as have been described above. Her stable currency, her keen business tradition, especially in German-speaking Switzerland, and her reputation for fine workmanship often achieved by long hours of concentration on most exacting tasks, have enabled her to sustain her position not only in competition with the Common Market group, Great Britain and the U.S.A., but also as a member of the E.F.T.A. Her command of the central Alpine passes, especially those pierced by the St. Gotthard and Simplon tunnels has facilitated transit trade (Fig. 47) between Central Europe and Italy. The modern roads utilizing these passes, as well as the St. Bernard with its recently opened road tunnel, also carry an increasing amount of traffic each year. Basle functions as a major transport node, in view of its frontier position at the head of Rhine navigation where freight converges, whether borne by rail from France or Germany, by river barge from the

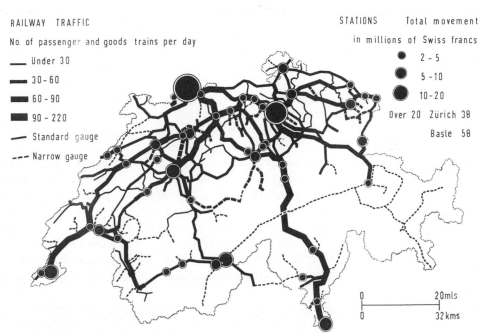

RAILWAY TRAFFIC

No. of passenger and goods trains per day

—— Under 30

▬ 30 - 60

▬ 60 - 90

▬ 90 - 220

—— Standard gauge

--- Narrow gauge

STATIONS   Total movement

in millions of Swiss francs

● 2 - 5

● 5 - 10

● 10 - 20

Over 20   Zürich 38

Basle 58

0   20mls
0   32kms

Fig 47   Rail traffic in Switzerland
(based on inset map by H. Boesch, *Die Industrie der Schweiz*)

Netherlands and Germany, by German *Autobahn*, or by air. Similarly Zürich handles a great deal of freight through its large marshalling yards along the lower Limmat; while its airport at Kloten, like that at Geneva, has been adapted to the 'jet' age. New national roads are under construction across the Mittelland, designed to speed up internal movement and Zürich has its new 'Europa' bridge. In recent years, Switzerland has developed several electric express train services which connect the chief cities, apart from the international luxury express trains, known as *Trans-Europa* Expresses.

Regional Geography	The three physical regions of Switzerland have already been clearly defined (p. 243–5) and it only remains to relate the basic features to the human geography. Further details, especially of the Alps, may be studied by reference to the official Swiss geological and topographic maps, which are some of the finest in the world.
THE SWISS ALPS	The complex structural features of the Alps, overridden as they generally are by features resulting from the Pleistocene glaciation, have little bearing on their human geography. This is a region of steep slopes, high altitude and poor or non-existent soils. It is, moreover, a region of difficulty on account of the harsh winters, with prolonged frost and heavy snowfall,

often barring access to villages by road, though the railways operate all the year at high cost with the aid of rock tunnels and with snow ploughs to keep the lines clear. Permanent settlement is, therefore, mainly in the more accessible valleys, though there are some remarkable examples of villages over 6,000 ft. (1,970 m.) high, as in Valais and the Upper Engadine (p. 252–3). Life in the Alps remains traditional with an incomparably lower living standard than in the cities of the Mittelland. It is concerned with stock farming on what are virtually small holdings, worked by the farmer and his family. Some subsistence crops, like rye, barley and potatoes, are also grown, usually in long, narrow strips on sunny terraces, as in the Lower Egadine around villages such as Guarda and Sent (Plate 50), and in irregular patches high above the valley gorge, as in the Val d'Anniviers. Most peasants also cultivate a garden plot, for the production of summer vegetables, fruit and salad crops.

The development of hydro-electric power in remote Alpine sites, first to serve railways such as the Gotthard, and later local industries, as at Visp and Chippis-Sierre, and now the cities and manufacturing centres

Plate 50   The Lower Engadine trench of the Inn River.
Terrace settlements, such as Guarda at 4,000 feet, are on the sunny, south-facing slope.

of the Mittelland, has done a little to check rural depopulation, but more industries are needed in Alpine valleys, especially in Graubünden and Valais. Huge modern power developments have taken place, first near the Grimsel Pass, where two great dams impound a lake seven miles long below the Aar Glacier. In Valais, La Grande Dixence project includes the highest dam in the world (934 feet or 285 m.) across the Dix and miles of underground rock tunnels lead water from high level glaciers to the vast reservoir behind the dam. A similar barrage has now been completed above Mauvoisin, in the adjacent Val de Bagnes.

Tourism has, for the past century, brought seasonal foreign visitors to the Alps; some villages, like Zermatt, being but a collection of wooden chalets before the 'golden age of mountaineering' pioneered by the Swiss Alpine Club a century ago. St. Moritz has long been a resort of international renown, as are Pontresina and Interlaken in a less ostentatious way. There are also the health resorts where medicinal springs occur, and these bring their quota of Swiss and other visitors who come to 'take the cure' at Scuols-Tarasp in the Engadine and at Bad Ragaz, near Sargans in Graubünden. A major asset in terms of unique and unspoilt scenery is the Swiss National Park, accessible to motor traffic only *via* the Ofen Pass, between Zernez in the Engadine and the Adige Valley in Italy.

THE JURA In north-west Switzerland, the long fold ranges of the Jura die out against the plateau Jura which extend from the Rhine Falls at Schaffhausen to the vicinity of Basle. The Jura mountains form a barrier to movement between the Saône Basin and the Swiss Mittelland, overcome by the building of a series of long tunnels along the line from Basle to Olten and from Delémont to Biel. The landscape contrasts in the Jura are between the dark forested slopes and the long valley floors, with their meadow grazing and parallel strips of arable. Mention has already been made (p. 251–2, 258–60) of the modern industrial products of the Jura townships, and these masterpieces of Swiss craftsmanship may be seen displayed in the jewellers' shops of the world's great cities.

THE MITTELLAND This is the heartland of Switzerland. Its landscapes are varied and picturesque but seem subdued when compared with the panorama of the Alps which can be seen on a clear day from the terrace of the *Bundeshaus* in Berne, or when set against the dark green forest ridges of the Jura. This is the region where the 'typical' Swiss wooden chalet abounds, usually set amidst meadow grasses, used for spring and summer grazing by the ubiquitous Swiss brown cow, and often interspersed with fruit trees, especially apple, cherry, pear and plum. Here farming is prosperous and progressive; the traditional strip cultivation is fast disappearing with increasing mechanization. The density of rural settlement is high; a figure which is increased by the growing number of factories which have spread over the region, mainly concerned with light industry, such as shoe manufacture (Bally), porcelain (Langenthal), and food processing (Maggi and Knorr).

Plate 51   The Swiss Mittelland.
The view shows regular field patterns and the meanders of the Aare, with the forested ranges of the Jura in the distance.

The Mittelland is a region of historic and picturesque cities, many of which date from the Middle Ages, when they were incorporated in the Holy Roman Empire. Some, like Basle, Augst, Avenches, Winterthur and Zürich are of Roman origin. Berne has served as the federal capital since 1848 but it originated like Fribourg in the twelfth century. Its medieval streets, with their fountains and luxury shops under arcades ornamented with colourful window boxes, make it unique as a capital city. St. Gallen retains its early monastic nucleus; Bremgarten its defensive walls. Both Basle and Zürich have preserved a number of buildings of Renaissance date, amidst the rising blocks of steel and concrete. In Zürich, as in Basle, the universities are partly accommodated in ultra-modern buildings, as are the hospitals. In the suburbs, once outlying villages, new skyscraper blocks of flats are rising, designed to cope with the great shortage of living accommodation.

CONCLUSION   Switzerland, spared armed combat since her neutrality was guaranteed after the Napoleonic Wars, has today achieved the highest standard of living in Europe. This remarkable achievement is the outcome of a long tradition of thrift, business acumen and a legacy of skilled craftsmanship, whereby scant internal resources are made to yield the maximum profit. High average incomes in the cities must be set against high prices for consumer goods and services. There is a growing increase in the shortage of unskilled, semi-skilled and skilled labour, the gap being filled largely by Italian and other south European immigrants.

The attraction of the New World, which led to the Swiss development of dairy farming in Wisconsin, U.S.A., has its counterpart today in the highly skilled engineers and technicians who emigrate to work in the industries of southern California, especially in aircraft and electronic plants, as well as in those of an older generation who designed the Golden Gate bridge at San Francisco, the Washington and, recently, the Verrazano-Narrows bridge in New York, linking Brooklyn with Staten Island. Swiss skill, precision and reliability are thus at a premium throughout the world.

FURTHER READING   E. H. Carrier, *Water and Grass*, 1932.

E. Egli, *Swiss Life and Customs* (transl.), 1949.

J. Früh, *Geographie der Schweiz*, 3 vols., also in French, 1930–1945.

H. Gutersohn, *Geographie der Schweiz*, Vol. I, *Jura*, 1958; Vol. II, Part I, *Alps*, 1961.

A. F. A. Mutton, *Central Europe*, 2nd ed., 1967.

Schweizer Heimatbücher. A series of monographs on aspects of Switzerland, with pictures and some maps and diagrams, in progress.

Schweizerische Alpenposten. Guides with maps and pictures published by the Swiss Postal Service.

A. Siegfried, *Switzerland* (Transl.), 1950.

Maps, Relief Models and Atlases

H. Boesch, *Die Industrie der Schweiz*, 1954.

Geotechnische Karte der Schweiz, 1:200,000, 4 sheets, 1934.

Kümmerly and Frey: *Relief Model*, 1:500,000, 1962.

Swiss National Atlas, in progress.

Topographic maps (Landeskarte), 1:50,000 and 1:25,000 (*Mittelland* only), in progress.

Uebersichtskarte der Schweiz, 1:500,000, 1965.

Vegetationskarte der Schweiz, 1:200,000, 1949.

Zürich, Bild- und Stadtplan, 1963.

The Benelux Countries

The Physical Environment

The three smallest countries of North-West Europe lie in a central position within the area discussed in this book. It is not possible to assign them to one single natural region of the continent of Europe but the lower basin of the Meuse (Maas to the Dutch) and the delta reaches of the Rhine provide an initial framework.

Taken together, the three countries cover a surface area of only some 26,000 square miles (67,000 sq. km.), less than that of Scotland. The most northerly parts of the Netherlands are in the same latitude as Hull and the southern tip of the Grand Duchy of Luxembourg is on the parallel of Le Havre. The longer axis is thus less than 300 miles from north to south whilst the greatest east-west distance is under 200 miles. By road, it is possible to cross the widest part of Belgium in a half-day.

This area has for long been a meeting point of North-West Europe; trade routes from the Baltic, the North European Plain, the North Sea and the French lowlands all cross here. To the historian this area includes the 'cockpit' of Europe and the soil of all three countries has been trampled by the armies of many an alien country.

The grouping of the three countries is a product of the twentieth century. The Benelux Customs Union was established in 1947 and by it customs duties were to be abolished within the union and uniform duties levied on goods imported from without. It was the extension of an older customs alliance, that of the Belgium Luxembourg Economic Union which was established in 1922 and preceded the larger economic groupings of the European Coal and Steel Community and the European Economic Community.

However, the three countries have been separate nations for a comparatively short period. Holland and Belgium have pursued different courses since 1609, when the seven northern provinces (Holland, Zeeland, Utrecht, Groningen, etc.) emerged as the free United Provinces. Prior to that, these lands formed in turn part of the 'middle kingdom' between the lands later to become France and Germany, a section of the Burgundian realm and the Spanish Netherlands.

Earlier, this was a Roman frontier region but during the fourth and fifth centuries two separate linguistic areas emerged peopled by races of different origin. These were Frankish to the south and Germanic to the north, separated by the Flanders and Brabant forests. During succeeding centuries these very forests were to become prosperous areas, and the Flanders area in the fourteenth century was probably one of the most urbanised areas of Europe. The linguistic boundary still follows a course through this area but it is noteworthy that although some of the rivalries of later centuries were based on religious differences neither this nor language differences were entirely responsible for the separation of the northern and southern provinces in the early seventeenth century. Political independence of the Dutch states and their greater commercial prosperity contrasted with the provinces of the south, which made only slow economic progress in the eighteenth century. Thus the impact of the Industrial Revolution and the growth of coalfield-based-industries during the nineteenth century was all the more marked in the Walloon region of Belgium.

Although the Netherlands, based on the core of the United Provinces, came into a form of independent existence in the early seventeenth century, the national boundaries and the establishment of three distinct states as we know them date only from 1831. At this date Belgium emerged as an independent neutral state and the Grand Duchy of Luxembourg assumed the shape it now has. This latter country took on a very much reduced size from its forbears; the province of Luxembourg which was then transferred to Belgium is larger than the Grand Duchy. This little land-locked country has an area of only some 1,000 square miles (2,580 sq. kms.) and a population of one-third of a million.

All three countries have always filled the rôles of 'buffer states' in the European balance of power, and especially between France and Germany; this has been particularly true of Luxembourg. In the last war the initial German advance followed the natural route of the Moselle Valley and across the Bon Pays; the final German offensive in 1944 in the Ardennes left a number of relics of war, as in the little Luxembourg towns of Wiltz and Clervaux and around the besieged Belgian town of Bastogne.

The chief linguistic boundary in Benelux is that across Belgium, between the French-speaking Walloons to the south and the Flemish population to the north. The official language in the Flemish areas is standard Dutch but there are various dialect differences within Flemish Belgium and in the Netherlands. The boundary in the east between Dutch or French and German speech is most clearly marked in Belgium; the Luxembourg tongue, *Letzeburgesch*, is a Germanic one. The largest section of Belgium in which German is spoken is the Eupen-Malmédy area which was regained from Germany in 1919.

GEOLOGY AND STRUCTURE

Within the Benelux countries the geological record is nearly continuous since Cambrian times. The record is however particularly comprehensive for some geological eras; notably the Devonian and Carboniferous of the Ardennes and Sambre-Meuse Valley; the Eocene of Brabant and the Flanders Plain, and the Pliocene, Pleistocene and Holocene of the Netherlands. Mesozoic strata are generally covered by later rocks but give rise to important outcrops in Belgian Lorraine and the south of Luxembourg.

A three-fold pattern is to be seen in the structural forms of Benelux. The oldest rocks, of the Hercynian block of the Ardennes, have been much folded and faulted (Fig. 48) and the younger strata lie nearly horizontally against or even partly over them to the north in the Netherlands basin of accumulation, and dip gently southwards in Lorraine, which marks the north-eastern limit of the Paris Basin.

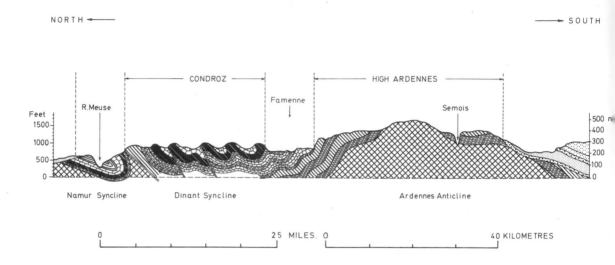

Fig 48   Cross-Section of the Ardennes

Rock types are extremely varied, ranging from slates and quartzites of the Cambrian to unconsolidated river alluvium of Recent times. The Devonian, which outcrops over an extensive area, includes hard siliceous rocks, although limestone bands are locally important. The Carboniferous also includes limestones but the sequence is chiefly of sandstones, shales and Coal Measures. The seams are frequently much distorted by faults and folds, whilst their thinness (generally less than 3 feet) and their shattered nature makes some suitable only for the making of briquettes. The workable seams are deeper in the western basin of the coalfield 'furrow' and also in the Campine field than in the Liège or eastern basin; depths of more than 4,200 feet (1,300 m.) being recorded in the Mons district. The Campine field is overlain by some 2,000 to 2,600 feet (600 to 800 m.) of younger rocks, notably Cretaceous and Tertiary in age, which provide difficulties for boring as there is a high water table and content.

Sandstones, marls and limestones of Jurassic age are represented by surface outcrops in Lorraine, and they are also encountered in borings in the eastern Netherlands. Cretaceous rocks include sandstones and marls, with characteristic limestones in the Hesbaye, Borinage and South Limbourg areas. Older rocks appear as inliers within these areas, and also in the Brabant Plateau where the main surface rocks are of Tertiary age.

Deposits of the most recent periods of the geological column can be divided into the following groups:

a   Those of marine deposition, such as the young sea clays of the Netherlands, of post-Roman date and characterising the delta region of Zeeland.

b   Deposits of fluvial type, such as sands and clays of the river floodplains, sands and gravels of river terraces.

c   Wind-blown deposits such as limon, and the dunes of the Netherlands and Belgian coasts.

d   Varied deposits, ranging from clays (till) of the ground moraine to sands and gravels of the outwash fans associated with the Riss ice-sheet in the eastern Netherlands.

e   Peat, in hollows formerly occupied by lakes.

SURFACE FEATURES   The configuration of the Benelux lands can best be appreciated by considering the major physical divisions of the countries taken together.

Within the three countries there is a great diversity of physical regions (Fig. 49). These range from the extensive polderlands formed by re-

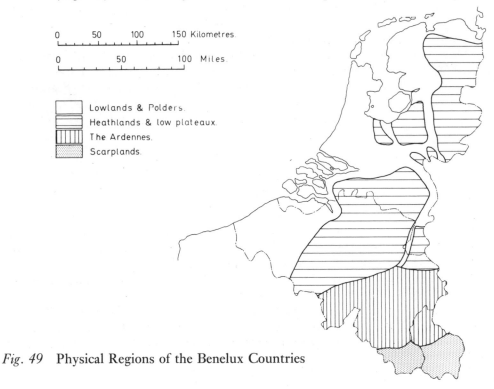

Fig. 49   Physical Regions of the Benelux Countries

clamation of the former Zuider Zee area of the Netherlands to the highest sections of the Ardennes which occur in Belgium and exceed 2,000 feet (655 m.). A series of broad zones can be recognised:

1 The lowlands of Belgium and the Netherlands.
2 The low plateaux and heathlands of middle Belgium and the eastern Netherlands.
3 The Ardennes.
4 The scarplands of Belgian Lorraine and Luxembourg.

1 *The lowlands of Belgium and the Netherlands.*

This region is primarily that of the Rhine-Meuse Delta; it is very low-lying and includes large areas of polderlands below sea level. In Roman times the land area was more extensive and the early centuries after Christ were, in the Netherlands, a time when the encroaching waters of the North Sea gained on the land. The low-lying areas are in places protected by a belt of sand-dunes varying in width from 100 yards (90 m.) to nearly five miles (8 km.). These dunes are formed on sand bars representing two stages in the evolution of the coastline. The older bar can now be traced north of The Hague but south from there it has been destroyed and the coastline is now some four miles farther inland than during Roman times. The newer bar lies seaward of the older one from The Hague to the island of Texel and through the Frisian Islands.

In addition to the dunes and polders and included within these lowlands are a series of sub-regions: they include the plains of Flanders and the river valleys of the Scheldt, Meuse and Rhine. The natural southern boundary of these lowlands is in northern France, on the edge of the chalk hills of Artois. French Flanders in fact has a coastline of over thirty miles compared with forty-two in Belgium. The recent sand dunes of the coast continue westwards to near Calais in France but the dominant formations of this area are the Eocene clays. The inland limit is marked by a gentle rise to the next zone, and this is generally at about the 80 feet (25 m.) contour.

2 *The low plateaux and heathlands of middle Belgium and the eastern Netherlands.*

These form a nearly continuous zone between the North Sea lowlands and the Ardennes uplands. The zone is broken by the valleys of the Lys, Scheldt, Meuse and Rhine but much of the region is in fact formed by high terrace deposits, the relics of predecessors of these rivers. On the basis of surface geology it is possible to recognise several divisions:

(a) *The limon-covered hills of middle Belgium.* The underlying geology varies here from Eocene clays in Interior Flanders to patches of Primary rocks in Brabant and also includes chalk in Hesbaye and the Pays de Herve. The loess or limon cover is widespread and in places reaches a thickness of 65 feet (20 m.). There is a general rise in altitude from west to east. The highest points in east Flanders are on a marked crest between the Dendre and Scheldt valleys where isolated patches of Pliocene sands form a capping; they reach 515 feet (157 m.) in the Pottelberg. Similar heights are found in the continuation of this ridge into France; this was a zone of military significance in the battles of the Western Front in the First World War.

(b) *The Belgian Kempenland (Campine).* The distinctive feature of this region (which extends into the Netherlands) is its lithology, which is that of the Pliocene sands and gravels, in places capped by somewhat coarser limon deposits than those farther west. The northern extensions of this, into Nord-Brabant, show a clear terrace sequence of the Pleistocene predecessors of the Rhine and Meuse. The altitude just reaches 330 feet (100 m.) and there is a marked bluff on the east and south-western sides where the plateau proper descends to the valleys of the Meuse and Demer respectively.

(c) *The plateaux of the central and eastern Netherlands.* In part these plateaux represent the terraces of Pleistocene rivers and consist of sands and gravels. However, the Riss ice-sheet covered some of the country and in the east these low uplands are formed of extensive sheets of till, or ground moraine. The higher regions occur in the Veluwe and in the extreme east of Overijjsel province where heights of 330 feet (100 m.) are reached by some rounded summits. In East Gelderland the deposits show clear evidence of being the terminal moraine of the Riss ice and exhibit the contorted and kneaded appearance of 'push-moraines'.

3   The Ardennes

The high ground of the Benelux countries lies in a broad zone across southern Belgium and northern Luxembourg. Elevations exceeding 2,000 feet (610 m.) occur in the east where this Hercynian highland continues into the Eifel section of the Rhenish Uplands. There is a gradual descent to the west where the Ardennes continue into France at a little over 1,000 feet (300 m.). A number of sub-regions may be recognised within the Ardennes, principally on the basis of differing physique. Geologically, these uplands are formed on the oldest rocks of the three countries, and it is convenient to draw the northern boundary of the area where the Palaeozoic rocks emerge from beneath younger rocks along the crest of the Brabant-Hesbaye Ridge. Considering the sub-regions in turn from north to south: the first is the trough-like valley followed by the east-north-east-flowing section of the Meuse and its left bank tributary, the Sambre, which has the same alignment. This too is the main structural 'grain' of the Ardennes—the Armorican trend line. The rocks in this section of the Ardennes are of Carboniferous age and the valley is cut in

Coal Measures; the rocks are much folded and faulted.

The rise on the southern side of the 'coal furrow' leads to a foothill zone rising from about 600 ft. (180 m.) to over 1,000 ft. (300 m.) on its southern edge. This region, of Condroz and Entre-Sambre-et-Meuse, is marked by a series of parallel ridges and valleys following the grain of the upland. The ridges are generally of sandstone whilst the intervening vales are in the softer shales and limestones, of the Carboniferous and Devonian systems. Pockets of coal have long been exhausted.

A broad vale, the Famenne Depression, generally below 600 feet (180 m.) succeeds the Condroz region. This vale crosses the entire Ardennes, and in its eastern section is drained by the Ourthe to its confluence with the Meuse and Vesdre at Liège. On the southern edge the Devonian limestones give local karstic features. The High Ardennes occupy the remainder of the region and these too may be sub-divided into a series of minor regions such as the Plateau des Tailles and the Hautes Fagnes. The oldest rocks, of Cambrian and Pre-Cambrian age, occur in two sections, the Rocroi Massif in the west and in the Hautes Fagnes (Hohe Venn) around Malmédy in the east. The underlying rocks of the High Ardennes are principally of lower Devonian age and include schists, sandstones and quartzites. One particular zone of the last rock comes to the surface in the centre of the southern syncline, the Wiltz or Eifel syncline. The rivers of the Ardennes are generally deeply incised and often follow extremely sinuous courses; abandoned meander sections provide valuable additions to the fertile alluvial plains which provide such vivid contrasts to the steep, wooded valley slopes and the exposed uplands.

4   *The Southern Scarplands.*

A comparatively small section of Belgium and over one-half of the Grand Duchy of Luxembourg lie south of the Hercynian massif of the Ardennes. They are formed on rocks of Mesozoic age and represent part of the scarplands of Lorraine (see Ch. 14). As such they form a unique appendage to Benelux and, in the case of Luxembourg, a very valuable one which is known as the Bon Pays or Gutland. The southern edge of the Ardennes shows a somewhat steeper descent than the northern zones; but the scarps, vales and plateau of the Luxembourg Bon Pays and Belgian Lorraine attain elevations up to 1,300 feet (400 m.). The lowest sections, in the Moselle Valley, descend to just below 650 feet (200 m.). Over a large section of Luxembourg the rocks are of Triassic and Liassic age, the Keuper Marl flooring many valleys and the Lower Lias or Luxembourg Sandstone lying horizontally on top of this and producing a plateau landscape. (The Lower Lias in the British geological succession mainly consists of marls and the landscape is a lowland in front of the Tees-Exe line.) In the extreme south the more typical Jurassic scarp is formed by the outcrop of the Inferior Oolite: this contains the minette iron-ore, is sometimes referred to as the Dogger, and its scarp here just reaches 1,300 feet (400 m.). The successive scarps of the Luxembourg Sandstone and the Longwy-Esch section of the Inferior Oolite face northwards. Just east of Dudelange the latter makes a sharp turn to form the eastward-facing scarp of the Côtes de Moselle.

DRAINAGE   Two factors have chiefly influenced the drainage pattern of these lands. One is the regional slope from the higher ground of the Ardennes to the basins of the North Sea and Paris Basin. The other is the detailed structure

Fig 50   Drainage of the Benelux Countries

of the massif and in particular the grain from west–south–west to east–north–east. Both these factors are structural and the stage to which erosion has proceeded has determined the degree of adjustment to structure which has been attained.

Two principal rivers in this region cross the Hercynian massif, the Rhine and the Meuse; these lines are obviously transverse to the main structural grain. A similarly transgressive course is followed by sections of the Moselle, the Ourthe, the Sûre and the Our in Luxembourg. Courses in accordance with the structure are taken by sections of the Vesdre, Semois, the east and west branches of the Ourthe, the Sambre and the Meuse below Namur. Although some of these river patterns may be explained by superimposition from a cover of younger rocks—and the incised meanders of some sections of many streams lend weight to this—the evolution of the present pattern is much more complex.

The evolution of the Rhine has been shown to involve the combination of earlier streams flowing from the Rhenish uplands. Similarly the Meuse has attained its present pattern as a result of the capture of streams formerly flowing to the Paris Basin. It is noteworthy that only two streams in this area flow north and south from the Ardennes watershed; these are the headwaters of the Ourthe and the Sûre-Our network respectively.

The streams of the lowlands of Belgium and Netherlands exhibit a number of complex patterns. Those of the Netherlands have been either much altered by artificial drainage and defence works or brought into being by polder construction. In Belgium two principal groups of streams can be recognised: those of the western Lys-Scheldt (or Escaut) basin, and those flowing from the hills of Brabant to the Rupel-Demer axis.

CLIMATE   The Benelux countries lie within the West Coast Marine climatic region and as such show features of mild winters, cool summers and moderate rainfall throughout the year. There are a number of local variations and these are particularly marked across the breadth of Belgium. Mean winter temperatures range from 3°C (37°F) on the coast to around freezing point in the Ardennes. Mean minimum temperatures over much of the area away from the coast are below freezing point for up to four months: the mean January minimum temperature at Bastogne is −11·2°C (12°F). The number of days with frost increases rapidly south-eastwards across Belgium to over 120 in the High Ardennes. There is a similar easterly increase across the Netherlands to over 80 days of frost in Overijssel Province.

Summer temperatures are generally warmer inland than at coastal locations and there is a steady rise in the mean July temperature south-eastwards over the Benelux countries to the Moselle Valley. Temperatures on the uplands are somewhat lower than the low plateau and a particularly warm area is the Meuse Valley north of Liège, where more than 30 days per year enjoy temperatures over 25°C (77°F).

Rainfall totals exceed 40 inches (1,000 mm.), in the highest areas of the

Ardennes and descend to about 22 inches (560 mm.) per annum in the rain-shadow lowland around Maastricht. Rainfall decreases south of the Ardennes crest but rises to 40 inches (1,000 mm.) on the Oolite scarp of Longwy-Dudelange. Totals in the Netherlands are greatest on the low hills of the Central Heathlands and the polderlands of Holland but do not exceed 32 inches (800 mm.) p.a. Rainfall is fairly well distributed throughout the year, with a tendency towards a late summer maximum over much of the Netherlands and Belgium north of the Sambre-Meuse Valley. South of this line the precipitation is heavier and unevenly distributed, but with a marked winter maximum. Some of this falls in the form of snow, and parts of the Ardennes enjoy a skiing season. During many winters ice sports are followed on the frozen minor drainage canals of the Netherlands.

SOILS The soils of the three countries reflect the physique and parent materials rather than the climate conditions under which they were formed. They range from the fertile heavy alluvial soils of the low-lying polders and river flood plains to the rather thin brown earths of parts of the Ardennes Uplands. The zone of heathlands which crosses the centre is marked by extensive podsol development, on both the limon and the glacial gravels and tills. Somewhat richer brown-earths are found in the south of Luxembourg and the lower zones of the Ardennes; whilst patches of wet bog soils mark the higher and ill-drained glacial plateaux of the eastern Netherlands. Usually there is no development of soil on the newer sand dunes of the coast but, as a result of careful manuring and treatment, the soils of the older dunes inland and northwards from The Hague are particularly fertile and valuable for horticulture. Soils of the reclaimed polder lands pass through stages of salinity and bog conditions before attaining alluvial soil conditions. Many of the brown earths of central and southern Belgium are well leached.

Population Distribution The Benelux countries have a total population less than one-half that of the United Kingdom but, like that country, it is predominantly an urban population. There are vivid contrasts between the heavily-populated urban regions and the less densely peopled rural areas. This is to some extent shown by the national figures for population density, the Netherlands and Belgium ranking respectively first and second in the world with 950 and 780 persons per square mile (365 and 300 persons per sq. km.). Luxembourg, however, has only 320 per square mile (124 per sq. km.) and the comparable figure for the United Kingdom is 550 per square mile (212 per sq. km.).

Statistics of the natural increase in population show that the Netherlands is increasing rapidly whilst Belgium is doing so only slowly—13.7 and 5.0 per thousand respectively, compared with 5.1 per thousand for the

0 ⎯⎯⎯⎯⎯⎯⎯⎯⎯⎯⎯⎯⎯⎯⎯ 50 Miles.

0 ⎯⎯⎯⎯⎯⎯⎯⎯⎯⎯⎯⎯⎯⎯⎯ 80 Kilometres.

Leeuwarden Groningen

Winschaten

Assen

Den Helder

Steenwijk

Meppel

Alkmaar

Kampen

Zandaam Zwolle

Haarlem

Almelo

Deventer Hengelo

AMSTERDAM

Bussum Enscheae

Hilversum Baarn

Apeldoorn

Leiden Amersfoort

Utrecht Zeist

THE HAGUE

Arnhem

Delft Gouda

ROTTERDAM

R
A
N
D
S
T
A
D

Nijmegen

Dordrecht

Hertogenbosch

Breda

Tilburg

Eindhoven

Venlo

Knokke

Turnhout

Ostend Bruges Eeklo St. Niklaas ANTWERP

Lokeren

Ghent Mechelen

Aarschot Diest

Roeselare Aalst Vilvoorde Hasselt

Ypres Maastricht

Courtrai Louvain

BRUSSELS St. Truiden

Menen Ronsé Halle Tienen Tangeren

Tournai Leuze Eupen

Soignes Nivelles Liège Verviers

La Louviere Huy

Mons Namur

Binche Charleroi

Bastogne

Arlon LUXEMBOURG

Esch

Fig 51 Principal towns of Benelux

United Kingdom. Again, Luxembourg lags behind with a rate of only 3.6 per thousand.

A number of major features can be noted on the map of population distribution of the Benelux countries:

1 There are a number of major concentrations of population: the agglomerations of Groningen, Randstad Holland, Eindhoven, Antwerp, Ghent, Brussels, Charleroi, and Liège, whose population exceeds 150,000.

Within this group can be noted contrasts between the older industrial centres in Belgium, and the modern looser-knit centres of the Netherlands.

2 The rural areas all support a moderate population; there are many small towns or large villages, and where the pattern is dispersed the separate farmsteads are numerous. Nevertheless, the Netherlands has more urban centres; there are at least 80 towns or municipalities with a population of 25,000 or more in that country but only some 30 in Belgium, and just two in Luxembourg. Within the Netherlands there are greater concentrations of such towns in the western and central areas.

3 The areas of low density are fairly clearly defined; they are the Veluwe, parts of Overijssel and Drente, eastern North Brabant and the High Ardennes. The rural population in these areas generally shows some form of nucleated settlement, especially in the bleaker areas of the Ardennes.

These countries contain some of Europe's oldest established towns. Flanders in the fourteenth century presented a highly urbanised aspect, but many of the towns of the Netherlands owe their origin to the succeding two centuries. Commercial development, based on towns, favoured their growth throughout Belgium and the Netherlands north of the line of the Sambre-Meuse Valley.

The stimuli to development of towns were primarily commercial; although centres such as Luxembourg, Namur and Liège also grew by reason of their fortress functions. In the low-lying regions defence against the sea was frequently more vital than against alien armies; the terpen sites of the province of Groningen and the dyke towns of Holland and Zeeland form good examples. Modifications of the latter involved the construction of a dam and the original site of Amsterdam is a prime example of this type (Fig. 68). The medieval town is well illustrated by Bruges with its closely compacted nucleus around the market place and town hall; the 'boulevard' pattern of concentric growth rings is seen in the plan of Brussels and to a lesser extent in Liège. Here an abandoned section of river course initially formed a bulwark for the lower town below the fortress; now, as in many European cities, it is principally an open space.

The nineteenth century industrial town is well illustrated on the Sambre-Meuse Coalfield by Charleroi. The modern industrial centre is typical of some of the urban growth points of the Netherlands and the sprawling city of Eindhoven is perhaps its most obvious example. Smaller towns of almost-entirely twentieth century origin are found in the new coalfield areas, such as Mol and Genk in the Campine.

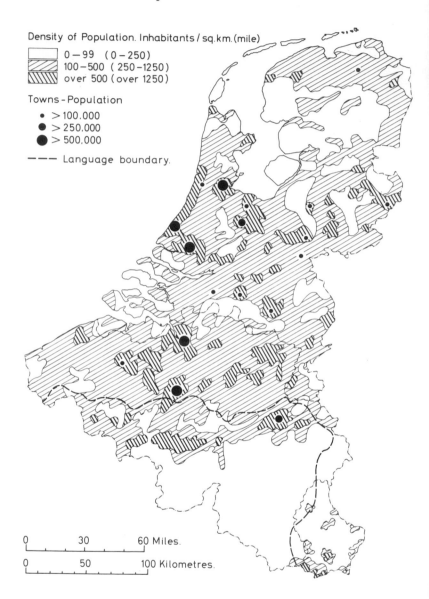

Fig 52 Population Density of the Benelux Countries

Economic Development

AGRICULTURE AND FORESTRY

Agriculture in the Benelux countries as a whole contributes less than 10% to the gross national product: it is most significant in the Netherlands and least in Belgium. Farms are small, over 75% of them being of 25 acres (10 ha.) or less, and the majority of the larger units occur in the zone of limon-covered hills which stretches across Middle Belgium. Although many farms are worked on the basis of small family units, more than half of the individual holdings in Belgium and the Netherlands are rented, but in Luxembourg nearly three-quarters are worked by the owner's direct labour.

There are many regional specialisations within Benelux, particularly in the lowlands of the Rhine-Meuse delta, where local horticultural concentrations occur, such as the cultivation under glass of Westland and the market gardening zones of the Betuwe and Zeeland. However, over most of the three countries agricultural activities can best be described as intensive mixed farming in which stockbreeding and the production of meat and dairy produce rank high. Ancillary livestock rearing of pigs and poultry is also important, with the former particularly dominant in the Netherlands. Arable cultivation includes a high percentage of fodder crops and there is usually more grassland than any other category in the annual land utilisation statistics.

Agricultural land use—Benelux 1964 (in 1,000 ha.)

	Belgium	*Luxembourg*	*Netherlands*
Arable cultivation	708	69	799
Horticulture	54	—	139
Grassland	839	64	1,342
Vineyards	—	1	—
Woodland	610	82	280

Number of Livestock (1964) *in thousands*

Cattle	2,663	161	3,317
Pigs	1,833	101	3,525

Differences in emphasis in agriculture between the three countries are chiefly a reflection of the varying characteristics of the land and climate. Thus the emphasis on woodland in Belgium and Luxembourg is due to this land use occupying over half the area of the Ardennes Massif whilst relatively few acres have been afforested in the low, level Netherlands. Similarly, the grasslands of the Dutch polderlands and riverine areas are the most extensive of the Benelux lands.

Forest management is an important aspect of the rural economy in the Ardennes regions and, to a lesser extent, in the central heathlands such as the Campine. Much of the natural woodland, in which oak predominates but beech is also extensive, has been replaced by plantations of coniferous trees, particularly Scots Pine. Nurseries are established in sheltered valley lowlands and the plantations cover the slopes and the less-exposed upper surfaces.

MINING AND INDUSTRY

The Industrial Revolution began in Europe with the development of the Belgian Coalfield. Pits had been worked in the Liège basin for some centuries before that and primitive metal industries had been based on Ardennes minerals and charcoal from the forests.

The Belgian or Sambre-Meuse coalfield contains a series of separate basins (see pp. 297–303) forming the site of the largest continuous industrial area of the Benelux countries. More recently-worked coalfields are in the Campine and Limburg regions and there are other coal reserves in the Peel district, east of Venlo, and in the Overijssel area. The older coalfield areas, in Walloon Belgium, are no longer of prime importance; the Campine coalfield, in the Flemish-speaking section of Belgium, has grown rapidly since its initial exploitation in 1917 and now produces over one-third of the Belgian total. There are thus problems associated not only with the changing industrial patterns in these areas but with the economic balance of the two linguistic divisions of Belgium. In the Netherlands, the Limburg coalfield's planned expansion has been halted by competition from natural gas and since 1960 the output has decreased.

The Belgian and Luxembourg iron-ore fields are geographically part of the Lorraine iron-mining area. The ore is of Jurassic age and has been worked since the last quarter of the nineteenth century. The orefield provides the site of integrated iron and steel plants at Athus in Belgium, Esch-sur-Alzette, Dudelange, Differdange and Pétange in Luxembourg. The other iron and steel plants of Belgium are sited adjacent to the coalfield and a number of integrated plants occur around Charleroi and Liège; the ore was at first obtained from the Carboniferous strata but is now brought in by canal from Lorraine. The major iron and steel works of the Netherlands depends entirely on imported supplies of ore and coke and is at the port of Ijmuiden at the coastal end of the North Sea Canal. Coke for the Luxembourg and Belgian Lorraine industries is also imported and comes chiefly from the Ruhr and the Saar.

Heavy industry in Belgium is confined to the older industrial areas and to the Brussels-Antwerp axis, where the Antwerp-Brussels-Charleroi canal provides an important means of transport of materials and finished goods. Similarly, heavy engineering in the Netherlands is sited at the major ports or where water-transport is available. Utrecht, for example, with a steelworks and rolling mill, has machinery and railway works.

The chief centres of the petro-chemical industries of Benelux are located at the major ports: Antwerp and Rotterdam being paramount but minor works are also found at Flushing and Ostend. Rotterdam is the site of the main oil refineries and associated plants of Benelux and surpasses every other site in Western Europe. Smaller centres are at Amsterdam (adjacent

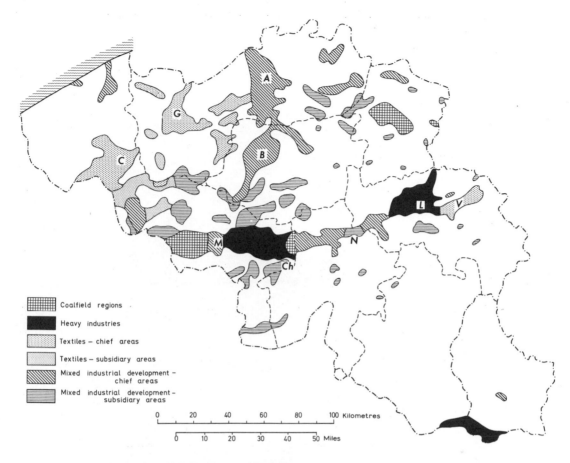

Fig 53   Industrial Regions of Belgium
Towns indicated by initial letters: Antwerp, Brussels, Charleroi, Courtrai, Ghent, Liège, Mons, Namur, Verviers.

to the North Sea Canal) and Ghent. Unlike Britain the textile centres of Benelux are not sited on the coalfield zone, although the nineteenth century did see the establishment of an industrial area around Verviers based largely on the woollen industry and at no great distance from the Liège coal basin. The traditional Flemish textile areas around Courtrai and Tournai utilise a proportion of local grown flax as well as imported cotton. The industry, however, remains scattered, as can be seen in Fig. 53, but the Ghent region has expanded greatly on the basis of man-made fibres.

Industrial development during the present century, and more particularly since the Second World War, has been of many light industries, based on metals, plastics and chemicals. This has taken place around some of the older industrial areas in Belgium but more particularly in the Netherlands. There is thus a pattern of increasing 'urbanisation' in many parts of that country, shown in Fig. 54 (over).

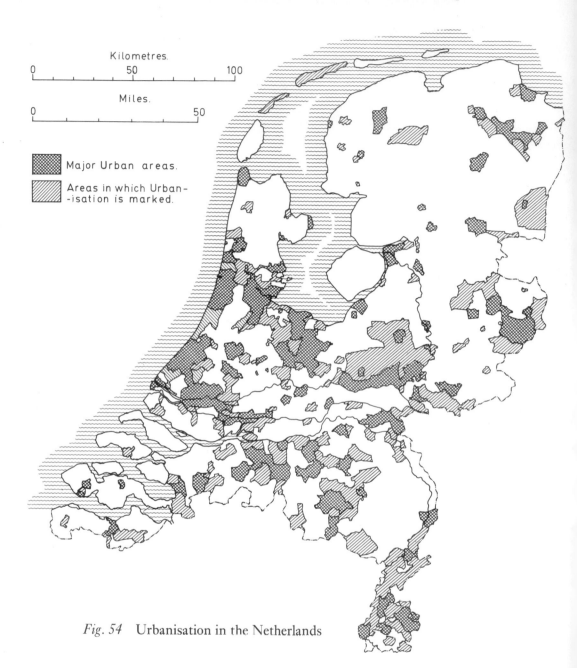

Fig. 54 Urbanisation in the Netherlands

TRADE   The three Benelux countries are all vitally dependent on trade connections both within the narrow groupings of their own customs organisation and the somewhat wider European Economic Community, as well as with many lands overseas. Many of the towns of the Netherlands and lowland Belgium were founded on a basis of commerce and trade links, initially between European partners such as those within the Hanseatic League and later also with colonial dependencies, particularly those in the Far East and Africa. The principal foci of trade routes are thus the major ports of Antwerp, Amsterdam and Rotterdam, which serve home interests as well as a large entrepôt trade.

Important movements of raw materials, such as those concerned with the iron and steel industries, also enter into the external trade of Benelux and both France and West Germany are important trading partners.

Value of trade between selected countries (%) (1964)

	Exports	Imports
BELGIUM AND:		
Netherlands	23	15
France	15	15
W. Germany	21	20
U.K.	5	8
U.S.A.	8	9
NETHERLANDS AND:		
Belgium	15	19
France	9	5
W. Germany	27	24
U.K.	9	7
U.S.A.	4	12
LUXEMBOURG AND:		
Belgium	23	39
Netherlands	9	4
France	10	12
W. Germany	28	35
U.K.	1	2
U.S.A.	6	3

COMMUNICATIONS   *Inland Waterways*

These have two main foci, Antwerp and Rotterdam, and the canal networks include the canalised distributaries of the Rhine and Meuse as well as a complex of canals, some capable of carrying vessels up to 4,000 tons (Fig. 55). Rotterdam handles the greatest volume of merchandise and serves as a transhipment and entrepôt port for the Rhine upstream to Basle, as well as for the Netherlands. Routes from Antwerp serve a more dispersed area and include canals of smaller capacity. Waterborne traffic comes from northern France via the Scheldt and Ghent, from Charleroi via Brussels and from Liège and the Campine via the Albert Canal,

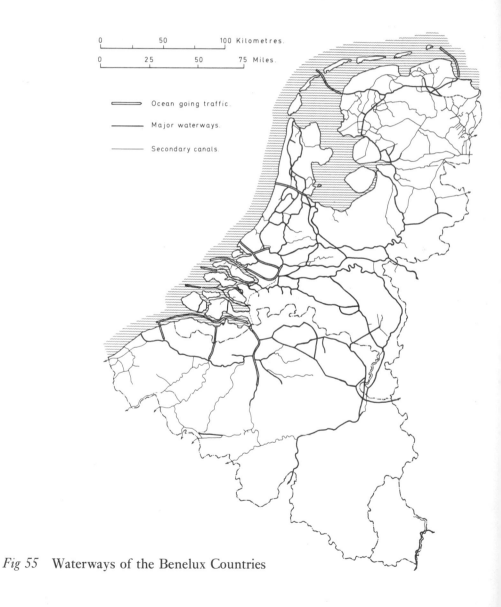

Fig 55   Waterways of the Benelux Countries

completed in 1940. Improved connections between Rotterdam and Antwerp will be provided by the canal in the Delta Plan (Fig. 66). Should the proposed Canal Vent Debout eventually materialise, linking the Rhine and Meuse from north of Cologne via Aachen to Liège, it will enlarge Antwerp's hinterland still further. Major canals link Bruges with its North Sea outport of Zeebrugge and Ghent with Terneuzen on the estuary of the west Scheldt. The Moselle canalisation project from Metz to Koblenz was opened in 1965, as was also the improved section of the Sambre Canal from Namur to Charleroi. Substantial traffic is carried on many other routes in these regions, the Meuse above Namur, the Scheldt-Lille canal and the numerous links across the Netherlands.

Railways

The rail routes of Benelux show interesting comparisons between the various national rail organisations; that in the Netherlands is operated by a non-government body whilst those of Belgium and Luxembourg are state run. The total mileage in Belgium is 3,188 (5,134 km.), but in the Netherlands only 2,018 miles (3,227 km.). Well over one half this total is electrified because of its high passenger traffic but only one-fifth of the Belgian line is so equipped. Both rail networks were extensively modernised after the Second World War; that period saw the extinction in Belgium of a network of local tramways which had reached a maximum mileage equal to that of the main railways in their heyday.

Roads

The trunk roads of Benelux are quite good but a pattern of main 'auto-routes' or motorways is a product only of the 1960's. Several patterns can be seen; the chief of these is the extension of the German *Autobahn* network across both countries to the North Sea. Thus the Antwerp-Liège-Aachen motorway connects with Cologne and the south German routes, and the Utrecht-Arnhem line leads from the Randstad Holland to the Ruhr network. North-south traffic within Benelux is chiefly between the industrial regions such as the Randstad Holland and the 'Stedendried-hoek' or urban triangle formed by Antwerp, Ghent and Brussels. From Brussels routes radiate to Ostend, the northern France industrial area, Charleroi and south-eastwards via Namur to Luxembourg. A similar, radial pattern characterises the road network of Luxembourg from the capital city.

Fig 56   Motorways and Main Roads in the Benelux Countries

Regions of the Benelux Countries

Regions of Luxembourg Luxembourg conveniently divides into clear natural regions; to the north is the Oesling or Luxembourg Ardennes and to the south, on the lower relief and younger rocks, the Gutland or Bon Pays.

OESLING The Oesling accounts for approximately one-third of the country's land area but supports only a fraction of the population. Many of the features of the Belgian Ardennes and also of the German Eifel are to be found here but it is distinctive in a number of ways. Although the river valleys are frequently deeply incised, and there is clear evidence of their polycyclic evolution, the main streams drain southwards to the Moselle and have smaller basins than the Meuse or the Ourthe. Nevertheless, their catchment areas are sufficient to make it economic to build reservoirs. Domestic and industrial water supplies are provided by one such reservoir at Esch-sur-Sûre, which is also a tourist attraction for yachting and fishing. A further reservoir, at Vianden, is part of a pump-storage hydro-electricity plant which commenced operation in 1964 and was then the largest of such schemes in Europe; it provides peak-hour supplies for the North Rhine-Westphalia electricity undertaking.

The highest point in Luxembourg is the Burgplatz (1,847 feet, 552 m.) but the upper surfaces of the Ardennes generally only slightly exceed 1,670 feet (500 m.). At least two partial erosion surfaces have been described for the highest levels, and the landscape is of an undulating upland plain. The underlying rocks include Devonian sandstones and schists but a series of quartzites, associated with a synclinal structure through Wiltz provides one variation. These have been quarried for road-metal. In the extreme north of the Grand Duchy the river valleys are only slightly incised but as they are followed downstream they become more deeply incised. Considerable quantities of drift material are found in these valleys but, although the flood plains have fertile alluvial soils, they are damp and generally remain in pasture. The upper surfaces have a somewhat thin soil cover which is generally a leached brown-earth. The large number of holdings and the resulting 'strip' field pattern is gradually changing to one of large fields; mechanised agriculture, producing wheat and other cereals, may be seen as well as bullock-drawn farm wagons.

The slopes of the valleys are generally too steep for any cultivation and remain in woodland, much of which is planted and managed for construction and fuel purposes. The dairy farming of the valley floors is on a very small scale of individual herds, these being generally less than ten head and frequently only of single animals. The milk is handled by a co-operative system with various collecting centres and a major plant near Ettelbruck; all the animals are tuberculin attested. A number of small tourist centres exist and some minor industries, but the traditional leather tanning is reduced to one example, at Wiltz. The tourist attractions, besides magnificent scenery, include camping sites, old chateaux, boating and fishing; Vianden and Clervaux are towns particularly engaged in tourism. The southern edge of the Oesling is marked by a descent into an east-west vale, drained by the Sûre and minor tributaries, known as the 'pre-Ardennes furrow'.

GUTLAND

The lowlands of Luxembourg are in fact a complex of scarps with intervening vales, the former facing north or east and being formed by such rocks as the Lower Lias (Luxembourg Sandstone), the Muschelkalk and the Inferior Oolite (Dogger) Limestone. The Luxembourg Sandstone underlies a large plateau region in the centre of the country and is often eroded into a landscape of deep defiles and cliff scarps. The upper surfaces are generally well-wooded, although much has been cleared and agriculture developed from nucleated villages. Scenic attractions provide a further advantage to this area, as in the Müllertal, and the Luxembourg Sandstone is also a valuable source of water. The Muschelkalk outcrop (Plate 52) is much faulted; its principal occurrence is on the west bank of the Moselle, here forming the eastern boundary of the state, and on these slopes a viticulture industry has grown up. This has suffered from German and, more especially, French competition since the establishment of the Common Market. A number of villages on the banks of the Moselle have their co-operative cellars, as at Remich, Wormeldange and Grevenmacher.

South-west of the Luxembourg Sandstone is a broad vale floored by clays, muds and shales of the Middle and Upper Lias and which is crossed before reaching the Jurassic scarp (which contains the minette ironstone) on the French border. In the south-east the lowland, between the Luxembourg Sandstone and the Muschelkalk slopes of the Moselle, is principally on Keuper Marl.

Agriculture in the Gutland is more prosperous than in the Oesling: there is a greater dependence on arable, especially in the southern sections where woodland and pasture are least. Even so, the economy is still little more than a peasant one, chiefly by reason of the small size of holdings and their scattered disposition. Villages are mainly nucleated although some isolated farmsteads are found; most villages are small and entirely rural, the exceptions being the spa of Mondorf-les-Bains, the wine-making centres on the Moselle mentioned above, and the small towns of Echternach, Diekirch and Ettelbruck situated in the valley of the Sûre or the pre-Ardenne furrow. These are route centres and have miscellaneous industries of which brewing at Diekirch is the largest. A further group of settlements in the extreme south are connected with the iron and steel

Plate 52 Moselle vineyards in Luxembourg.
The village of Ehnen, on the left bank of the Moselle, looking south. Note the terraced vineyards on the outcrop of the Muschelkalk.

industry, the largest single item in the Luxembourg economy.

Iron ore has been worked and used in Luxembourg for several centuries. Initially alluvial sources and charcoal from the extensive woodland were the bases of an iron industry. The use of the 'minette' ore from the Jurassic 'dogger' scarp in the extreme south began in the mid-nineteenth century in the steelworks at Eich on the northern outskirts of Luxembourg city. The patenting of the Gilchrist Thomas process was quickly followed by the expansion of the industry in Luxembourg (the first European licence was granted there, in 1879). Initial permission to exploit these deposits was conditional on smelting the ore in Luxembourg. The chief centre of the industry is Esch-sur-Alzette (Plate 53), the Grand Duchy's second town, and the industrial concerns here are combines such as A.R.B.E.D., associated with mines and works elsewhere, in the Lorraine, Saar and Ruhr. Coking coal is needed from the last-named area and is brought by

L

Plate 53 Esch-sur-Alzette, Luxembourg.
Esch-sur-Alzette, the second town of the Grand Duchy of Luxembourg. View
northwards from the slopes of the 'minette' scarp.

rail. With the completion of the Moselle canalisation and a new river harbour near Wasserbillig increased coke movements between the Ruhr and Luxembourg are likely. The orefield is divided into two basins: in the west between Differdange and the French and Belgian frontiers, and eastwards from Esch to Dudelange. Integrated works, blast furnaces, steelworks and rolling mills, are located at all these towns and at Belval and Rodange.

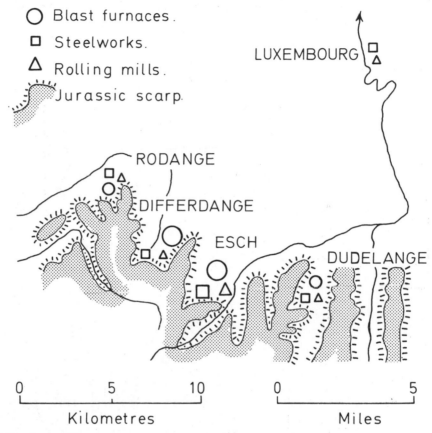

Fig 57 The Luxembourg iron and steel industry
The size of the symbol is proportional to the number of works, blast furnaces, etc. in the basins named.

Luxembourg city

Although a small city by comparison with the other capitals and provincial centres of Benelux, Luxembourg city is an important settlement. The major growth patterns and functions of the city are indicated on Figure 58; its initial site on a meander of the Alzette deeply incised into the Luxembourg sandstone is believed to be Roman (Plate 54). The site was turned into a magnificent fortress by Vauban in the early eighteenth century and the ruins of these 'casemates' are still to be seen. Luxembourg city has grown much in recent years; prior to the nineteenth century it was little more than a fortified town strategically placed on the route between the Paris Basin and the Moselle Valley; industrial and commercial growth followed the arrival of the railway, in the last two decades of that century. Luxembourg is the centre of many international organisations and is the chief market centre for the entire country and also for parts of the Belgian province of Luxembourg. The industries of the capital include a number of engineering works, foundries, chemicals, printing, clothing, furniture manufacture and food processing.

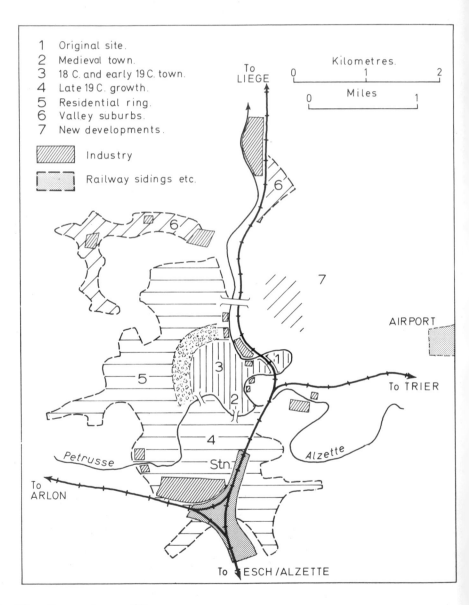

Fig 58.   Luxembourg City

Plate 54   Luxembourg City.
Aerial view showing the valley of the Alzette at top right, and its tributary the Petrusse in the left foreground. Remains of the eighteenth-century fortifications are in the centre of the picture.

Regions of Belgium

THE ARDENNES

The Ardennes Massif is divided by the line of the Meuse above Namur into the smaller western section of Entre-Sambre-et-Meuse, which extends into France, and the main south-eastern massif. This latter includes the Condroz, the Famenne and the High Ardennes or Ardennes *sensu stricto*, and extends across the Luxembourg Oesling to the German Eifel.

Typically, the Ardennes is a forested windswept upland, into which deep valleys have been cut, with a poor soil formed on hard rocks (Plate 55). The river valleys, notably those of the Lesse, Ourthe, Aisne, Amblève and Semois, provide a number of routeways into the massif but even so this area has never been densely populated. It is now an area of declining population.

The poor soils of such upland areas are frequently over-emphasised; in the case of the lower surfaces of the Ardennes, between 1,400 feet (430 m.) and 1,700 feet (510 m.), the alternation of sandstones and schists has tended to yield mixed soils of reasonable permeability and fertility.

The upper levels, over 1,800 feet (550 m.), contain areas of peat bogs, some of which have been used in the past for fuel supplies, whilst other areas are being deep-ploughed and used for pine plantations.

The climate of the Ardennes is also bleak. Rainfall totals are generally well above 40 inches (1,000 mm.) and reach maxima of 55 inches (1,400 mm.) per year in the Hautes Fagnes and the plateau area north of Bouillon. Although much of the region presents a well-wooded appearance, the southern and western areas along the French border and around the French town of Revin, are particularly heavily forested. This woodland is no longer the original oak cover, although some may still be seen near Anlier and Chiny. Beech and Pine (*Pinus sylvestrus*) have been planted and the forest management is of considerable importance.

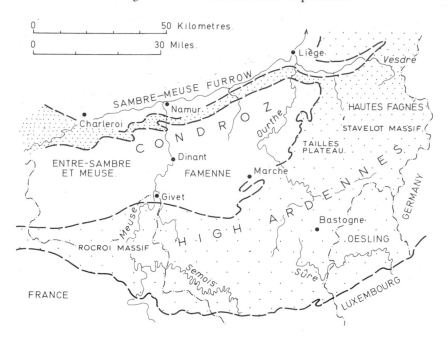

Fig 59 The Ardennes

Settlements in this area are small and generally sited in forest clearings; buildings are simple and include stable and barn in a longitudinal pattern. Farms are small, less than 50 acres (20 ha.) in size and the fields are chiefly in pasture, amounting to some 80% or more of the cultivated area in the north-east. Cereals are either rye, oats or barley; potatoes and some fodder are also grown. The alluvial soils of the Semois Valley (Plate 55), in particular such areas as abandoned meanders or the slip-off sides of the river loops, form fertile areas for these crops, and also for the local speciality of tobacco. The field-pattern is one of many small strips, separated by wire fences; the entire section being bounded by the forest edge on the steep valley sides.

Plate 55   The Semois Valley in the Ardennes.
The level skyline of the Ardennes Plateau and the wooded slopes contrast with
the cultivated flood plain. Note the tobacco-drying sheds in the fields.

This is the least-densely populated area of Belgium; there are less than
200,000 in an area of more than 5,000 sq. kms. Some well-sited towns have
been able to develop tourism, such as Dinant, Laroche, Houffalize and
Bouillon and there are a number of designated parks and nature reserves.
Other towns, Bertrix, Vielsalm, St. Vith and Bastogne for example, are
small market centres. Industries are almost completely lacking, apart from
some traditional ones, like tanning at Stavelot. Quarrying is important
in some sections, such as of limestone for cement manufacture at Jemelle
on the main north-south railway route from Namur to Luxembourg.

Hydro-electricity development is a source of power for this area, and
the rivers Ourthe, Amblève and Warthe have been used to a small extent
but there is considerable remaining potential.

The chief routeway across the area is that from Namur to Luxembourg:
this is the main electrified rail route leading south and its line is paralleled
by a main trunk road. The other, converging route, from Liège to Luxem-

bourg avoids the bleakest parts of the Hautes Fagnes; the rail route, which is not electrified, follows a more tortuous line along the valley of the Clerf through the Oesling and neither it nor the companion road route carries as much traffic.

Namur is the administrative centre for the south-east of Belgium: secondary centres are at Dinant and Bastogne but the Pays de Herve, Vesdre Valley and lower Ourthe areas are in the hinterland of Liège. Namur is in the centre of the Sambre-Meuse trough, at the confluence of these two rivers, and well sited for communications both along and transverse to the valleys. It is on Carboniferous limestone midway between the two chief coal basins of the trough. Food manufacturing, flour mills and a paper industry are important, together with light engineering.

To the west of the Meuse the Ardennes Massif is generally lower; the highest part, the Rocroi massif, only just exceeding 1,330 feet (395 m.) near the French boundary. This upland is half in Belgium and half in France, and descends westwards to the clay-covered region of Thiérache which is typically a pastoral region. In most respects this section of the Ardennes presents a similar wooded aspect to that east of the Meuse. It is, however, somewhat more difficult of access, with fewer routeways: the principal artery is that of the Cambrai-Hirson-Mezières road and electrified rail routes. The Chimay-Petigny area is a noted tourist region and marks the northern edge of the massif, where Devonian limestones produce karstic scenery. This is also the southern continuation of the Famenne, sometimes referred to as the Fagne. This band of limestone also yields somewhat more fertile soils than the adjacent area to the north and is picked out across the entire Famenne by increased arable cultivation. North again the higher land of the Condroz is continued by the Entre-Sambre-et-Meuse region and, in France, the plateaux of the Pre-Ardennes. The ridges are well wooded and the intervening vales are chiefly devoted to pasture, but the region is surprisingly thinly populated considering the nearness of the industrial belt to the north. Nevertheless, there is a considerable amount of commuting to work in that area by residents of this rural zone.

BELGIAN LORRAINE This area is but a small zone of Belgium; its local name is the *Guame*. It is an extension of French Lorraine and shows some of the characteristics of that area, which contrast markedly with the Ardennes to the north. This is particularly true of the climate; only 90 days of frost on the average per annum compared with over 120 days in the High Ardennes and an annual rainfall which decreases from 48 inches (1,200 mm.) to under 35 inches (900 mm.) at Torgny in the south-west. Conditions are generally similar to those of central Belgium in the vicinity of Brussels.

The landscape is dominated by a series of cuestas and intervening vales, produced by the alternation of sandstones, limestones and clays. There are three north-facing scarps, formed respectively by the Florenville Sandstone (the continuation of the Luxembourg Sandstone), the Aubange sandstone, and the Longwy Limestone ridge (the Inferior Oolite iron-bearing strata which continues into southern Luxembourg).

The ridges generally attain 1,300 feet (400 m.) and are often forested; the dip slopes are well dissected by small tributary streams. In the east, towards the Luxembourg frontier the ridge and vale pattern dies out in the headwaters regions of the Semois.

Typically, settlements are small and strung out in a 'street-village' pattern, with small terraced houses; agriculture follows the pattern of the Ardennes to the north with the emphasis on forestry and in the northern vales the settlements are nucleated. The Semois Valley is primarily devoted to pasturage but some 30% of the farmland produces rye, potatoes or fodder crops and sometimes other cereals.

The chief feature of this area is its industrial zone, which results in an overall population density double that of the Ardennes. The centre is Arlon which combines the functions of commercial, administrative and provincial centres. Industry is based on the iron ore from the Longwy ridge, especially at Halanzy and Musson, and there are a number of blast furnaces in the vale. The main steelworks are at Athus.

There is thus an important sub-region in the south-east with several semi-urban agglomerations, Athus, Halanzy, Aubance, Messancy, in a zone whose population density is treble that of the rural section of Belgian Lorraine.

THE HAINE-SAMBRE-MEUSE AXIS

Stretching across the centre of Belgium for a distance of some 95 miles (150 km.) is a nearly continuous zone of industrial towns. This follows the outcrop of the Carboniferous Coal Measures and for nearly three-quarters of the way the zone corresponds to the valley of the Meuse and its major tributary the Sambre. This region is frequently referred to as the Sambre-Meuse coalfield, coal-furrow or trough.

A clear distinction can be made between the larger, western, basin and the eastern region around Liège. The former is the more extensive and continues into the northern coalfield of France and its industrial region.

Three distinct regions may be recognised in the western basin; the Borinage area whose chief town is Mons; the Central Basin, centred on La Louvière, and the Charleroi Basin. The first two are characterised by their decline in importance as coalfield areas and the introduction of new industries, especially following the accelerated decline of the coalfield since 1958. The Charleroi region is the more densely populated area and possesses the main heavy industries, iron and steel-works, chemicals, etc.

Borinage

This industrial area lies chiefly west of the town of Mons, provincial capital of Hainaut, and on the southern side of the valley of the river Haine, a westward-flowing tributary of the Scheldt, which it joins in northern France. The surface rocks are chiefly Cretaceous but a belt of Tertiary clays occupies the middle of the valley, which is open and level.

L*

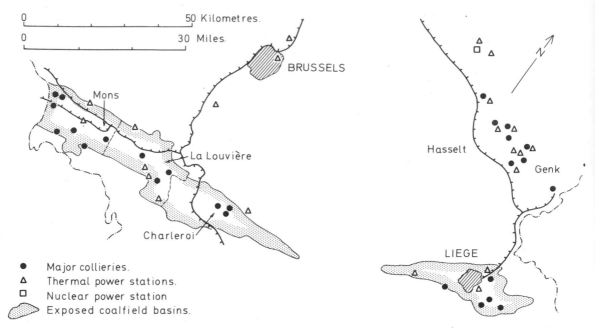

Fig 60   Coalfield Regions of Belgium

The valley-sides are characterised by wooded bluffs, particularly to the north. The industrial agglomeration consists of some twelve medium-sized coalfield towns and villages each of about 10,000 population, which mark the earliest stage of the basin's development. To the north a smaller group of more dispersed towns followed the second stage, of deep-shaft collieries; the best coking coal occurs at depths of 2,600 to 4,400 feet (800 to 1,400 m.). These towns are associated with the canal from Nimy (on the northern outskirts of Mons) to Tournai. The chief canal, however, is the straight Condé-Mons section of the waterway which links north France with Charleroi. Production of coal from the Borinage district has steadily decreased since 1951 and new industries such as paper manufacture, food processing and light engineering have been established to diversify the economy of the area.

Central Basin

This area lies at the head of the valley of the Haine; the Coal Measures are here overlain by both Mesozoic and Tertiary rocks, the latter forming the higher ground (about 470 feet, 160 m.) of the Haine-Sambre watershed. Coal production in this area has declined less than in the Borinage and about one-tenth of the Belgian total comes from the Central, or La Louvière, basin. The coal is a good coking one and there is an integrated steelworks at La Louvière. Glass manufacture and industrial ceramics are other activities of the conurbation centred on this town, also gas and chemical industries associated with the coalfield.

Charleroi

The chief town of the industrial south-west is Charleroi which, with its agglomeration of surrounding towns, makes up an urban and industrial region with a population approaching 400,000, although the actual town of Charleroi accounts for only a small fraction of this.

Charleroi is at the point where the Sambre enters the coal furrow from the south-west. The valley widens as it receives two minor tributaries one of which, the Pieton, provides the valley followed by the important canal and rail route northwards to Brussels. The river terraces downstream provide good sites for industries but this industrial area is much more compact than that of the Central basin.

As in many other areas coal production has markedly dropped since 1951; Charleroi, however, is primarily important for its iron and steel industry. The major works are sited close to the town centre and adjacent to the canal: coke is received from the Campine and the Ruhr as well as from the Borinage whilst ore comes from French Lorraine. Downstream are further iron and steelworks but the industrial pattern here is undergoing changes: at the most easterly point of the area is Jemeppe where a large plastic factory has been established. Chemical works are also sited along the Sambre valley between Charleroi and Jemeppe.

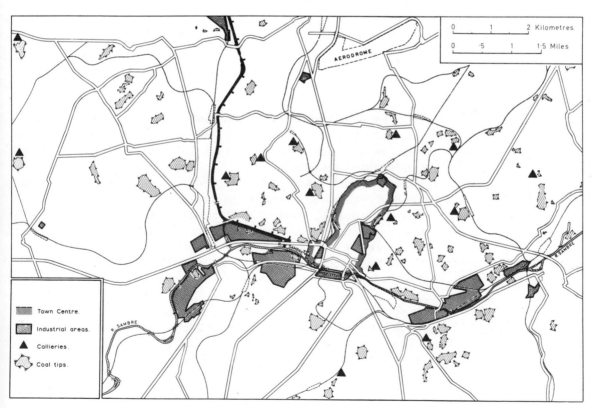

Fig 61 Charleroi

The traditional centre of the glassware industry, based on sands from the Entre-Sambre-et-Meuse region, was also at Charleroi; the industry continues at Roux, near the Brussels-Charleroi Canal, and at Auvelais on the Sambre downstream from Charleroi as well as in a number of small factories within the city. The newer glass industry of the Campine area now provides acute competition. The industries of Charleroi are sufficiently diversified to permit the continued growth of this area. The canal to Brussels has been enlarged to take vessels up to 1,350 tons, and that to Namur has been improved by straightening and a reduction in the number of locks.

The eastern basin

Centred on Liège, the Walloon centre of Belgium, this area provides both contrasts and similarities with the western industrial regions of the Sambre-Meuse trough. The underlying coal basin is smaller and shallower than the western one; it is also the coalfield with the longest history of working, having been exploited by shallow adit workings at least as early as the seventeenth century to provide fuel for the smithies of Liège. A number of sub-regions of Belgium are closely linked here: the industrial districts of the Liège conurbation and the Verviers areas: the Hesbaye and Campine heathlands; the Pays de Herve and the Ardennes foothills. To all these areas the town of Liège is the regional service centre; its influence is least in the Campine because of the language boundary, which crosses the Hesbaye, and also this is an area of relatively recent development.

Liège

Liège has a long history: it contrasts with the industrial centres of the eastern basins which are principally products of the last two centuries whereas the bishopric of Liège existed as a semi-independent state before the emergence of the Benelux states. The town is sited below the confluence of the Ourthe and Vesdre and the modern town spreads across the interfluves of these streams as well as the flood plain and river terraces of the Meuse (Plate 56). The basis of industrial expansion was the eastern coalfield but this is declining: the collieries in the east and south, where the coal is more suitable for coking, now being of chief importance. Supplies of coking coal are also brought via the Albert Canal from the Campine, and iron ore comes from Lorraine and Luxembourg. The steel works are mainly situated downstream but the blast furnaces are upstream and the river provides a valuable means of transport for both pig iron and molten steel. A number of specialities, tubes, cables, heavy electrical machinery, etc. are to be found and also the completely separate industry of zinc reduction and manufacture. Chemical works, tyre manufacture and crystal glassware manufacture are also represented in Liège. Despite this diversity the contraction of coal mining has presented the area with problems but good communications by river and the Antwerp-Liège-Aachen motorway should facilitate industrial expansion here.

Legend within figure:

BUILT UP AREA

INDUSTRIAL AREA

COAL MINES

COAL TIPS

CITADEL

R. MEUSE

R. MEUSE

OURTHE

Kilometres
0   1   2

Miles
0   1

Fig 62 Liège

Plate 56   The Liège industrial area at Seraing.
             Seraing is on the western outskirts of Liège. The Meuse is in the centre of this
             view looking westwards.

Eastwards from Liège, along the Vesdre Valley, is a discontinuous industrial zone; compared with the Liège Basin this is on a small scale although its centre, Verviers, is the chief woollen town of Belgium. The textile industry is based on a number of small settlements between Nessonvaux, midway between Liège and Verviers, and Eupen. Two reservoirs, at Lake Gileppe and Lake Eupen, were constructed in 1875 and 1935 respectively to provide water for the industry. Since 1960, the industry, which uses a considerable proportion of Australian wool imported via Antwerp, has shown little growth in the face of strong competition from man-made fibres. Other industries in the valley include food preparation, (chocolate production in particular), engineering and, at Welkenraedt in the extreme east, a ceramic industry.

The Vesdre Valley extends westwards between two dissimilar hill regions. To the south, between the Vesdre and the Amblève, are the plateaux of the High Ardennes, whilst to the north are the lower hills of the Pays de Herve. These latter are underlain by Cretaceous rocks, which rest unconformably on the Carboniferous strata, and the region is somewhat similar to the Hesbaye area.

The region to the south shows a complex geology, in which the Devonian sequence is crossed before the Cambrian (underlying the Hautes Fagnes) is reached. This is a more densely populated region than the typical Ardennes areas farther south; towns such as Theux and Spa are within commuting distance of the Liège conurbation, as too are the smaller villages of the Amblève and lower Ourthe Valley. Spa is also an old-established resort, based on its mineral spring (it has given its name to all spas), and this region has a tourist rôle greater than its agricultural potential. Woodland and mixed farming (but little cereal cultivation) are the main features of the rural land use.

The Pays de Herve, rather contrastedly, is a dairy farming region of some importance. It too is within easy reach of the Liège conurbation and is served by a good main road including the Liège-Antwerp motorway. The farms are generally small, less than 12 acres (5 ha.) in size and the landscape is an undulating one of *bocage*. The dairying is intensively organised with a rotation of pasture land and fodder crops; the herds are of high-quality animals, butter and cheese are produced and there is a concentration on pigs as a secondary livestock. In the sheltered valleys fruit farming is also important, orchard fruits predominating; cider is produced at Thimister.

THE CENTRAL
HILL REGIONS

To the north of the Sambre-Meuse industrial region the land rises to elevations of about 650 feet (200 m.) or a little less, and then gradually descends northwards and westwards to the lowlands bordering the North Sea. These hills are formed on various rocks; nearest the Sambre-Meuse they are Palaeozoic strata but some Mesozoic rocks occur both in the east and west. An almost continuous covering of limon characterises the hills as also their extension eastwards across the southern Netherlands into Germany.

Northwards again, the hill region extends into the distinctive Campine (Flemish Kempenland) where the underlying geology is of rocks of Pliocene age. Altitudes here are between 160 and 320 feet (50 to 100 m.).

These hill regions have been given various regional or pays names; from west to east they are Hainaut or the Pays d'Ath, the Brabant Plateau and the Hesbaye, with the Pays de Herve on the eastern side of the Meuse beyond Liège. The entire zone is sometimes referred to as Middle Belgium.

The Campine

Of the heathland regions of Benelux this area is distinct and unique in several ways; primarily this can be ascribed to the basic physique and geology. Before this century the Campine was a typical frontier zone; the natural soil development from the coarse Pliocene sands and gravels being infertile with contrasting pockets of peat bog and marsh. The natural vegetation is of heath and scrub, and these covered the entire region as recently as 1850. A century later this had been reduced to about one-seventh and the landscape transformed into one of pasture and cultivated fields. The agricultural pattern is similar to that of Flanders, but the individual farms are larger, generally between 12 and 25 acres (5–10 ha.), and nearly three-quarters are worked by the direct labour of the owner-occupier and his family.

The field pattern, as in Flanders but contrasting with that of the Ardennes, is in blocks and not divided into scattered strips: woodland is still a notable feature of the landscape, in particular, plantations of Scots Pine have been made often as wind-breaks. Here is a developing region in terms of agriculture and new hamlets are taking shape; this is particularly true of the central and southern zones.

On the higher eastern margin, which rises to just over 330 feet (100 m.) there remains a higher percentage of woodland. Also on this eastern sector is the important and developing coalfield area. The presence of a concealed basin of coal seams beneath the Pliocene and underlying Cretaceous strata was known early in this century but it was little developed until after the First World War. Production is of good quality coal, suitable for coking, from seams which are little faulted, frequently more than three feet (1 m.) thick, but at depths of 1,600 to 3,300 feet (500–1,000 m.). The coalfield zone extends from Pessenderloo to Hasselt, Genk and Eisden; the three first-named are adjacent to the Albert Canal and the last town is on the South Willemsvaart Canal. Other industries include zinc and copper refining, glass-making at Mol-Gompel using local

Plate 57   Zinc processing plant near Mol, Campine.

Balen is a major zinc processing plant sited on a branch canal south-east of Mol in the Campine. Belgium is the world's second exporter of zinc, and is prominent in the production of other non-ferrous ores.

sands, brickmaking, generally adjacent to the Bocholt-Herentals Canal, and chemical industries. The original isolation of this area led to the establishment of such works as the somewhat insalubrious ones associated with lead, and the dangerous explosives industries at Lommel and Balen.

The coalfield is ultra-modern in equipment and methods; practically all the collieries and industries of the Campine are arranged in garden-city style with their associated dwellings. The Campine has a high proportion of foreign labour, especially Italian workers, and there is also a considerable movement of commuters between towns within the area and across the Dutch border to towns such as Breda, Tilburg and Eindhoven.

Hainaut

To the north of the Mons-Charleroi industrial regions lies a hilly region which north of Charleroi reaches 570 feet (160 m.) but which is generally at little more than 330 feet (100 m.) before descending slowly north-westwards towards Interior Flanders. This is the low plateau of Hainaut or the Pays d'Ath, and it is underlain by the Eocene Flanders Clay which here rests on the northern limits of the coal syncline. Carboniferous limestone appears at the surface in places and Cretaceous rocks form the southern boundary in the west, where they overlie the Borinage coal basin. The limon cover which is found on all these hill regions of Middle Belgium is somewhat variable in thickness in this region.

Hainaut is an area of large nucleated settlements with diverse characteristics: Soignies, on the main Mons-Brussels route, has tanneries and also extensive quarries in the Carboniferous Limestone. Ath marks the southern extension of the Flemish textile region, and is noted for furniture manufacture. To the south the chalk is quarried for cement and there are cement-works near Mons. A line of wooded country marks this southern edge and continues westwards into France.

Agriculturally, the region is a prosperous one, with mixed farming and cattle rearing. Cereals and sugar beet become more important to the east, flax to the west, and dairying and some market gardening in the regions nearest the main centres of population.

South of the Mons basin is a further limon-covered chalk zone which rises to 650 feet (200 m.) generally and which resembles the Hesbaye with its compact villages, large farms and a concentration on grass and fodder crops. Sugar beet, grown in the rich agricultural zone farther south, bordering the Entre-Sambre-et-Meuse region, is refined at Thuillies.

Brabant

The central hill region of Belgium shows a number of contrasting landscapes. These are particularly marked between the areas east and west of the River Senne. To the east, and upstream from Brussels, there is a marked rise to the plateau of Brabant, formed by the Brussels Sands which rest upon the Flanders Clay; the limon covering is here much more discontinuous. To the north this gives way to a plateau capped by Pliocene materials, an extension of the Campine area which is known as the Hageland. West of the Senne the plateau is lower, *c.* 200–300 feet (60–90 m.) and there the geology is mainly of clays with some limon capping. Older rocks, of Silurian or Cambrian age, outcrop in valley exposures and are quarried for building stones, setts, etc.

The northern section of this region is known as the *Region Mixte*: it is diverse in agricultural activities, industries and settlement characteristics, but the economy is oriented towards Brussels. The rather larger than average farms to the west of the Senne carry on market gardening and dairying; fruit cultivation marks the zone west of Brussels in a sector between the routes to Ghent and the Senne Valley. Settlement in this lower area is along the roads whereas on the Brabant Plateau to the east it is typically of nucleated villages and small urban centres, with a greater percentage of woodland, in the clearings of which these settlements had their origin. The isolated large farm, arranged around a closed courtyard is typical, and there is a higher percentage of grassland.

Within the entire zone there is a daily movement of labour from the rural regions to the industrial centres, particularly to those of the Senne Valley and Greater Brussels. There are also movements to local industries such as at Enghien with light engineering, Ath with furniture manufacture and Louvain with varied industries. This last town is considerably larger than any of the others, and is served by a canal spur from Malines on the Antwerp-Brussels canal. Industries tend to be developing along this canal and include those associated with agriculture, such as flour milling and vegetable canning; metal and electrical industries also exist at Malines and the car assembly plant of Standard-Triumph is here.

North of Louvain and south of the Demer Valley lies the Hageland: a zone of Pliocene heathland intersected by many valleys and having marked similarities to the Campine. It is an area of small market garden holdings and of a commuter population travelling to one of the peripheral towns—Aarschot, Diest, Tirlemont or Louvain.

The Hesbaye

West-north-west from the Liège conurbation the central hills of Belgium are formed on the Cretaceous Chalk subsoil. There is generally a thick covering of limon and the surface configuration is of an undulating plateau at some 650 feet (200 m.), limited by a sharp descent on the south to the Meuse Valley. This is *la Hesbaye sèche*, an area of dry valleys and little surface water, with belts of woodland along the minor roads, of large open fields and large nucleated villages as well as dispersed farmsteads. Farther north the plateau is lower and the sub-soil is clay; this is *la Hesbaye humide*. Most of the Hesbaye farmers practise a rotation of crops in which sugar beet, a cereal (wheat, barley or rye) and fodder crops alternate. A number of sugar beet factories occur within the area or on its edges, as at Tirlemont (Tienen).

THE
BRUSSELS-ANTWERP
INDUSTRIAL AXIS

The most densely populated region of Belgium is that of the industrial zone from Antwerp to Brussels. This lies at the heart of the country; it lies in the north of the province of Brabant and in a central position relative to Benelux routeways. The sphere of influence of Antwerp extends to the western Campine and over some of the polderland west of the Scheldt estuary, the Pays de Waes. Brussels fills a local provincial capital rôle for the northern part of Brabant as well as the specialised functions of a national capital.

Antwerp

The port of Antwerp is third in rank in North-West Europe, after Rotterdam and London. It is some 49 miles (78 km.) from the sea but has a

Plate 58 Antwerp.
An aerial view showing a section of the old town in the foreground, modern development on the far side of the Scheldt, and the extensive port developments in the distance. New works will extend these farther downstream to accommodate 100,000 ton vessels.

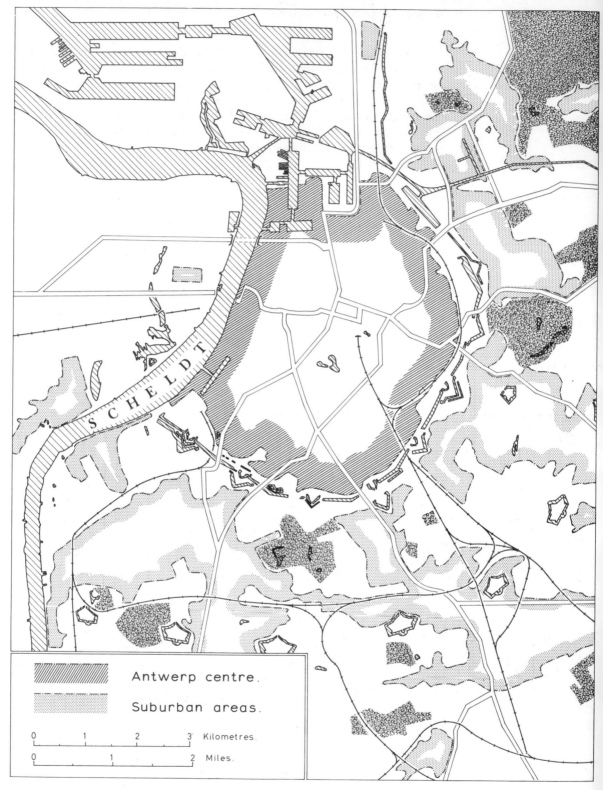

SCHELDT

Antwerp centre.

Suburban areas.

| 0 | 1 | 2 | 3 | Kilometres. |

| 0 | 1 | 2 | Miles. |

Fig 63   Antwerp

comprehensive and spacious development of basins and quays downstream from the town, in addition to several miles of river and canalside quays. Canal links with Brussels, Charleroi and the south, the Campine, Liège, and the Meuse make Antwerp an international port for a hinterland with a radius of up to 250 miles (400 km.); extending from northern and eastern France to Aachen in Germany and parts of the southern Netherlands. Improved waterway connections with Rotterdam will be one of the results of the present Dutch Delta Plan.

Antwerp is sited on the east bank of the Scheldt (Plate 58) and shows a clear series of growth rings. The line of walls and fortifications which contained the sixteenth century town is marked by boulevards, but outer defensive sites dating from the nineteenth century and the recent World Wars may still be traced. Modest growth of new industries and, mainly, residential regions on the west bank are developments chiefly since the Second World War, although the first road tunnel under the river dates from 1931.

The Antwerp conurbation extends southwards along road and rail-routes to Brussels almost as far as Malines; in fact urbanisation is practically continuous along this route from Antwerp to Brussels. To the north, the city is bounded by its dockland and associated industries: refineries and car assembly plants. The industries of Antwerp are many and include those associated with an international port such as shipbuilding and the processing of tropical products. A variety of heavy industries are sited upstream from the city and along the Scheldt or canal banks from Hoboken to Willebroek. These include cement, industrial ceramics, textile and chemical industries. At Willebroek and Boom there is a concentration of brickworks along the river Rupel.

The industrial growth of Antwerp has followed its growth as a port, and other industries such as diamond cutting (which employs some 10,000 workers), photographic works, telephone, wireless and other precision industries have established and expanded here. The Antwerp agglomeration altogether has a population approaching three-quarters of a million and is one of the fastest growing sectors of the country.

Brussels

The Brussels agglomeration extends for some twenty-five miles (40 km.) along the valley of the Senne and has a population of over a million. The city itself stands as a bi-lingual island in the Flemish-speaking part of Belgium; the main linguistic boundary being 8 miles (13 kms.) away at the nearest point to the south-east. The city's expansion has crossed this boundary in several places and the resulting linguistic problems are considerable.

Brussels stands at the northern edge of the low Brabant plateau, and the city centre has a polygonal pattern embracing an upper and lower town area. The pattern is made by a line of boulevards and is crossed on its western side by the river Senne and the Willebroek to Charleroi canal. The main railway tunnels through the city centre, although the chief

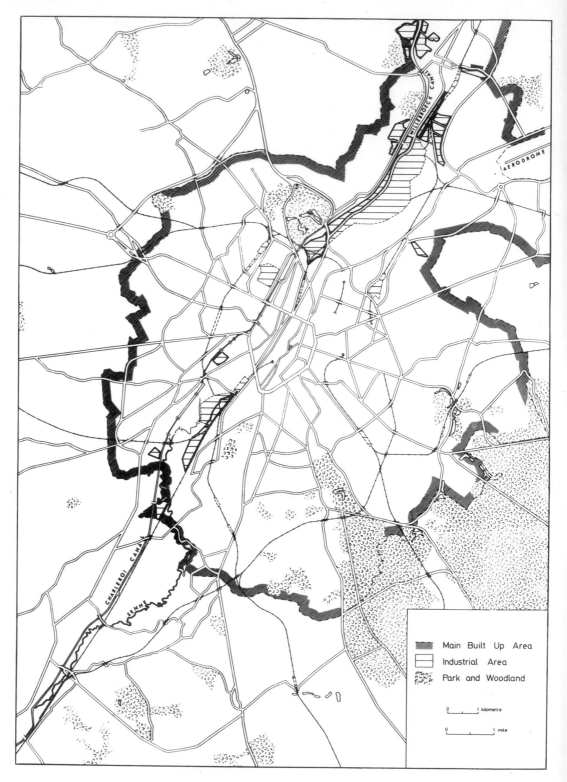

Fig 64 Brussels

Plate 59 Brussels.
Older buildings in a corner of the Grand Place in the foreground contrast with newer commercial properties on the slopes of the higher town.

stations are on the northern and southern sections of the boulevards. The division between upper and lower town is reflected in the urban functions, the lower region being the oldest sector and the chief commercial and shopping district, whilst the upper town houses the administrative sector. Industrial zones follow the valley north-east and south-west whilst the suburban tentacles of Brussels have moved south-eastwards (Fig. 64) towards and beyond the forest of Soignes, which forms a 'green wedge' in this sector. Dispersed areas of suburban style commuter settlements lie in a broad zone around the city and especially to the south. Market gardening development is to the north and west, but a notable exception is the glass-house area of Hoeilaart some 6 miles (10 km.) south-east of the city centre where the growing of dessert grapes is a speciality (Plate 60). Beyond this, and across the linguistic boundary, further residential development is taking place.

Plate 60   Market-gardening at Hoeilaart, Brabant.
A section of the market-gardening glasshouse region at Hoeilaart, south-east of Brussels. There are some 340,000 glasshouses in this district producing mainly black grapes and vegetables. About 15% of the produce is exported.

The industrial activities of the Brussels region are immensely varied; they include miscellaneous light industries and food manufacture, clothing, tobacco and pharmaceutical goods, printing, jewellery and electrical ware. Along the line of the Willebroek Canal, to the north of the city, industries are chiefly connected with goods imported into the area; timber, flour, chemicals and heavy metals. By contrast, the Charleroi canal has more varied industries, including textiles and cable works. Finally, in the extreme south, at Clabecq, there is an iron and steel works with blast furnaces and steel converters.

FLANDERS   Within this region, which extends southwards into France and northwards into the Netherlands, may be recognised a series of physical subregions roughly parallel to the coast. From the coast inland they are:

(a) *The Dunes.* A narrow strip of coastal land in this area, generally less than $\frac{1}{4}$ mile (400 m.) in width but reaching about 1 mile ($1\frac{3}{4}$ km.) in the west.

(b) *The Polders* and the maritime lowlands of Quaternary deposits.

(c) *Interior Flanders.* A region rising to inland summits in the Tournaisis district of nearly 500 feet (150 m.) but generally undulating land between 80 feet (25 m.) and 160 feet (50 m.).

Urban and industrial developments have taken place in all these areas to produce a pattern which cuts across the physical regions and also the international boundaries. The main areas are: Ghent-Terneuzen, Lille-Roubaix-Courtrai, and the coast.

Towns in Flanders were first established some ten centuries ago; Ghent had developed as an inland port by the early ninth century as a trading and manufacturing settlement at the confluence of the Scheldt and the Lys. During succeeding centuries Bruges grew to great importance and the two towns were linked by canal in the thirteenth century. Antwerp, however, dominated the area in the sixteenth century and an attempt to revitalise Ghent led to the construction of the small Sasse Canal in 1549. The dominance of Amsterdam as the port serving the Netherlands was a result of the Treaty of Westphalia in 1648 which closed the Scheldt and all outlets to the sea via the Scheldt. It was not until the early nineteenth century that Antwerp and Ghent were to be given new life. In the case of Ghent the Sasse Canal was deepened and brought into use between Ghent and Terneuzen in 1827 and it has been progressively improved ever since: it will in future be able to handle ships of 50,000 tons.

The Flemish industries had declined in the eighteenth century and workers travelled great distances, e.g., to northern France. The position was made worse by the early communications, in particular the railways, being chiefly north-south, e.g., Antwerp-Brussels-North France, the development of east-west lines coming later.

Nevertheless, Ghent is a growing industrial centre at the heart of an agglomeration containing over $\frac{1}{4}$ million people, with waterway links to Bruges, the upper Lys and the Scheldt, as well as the ship canal to Terneuzen. Of first importance are the cotton textile and the expanding man-made fibres industries. Other industries, along the ship canal and in Netherlands territory as well as in Belgium, include a shipbuilding yard, chemicals, refineries, electrical goods, paper, and there is a project for an integrated iron and steel complex.

Plate 61   Flanders landscape near Ghent.
Industrial development along the canal west of Ghent, in the close pattern of mixed farmland and woodland of interior Flanders.

The major industrial conurbation of Interior Flanders includes both French and Belgian towns in the Lille-Armentières-Courtrai-Tournai area. By reason of the international boundary two textile industries are found here, the one in Belgium being part of the typically scattered pattern of Flanders, whilst that of France is the more concentrated.

The Flemish textile industry is an old established one but the materials woven have changed over the centuries. Initially a woollen-using industry, it transferred to linen and, in the nineteenth century, to cotton. Flax is an important crop in the Flanders Plains, and particularly on the low hills of Interior Flanders.

This is an area of intensive agriculture, generally organised in many small family farms, the average size being 12½ acres (5 ha.). These farmsteads are scattered but there are also many small villages and towns, particularly in the west, and their industries derive much of their labour force from the farmer's family. The farming is of a mixed type and con-

Plate 62 Flax farm in western Flanders.

centrates on livestock: the rotation includes roots and legumes, rye, oats and barley, much of which is for fodder purposes. Industrial crops are flax, chicory, and hops; these are most typical of west Flanders and the higher regions of the centre.

The coast of Flanders is an important tourist asset to Belgium and, to a lesser extent, northern France. Many seaside resorts have been established along this dune coast, from La Panne near the French border to Knokke near the Dutch. There are also a number of ports, each of which has its own special function: the two most important are:

Zeebrugge—the outport for Bruges and a ferry head for rail and road traffic with England; primarily in goods but with some passenger and car traffic. There are a number of industries including glass manufacture.

Ostend—the main packet port for cross-Channel traffic to England in passengers and road vehicles, and a fishing port. Some 80% of the Belgian fishing fleet is based here. There is a chemical industry at Zandvoorde.

The most marked feature is the seasonal variation in population associated with the tourist and holiday industry. In winter many large apartment blocks, hotels and shops are completely closed and the summer population may rise some ten or twenty times that of the winter. There is also a considerable movement of people through this area; this is not only from across the Channel but also along the coast.

Plate 63   Ostend harbour.
Part of the older harbour with shrimping vessels. Entrance to the newer section, ferry terminal, etc., is in the right background.

The dunes region is a recreational zone and also forms a line along which road and rail routes operate; it has no agricultural value and is marked by dispersed settlements, even villas, away from the somewhat rectangular pattern of holiday towns, many of which are products of the twentieth century.

The polderlands behind the dunes are a somewhat narrower continuation of those in the Netherlands. This is a landscape that is almost devoid of trees, and is intersected by numerous drainage channels. It is entirely a man-made landscape; since the eighth century it has been gradually reclaimed by peasants and by the larger land holders, religious houses, etc. There are thus contrasts between the irregular pattern of banks and ditches of older reclamation lines, and the rectangular pattern of more recent work, as seen south of Ostend and north-east of Bruges. There are also contrasts in the agricultural pattern, ranging from small family farms of less than 12 acres (5 ha.) to large opulent farms of up to 125 acres (50 ha.). These latter are generally well-equipped and productive dairy farms; the highest density of cattle in Belgium is in this area, up to 70 cows per 100 acres (180 cows per 100 ha.) and also a concentration of ancillary pig-farming. Sixty per cent of the land is devoted to dairy cattle pasture, and much of the remainder to fodder crops. Cereal production of barley, oats and wheat is also carried on and the highest yields of the country are recorded here.

The main market centre in the polderlands is the historic town of Bruges. There are industrial regions of Bruges particularly near the ship canal to Zeebrugge and it has light engineering and food processing industries.

Regions of the Netherlands
NORTH BRABANT

This area is part of the Benelux Central Region, a frontier zone of both Belgium and the Netherlands which has many points of similarity across the national boundary. It has been partly described under the Campine region of Belgium, pp. 303–5. It is a somewhat undulating plateau area in which sands form the main surface material; the higher sections occur in the Campine, which reaches nearly 330 feet (100 m.) whereas the North-Brabant region of the Netherlands does not much exceed 100 feet (30 m.).

This area of the Netherlands is bounded by a ring of large towns, which begins on the Meuse Estuary with Bergen-op-Zoom and continues with Roosendaal, Breda, Tilburg and Eindhoven to Weert.

Agriculture is most important as the occupation of rural areas in the north-east of North Brabant and is a mixed type of family-farming, on the sandy soil regions. Holdings are small, averaging less than 12 acres (5 ha.), and there is little difference across the national boundary here. Farther east there is a greater concentration on arable whilst to the west and in most valley situations pasture is predominant. Around Breda horticulture is important.

The industrial activities of the growing towns of North Brabant are varied; the local resource-basis for industry is almost lacking and raw materials must be brought in. There is thus a concentration on skilled engineering industries rather than on heavy industries; the initiative for the establishment of industries has been both governmental and private.

Plate 64   Eindhoven.
Aerial view of the town centre. The chief works of Philips electrical industries
are in this town, and modern spacious factories and suburbs surround the small
core of the old town.

Eindhoven (Plate 64) is the largest town of this group, with a population
of about one quarter of a million and with a number of industries: electrical
(Philips, founded here in 1908), car manufacture (D.A.F., started in 1928),
tobacco, textiles and woodworking. The population of Eindhoven in 1900
was only 5,000 and in 1964 exceeded 178,000; the site is on the 'flat'
provided by the wide terrace-spread of an earlier course of the Meuse at
about 45 feet (17 m.) above sea level.

Other towns in this zone are Breda and Tilburg, both noted for textile
industries, wool at Tilburg and synthetic fibres at Breda. The site of
Breda is on the extreme limit of the low plateau of North Brabant and at

the edge of the flood plain, whereas Tilburg is near the head of a minor tributary stream draining from the terrace to the Meuse.

The growth of mining communities in the Belgian Campine coupled with a decline in agriculture and rural population generally has led to a surplus of labour in some of the rural regions of this area; this has been accentuated by the natural increase of the mining settlements. There is a pattern of commuting from the Belgian area to the towns of the adjacent Dutch area and particularly to Eindhoven. Other industrial activities are strengthening in the Campine and the traffic may become less one-sided as a result.

The provincial capital of North Brabant is 'sHertogenbosch, also on the northern limit, at the edge of the Meuse lowlands. It has mixed industries, including machinery, cigars and footwear. The last-named is a particular feature of a zone, the *Laangstraat*, of small towns and villages which stretches westwards from here for some 25 miles (40 km.).

LIMBURG

This is a separate sub-region of the Netherlands, an appendage east of the Meuse, which contains the chief coalfield and the highest land areas of the country. The area was gained by the Netherlands in 1839 in exchange for cession by the Dutch crown to Belgium of part of Luxembourg (now the Belgian Province of Luxembourg). Limburg includes the narrowing Meuse flood plain around Maastricht but otherwise is an upland area between 400 and 600 feet above sea-level (120 to 180 m.).

The flood-plain area is distinguished by industries such as glass, earthenware and cement manufacture, related both to local deposits and the coalfield farther east. Maastricht is overshadowed as a regional centre, however, by Liège and Aachen; the major international routes pass either to the south, in Belgian territory, or well to the north. Routeways along the Meuse valley are to some extent duplicated, there being a major canal linking Liège and the Campine (the Albert Canal) entirely in Belgium, whilst the older Zuid-Willemsvaart Canal serving the northern Belgian Campine leads from Maastricht. Northwards from here the Meuse is unsuitable for barge traffic and the Juliana Canal carries traffic for some 22 miles (35 km.) from Maastricht to a point on the Meuse above Roermond.

The Limburg coalfield is suffering from the competition of other sources of power, especially oil and natural gas. Planned expansion of this coalfield was suspended in 1961 and in 1966 the number of state coal-mines was reduced by one-third, chiefly by the closing of the older and more costly pits to operate. Other industries have been developed (Plate 65), notably chemical products and plastics (polyethylene) at Geleen. Heerlen, in the east, is the chief town of the coalfield; it has grown rapidly since 1900 and has a planned layout.

The agriculture of this low plateau, which is contiguous with the Pays de Herve of Belgium (see p. 302), is similar to that of the Hesbaye region of Belgium, being based on limon-covered chalk hills. Mixed farming in small family units is the chief feature, with local concentrations of market gardening.

Plate 65   South Limburg colliery.
Lutterade, near Sittard in South Limburg. A modern colliery and nitrogen-fixation plant are in close juxtaposition with a mosaic of strip arable fields.

THE EASTERN
HEATHLANDS

The eastern Netherlands provide a convenient unit for discussion as they include the main upland areas of the country; they are also the less densely populated regions and have the more 'rural' aspect, compared with the 'urbanised' western Netherlands. Although a number of sub-divisions may be distinguished, due to differences in occupations, landscape and physique, this region will be taken as a whole.

In the extreme north, in the provinces of Friesland and Groningen, is a region of lowland marshes where agricultural activities are chiefly based on cattle and dairy farming. Leeuwarden is the centre of this area, and the produce is exported both within Benelux and outside: eastwards, the pattern of farming becomes more mixed and in the Oldambt area on the German borders wheat is the dominant crop. Settlement in both areas is strongly nucleated with a large number of 'terpen' sites (see also pp.182–3).

These are man-made mounds of earth some 15 to 30 feet (5–10 m.) high which provided a defensive site against inundations by the sea; many are of considerable age and they were described by Pliny in the first century A.D.

The heathlands of Drente and Overijssel provinces include a considerable proportion of glacially-derived materials in their subsoil. This has resulted in some areas of upland peat bogs. These were gradually reclaimed by the simple expedient of establishing settlements on the banks of a canal, and gradually cutting out the peat. A long strip of ground at right angles to the canal was thus cut down to the sandy sub-soil, which was then well manured and is now used for the cultivation of potatoes and vegetables. Horticulture is most important but rye and oats are also grown as fodder cereals for the home market, and there is an agricultural industry of strawboard manufacture. South of Groningen dairy production is important, and this gives way to a grassland region centred on Zwolle which exports dairy products. Groningen itself is a market and service centre with an extensive hinterland. It has a number of small industries associated with agriculture-food processing, light engineering and machinery.

From Zwolle south and south-east to the German frontier the province of Overijssel is a predominantly pastoral region with small hamlets and isolated farmsteads. The farms are sited in the centre of their block of fields and there is also a higher percentage of woodland than farther north. The natural vegetation is of heathland or oak forest and there are considerable areas of this vegetation remaining, especially between the settlement groups known as 'es-dorp'. These hamlets or villages became established on patches of fertile land (or 'esch') which were originally farmed on the open field system. The individual farms are small, the average size is only 20 acres (8 ha.) and nearly one-half are 12 acres (5 ha.) or less. The average herd is of 9 to 10 cows, 4 or 5 calves, some pigs and up to 200 or so chickens. This region has been losing population by migration to such areas as the Randstad Holland: although new industries have been introduced to the area and 'development' regions have been designated.

A region in which industrialisation has already taken place is that of Twente; it is based on the textile industry of cotton and also includes the making of machinery. The chief centres are Hengelo, Emschede and Deventer. Emschede, with a population exceeding 150,000 is the centre of the cotton industry, but also manufactures textile machinery and has other engineering activities. Cotton manufacturing is widespread amongst the smaller towns of the region but there are no great local specialisations. Nevertheless, this is the main example in the Netherlands of one area with a single dominant industry. The brown-coalfield of the upper Ijssel is in the south of this area but industrial power derives from the Dutch electric grid.

These eastern regions are terminated by the valley of the River IJ on the west, beyond which is a further area of heathland formed on the poor sandy soils of glacial outwash. This is the Veluwe, whose major function is as recreational land, although some improvement for agriculture has taken place.

M

An important factor in the eastern Netherlands since 1960 has been the development of the Groningen gas field; indeed this is important to the whole country. Pipelines were constructed in 1964 and later years southwards to Zutphen, Arnhem and Maastricht, with spurs to serve Eindhoven, the extreme south-west of the country, and the Randstad cities. Additional lines were installed in 1966 to lead directly to Ijmuiden and the Randstad area via the polderlands and the Ijsselmeer.

In the extreme south-east of Drenthe Province, almost on the German border, is the oil field centred on Coevorden and Schoonebeck. This is the richest oilfield of North-West Europe but even so produces less than one-quarter of the Netherlands' requirements. The oil bearing strata are in an anticline of the Lower Cretaceous rocks at a depth of some 2,500–3,000 feet (800–900 m.) and production started in 1945. A second oilfield between The Hague and Delft produces only about one-half the output of the Schoonebeck field.

LOWLANDS
AND POLDERLANDS

The provinces of Gelderland, Utrecht, South Holland and Zeeland include large areas of low-lying land adjacent to the rivers of the Rhine-Meuse-Scheldt system. These are chiefly formed on clays which are fluvial in origin as far downstream as the longitude of Gorinchem. Below there they are of marine origin. The Rhine divides into northern and southern distributaries, the Lek and the Waal respectively, and between these and the Meuse are a number of pastoral regions.

The river clay areas present drainage difficulties; water meadows are typical, and the level of water fluctuates with the regime of the river. Some of the earliest areas of reclamation in the Netherlands are here, one such being the Betuwe, between the Lek and Waal, a rich pastoral area which also specialises in market gardening. Permanent grassland and little tree growth, level fields broken by drainage ditches, and isolated farmsteads or groups of farms in small hamlets are the main features of the landscape. The holdings are generally small, over 50% being 12½ acres (5 ha.) or less, and the level of production small, as too is the density of population. Farther upstream cultivation becomes more varied as market-gardening and orchards appear. The chief industry in this zone is that of brick making.

The marine clay regions contrast with the riverine areas in that cultivated fields are twice as important as grassland; with some areas, such as South Beveland, having a concentration on horticulture. Grassland is more important on the island of Walcheren (Plate 66) than in many other parts of this region; the coastal fringe, with a dune coastline, has a service function, that of recreation.

Towns in these lowlands are generally small but include two large cities, Nijmegen and Arnhem. Both have riverside sites and grew at crossing points of the Waal and Lek respectively. Arnhem is on the north bank where the ground begins to rise towards the low infertile heathlands of the Veluwe. Synthetic textile fibres, food industries, and various metal

Plate 66   The North Sea coast of Walcheren.
The village of Zoutelande is in the foreground.

industries here provide employment as do service functions for an area stretching northwards into the province of Overijssel.

Nijmegen is a town of similar size to Arnhem: it is sited on the south bank of the Waal where high ground of the Meuse-Rhine watershed descends to the flood plain. Like Arnhem, it is a Roman foundation and has a history of continuous occupation since then, Charlemagne having a palace here, and it was also one of the Hanseatic League towns. Textile, chemical and food industries (sugar refineries, breweries, etc.) are sited here.

Between the north-flowing Rhine distributary, the IJ, and the main river lowlands is a low upland region, the Veluwe, which marks the most western extent of the Pleistocene moraines in this district. As a result of

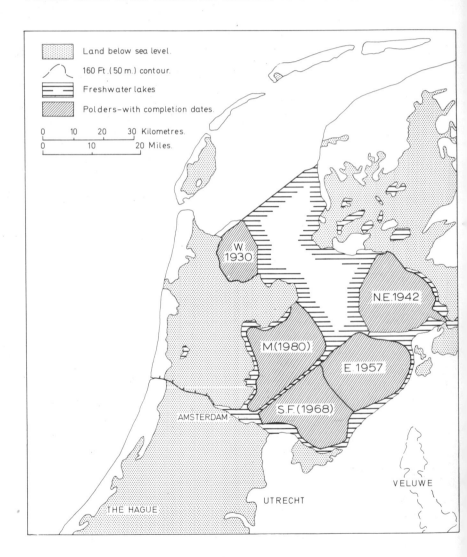

Fig 65   The Polderlands of the Netherlands

the poor soils this is chiefly a heathland, with considerable areas of semi-natural woodland, scrub and sandy heath. It provides the site for Arnhem's airport and is a valuable recreational district for the surrounding towns, Arnhem, Ede, and Appeldorn. The general upper level of this region is around 130 feet above sea-level (40 m.).

A similar wooded upland area lies south of Hilversum, extending between Utrecht and Amersfoort to the banks of the Lek. This is generally much lower than the Veluwe, but does reach 160 feet (50 m.) south of Amersfoort. Some of the woodland in this region is maintained in plantations.

The Delta Plan

Reclamation of the lowlying regions of the Rhine-Meuse Delta has continued since the inundation of this region in the early Middle Ages, with a great impetus after the particularly disastrous floods of 1953 and

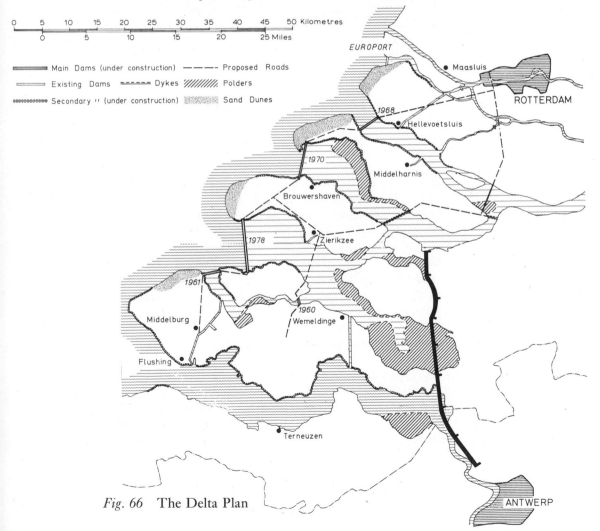

Fig. 66 The Delta Plan

the growing encroachment of saline water into the fresh-water areas. The plan is simple in outline; it is to construct a continuous coastline from Flushing to Europort by building five dams across such inlets as the Haringvliet and the East Scheldt. The coastline exposed to the action of the sea will be shortened by some 440 miles (700 km.) and an area of 25–35,000 acres (10–14,000 ha.) will be available for reclamation. Polderland will not be the chief feature but the area to be devoted to fresh-water lakes is considerable (Fig. 66) and these will provide water supplies for agriculture as well as reduce salinisation of the areas farther inland. This is a real threat if the present rate of increase of pumping from the (fresh-) water-table continues.

These lakes will also provide recreational facilities and it is further proposed that improved communications to Zeeland Province should follow some of the dikes. A new canal between Antwerp and Rotterdam will be constructed on the inland side of the Delta plan area. The outer dikes are to be built in stages and are scheduled to be completed by 1970 at which time only the New Waterway and the West Scheldt will remain open for navigation into the Rhine-Meuse-Scheldt delta area, although a lock will give access into the Haringvliet.

The Frisian islands and North Holland

This isolated region is marked by a lack of industrial development and by a sparse population. Nevertheless, on the Frisian island of Vlieland in particular and also around Den Helder there are signs of urbanisation; either by reason of a higher population density, or by the fact that few of the working population are engaged in agriculture or fishing. This is brought about by the recreational and tourism functions of this sub-region; apart from this the area supports a pastoral-farming industry with mixed farming and market gardening locally more important in the south of the Den Helder peninsula. The Streek, or Drechterland, area north-east of Hoorn has a concentration of flower-seed production, whilst the polder land area of the interior of North Holland is one of the milk and dairy produce areas for the Amsterdam conurbation. In the south there are signs of urbanisation in a growing commuter-region linked with that conurbation. The North Sea coastline is backed by a broad zone of dunes but this is less intensively used for recreation than the North Kennemerland section to the south.

The Polderlands

Reclamation of land from the sea has been a feature of Dutch geography and history but various techniques have been used in different areas. In Zeeland, islands were linked by dikes to enclose land which could then be pumped dry; in North Holland lakes were separated by dikes closing sea-inlets and these lakes were then reclaimed. Along the whole coastline it has often been necessary to supplement dunes by massive sea-dikes. The actual reclamation process is slow: it involves the pumping of water into a network of drainage channels at different levels and ultimately through sluices into the sea, and then the de-salination of the exposed land. The pumping was first done by windmills, whose use became widespread in the fifteenth century, then steam and now electrical pumping. The principal drainage canals are referred to as ring-dikes and both the dikes or areas into which the water is then evacuated are called *boezem*. From these the water is released into the sea at an appropriate state of the tide.

Complications occur due to movements of the land, principally its consolidation and shrinkage. The slow eustatic sinking of the Netherlands region must not be forgotten but it is not a major complication.

In the history of the reclamation of the Netherlands the earliest stage was the isolating of the many lakes of North Holland from the sea; this was started in the late fourteenth century. The lakes were then pumped dry, and the polders divided by a series of dikes and intersected by drainage ditches. The pattern of such reclamation of the older lakes was frequently piecemeal and irregular in shape.

Reclaimed lands were, and still are, in continual danger of inundation, not only from the sea but from the embanked rivers which cross the area and which have been steadily straightened over the centuries, and also from the many remaining lakes. A large number of these lakes, especially in the Amsterdam–Utrecht–Hilversum area are the relics (like the Norfolk Broads) of peat extraction and date from the Middle Ages and later. They are marked by a long, narrow and rectangular pattern. The provinces of Holland and Friesland were particularly lacking in wood for fuel; most settlements therefore extracted peat and this was used for domestic and industrial purposes. Other inland bodies of water were created by the various inundations of the sea; the most extensive such lake was the Haarlemmermeer, covering an area of 45,000 acres (18,000 ha.) between Haarlem, Amsterdam and Leiden. Plans for the reclamation of this lake were considered from the seventeenth century onwards, but it was not completed until 1852 and has many regular patterns of the modern reclamation style.

The most striking feature of land reclamation in the Netherlands is that of the Ijsselmeer, which was enclosed by a main dike in 1932 and sub-divided into large polders. The first to be completed was the North-West, or Wieringermeer Polder and this is now fully integrated within the agricultural region of North Holland. Mixed soils here have helped in both arable and dairy farming, farms vary in size from 50 to 150 acres (20 to 60 ha.); urban functions are provided by three modern villages within the region.

The north-east polder is more recent, whilst the neighbouring polder of East Flevoland is not fully reclaimed. Only the initial diking is in progress for the remaining polders of South Flevoland and Markenwaard. A large body of fresh-water lakes and wide channels will remain when all are completed.

The major landscape feature of these new polderlands is the regular field pattern; the basic unit in the North-East Polderland being one of about 60 acres (24 ha.), surrounded on three sides by drainage ditches and

Plate 67   Aerial view of the North-East Polder.
Note the regular spacing of farmsteads.

by a road on the fourth. Farm-holdings are made up in combinations of
whole or half units (but not less than half) and the farmsteads are associated
with each holding, giving a dispersed settlement pattern. Some ten villages
have been built for minor service functions and a regional centre, Emme-
loord, has been established. The future of some at least of these villages is
uncertain as they show a depopulation tendency.

The land use is mixed; there is a high proportion of grassland on the
peripheries but the majority of farms are engaged in arable production.
About 5% specialise in horticulture and a similar number in woodland
cultivation. A fishing village, Urk, has been maintained on the south-
western extremity of this polder.

RANDSTAD
HOLLAND

The urban settlement and its commercial functions have been typical of the Dutch scene for many centuries. In the provinces of Holland several large urban areas emerged in fairly close proximity: towns such as Amsterdam, Rotterdam, The Hague, Utrecht, Leiden, and Haarlem all lie within a circle of radius 20 miles; an area comparable in size with that of Los Angeles.

These towns make up the 'Randstad Holland' or 'Dutch Urban Ring' and the region is an example of a conurbation with a rural heart. This centre is one in which agriculture is oriented towards the chief towns; it is a polder land mostly below sea level, in which the subsoil is either peat or marine clay which generally indicates areas of reclaimed lakes (e.g. the Haarlemmermeer). The peatlands are characterised by cattle rearing and the production of dairy produce and the old lake floors by market gardening.

The outer ring is not entirely urbanised (Fig. 67) but includes a number of sub-regions in which various forms of agriculture are locally dominant. Thus, between the agglomeration of industries of the lower Meuse below Rotterdam and the urban area of The Hague there are market gardening regions of Westland and Berkel. Both of these are dominated by cultivation under glass: in the Westland region there is a concentration on tomatoes, grapes and cucumbers (Plate 68).

Plate 68   Glasshouse concentration in Westland.
Aerial view of part of the Westland glasshouse concentration.

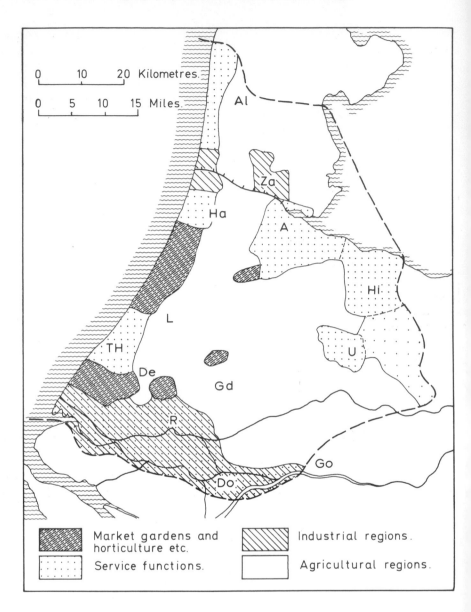

Fig. 67 Regions of Randstad Holland. Towns indicated by initials e.g. Gd = Gouda.

Residential areas are interspersed with areas of market gardening and industry and there is a strong element of commuting to the principal work centres—Utrecht, Rotterdam and Amsterdam. The region of South Kennemerland (around Haarlem) on the North Sea coast is one such residential area for Amsterdam.

There are notable contrasts between the major centres of the Randstad, and it is worthwhile examining each of these in turn.

Amsterdam

The original nucleus of this city was a market place and harbour site at the junction of the small river Amstel and the IJ (Fig. 68). The initial site was on a dike but in 1240 a dam was made across the Amstel, diversionary streams were led to east and west, and Amsterdam emerged as a prime example of a dike-and-dam-town. The area available for building was successively extended by the building of other dikes, the creation of a series of concentric canals, and the characteristic layout of the city emerged. In modern times Amsterdam is the centre of a continuous group of settlements stretching along the North Sea Canal (built in the 1870's) and on the shores of the Ijsselmeer.

It is possible to recognise several distinct zones in the functions of Amsterdam. The older heart of the city, much of which dates from the seventeenth century, is given over to commercial functions; it is the financial centre of the Netherlands. Even so there are many areas of a residential character as well as a mixture of cultural amenities, shops,

Plate 69 Amsterdam.
Aerial view showing the town centre with its pattern of canals, Central Station and part of the inner harbour on the River IJ.

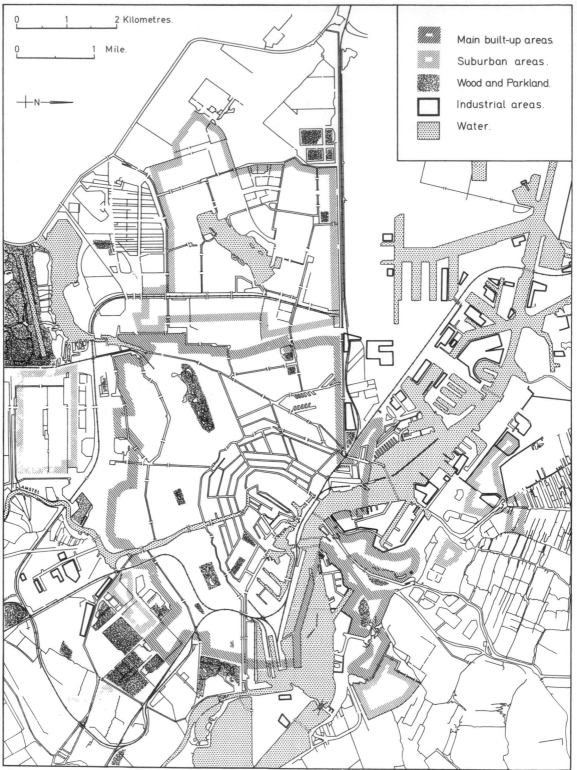

Fig 68 Amsterdam

offices and light industries. This is the area of canals lined with quays and tall houses. Southwards there stretch further residential zones and in particular the 'New South' region of modern blocks with green open spaces, essentially a region of post-Second World War development. To the west and northwest lies the chief industrial zone with shipyards, sugar refineries and other food-processing industries, particularly of tropical products such as rice and chocolate.

The North Sea Canal links Amsterdam with the North Sea and at its western end is the town of Ijmuiden with its large integrated iron and steel-works which depends, like that at Dunkirk, on water-borne supplies of all its raw materials. Other industries in the region are those of aeronautical works (Fokker), precision engineering and chemicals. In terms of industrial employment in this region, the various metal industries employ about as many workers as the clothing and food industries together. Amsterdam remains only a national port compared with the international functions of Rotterdam; it has some entrepôt functions, and is linked to the Waal by canal.

Rotterdam

Of the growing centres within the Dutch Urban Ring, the international port of Rotterdam shows the most striking growth, both in economic functions and in physical size. Rotterdam lies at the junction of a small tributary, the Rotte, with the distributary of the Rhine known as the New Meuse. The original dike-and-dam town pattern is no longer easily seen and the present town centre is almost entirely new, having been rebuilt after the extensive damage it suffered during the Second World War. The town centre is on ultra-modern lines with all-pedestrian shopping precincts, skyscraper commercial blocks and apartments, wide streets and open spaces.

The growth of Rotterdam is comparatively recent and dates mainly from the time of construction of the New Waterway connecting the New Meuse to the sea at the Hook of Holland, which was opened in 1872. This gave a deep channel compared with the natural route which was then silting, but it does require continual dredging. At the same time new quays and dock basins were constructed on the left bank of the New Meuse, at Feijenoord. Later, docks were constructed at Waalhaven, farther downstream and in the junction area of the two Meuse streams and the New Waterway. All the later development of port facilities have concentrated on the left-bank downstream whilst the oldest were on the right bank in the city centre. The ultimate development is at the mouth of the New Meuse, at Europort. There is thus a conurbation, based on the ports, which reaches from the Hook of Holland via Maasluis, Vlaardingen and Schiedam to Rotterdam.

The industries of Rotterdam are mainly those linked with its functions as the chief sea port of North-West Europe, ranking equal with New York in terms of trade. Of prime importance are the transit facilities for handling grain and oil; the refineries are the main ones of the Benelux

Plate 70 Rotterdam.
Aerial view eastwards with the town centre at top left and a small section of the port installations which line the Meuse.

countries and are linked by pipeline with Cologne and the Ruhr. Most heavy goods, minerals, wood, fibres, rubber, vegetable oils, etc., destined for the large hinterland of Rotterdam pass through here. The hinterland extends up the Rhine to Basle, and thus includes several important industrial areas, of which the Ruhr is most important, and with which there are links by motorway and electrified railway.

Other industrial activities are those of food processing, milling, brewing, distilling, car assembly and shipbuilding. A large area for future industrial expansion lies on the southern side of the New Waterweg between the Botlek and the North Sea. This includes Europort, an extension of the facilities of Rotterdam, and amongst the industries to be developed here will be an integrated iron and steel works and petro-chemical complex (Fig. 69).

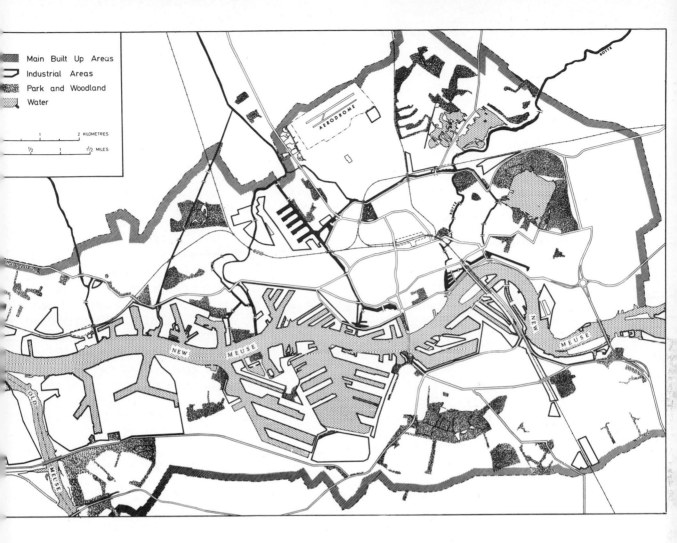

Fig 69 Rotterdam

The Hague

In comparison with other regions of the Randstad this is uniquely different: it has been described as the 'largest village in Europe'. It is essentially a residential town, sited on the inland side of the dune coastline in a wooded region, and unlike other Dutch towns is neither on a branch of the Rhine nor owes its origin to commerce, but to being favoured as a hunting lodge of the Counts of Holland in the thirteenth century. It was established as the administrative capital in 1618 and is the centre for many organisations, both national and international. Continuous with The Hague is the coastal resort of Schevingen and, between The Hague and Rotterdam, is the town of Delft, with steelworks and man-made fibre industries.

The other urban centres of the Randstad are all on distributaries of the Rhine, chiefly on the Oude Rijn (Old Rhine) which in former times was the most important. Utrecht, a city of over a quarter of a million inhabitants was founded by the Romans, and is an important religious and university centre with steel and phosphate industries. It is of increasing importance at the eastern apex of the Randstad, and is at a junction of rail and road routes.

CONCLUSION

Within the Benelux countries there are many minor regions with unique characteristics, a feature not surprising in view of the variety of physical landscapes, the long history of human occupance and the high population density. It is not possible to distinguish national contrasts; there is not 'an industrial Belgium complementing an agricultural Netherlands', but rather a complex mixture of both rural and urban facets in all three countries.

A number of basic factors may be found in many of the problems of these lands. The influence of water, be it as an enemy to be kept back or as a friend to provide power or transport, is one such factor. Another is the relationship between two linguistic groups, the Flemish and Walloon, but it should be noted that taking the three countries together, out of a total population approaching 22 million only some 4 million are French-speaking. Thirdly, and basic to the entire geography of this area, is the situation of these lands at a series of geographical junctions; routeways across the North European Plain, via the Rhine to Central Europe, to the Paris Basin and westwards via the English Channel or across the North Sea, all converge here. The North European Plain is here at its narrowest and lowest, in the delta of the Rhine-Meuse-Scheldt system, but rises quickly to the old rocks of the Hercynian Ardennes, so in yet another respect is this a junction region.

Although in the past many of the separate regions and individual towns, particularly the ports, have pursued independent ways, the trend of the last century or so has been for unification. In the twentieth century this has taken the form of economic grouping: it is only in this way that the prosperity of these small states of Western Europe can continue in the van of progress.

FURTHER READING

G. B. G. Bull, 'The Netherlands Delta Plan', *Geography*, 1962, pp. 87–89.

K. C. Edwards, 'The Luxembourg Iron and Steel Industry', *Transactions and Papers, Institute of British Geographers*, 1961, pp. 1–16.

T. H. Elkins, 'Liège and the Problems of Southern Belgium', *Geography*, 1956, pp. 83–96.

J. M. Richards, 'New Towns in the Netherlands', *Progress*, 45, 1956, pp. 147–157.

R. C. Riley, 'Recent Developments in the Belgian Borinage', *Geography*, 1965, pp. 261–273.

L. D. Stamp, 'The Geology of Belgium', *Proceedings Geologists' Association*, 33, 1922, pp. 1–38.

S. W. E. Vince, 'The Agricultural Regions of Belgium', *London Essays in Geography*, 1951, pp. 255–288.

France

The Past
in the
Present
'Everyone has two countries—his own and France' runs a saying, and there can be few for whom that country is not attractive for its landscapes, its wines and foods, the people and their art. The French are justly proud of their beautiful and expressive language, while history has left so profound an imprint and the sense of history and cultural tradition is so strong, that certain legacies of history upon the environment and people must be outlined.

France has had a very long period of settlement in areas on or near well-defined routeways. The rich and easily-cultivated soils, especially of the Paris and Aquitaine Basins, were great attractions, as were the varied climates. The bluffs of the numerous limestone regions offered defensive sites. French names have been applied to certain phases of Palaeolithic culture e.g. Cros Magnon. Neolithic stone monuments such as menhirs, dolmens and cromlechs (the names are later Celtic ones) are common in certain areas such as Brittany. Permanent agriculture and settlement began at this time, 2,500 B.C. Iberians later penetrated south-western France, and Greeks settled at Marseilles about 600 B.C. In the fifth century B.C. the Celts came to France; like those in the British Isles they still have their distinctive language and culture.

The legacy of the Romans is impressive. There are great buildings such as the Pont du Gard, part of an aqueduct constructed long before Christ; the arenas in Nîmes, Arles and Paris itself; roads, and the basic street plans of very many cities and towns; and, last but not least, to the Romans the French owe the introduction of their most famous plant—the vine, and one of their delicacies—the edible snail. The Roman tradition of the good life was not lost on the French.

The decline of Rome brought decay in France. Gaul fell apart but the hope of unity persisted. The Franks were the most numerous new immigrants and began the first era of cathedral building. In the south the Visigoths enlarged the fortress of Carcassonne, which the Romans had constructed to guard the routeway between the Atlantic and the Mediterranean. However, the Arian heresy became a divisive force between southern and northern France, re-inforced by differences of dialect and of agricultural system.

On the death of Charlemagne, the greatest Frankish emperor, the empire was divided into Carolingia, Lotharingia and the German Realm at the Treaty of Verdun A.D. 843. Here were the seeds of later rivalry between the first and the last for Lotharingia (the 'Middle Kingdom'—

now the Low Countries and Alsace-Lorraine). Yet neither France nor Germany remained united, and France lapsed into seven seigneuries.

In the next century a new unifying movement came from the Capet rulers, dukes of the area around Paris. They were the heirs of the Frankish emperors, and were recognised as leaders by the other seigneurs. The development of a strong central government again became the aim, and remains a dominant aspect of modern France in contrast to, for example, Britain or the United States. More cathedrals were built, forests were substantially cut, parts of the Poitou and Flanders marshes were first drained, and the taming of the Loire was begun with *levées* or dikes.

The Normans brought new vigour into northern France, while southern France was riven apart by religious disputation. The Norman kings, however, also brought the link between France and England; Henry of Anjou who became Henry II of England in 1154 added to the English crown the west-central lands of Anjou, Touraine, Normandy and Maine, while his wife, Eleanor, former wife of Louis VII of France, brought larger areas in the south-west. All this led to fierce struggles over centuries between the English and French, and continued disunity in France. Both countries or their vassals built border fortresses or *bastides* in the south-west, with rectangular road plans. Montauban was the first French one (built 1144) and Libourne the most famous English one (built 1270). England carried on prosperous trade with south-western France, importing wine (especially claret) against wool.

Under the Capet Philip II (Philip Augustus), 1180–1223, the county of Toulouse was won back from the English, Paris was first surrounded by walls, Notre Dame consecrated, the Louvre Royal Palace was built (now the art gallery), and the Sorbonne established by Richard de Sorbon, now the Faculty of Arts (Letters) of the University.

The Second Hundred Years War brought anarchy, exhaustion of people and resources, and the Black Death. From this unpromising situation there emerged the petite but forceful Joan of Arc, intent on raising the spirit of the French monarchy and expelling the English. At her death in 1431 little but Calais remained in English hands, and by the middle of the fifteenth century Burgundy was absorbed, which for centuries had been as strong as any of the other seigneuries of France and might otherwise have become a European state.

Under François 1er, 1515–47, the Louvre was enlarged, the palace of Fontainebleau built, the Collège de France endowed as a forum for distinguished lecturers, and Calais, Metz, Toul and Verdun were brought within France.

Henry IV, 1589–1610, at first a Protestant, unwillingly started hatred and bloodshed between Catholic and Protestant (Huguenot) until in 1598 the Edict of Nantes recognised their civil rights. Huguenot towns, such as La Rochelle, became centres of vigorous industries.

The long reign of Louis XIV—*le Roi Soleil*, 1600–1715—saw national and overseas expansion, and economic development, despite autocracy, extravagance and crushing taxation of the peasants. France extended her domain to the Pyrenees, acquired the Franche Comté (Jura), and parts of the Rhine Valley and Flanders. In some of these lived non-French people who have ever since been instructed exclusively in French. More significantly, the ministers of Louis XIV who had claimed 'natural' frontiers or limits for France, as good defensive ones, allowed themselves to extend France beyond the high ridge of Artois and down to the Flanders Plain, so burdening France with her most easily-overrun boundary.

The first long canal was built in 1666–1681—the Canal du Midi, linking the Atlantic and the Mediterranean—the first roads constructed since the Roman ones, banks were established with the help—as in England—of the Lombards, and the state porcelain works at Sèvres and the Gobelins tapestry works in Paris were founded which continue to this day. Yet bigotry led Louis XIV to revoke the Edict of Nantes, and so the freedom of the economically-important Protestants was destroyed. They fled (like the Jews from Hitler), and took their part of the silk industry to Essex, Spitalfields and Wandsworth in England; they began the construction of Berlin; and some who emigrated to the young Dutch settlement at Cape Town introduced the vine to South Africa. The loss of these people to France was great.

So the 'Sun King' also cast a shadow over France, and lived so long that his grandson succeeded him. Under Louis XV France acquired all the Rhinelands she now possesses, and Corsica just in time for Napoleon to be born French rather than Genoese.

In the French Revolution the large estates of the Church, Nobility and Royal Family were broken up, and fell into the hands of the middle class. The aristocracy was eliminated from power and national tradition. The ordinary person was free to live where he wished and could, taxes were standardised, the provinces sub-divided into the small character-less *départements*, and the *paroisses* became *communes*.

Under Napoleon there was strong encouragement of science and engineering, and much incidental construction of roads and bridges. The Napoleonic Code of Laws instituted, *inter alia*, equal inheritance by all sons—the cause of the break-up of many farms and the dispersion of holdings in the name of equality.

Under Louis Philippe, 1830–1848, railways were begun and canals greatly extended. Industrialisation got under way half a century behind Britain.

Nice and Savoy were acquired as payment for French help against Austria in the wars of Italian unity, and so beautiful country became French under Napoleon III. Haussmann was commissioned to re-plan Paris by constructing wide boulevards, admitting light, improving health, enhancing the beauty of Paris and the prestige of Napoleon III. Wide avenues also prevented barricading, and so easy opposition to his regime. The radial pattern or *Etoile* (Star) from the Arc de Triomphe, the Champs Elysées, the Grands Boulevards, and much more in their present form are his work. Economic development particularly of railways, ports and the banking system went ahead.

Yet France was quickly overcome by Prussia in 1870–1; thereafter France had not only a united Italy on one doorstep but a far stronger unified Germany on the other. France was no longer the most populated country of Europe. Germany gained Alsace-Lorraine and was soon to make its iron-ore fields the basis of a large local iron and steel industry.

Thereafter, France was a frustrated power. Governments were short-lived and fierce antagonisms divided clerical from anti-clerical, right wing from left wing. The weak bases of France in the coal-age industrial revolution became evident as first Britain, then Germany, and the U.S.A. left France behind.

The First World War caused appalling national haemorrhage. Over two million men—those at the prime of life—were killed, one-fifth of them around Verdun. Vast areas near that town have never since been cultivated. The main coalfield, the North, was utterly devastated; as compensation the Saar was made over to France until 1935. Alsace-Lorraine was regained but the economic gain was less to the French than it had been to the Germans, since the coke was now separated from the iron ore by a political boundary and different currency; while Lorraine ore was never vital to the Germans as Ruhr coke was to the French.

In 1940 France was overrun by the Germans and brought to an armistice in under six weeks. Despite the rigours of the Occupation, the losses of the Resistance, the Free French, and renewed fighting in 1944–5, there were far fewer casualties than in the First World War, although much more intensive and widespread destruction.

The Monnet Plan of 1947–52 and Marshall Aid from America, plus a new national determination, brought fairly speedy recovery, notably in coal mining and the railways. Yet again the governments were weak coalitions until, after having left politics in disgust in 1947, the great war-time leader de Gaulle came back in 1958 to solve the Algerian question. Since then France has been politically stable and economically prosperous, perhaps as much due to her participation in the European Economic Community as to de Gaulle's policies, for the Community has opened greater markets and forced French industry to become more competitive.

The Environment in Tradition

The environment has also helped to shape French attitudes. Varied and often very fertile soils and climates that are, for the most part, kind to either Temperate or Mediterranean crops and sometimes to both, have encouraged a strong attachment to the soil and its produce. The peasantry is still powerful in France, sometimes too much so. The tradition of good and varied food in France encourages diversity in agriculture, though this variety is frequently inefficient and always costly—mainly because of under capitalisation and insufficient mechanisation, in turn often made difficult by dispersion of holdings and small farms.

When the industrial revolution was based on coal, France was at a disadvantage because of her relative paucity of that resource, of which she had to import large amounts until this mid-century. Thus there was a tradition of fuel economy with central rather than individual room heating, and the use of patent fuels made with coal dust or waste. With the advent of electricity, oil or natural gas-based industrialism France is better placed, for she has great home or overseas resources of these.

Because of modest supplies of coal and of iron from 1871–1919 France also had relatively less heavy industry than Britain or Germany, her industry was traditionally small in scale, and the ferrous and non-ferrous groups were poorly represented. This situation changed after the iron-ore deposits of Lorraine were regained in 1919, and as aluminium and chemical industries developed, for which she has good resources. However, despite the famous but few large-scale enterprises in automobile, tyre, chemical and aluminium production, French industry is still mostly small or medium scale. This must also, in part, be ascribed to French individualism, to the dislike and distrust of mass-production and distribution, to devotion to the small, individually-designed or unusual article, to the catering in consequence for varied tastes, as varied as the environment in which the French so fortunately live. Diversity and individuality are fundamental factors in the physical environment and culture of France.

The Physical Environment

France is by far the largest country in Europe (excepting the U.S.S.R.), and its area of 212, 659 square miles is more than two-and-a-quarter times the size of the United Kingdom. The southernmost point of France, in the Pyrenees, is about 42°N and the northernmost one, where the Franco-Belgian border meets the sea, is about 51°N. Only small areas of the United Kingdom are south of 50°N, yet little of France is north of that line. France is, therefore, well-situated to receive more sunshine than the United Kingdom and includes the totally different climatic régimes of the Short-Cold-Winter and Mediterranean. France is the only country in Europe with lands extending from the mild and usually humid North Sea, Channel and Atlantic coasts to the seasonally dry Mediterranean. There are, therefore, much greater agricultural possibilities in France than in most European lands, the more so as a result of her fertile soils. There have also been strategic implications for France in having both Atlantic and Mediterranean coasts, and a coastline separated by other countries, like that of the U.S.A.

France lies astride some of Europe's—indeed the world's—most important routeways. In the north is the Channel (*Pas de Calais*), a great artery for contacts with Northern Europe. The Vermandois Sill between the Paris and Brussels Basins is the watershed between the Somme, Scheldt (*Escaut*), Sambre and Oise. This is one of mankind's most ancient passage-ways between the Paris Basin, Flanders and the Rhinelands—especially Aachen (Aix-la-Chapelle) and Cologne. In the east is the narrow Saverne Gap through which there is just room for the Zorn River, the Rhine-Marne Canal, the railway and road to pass. The gap links the

Paris Basin with the upper Rhinelands and southern Germany. South-eastward lies the Belfort Gate between the Rhine, the Saône-Rhône Valley and the Paris Basin. A little to the south-west is the Burgundian Gate, a great artery for traffic between the Paris Basin, the Saône-Rhône Valley and the Mediterranean. The Saône-Rhône Valley is one of the great corridors of human movement, as witnessed by the wealth of archaeological remains and architectural monuments. From it there are routes eastward into and across the Alps, and south-westward to the St. Etienne Coalfield and the Central Massif. More significant again is the Naurouze Sill, within which is the narrower Gate of Carcassonne, whose fortress has guarded the Atlantic-Mediterranean through-way. Lastly, there is the Poitou Sill, between the Paris and Aquitaine basins, on the routeway to Spain and Portugal, long controlled by the town of Poitiers.

These routeways are the more important because of the compactness of France, the diversity and richness of many of its lands, and the importance of trade with neighbours, especially with the development of the European Common Market.

GEOLOGY, STRUCTURE AND SURFACE FEATURES

The British Isles and France are the world's most geologically diverse countries; all the great geological eras and formations are represented in France. The most ancient rocks of Archaean and Pre-Cambrian age, composed of sediments transformed by heat and pressure into schists and gneisses, as well as eruptive granites, largely compose the ancient massifs of Armorica in the north-west, the Central Massif in the south-centre, the Vosges in the east, and Corsica in the south. In the great Alpine earth storms, more of such rocks were heaved up to form the cores of the central and eastern Pyrenees, and the Alps; because of subsequent foundering the core of the Maritime Alps is well exposed in the small Maures and Esterel massifs.

On and around the large massifs the Primary (Palaeozoic) rocks were successively laid down; Cambrian and Silurian schists survive in interior Armorica, in the south-west of the Central Massif and in the Vosges; as do the Devonian series in the Morvan of the north-east of the Central Massif, and in the Ardennes. The Carboniferous, with or without coals, is also found in all massifs. During the middle of the Primary period the massifs were subjected to folding, first in the Caledonian trends with their north-east to south-west direction, so characteristic of the Vosges and of the eastern edge of the Central Massif. In late-Primary times came the Armorican movements, well revealed in the relief trends in Armorica itself, in the Limousin of the Central Massif, and in the Ardennes.

These massifs were raised again in Permo-Triassic times, much eroded, and mostly submerged again under the later Secondary (Mesozoic) seas that deposited limestones (from sea shells), sandstones (from shore areas), and clays (from lagoon vegetation conditions). Some areas remained dry land and so are bare of these sediments; many more are as bare because these sediments have since been eroded e.g. from the southern Vosges, from most of the Central Massif except the level *causes* in the south, and from all Armorica except the Rennes Basin. Secondary deposits are best preserved in the great sedimentary basins of Paris and Aquitaine.

The vast upheavals of the Mid-Tertiary (Cainozoic) Alpine movements, pointing up the Pyrenees, Jura, and several alpine chains, rejuvenated the rivers, and tilted and cracked the otherwise-resistant massifs. On the north of the Alps the Vosges-Black Forest, until then one block, and the Bohemian Massif together kept the Alps to their present northward extent. However, in the process the Vosges-Black Forest Massif split apart, each segment was tilted up on its southern edge by the Alps, the great Rhine Rift Valley was formed between them, and the upper Rhine diverted into it. The Central Massif took the strain of the westward thrust of the Alps, was likewise tilted up on its eastern and southern edges, and severely fractured mainly where the Allier and Loire now flow in fault-guided valleys. With the faulting went volcanic activity, especially in the Central Massif. Armorica was virtually unaffected, remoter as it was, and protected from the earth storms by the Central Massif. However, the several Secondary sedimentaries of the east and south-east of the Paris Basin were most raised up precisely where, between the Vosges and the Central Massif, they were least protected from the Alpine movements. Likewise, the Pyrenean movements caused parallel ridging far to the north-east, even in the north of the Paris Basin in the Bray anticline and Somme syncline. In both cases there was rejuvenation of rivers, and since the raised sedimentaries were of varying resistance a scarp-and-vale topography developed, well seen on the east and south-east where the tilting had been greatest.

Yet there was also extensive deposition by seas in Tertiary times, especially in the Paris and Aquitaine Basins, in the Rennes Basin of Armorica, in the then-new fault basins of the Central Massif and the Rhine Rift Valley, and in the Saône-Rhône Valley.

Volcanic activity persisted in the Monts Dômes of the Central Massif (west of Clermont-Ferrand) until late Quaternary times, indeed until some 8,000 years ago, and many of the volcanoes look exceedingly fresh. There was also glaciation in the Cantal of the Central Massif, the Vosges and, of course, in the Pyrenees and Alps, still persisting in the latter (Plate 83). Wind-borne loess (or limon) was extensively deposited in the areas mentioned in the previous paragraph, and is largely responsible for their present fertility. There has been much other accumulation in the Somme Valley, probably a consequence of the Channel break some 5–20,000 years ago, in the Poitou Marshes, and in the Landes of the Aquitaine Basin, though there has also been submergence of the Breton and Mediterranean coasts.

Finally, man has gained land by assisting nature in the reclamation of Maritime Flanders, the Somme *hortillons*, the Seine Estuary, the Vendée and Médoc (west side of Gironde Estuary), and by thwarting or taming floods through constricting and embanking the Loire over some seven centuries with successive dikes. Inland marsh, like the fertile Bresse south of Dijon, has been reclaimed; although its southerly neighbour the Dombes remains ill-drained because its clays do not warrant the cost. With so much good land available in France, the urge to reclaim heathland has been less than in other countries of North-West Europe. More attention has been given to clearing woodland from rich areas like Brie, but it remains in the poor and widespread Tertiary sand areas of the Paris Basin.

Varied geology has given a remarkably diverse landscape, with equally varied soils and agricultural possibilities, further enhanced by contrasted climates. There is, in fact, a truly remarkable regional variety, imprinted in the very names of settlements such as St. Jean-de-Maurienne, Bourg-en-Bresse, and hundreds more. Farmers and rural dwellers are, indeed, far more conscious of these regional names than they are of the départements. These regions are known as *pays*, and have been studied in detail by French and other geographers but are not their creation.

DRAINAGE France has a remarkably fully developed pattern of drainage. As would be expected in a country of such long geological and structural evolution and variety, there have been spectacular captures and changes of course. The ancient massifs are the original sources of a primitive radial system of drainage, which has been modified by prolonged sedimentation, especially in the Paris and Aquitaine basins, and by the Alpine Orogeny through its effects upon the massifs and their drainage networks. Except for the Morvan, the Central Massif is no longer drained northwards to the Seine, whose headwaters here have been diverted to the westward-flowing Loire. Streams draining the Vosges have been captured by the Meuse and especially by the Moselle, whose vigour has been increased by the uplift of the Ardennes and Rhine Highlands. Nevertheless, the Meuse lost its former left bank Aire tributary to the Aisne and, more dramatically, a right bank headwater to the Moselle, so leaving a classic dry gap at Toul. Until late Pliocene times the Rhine flowed south-west from the site of Basle to a lake in the Bresse area north of the site of Lyons; earth movements then diverted the Rhine into the new rift valley, and the now upper Doubs was at first its tributary.

There are now three great fan-shaped systems, those of the Seine, Loire and Garonne. Less wholly French, more peripheral and linear are the Saône-Rhône group, the Rhine, the Moselle, the Sambre-Meuse, the Scheldt and Lys. All but the Rhône and some lesser rivers flow into the Atlantic or its seas.

Many rivers rise in impermeable rocks of the Hercynian massifs e.g. some Seine tributaries have their source in the Morvan; the Allier, Loire and many Garonne affluents rise in the Central Massif; the Saône and some of its tributaries, the Moselle and its upper affluents issue in the Vosges. However, the Tertiary Folded Mountains are also a great source of rivers. Most left bank tributaries of the Garonne rise in the Pyrenees; the Doubs—now an affluent of the Saône—issues in the Jura; the Rhône and the Rhine rise in the Alps—both in glaciers. Lastly, the Seine and most of its affluents issue from the various clays of the Paris Basin.

French rivers likewise rise in areas climatically more diverse than those of other countries of North-West Europe, so that régimes and profiles (especially of the Seine and Saône) are better for navigation and water supplies than those of most European rivers. However, the Rhône is a notable exception, for it has a variable discharge which increases sharply with the Alpine snow melt. The river has needed costly control for safe navigation. And if severe storms over the south-western Central Massif coincide with the spring and early summer snow melt in the Pyrenees, then all the Garonne system may be in flood. Lastly, as the Loire and its tributaries rise in the Central Massif, they are also subject to sudden and severe floods due to rapid run-off. The central and lower Loire has been embanked by successive levées since the thirteenth century; the French used this experience in their initial efforts to control the Mississippi.

CLIMATE Unlike the United Kingdom, the higher areas of France are mostly in the east and south-east, so that France is wide open to mild oceanic influences but well protected from severe continental ones. The east and south-east are wetter or have more snow than comparable areas in Britain. Annual temperatures are modest, and the high precipitation has a summer or autumn maximum, as at Besançon or Grenoble. Wind is often a significant factor, and there are sharp differences according to aspect. This is well seen in west-east valleys where the northern side facing south has far more sun, is known as the *adret*, and is usually settled and farmed; while the south side which faces north is necessarily colder, has the chilsome name of *ubac*, and is usually still under forest or pasture. Many Alpine valleys show this phenomenon, often clearly evident on maps.

Because of the latitudinal and longitudinal extent of France, it inevitably has the West Coast Marine climate in the north-west, the Short Cold-Winter type in the east, and Mediterranean conditions in the south. The first is well-shown in Brittany, notably at Brest. There is a small diurnal and annual range of temperature, and a rainfall maximum in autumn or winter. Yet for all the frequency of rain the total fall is fairly modest, because so much is drizzle, although relative humidity is high. The mild temperatures are advantageous to early crops of potatoes, cauliflowers and the like, but the frequent rainfall and high humidity cause rather leached and so lime-hungry soils, and these and the climate are disadvantageous to many other crops.

The Short Cold-Winter type occurs in deep eastern valleys such as the Rhine Rift Valley, and in the fault basins along the Allier and Loire rivers in the Central Massif. This type is well illustrated by Strasbourg. There are substantial yearly ranges of temperature, rainfall is often less than in other areas, and the maximum falls are in Spring and early Summer. Such conditions are propitious for many crops.

Climatic statistics for typical French climatic zones and stations.[1]

Zone and Station	Days of		Mean Temps.			
	Frost	Rain	Jan.		July	
			°C	°F	°C	°F
Mountain						
Besançon	71	189	1.2	34.2	18.8	65.9
Grenoble	n.a.	136	1.4	34.5	20.2	68.4
West Coast Marine						
Brest	7	196	7.2	45.0	17.5	63.5
Short Cold Winter						
Strasbourg	87	171	0.7	33.4	19.0	66.2
Mediterranean						
Perpignan	13	80	7.3	45.2	22.9	73.2
Marseilles	37	82	6.6	44.0	22.4	72.4
Cannes	6	82	8.5	47.4	23.6	74.5
W. Coast Marine–Short Cold Winter Transition						
Caen	8	155	4.6	40.3	17.3	63.2
Paris	49	166	3.4	38.0	19.0	66.2
Nancy	80	170	1.3	34.4	18.1	64.5
W. Coast Marine— Mediterranean Transition						
Bordeaux	45	170	5.4	41.8	20.5	68.9
Toulouse	39	144	4.9	40.9	21.2	70.2
Short Cold Winter— Mediterranean Transition						
Lyons	62	150	2.9	37.2	21.3	70.4

[1] From *Agricultural Regions in the European Economic Community*, European Productivity Agency, Organisation for European Economic Co-operation, 1960, p. 45.

Rainfall in ins. and mm.									
		Quarter							
Annual		1		2		3		4	
ins.	mm.	ins.	mm.	ins.	mm.	ins.	mm.	ins.	mm.
42.8	1088	9.0	229	10.5	267	11.5	293	11.8	300
38.5	978	7.9	201	9.7	246	9.9	252	11.0	279
33.2	842	9.0	225	5.7	146	6.3	160	12.2	311
27.4	696	4.4	114	7.3	185	9.2	233	6.5	164
23.1	587	5.8	146	4.9	125	3.7	94	8.7	222
22.5	572	5.4	137	4.5	114	3.6	92	9.0	229
31.3	796	9.4	240	5.7	144	4.1	104	12.1	308
26.8	681	5.8	147	6.1	156	6.4	162	8.5	216
23.9	607	5.0	128	6.1	154	6.0	153	6.8	172
29.0	737	6.2	158	6.8	174	7.6	192	8.4	213
32.8	833	8.4	214	7.6	192	6.1	154	10.7	273
26.9	684	5.9	151	8.2	208	5.8	148	7.0	177
32.6	827	5.3	135	8.7	221	9.2	233	9.4	238

°C are quoted first, following modern British usage, but inches before millimetres, as still traditional.

The Mediterranean is the third climate and is restricted by mountains to coastal pockets east of the Rhône but is found over a wider coastal plain west of it. The highest summer temperatures usually occur in this climatic region. The rainfall maximum is in Autumn, but much is lost on steep slopes and by rapid percolation. There is a semi-drought in summer, pleasant for tourists, but difficult for farmers who must pay for irrigation if they are to grow the more remunerative crops. The area is also liable to receive the cold Mistral wind in winter, which blows furiously when there is high pressure in the Paris Basin and low pressure in the Gulf of Lyons. The low temperatures are unpleasant for tourists (and originally the Riviera was a winter resort), so that the well-known towns with a winter season are precisely those protected from the Mistral by distance from the Rhône Valley and by southward projecting promontories of the Maritime Alps. The wind may also damage early crops in the lower Rhône valley, so farmers protect the western and northern sides of their fields with cypress and wicker hedges, and may use automatic heaters to counter the cold. Conditions in the relatively wet eastern sector are well illustrated by Cannes, and in the drier centre and west by Marseilles and Perpignan.

Important as are these climates, and the areas in which they occur, the transitional types are far more beneficial to agriculture, the more so as they occur widely, and over mainly fertile lowlands.

The first transitional climate is the West Coast Marine-Short Cold Winter found over much of the Paris Basin. The western side is naturally more oceanic, the east more continental, although the greater relief of the east extends the oceanic effect eastward, particularly with respect to rainfall. The transitional area has a fair range of temperature, the rainfall is fairly evenly distributed between the months, and the area avoids the excessive humidity of the west and the sharp winters of the east.

Another remarkable transitional type is the West Coast Marine-Mediterranean, more oceanic in the north-west as Bordeaux demonstrates with its rainfall maximum in Autumn, more Mediterranean to the south-east, although Toulouse has most rain in Spring. The area has a rainfall minimum in summer but avoids the semi-drought of the Mediterranean, so that there is less expense on irrigation. Although summers are cooler than there, they are sufficiently warm to ripen almost all Mediterranean crops. The winters are much cooler, but this is of little significance.

Lastly, there is the Short Cold Winter-Mediterranean transition found in the Saône-Rhône corridor, more continental in the former valley, more Mediterranean in the latter. Lyons represents the perfect transition. Again, the disadvantages of both climates are avoided, but their merits are combined. The cold winters of the first are tempered, and the semi-drought of the Mediterranean does not occur. There is a long growing season, with adequate rain in spring to promote growth.

VEGETATION   While it is true that the vegetation of France, like that of all inhabited countries, has been much changed, it is still more varied than that of any other country of comparable area and situation. This is because of great geological, geomorphological and pedological variety, and of the altitudinal range from sea level to 15,711 feet (Mt. Blanc). Some regions are near several seas, others are remote from them (Rhine Rift Valley); while there is a remarkable variety of climatic conditions. As the population is relatively small there has been only modest pressure upon the land and its resources, while substantial areas are preserved as state forests. France, alone in Europe, has both Temperate Vegetation of Atlantic, Middle European and Mountain subtypes, as well as varied Mediterranean vegetation.

SOILS These have been described on p. 38. It suffices here to emphasise not only the immense variety of soils in France as a whole, but in its regions as between valley bottom, valley slope, plain, plateau or mountain. Wind-borne loess or limon is of great importance in the Paris Basin, Flanders, northern Brittany, the Rhine and Rhône valleys, as is waterborne molasse in central Aquitaine. Alluvial soils are also of great significance in the major river valleys; while in Sologne, the Landes, Dombes and Bresse great differences result from the relative efficiency of drainage. Man has made drastic changes to soils by drainage, and the application of lime, basic slag or fertilisers. The soils of coastal Brittany have been vastly improved by the application of seaweed and shells, those of interior Flanders by the application of manure.

Population Distribution

The population of France (46,520,271 at the census of 1962) is low. The average density of 218 per square mile (87 per sq. Km.) is much less than that of the Netherlands, Belgium, the German Federal Republic or the United Kingdom; indeed, it is little more than that of mountainous Austria. France has neither conurbations comparable with those of the Ruhr or West Midlands, nor a continuous ring of towns like the *Randstad Holland*, despite an even longer history of urbanisation in France. This is because it has not been a great trading nation like the Netherlands, or a country with as much heavy industry, relative to area or population, as the German Federal Republic, Belgium or the United Kingdom. Nor are there many areas of dense rural population in France; exceptions are parts of the valleys of the central Loire, Rhine, Rhône, Garonne and some of its tributaries, and coastal Brittany. Many areas of France are underpopulated, and could be more productive with more people, such as some fertile areas of central Languedoc and central Aquitaine.

This is a reflection of the slow growth of the French population in the two centuries up to the Second World War. By contrast, in many other countries the population was then increasing rapidly, consequent upon mining and industrial developments, political unification as in Germany and Italy, and the opening of vast new areas to trade. France was left aside from much of this. She lost some five million men in the Revolutionary, Napoleonic, Franco-Prussian, First and Second World Wars. Furthermore, there were three million fewer births than might otherwise have occurred. There were other causes, such as family restriction among peasants to avoid further sub-division of their small farms, whilst in urban areas poor housing had the same effect. Partly as the result of bad housing there was much tuberculosis, and as the result of alcoholism much liver cancer, so that the death rate was high. There was a general atmosphere of frustration and disinterest.

All this changed dramatically after the Second World War. The birth rate increased—mainly, perhaps, because of extremely generous, progressive and untaxed family allowances, and numerous other advantages for the parents of large families. There has also been a great reduction in the death rate through the virtual elimination of tuberculosis as a killer, and with better housing, living standards and medical care. The population grows by about half a million a year, while in eighty years up to 1946 it increased by only $2\frac{1}{2}$ million—and that as the result of the immigration of foreigners with their higher birth rate. Between the last censuses of 1954 and 1962 immigration accounted for one-third of the great increase, but natural increase for two-thirds.

The areas of low density are, naturally enough, the high Alps and all the southern Alps (except the Durance Valley), the higher and bleaker parts of the Jura and Pyrenees, the Causses and granitic areas (especially the Cévennes) of the Central Massif, the Vosges and interior Armorica. They also include the poor lowland areas such as the Landes, Camargue, Dombes (north of Lyons), Sologne and Dry Champagne.

Pockets of denser rural population have been mentioned. Other clusters are the mining and industrial areas, Greater Paris (one-sixth the French population), the ports, and the tourist zone of the Riviera from Cannes eastward.

Natural increase is greatest north and east of the line from Geneva-Dijon-Sens-Orleans-Nantes-Rennes-Cherbourg, but there is outward movement from some of these areas e.g. the poorer ones of the Paris Basin especially between Paris and the Lorraine industrial area, and from western Normandy. Migration also continues from the poor areas cited earlier, and from almost all of Brittany.

The counterpart is the influx to Greater Paris, the Riviera, and the developing industrial areas such as Lacq, Toulouse, the Rhône Valley, Grenoble and Lorraine. Thus some parts of the south which have low rates of natural increase nevertheless attract migrants and immigrants.

France has long been attractive to immigrants, especially to Poles, Belgians and Spaniards before the Second World War, to Italians, Spaniards, Portuguese and Algerians since then. They are prominent in unskilled work in heavy industry, building work and transport, and often live in grim shanties or *bidonvilles* (literally 'petrol-can towns', after some of the materials used for housing). The nearly one million better-off *pieds noirs* (or French who left ex-French North Africa—especially Algeria) settled almost entirely in Aquitaine, Languedoc or the lower Rhône Valley where many bought farms. The older or richer ones settled largely on the Riviera.

TOWNS France has few large cities. Paris alone has over one million people (against four such cities in the United Kingdom), and is three-and-a-half times larger than the next largest city—Marseilles. There are only five towns of over a quarter-of-a-million people (against 17 in the United Kingdom), or 27 over 100,000 (71 in the United Kingdom). Even if built-up areas are considered, there are only 13 over 250,000 and 32 over 100,000 in France.

These few large towns also reflect the relatively modest development of French industry, and the low rate of population increase over the last two centuries. Under one-half the French live in towns of over 20,000 people; more than two-thirds do so in England and Wales. Moreover, except for Paris and Lyons, the largest towns are peripheral, because mineral development and industry are likewise so, in contrast to the situation in Germany, Benelux and England.

The problems of Paris are discussed on p. 428. The central districts of the city are losing people but the Paris Region grows apace. Certain other towns have also grown fast, some mainly because of reconstruction (often with new high-rise centres) after war damage e.g. Dunkirk, Caen, Brest, greater Marseilles (the town itself is not growing), Toulon and Orléans. Nîmes and Montpellier have grown mainly by immigration of French repatriates from North Africa, and Nice by its attraction for retirement. Other towns are growing by normal economic development, notably Toulouse, greater Lyons, Grenoble, Besançon, Dijon, Le Mans, Tours and Rennes—the latter mostly as the result of governmental encouragement of industrial dispersion.

There are no New Towns as in Britain, the Netherlands or Yugoslavia. Where there has been a creation like Mourenx (Plate 73), it is really a housing complex rather than a true town with diverse industries and regional functions. Instead, some towns of about 100,000 inhabitants or more are being developed as regional metropolises, capable of taking some decisions away from the central government, and having specialist functions e.g. large hospitals. Such are Lille, Nancy, Strasbourg, Lyons, Marseilles, Toulouse, Bordeaux and Nantes. Others would be centres less fully equipped, but having important spheres of influence and diverse services. These are Rennes, Caen, Rouen, Dijon, Grenoble, Nice, Montpellier, Clermont-Ferrand and Limoges.

Meanwhile, three-quarters of French towns have under 30,000 inhabitants. They are common and typical throughout France, and for centuries were static in population and area, often confined by walls. Although these are now usually replaced by roads, the old core is often clear, and growth beyond it quite modest, except in towns in industrial or mining districts. Areas occupied by most of the large towns are also usually relatively small, because so many people live in flats or apartments. And this despite the fact that France, through a lower density of population, has far more space than England, Belgium, the Netherlands or the German Federal Republic. The French have traditionally been unwilling to pay adequately for housing, and it has also been fashionable to live in town centres rather than in suburbs. Hence urban concentration and modest suburban extension are still typical. Until recently there was little urban or industrial planning in France, unlike Scandinavia, the Netherlands or Britain.

The Development of the Environment

AGRICULTURE

Agriculture is more important in France than in most west European countries. The value of farm produce is four times that of car production, that of meat is greater than that of steel, and that of milk larger than that of coal. France could be virtually self-sufficient, and although she imports more agricultural products than she exports, the latter are important and numerous. They embrace wine, wheat, barley, maize, meat, cheese, fruit, vegetables and flowers.

The importance of agriculture is a reflection of the variety and advantages of French climates, of the sedimentary basins and valleys which occupy over one-half of the country, and of the varied and often exceptionally rich soils e.g. limon and molasse. Economic and social factors also play their part—the lesser development of heavy industry than in the German Federal Republic or the United Kingdom, the tenacious survival of the peasant, and the French cuisine with its exacting demands upon the farmer.

Yet France is often an inefficient agricultural producer. The farming fifth of the labour force produces under one-eighth of the gross national product. Yields are sometimes low by comparison with other west European lands like Britain or Denmark; agricultural exports from the latter are greater than from France, thirteen times the size of Denmark. Quality of produce and its presentation often leave much to be desired.

One-half of the farms are under 25 acres (10 h.) in size, and over three-quarters are under 50 acres (20 h.), although farms are usually smaller in many other European countries. French farms often comprise scattered holdings, but substantial consolidation has been achieved, especially in the Paris Basin.

Farm equipment and methods are often poor. Housing (of man and beasts), water provision and sanitation are frequently lamentable, although electricity is almost universal. New methods, new crop varieties or species, better equipment and rational marketing are adopted slowly by the peasants who comprise about one-half of the farmers.

The contrasts in the table opposite demonstrate something of the duality of farming (as of much else in France) between north and south or, more accurately, the south-centre. The north is comparable with countries in that latitude. The south-centre and south have considerable physical difficulties such as much rugged upland, poor soils and a summer rainfall minimum, lower yields and usually poorer methods. What gives France poor national figures is the averaging of two agricultural zones, for it

French land-holding systems[1]

Type of holding	% of holdings	% of area	Main location
Ownership	53	55	Small farms. Widespread, especially in the south.
Tenancy	17	38	Large farms in Paris Basin. Small ones in Armorica.
Mixed Ownership and Tenancy	25	Included above	Farms partly owned, partly rented. Common in Picardy and Artois.
Share cropping	3	6	Large farms. Giving way to Tenancy. Important on north and west of Central Massif, Vendée, Aquitaine.
Other	1	0	State farms and research stations.

[1] Figures for 1955, from P. Pinchemel, *Géographie de la France*, Tome 2, 1964, p. 386. Percentage discrepancies due to rounding.

should be remembered that France alone among European countries extends from the North Sea to the Mediterranean.

Improvement is slow, not only because this is the case in most old farming communities but because of high tariff protection in France and the strength of the peasant vote. French-produced foodstuffs are costly—one of the factors in the high cost of living in France, and they have been a source of dispute between France and her Common Market partners, who would prefer to buy cheaper farm produce from elsewhere.

Livestock Produce

This accounts for two-thirds of agricultural sales. Three-quarters of the animals are cattle, beef and dairy animals being about equal in number. Meat accounts for one-third of agricultural receipts, and milk for one-fifth. France is the third or fourth world producer of meat, but its cost is high and the quality only moderate.

The French eat much beef and veal, pork and poultry, but little lamb or mutton. Famous beef breeds are the Charollais, Limousin and Armoricain, whose home areas are beef-cattle rearing regions. Fattening takes place either in areas like the Paris Basin where fodder crops are grown in rotation with cereals, and markets are near, or in coastal areas where marshland pastures are rich.

Dairy cattle are kept on pastures of the damper coastal areas of Flanders,

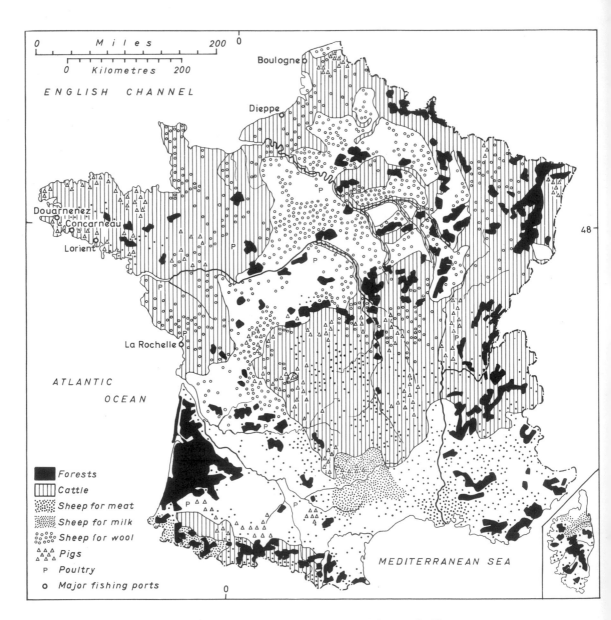

Fig 70 Livestock, major fishing ports and forests in France
(Simplified from map by Direction de la Documentation, Paris)

Normandy, Armorica, the Poitou and Vendée marshes, the Charente, and all clay vales. Dairy cattle are also important in the Vosges, Jura, northern Alpine valleys, and in the volcanic Cantal (Central Massif), where they spend winters in the valleys and summers on upper pastures. The milk is converted into cheeses such as Munster, Gruyère, Tomé de Savoie and Cantal, to name only one from each of the above areas.

Little milk is directly consumed; many French never drink or use it. A French Premier once chided a labourer for drinking too much wine and spirits; the labourer replied 'after a hard day's work in the fields I just don't feel like drinking milk, it makes me wobbly'. The bottling or packaging of milk is far from universal. Milk produced in western Normandy and especially in the Charente is largely made into butter—itself used mainly for cooking in France. Most of the rest of the milk is used in making some 300 varieties of cow's milk cheese.

Sheep are kept in areas of mixed farming such as Beauce or Dry Champagne, or in the drier salt marshes of the Vendée and Camargue (Rhône Delta). They are also important in poor upland limestone areas such as the Causses of the Central Massif (Plate 78), the outer Pyrenees, the southern Alps and Corsica, in all of which they are kept primarily for milk for Roquefort cheese. There are nearly a hundred more cheeses made from sheep's or goat's milk.

Pigs are kept by peasants for food, and so are common on small farms. They are also numerous in dairy cattle areas, since they are fed on skimmed milk, and near towns where restaurant 'swill' is available.

There are famous poultry areas such as Bresse (Saône Valley) and Beauce for chickens, the Vendée for ducks, and Sologne for geese. Brittany has developed the battery system. Poultry and eggs account for about one-tenth of agricultural sales.

Fruit, Flowers and Vegetables

These are the most valuable output of arable farming, and annual sales are worth about the same as those of poultry and eggs. Production is highly varied because of the physical and climatic diversity of France, and is much encouraged by good transport, the French cuisine, and rising living standards. However, competition from Spain and Italy is severe.

Fruit production comprises, first, the southern fruits such as table grapes, peaches, apricots and melons from the Aquitaine Basin, the Rhône Valley and Lower (i.e. coastal) Provence. Olives are also grown in the latter two areas but are not important. Temperate fruits such as pears and plums may be grown early e.g. the former in Conflent (Plate 81), and the latter in Aquitaine for early sales or for drying as prunes. Main crop areas for such fruit are in the north. There are many local specialities such as strawberries around Plougastel (Brittany) or blackcurrants around Metz and Dijon.

The cultivation of vegetables is often intensive and occurs in the following type regions (Fig. 71):

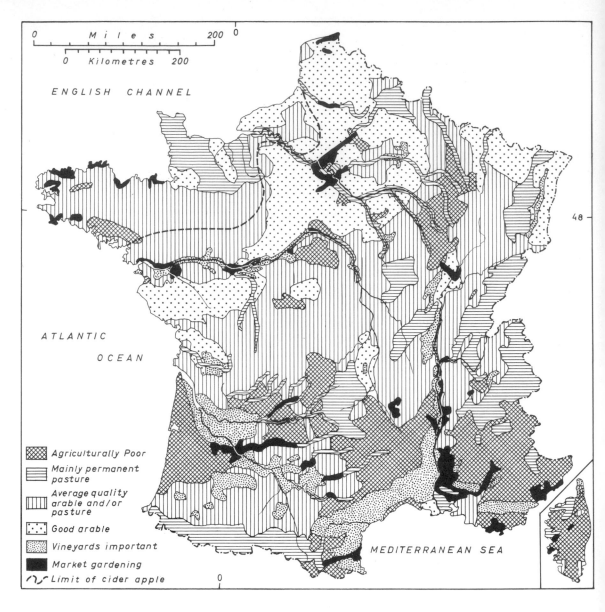

Fig 71 Land Use in France.
(Simplified from map by Direction de la Documentation, Paris)

(a) Very early areas such as the Roussillon, Provence and Corsican plains for salad crops, artichokes, peas and beans.
(b) The bulk early and main season areas of the Garonne and lower Rhône Valley.
(c) The early northern areas for potatoes, cauliflowers, brocolli, onions and artichokes in coastal Brittany (Plate 77); and for salad crops, peas and beans in the Loire vales.
(d) Bulk production northern areas of the Paris Basin.
(e) Highly intensive production around cities, especially Paris.

Flowers are grown early for cutting and potting, and all the year round for perfume distillation around Grasse and on the Riviera; for cutting, potting and for seeds in the Loire vales and, as for fruit, there are local specialities such as the roses of Brie and the violets around Toulouse.

Cereals, Sugar Beet, Potatoes and Fodder Crops

These may be considered together since they are so often grown in rotation. Cereals account for one-tenth of agricultural revenues, and occupy one-half the arable area. France is a major producer of wheat and usually has a substantial surplus, although it has too high a cost to compete on open world markets—hence the French insistence upon sales in the European Economic Community.

Wheat occupies one-half the cereal area and is outstandingly important in the Paris and Aquitaine basins, in the Rhine and Saône-Rhône valleys. It comes mainly from large, mechanised farms, and the quality is good. The barley output is about one-half that of wheat and, as in England, is much grown as an animal food. It is also used for brewing beer in the north and east, and some is exported. Maize has likewise increased in area and output, mainly through the use of profitable American hybrids e.g. in Beauce, but has long been important in southern Aquitaine, and in Alsace for fodder. The maize output is about one-half that of barley, and there is a large export surplus. Oats are grown in wetter or poorer areas for animal feed, as is the little-grown rye. Rice is important in the Rhône Delta.

Sugar beet was introduced during the British blockade of Napoleon, and so over a century before it was grown commercially in England. It is grown for sugar and pure alcohol production, and other varieties are grown for animal and human consumption. All are excellent in rotation with wheat, barley or maize, but the area occupied is but one-tenth that under wheat. Potatoes and fodder crops are other crops grown in rotation with wheat and barley, especially in the Paris Basin, where mixed farming is important.

The Vine

This is the most famous crop in France, which is the leading world producer of wine by value and variety of output. Although France has one-quarter of the mass-production vineyards of the world, the crop occupies no more than 7% of the arable area, and only in some seven *départements* is the vine the most valuable crop. Nevertheless, this is, per acre, one of the most remunerative agricultural pursuits; revenue from it accounts for about one-twelfth of farm income, about the same as from wheat which occupies over three and a half times as much space, while wine is a significant export. Because of over production of poor wines, quality is being improved and the vine restricted to the better areas, partly by competition for land from the also-profitable fruit, vegetable, tobacco or hop crops, and partly by law.

The vine requires well-drained but not rich soils, so that some areas useless for other crops are under the vine. It requires much sunlight and warmth, so that it is frequently grown on south-east facing river terraces, as of the Garonne and its tributaries; on valley slopes; and on porous chalk or other limestones such as Cognac and certain areas of Burgundy. Rain is required at the beginning of and during growth, but there should be a minimum (or else it should fall in darkness) in the later stages—otherwise the sugar content will be insufficient. High relative humidity causes mildew, and Médoc, west of the Gironde, ideal on other grounds, is

Plate 71   Two aspects of champagne production.

Left : Vineyards at Mailly. The Tertiary limestone outcrop is wooded, whilst the slope of mixed soils is almost entirely under the vine.

Right : The cellar is typical of many miles of such galleries in the underlying chalk. The full bottles on the left are tilted downwards and inwards in an A-shaped rack, and are turned slightly each day to drain the sediment towards the cork. White spots on the base of the bottles help to gauge the amount of turning required. When the sediment has accumulated, it is frozen, the cork removed, and the sediment is ejected. Sweetened liquor may then be added for demi-sec champagnes. When recorked the bottles are stacked horizontally, as on the right.

very prone; a copper-sulphate spray (popularly known as 'Bordeaux Mixture') was developed to counter it. In the nineteenth century French vineyards attracted a vine louse which attacked roots and spread the phylloxera disease, destroying two-and-a-half out of six million acres under the crop between 1860 and 1895. The commercial vineyards of Poitou, Auvergne and the Rhône Valley all but disappeared.

In the past commercial vineyards were of necessity in areas not only satisfactory on pedological and climatic grounds but near transport by water, or by short roads to it. English rule of much of Aquitaine from 1154 to 1454, the English aristocracy's appreciation of claret, and the ease

of its transport by river and sea through Bordeaux, were further factors in establishing the vine on river terraces and valley slopes. Bordeaux also levied heavy taxes on wines handled from other areas so as to restrict their development, while even now vineyards cannot be created without equivalent withdrawals from vine cultivation.

Wine production is also affected by the campaign against alcoholism in France (more the consequence of drinking spirits). Exports are influenced by the view of some non-Catholics that wine is evil, by occasional prohibition of its consumption in some countries, and especially by increasing competition from other producers (particularly Italy which usually produces greater quantities than France).

Maintaining a vineyard requires much capital, patience, skill and hard work. Not for nothing has there been called *une civilisation de la vigne*. There are about one-and-a-half million vine growers, cultivating some three-and-a-half million acres. Four-fifths have under five acres. There are extensive châteaux estates in Aquitaine and Burgundy, but the largest is about 900 acres. Small producers often sell their produce to large bottlers, especially in Champagne, and others sell through co-operatives.

The greatest areas for bulk production are the Languedoc *Costières* estates, which produce cheap red wines, one-half by quantity of French wines but a small fraction of the total value. The greatest area by value of output is easily Aquitaine (Fig. 71), and it alone has a wide variety of wines and spirits. The Médoc clarets produced on the left bank Gironde terraces are its finest product, indeed the world's finest wine. Almost equally renowned are the Graves terraces (producing mostly white but also some red wines) just above Bordeaux on the same bank. Then come Cérons and Barsac (both rather sweeter), followed by the Sauternes slopes east of the Ciron tributary of the Garonne famous for a sweet dessert white wine. On the right bank of the Garonne are the less-famous Côtes, and between them and the Dordogne the Entre-deux-Mers produces good and mostly red wines. Across the Dordogne are the districts of St. Emilion, Pomerol, Fronsac and Bourg—the latter by the confluence with the Garonne. All these produce mainly red wines but also some whites. On the central Dordogne are the less-renowned white wine areas of Montbazillac and Bergerac, and on the central Garonne and its tributaries such red and white producers as Gaillac-sur-Tarn. In the north of Aquitaine is Cognac on the Charente, while in the south is the district of Armagnac around the Baise and Gers tributaries of the Garonne; these are brandy areas.

Next in value of output comes Burgundy, with its vineyards on the narrow south-east facing slopes of the Paris Basin and Central Massif, with mixed and well drained soils. The area begins south of Dijon with the Côte de Nuits, and continues as the Côte d'Or north of Beaune, the Côte de Beaune south of it, the small and un-renowned Côte Chalonnaise south of Chagny, Mâconnais north and south of Mâcon, and ends with Beaujolais. Famous vintages apart, quality declines from north to south. North-west of Dijon is tiny Chablis, with vineyards on slopes of the Portland Limestone.

On the narrow, middle and lower slopes of the Tertiary Falaise de l'Ile de France, from the Aisne River to the St. Gond Marshes, and for some miles down the Marne Valley (Plate 71), is the Champagne area. Production is almost entirely from small farms, but bottling is mainly by famous large firms in Rheims or Epernay. The output is relatively small but the value high.

Lastly, there are the less important valleys. The central and lower Loire vales produce mostly still but some sparkling white and rosé wines. The best Rhine vineyards are on the steep eastern slopes and mixed soils of the Vosges between Thann and Sélestat (Plate 86), and their wines are dry whites. The few remaining famous vineyards of the once vine-covered Rhône Valley, such as Tain l'Hermitage and Cornas (both near Tournan) and Châteauneuf-du-Pape (near Avignon) are red wines, in style intermediate between a burgundy and a claret, although Tavel, also near Avignon, is a famous rosé.

In northern France, where the vine is not cultivated commercially, apples are grown in Brittany and Normandy for cider, of which France is the leading world producer. There is little evidence of this, however, because most is produced for consumption on farms. Cider-bottling firms are few and commerce in it small. Quite the contrary is the case with beer, of which France is also a major world producer. One-third is produced in the far North, one-third in Alsace-Lorraine, and a sixth in Paris. Most large towns have breweries and consumption is increasing at the expense of the cheaper wines. Hops come mainly from Flanders and the Rhine Valley.

FORESTRY   One-fifth of France is tree-covered (Fig. 70). The percentage is growing because of a vigorous policy of afforestation to reduce imports of timber and cellulose; to use poor land as in Sologne; to protect river sources and soils, to fix dunes, and to halt avalanches.

The physical variety of France is again evident in the forests and types of timber, of which two-thirds are deciduous and one-third coniferous. The most wooded areas are in the north-east but the largest forest—the Landes—is in the south-west. Forested areas are both natural (such as those of the Paris Basin) and planted (Landes), and upland (e.g. Vosges) or lowland (Harth of the upper Rhine Valley). They commonly remain or have been planted on areas too poor for agriculture, although areas such as the karstic causses or plans support neither crops nor trees.

Forests may be conveniently divided into Temperate Lowland, Temperate Upland and Mediterranean. In the first category, the Landes occupies two-and-a-half million acres—but this forest is only a century old. Pines were planted to reclaim ill-drained Tertiary sands; the trees have become a great resource, now mainly for paper (p.446). The pine and birch stands of the chalk Champagne Pouilleuse (Dry Champagne) are likewise planted, and are regularly cut. The forests on the Tertiary sands of the Paris Basin are natural, regularly cut and replanted in the case of Sologne with its pines, fir, oak and birch; but little disturbed in the state forests of Fontainebleau and Compiègne, which are more deciduous than coniferous. There are also great blocks of public forest—again mixed—on river terraces in the Rhine Valley.

Only certain Temperate Uplands are well forested, notably the Ardennes, Vosges, Pyrenees, Folded Jura, northern Alps, Argonne and some escarpments. The first two each have a quarter-of-a-million acres (in the first counting only the French Ardennes); in all there is exploitation of wood.

Mediterranean forests and woodlands have been severely degraded by nature, by man and by domestic animals, and defence of the frail forest is not easy. Almost the only real forest areas are the Maures (168,000 ac.; 65,000 h.), Esterel (67,000 ac. or 26,500 h.) and the rugged slopes of the western half of Corsica, mostly covered with pine, cork oak and chestnut.

FISHING

France has a long and varied coastline opening on several seas, with many harbours, and good land transport. Like agriculture fishing has to meet the calls of the French cuisine, and also of a catholic country requiring fish on fast days. Yet there are only some 50,000 fishermen, with another 20,000 people in ancillary occupations. Except near the coasts fish is not an important food, because before refrigeration only dried or salted fish could be carried far, and this was little favoured. Sea fish are sold inland only in major cities, because refrigeration is under-developed in restaurants and homes.

Although fish landings by weight are modest compared with Norway, Iceland, Germany or the United Kingdom, their value is more respectable because of the importance of valuable shell fish, sardines, anchovy and tunny. French fishermen catch lobsters and crayfish off Ireland, Brazil and Mauritania, sardines off Morocco, and tunny off much of West Africa. Freshwater fish, especially salmon and trout, are quite important because relatively rural and mountainous France has many unpolluted rivers, and fish-farming in ponds is common.

As elsewhere, sea fishing is becoming more capitalised. Ships are becoming larger but fewer in number, as are crews and ports (Fig. 70). Boulogne has emerged as by far the largest centre in terms of tonnage and value landed (mainly herring, mackerel and cod) because of the size of its harbour and excellent rail connections. Certain ports are static such as Dieppe, St. Malo and La Rochelle. Others have declined because they are ill-served by communications, such as Fécamp and Paimpol, although some have reacted by specialising—Fécamp in making 'roll mops' and Roscoff in keeping lobsters in tanks.

On the south Breton coast, Lorient (really Kéroman) and, more recently, Concarneau, while each landing less than one-half the tonnage of Boulogne, have rather more than that percentage by value because of their importance in shell and white fish, tunny and sardines. Douarnenez and La Rochelle have smaller tonnages but again relatively high-value catches. The eight French Mediterranean fishing ports handle only small catches, but because they are numerous and the climate unhelpful to the handling of fish, it does figure more in local consumption especially in the fish stew 'bouillabaisse'. As in Brittany there is still some part-time almost subsistence fishing; there was much more in the past.

FUEL AND POWER *Coal*

Most French coal resources are near her borders, for the largest field in the north is an extension of the Belgian-Sambre-Meuse fields, whilst Lorraine, the other major field, is an extension of the German Saar field. France developed coal-mining late, most of the coal was not only peripherally sited but restricted in variety, indifferent in quality, and costly to mine. During the whole of the coal-based industrial revolution, France had insufficient coal and has had to import huge quantities, 50 million tons in 1913 and one-quarter to one-third of that amount now. All western France was dependent upon imported coal, so that the paucity of coal-based industrialisation there—and elsewhere in France outside the coal-fields and Lorraine—is not surprising. Nor did France enjoy, except at Le Creusot and St. Etienne, that juxtaposition of coal and iron ore so common and helpful to early British industrial development.

In this century the situation has gradually improved, for France acquired the Lorraine field in 1919, and she also had the Saar as war reparations from 1919–35 and from 1945–56. The Northern Coalfield, though appallingly damaged in the First World War, was reequipped by 1925 along then-modern lines. Hydro-electric power has been greatly developed to offset the shortage of coal, and has encouraged electricity-based industrialism. Since the Second World War home and imported oil, and Lacq natural gas have made an even greater impact than hydro-electric power. Coal now contributes less than one-half of France's needs of energy; so coal output is being stabilised or reduced, especially in the Northern and Central Massif fields.

The Northern Coalfield (Fig. 72) extends west-east in a slight arc for some 75 miles, from west of Béthune to the Belgian border, and is about 10 miles wide. It produces about one-half of French coal but has adverse mining conditions. Shafts pass through water-bearing strata, the coal seams are thin, faulted, inclined and contorted, and there is danger from water and gas. The areas nearest to Belgium were the first to be mined, as their coal (mainly coking) was nearer the surface. Industries such as iron and steel (now using Lorraine iron ore or pig iron, imported ores and scrap), engineering and textile works were first developed on the coalfield. They were depressed in the thirties but were reorganised later. By contrast, the western sector around Lens was opened later because of the depth of its coal. It was less depressed in the thirties because of its more varied, better quality and cheaper-mined coal, but is less prosperous again because it is too exclusively concerned with coal production. The central and eastern areas are now most prosperous.

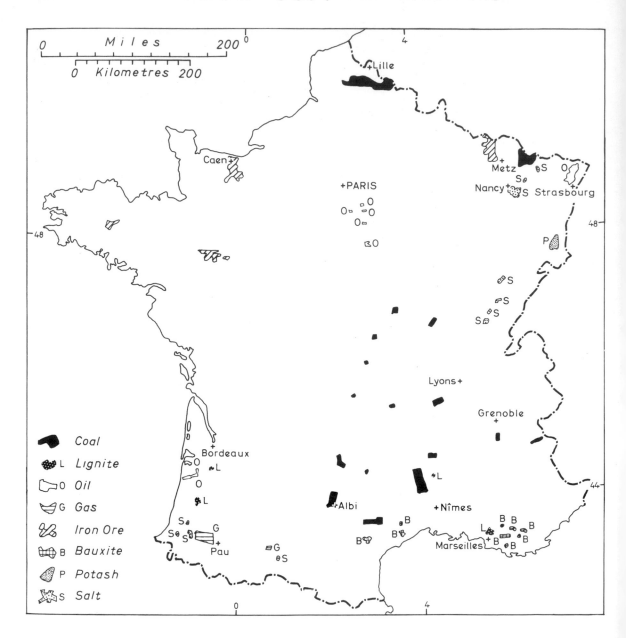

Fig 72   Minerals exploited in France

The coalfield has become one of France's most important areas for the production of electricity and gas, for the manufacture of coal derivatives (coke, patent fuels and chemicals), iron and steel; while the textile industry of Lille, Roubaix and Tourcoing uses the surplus of female labour which is taken long distances daily by coach. Unfortunately, the remarkable concentration of coalmining into two-fifths of the pits of 1945, and their modernisation, have not been accompanied by the advent of much new industry so sorely needed to diversify the economy. Poor urban amenities are the chief deterrent, and the area needs a New Town.

The Lorraine (Moselle) Coalfield has excellent gas coal but coking coal would have been far more useful in view of the proximity of the Lorraine iron and steel industry; hence the mixing of Lorraine coal with coking coal at Carling to make metallurgical coke (p. 370). Lorraine coal lies deep, but modern methods have offset this disadvantage and, with seams of up to 14 feet thick the output per manshift at the coal face is the highest in Europe. Indeed, whereas the 45 remaining modernised pits in the Northern Coalfield produce about 26 million tons, the 9 Lorraine pits produce about 14 million tons, or one-quarter the national total. Coal production will be increasingly concentrated in these two fields.

The Central Massif fields are dispersed in small fault or narrow synclinal basins on or adjacent to the crystalline rocks. Several were notable in early industrialisation because of occasionally associated iron ores e.g. at Le Creusot and St. Etienne; indeed the former had mainland Europe's first coke-using blast furnace, partly established by an Englishman. Unlike other coalfields these are also far from France's oft-overrun borders, and so they or nearby towns were favoured for armament works. Such was the case with Le Creusot, and Montluçon near the Commentry field. Almost all fields became centres of coal-using industries. However, mining costs are high and, but for the fact that much of the coal is coking coal, more pits would have closed. Total production is about 10 million tons.

A little anthracite is mined in Alpine valleys near Briançon, and at La Mure south of Grenoble.

Electricity

Because of the previous shortage of coal, thermal production has always tried to use poor coal or coal waste. More recently, oil or gas-fired and nuclear-power stations have been built, while there has been a massive development of hydro-electric power. Since 1947 hydro and thermal production have been challenging each other. The very largest stations are still mostly thermal, and new ones are still being built to use coal now unwanted by other concerns. Most thermal stations are located beside navigable water, by which they receive their fuel, on coalfields, or in the Lorraine steel areas where they may use coke oven or blast furnace gas. Others are fed with natural gas from the gas-grid, or use lignite from Hostens and Beylongue in the Landes, and from Fuveau north-east of Marseilles (Fig. 72). Almost all are in great urban areas.

The world's first hydro-electric power station was opened at Grenoble in 1869, and since then many have been built, most of them unknown because they are quite small and provide power only for a town and a few industries. They were economic in France because of the shortage and high cost of coal. Early developments were again peripheral, because existing falls in the Alps and Pyrenees were the first to be harnessed. Even before the First World War, their power was used to electrify railways, and electro-chemical and electro-metallurgical industries were also attracted by power to the Alps.

Large schemes were initiated in the thirties. The harnessing of the headwaters of the Truyère, the Dordogne and its tributaries was begun in the Central Massif, and has since been extended to other rivers. The winter maximum of these rivers compared with the spring and summer maxima of those in the Alps and Pyrenees was a great merit, but such is the seasonal variation due to this and to the rapid run off in the Central Massif that high dams have been necessary to impound large reservoirs or lakes. Little industry existed in the area, and little or none has been attracted by the power, for the Central Massif is less well sited for industry than the international routeways of the Alpine valleys. Central Massif power is largely sent by grid to Paris and elsewhere.

A start was also made on the harnessing of large swift-flowing rivers whose force and massive discharge (rather than fall) could be profitably developed. So on a deviation canal of the Rhine, the Kembs station was opened in 1932, and five more stations have been added since 1952. Much more important are the works of the Compagnie Nationale du Rhône, established in 1934 to harness that river for power, navigation and irrigation (Figs. 85 and 90). Génissiat was opened in 1948 (after war delays), near where the Rhône enters France, and with the then-highest capacity in Western Europe. In 1952 the almost as powerful Bollène station across a 12 mile deviation canal on the lower Rhône between Donzère (below Montélimar) and Mondragon was opened. Subsequently, smaller capacity but still large stations were opened at Châteauneuf (Montélimar) in 1958 and Le Logis Neuf (Baix) a little to the north in 1960 (Fig. 85 and Plate 72). Four more are under construction. In all, they will produce energy equivalent to 20 million tons of coal, so regulate the river as to make it easily navigable, and irrigate 750,000 acres (300,000 h.)—much of it already achieved below Bollène (Fig. 90). The tremendous quantities of power have also permitted the establishment close to Bollène of a radio-active isotope works, the most costly modern industrial unit in Europe. Regular water supplies also facilitated the establishment in 1956 of the first nuclear power station downstream at Marcoule. The Durance is also the subject of large power and irrigation development (Fig. 90), its largest station, Serre Ponçon, being comparable with those on the Rhône. Man has indeed made a new landscape in these two valleys.

Vast reservoirs have been created in the Alps to guarantee power at dams across valleys (e.g. at Tignes, upper Isère). Water is also being diverted from one valley to another e.g. from the Isère to the Arc for the Randens underground station (p. 414).

In 1966 France opened the barrage across the Rance Estuary in Brittany, just above St. Malo and Dinard, the world's first commercial station to generate power from the force of the tides, whose maximum variation here reach 44 feet, and whose discharge can exceed by four that of the Rhône. The capacity is 240,000 kw, about one-quarter of the largest thermal power station in Britain, and may encourage the advent of more industry to Brittany.

Plate 72 Baix-Le-Logis-Neuf power station on the Rhône.
View from the left bank over the deviation canal, power station, shipping lock, the wide bed of the Rhône and vineyards, to the Coirons—a volcanic outflow from the Central Massif.

Oil and Natural Gas

Oil has been obtained by mining at Pechelbronn, north of Strasbourg, since the fifteenth century, and by pumping since 1881, but it is now of very minor importance. The next significant oil discovery was at the Etang de Parentis (Lake Biscarosse) south-west of Bordeaux in 1954, and there are other producing areas nearby. In 1958 oil was discovered east of Orleans in the Paris Basin, and also east, south-east and south of Paris. Production from all of these is now 5–10% of French needs, while France also benefits from her Saharan and Middle East oil interests. Oil refineries are still mainly on the coast, navigable rivers (Gironde, Loire, Seine) and, more recently, the Rhine at Strasbourg and the Rhône at Lyons, both 'fed' by the Lavéra-Karlsruhe pipeline.

More significant than French oil is gas, mostly from Lacq, a reserve discovered in 1951 (Plate 73). At first it could not be distributed because of its exceptionally high sulphur content (15%), but since 1958 a vast gas

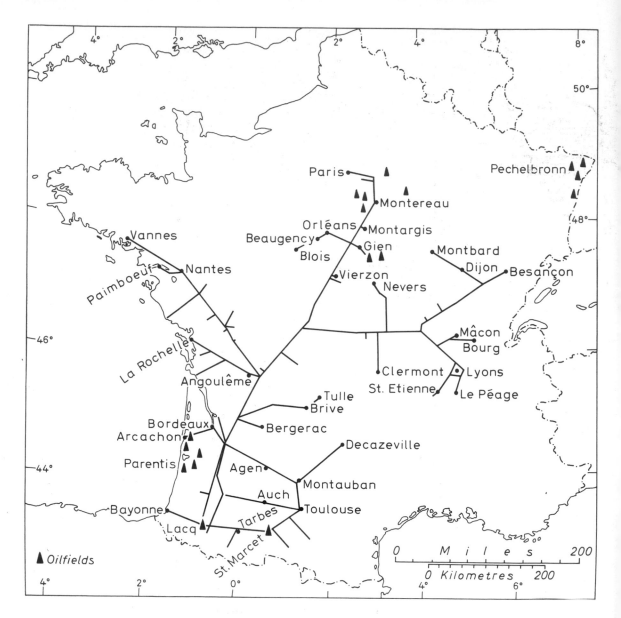

Fig 73 French oilfields and natural gas grid

grid (Fig. 73) has been laid over much of France. Coal-gas production has ceased in these areas, but the chemical industry—indeed many industries—has been greatly stimulated. Maximum output of Lacq gas will last until about 1977 but other reserves exist. France is also importing liquid gas from the Sahara via Lavéra (Marseilles) and from the Netherlands by pipeline through Belgium, as well as prospecting in the North Sea.

Plate 73   The sulphur extraction unit at Lacq.
In the centre-rear is the new apartment complex of Mourenx-la-Neuve, housing
12,000 people. Beyond are the Central High Pyrenees, 20 miles away.

France has indeed come far from the days when coal was the only
fuel, and she was desperately short of it; indeed, France is well placed
in the electrical and petro-chemical age.

MINERALS (OTHER
THAN FUELS) AND
ASSOCIATED
INDUSTRIES

Many minerals have been and are mined in France but only iron ore,
bauxite, potash, sulphur and salt are important at the national level. These,
and the fuel and power resources (see above) are almost all located on or
near the margins of France, so adding to the cost of their transport and to the
danger of loss at times of invasion. Thus most of the coal, iron ore and salt
were overrun in the First World War, and these as well as potash in 1940.

France enjoyed neither the wide range of commercially-exploitable
non-ferrous ores such as lead, tin and copper, nor the common juxtaposition of iron ore and coal so helpful to early British industrial development. Apart from coal, almost all the now-significant minerals have been

mined only within the last hundred years, several in less than half a century. Most of the iron ore is lean (30–33% *Fe*) and phosphoric, and could not be used in steel making until after the invention of the Gilchrist-Thomas process in 1879, by which time France had lost most of the then known easily-mined reserves. They were regained in 1919, only to be lost once more from 1940–45. Even when in French hands they were separated by a boundary from the best coal and coke in the Ruhr, while in German hands the iron ore and coke were within one currency and price zone. The advantages to France of the European Coal and Steel Community are that she has access without discrimination to Ruhr coke and coal, and enjoys a greater competitiveness for her steel industry.

Iron Ore and the Iron and Steel Industry

France is the second (though a very poor second) European producer of iron ore after the U.S.S.R., and the fourth European steel producer. Almost all the ore comes from the Upper Lias of the Côtes de Moselle west of Nancy and Thionville, around Longwy, and from the Briey Plateau dipping westward behind the scarp. A little comes from the same formation where it outcrops on the west of the Paris Basin near Caen. The ore is similar to that quarried in the English scarplands, although the French ore is less lean. About one-half is obtained by adit-mining (more or less level shafts), the beds may attain 30 feet, mining presents no problems, and cutting and transport are mechanised and efficient. Ore mining is commonly carried out by iron and steel companies whose works are adjacent (Plate 74).

The fields around Nancy (Fig. 72) were the earliest to be opened (by adits), at first for iron-making alone. After the Franco-Prussian War they remained French but the siliceous ore is sandy, friable and not self-fluxing. Transport of coke from the Ruhr, the French Northern Coalfield or from elsewhere is expensive; thus the associated industry has rather higher costs than those farther north.

The second mining zone is also at the foot of the Côtes de Moselle, beginning south of Metz and extending over the border into Luxembourg. The French (and main) sector includes the narrow obsequent Orne and Fentsch valleys of the scarp. This area, with almost entirely calcareous and thus self-fluxing ore, is by far the most important in Lorraine, and was mainly developed by the Germans, using Ruhr coke. When Lorraine became French again this district was put into the same situation as that of Nancy—it had either to pay foreign currency to buy Ruhr coke or get inferior and more expensive coke from the French Northern Coalfield. Nor was Ruhr coke always available after each of the wars; the Germans needed it themselves. Hence the intensive research undertaken to use French Lorraine or German Saar coal (which the French also possessed from 1919–35 and from 1945–56). At first only 30% of that coal could be used in a mixture with 70% of real coking coal to obtain metallurgical coke; now the proportions are reversed. Moreover, the smaller amounts of Ruhr or other coal or coke now required can be brought in more cheaply as a result of the European Coal and Steel Community's abolition of discriminatory prices and freights to foreigners, and because of cheaper transport by the canalised Moselle opened in 1964 (p. 379).

There are ten highly integrated works in this area, making wide use of oxygen-enrichment and other processes to make better steel than the normal basic Bessemer product. There is very considerable further fabrication through cold rolling to steel flats and tin plating (Plate 74). The factors which cheapened Ruhr coke have also cheapened the transport of finished products and widened their markets outside France.

Plate 74   The Sollac integrated iron and steel works at Sérémange, in the obsequent valley of the Fentsch, near Thionville.

The company has its own ore-mining adits (galleries) in the Côtes de Moselle behind. To the left are the iron-making blast furnaces, then come the steel furnaces where the white smoke rises, and there follow down the valley hot and cold rolling mills and tin-plating works.

The third area is the border one of Longwy, and here the ore is again siliceous as at Nancy, though cheaply quarried. However, the terrain is difficult because of the incision of the Chiers River, making level ground for large works difficult to secure alongside railways and roads. Nevertheless, there are five integrated works and as many blast furnace-sites, unlike the previous area or even the Nancy district. The Longwy area has been French ever since the ore was worked. Belgian and Luxembourg firms also have concessions or industrial interests in this area bordering their own works just across the boundary. Before leaving the steel-making areas of Lorraine it should be noted that they account for about two-thirds of French steel.

Lastly, there is the Briey Plateau where, since the ore (mostly calcareous) is dipping westward, extraction must be by shaft mines. Always French, industrial development has been minimal here, and the ore goes to the Thionville and Orne Valley areas whose firms mine it.

The Normandy orefield around Caen has siliceous deposits of higher iron content than in Lorraine, but the amount quarried is only one-twentieth that of Lorraine, because of faulting and steeply-dipping strata. There is an integrated plant at Mondeville, near Caen, using German and American coke, both brought by water transport. Normandy ore is also sent to an iron works at Rouen by sea, as well as being exported.

Almost insignificant now are the non-phosphoric but richer ores obtained from residual cappings on Ordovician sandstones in southern Armorica north-west of Angers, and on Silurian schists north-west of Alençon. Similar ores have been worked in the upper valleys of the Tet and Ariège in the Pyrenees, where they nourished long-standing iron and steel industries. However, these now depend upon pig-iron, scrap or semi-finished steels, usually from Lorraine, and brought in for further refinement in electric furnaces. There are similar but larger plants in Alpine valleys (Plate 83) e.g. of the Arc and Isère.

Like these Alpine valleys the other iron and steel-making areas are not on iron ore fields. One type of location is in areas with good coking coal in the Central Massif and Northern Coalfield. The once-important iron ores of the former have long been exhausted economically. Lorraine pig iron or scrap are melted at Montluçon, Commentry, Le Creusot, Blanzy, St. Etienne and nearby centres, in Siemens open-hearth furnaces. These use more fuel than Bessemer converters but make finer steels. The tendency of old centres to specialise is clear.

The Northern Coalfield steel districts are less highly specialised because their location is better and costs lower. They are able to bring in Lorraine, Swedish or other ores fairly cheaply, and so still have blast furnaces, unlike the Central Massif areas. The North also uses pig iron and semi-finished steels, usually from Lorraine, and steel scrap. A large slabbing mill is at Denain (south-west of Valenciennes), there are other plants nearby, and around Mauberge in the Sambre Valley. Smaller plants are at Isbergues on the Aire Canal, at Outreau—a suburb of Boulogne (originally using Jurassic ores from the Boulonnais), and east of Dunkirk.

Although works near the mouths of the Adour and Loire, and below Rouen on the Seine, have always brought in all raw materials, the vast *Usinor* integrated works on the west side of Dunkirk demonstrates a new trend (Plate 75). Rich haematite is imported from Mauritania, the works has oil-fired furnaces, and uses a minimum of coke. This great complex is akin to the Port Talbot and Newport works in Wales, and similar plants may be built near Marseilles at Fos, and elsewhere. Everywhere in the world the trend is to use richer ores, local or imported, and this puts in doubt the future of the lean Lorraine ores. In France the canalised Moselle

Plate 75 The Usinor integrated iron and steel works at Dunkirk, with its ore reception basin.

Beyond and behind is an oil refinery, the lock-basins and the town rebuilt after the Second World War. Beyond is the seaside suburb of Malo-les-Bains. Note the sand-dune coast.

will make it cheaper and easier to import richer ores to Lorraine, and to Luxembourg and the Saar, to which Lorraine currently exports its ore.

Steel making also exists in many ports and in Paris on a small scale, usually by or for engineering industries. The latter are important in all iron and steel-making areas and large towns. An important branch is shipbuilding, where the largest and most efficient works are on the Loire at St. Nazaire and Nantes; on the Seine at Rouen, Le Havre, and between the two; and at Dunkirk. Smaller yards at La Pallice, Bordeaux and especially on the Mediterranean have excess capacity because of competition from Japan, and their remoteness from large iron and steel producers puts their future in doubt. The great automobile, lorry and earth-shifting equipment firms are mainly in Paris (Plate 85) and Lyons where there is a large local market and transport is good. Some are in places like Sochaux near Montbéliard because of original family associations (like Cowley in Britain), or in places such as Rennes to which a firm has been encouraged to decentralise by the government (again as in Britain).

Bauxite

This hydrated oxide is one of several ores of aluminium, and takes its name from the village of Les Baux in the Alpilles, south of Avignon, where it was first mined. However, most is now quarried or deep mined in the limestone hills at Brignoles north-east of Toulon, but a little comes from north of Sète (Fig. 72).

France was formerly a major producer but her bauxite, though of high quality and easily quarried or mined, is expensive because it has been difficult to get conveniently-shaped mining leases. France now produces only a very modest part of world supplies; some is exported because of its good quality, but most goes to Gardanne near Marseilles for reduction to alumina (by boiling with caustic soda), the electricity for heating being generated by using local lignite. Some of the alumina is also exported, but most goes to Alpine valleys for conversion to aluminium with the use of vast amounts of hydro-electric power, or to Noguères, near Lacq, where natural gas is used for cheap electrical generation.

Potash

Although potash was long known to exist under the Nonnenbruch Forest north-west of Mulhouse, the concession was initially held by a German monopoly which mined only its original Stassfurt deposit. The return of Alsace to France in 1918–19 broke the monopoly, and France became a major producer. Potash is a base for fertiliser and other chemical industries in France, and some two-thirds of her potash is also exported.

Salt

Most of this is obtained by brine pumping east of Nancy, at Poligny and Salins (Jura edge), and in southern Aquitaine, wherever salt remains from evaporation of shallow gulfs of the Triassic seas, just as potash was formed in Rhine Valley gulfs in Oligocene times. Salt is used in many chemical industries—locally at Sarralbe, Dombasle, Nancy, Dôle, (Saône Valley—brine taken by pipeline from Poligny), and elsewhere. A little salt is evaporated on the Mediterranean and Biscay coasts, especially the former, mostly for domestic or export needs.

Sulphur

This occurs in such quantities with natural gas at Lacq (Plate 73) that its extraction was vital to use and pipe away the gas. From being an importer of sulphur, France now has five times her needs, and has become the second world producer.

With such diverse materials to hand it is not surprising that the chemical industry is well developed in France. Apart from branches immediately associated with the above minerals, or imported phosphates, there are those using imported oil to manufacture detergents and synthetic textiles e.g. at Croix-Sainte (entrance to Etang de Berre) and near oil refineries there and on the lower Seine, Loire and Garonne. Those based on coal and its derivatives are also important, such as dyestuffs produced on coalfields. Electro-chemical plants using great quantities of power are in the Arc and other valleys of the Alps, in the Gave de Pau and Ariège valleys of the Pyrenees, and the Rhône Valley. Natural gas, crude and refined oil pipe lines are likely to help old and new chemical industries; the nitrogenous products plant at Toulouse is one that has greatly benefited. Chemical industries are also important in and around the great urban centres e.g. Paris.

OTHER INDUSTRIES

Cement

This is the last French industry to be mentioned which depends upon quarried material. France is exceptionally well provided with limestones of the various geological ages and this fact, combined with her need for reconstruction after two world wars, and her invention of reinforced and pre-stressed concrete, has stimulated a notable cement industry. This is largely concentrated near urban markets, and where the raw materials and navigable rivers also exist e.g. in the Seine, Garonne and Rhône valleys.

Textiles

There is a long history of production of diverse textiles in France, which takes fourth place in world textile production after the U.S.A., the United Kingdom and the U.S.S.R., and also accounts for about one-fifth of European production. Textiles occupy nearly one-sixth of French workers but account for only about one-twelfth of the industrial output by value. As in other older industrial countries there has been much concentration in the older branches of production, especially cotton. Man-made fibres account for over one-quarter of the output, and their share is increasing.

Most of the textile industry is still concentrated in a few areas, long prominent in it. Flanders, so renowned for its hand spinning and weaving of local wool and flax, survives as a textile area because the opening of the Northern Coalfield brought the means of raising steam power to run machines. Now they are powered by electricity produced from the nearby coal, and are mostly using cotton, wool, mixtures of these, and artificial or synthetic fibres. Roubaix and Tourcoing, by the Belgian border, and formerly very dependent upon the daily advent of Belgian labour, are responsible for some 90% of wool combed in France (even for over 10% of world wool combings), and for over one-half of French wool, worsted and carpet production. As in other countries there are smaller centres of long-standing specialities, such as Rheims for flannel and Orleans for blankets.

Although Rouen and its environs spin most of the cotton, Rouen was originally a wool-making centre. Together with Le Havre it is the main cotton importer. Cotton weaving is largely in Lille, Armentières, Roubaix and Tourcoing, and again in lesser but highly specialised centres elsewhere e.g. east of the Vosges (for calicoes), west of the Vosges (voiles), or Troyes (knitwear and hosiery). The latter centres use cotton almost entirely in mixed fabrics.

Linen, although far less important than these other textiles, is still almost all spun in Lille, and woven in Roubaix and Tourcoing. Some local flax is used, but most is imported.

By comparison with these Northern areas, Alsace production is now of minor importance. It also originated as a hand industry in the eastern valleys of the Vosges using local wool, soft water from the granite for washing it, and the fast-flowing streams for power. Cotton and silk were later introduced for calico and muslin manufacture, in imitation of Indian fabrics and patterns. By the time of the Franco-Prussian War the industry was mainly in Colmar and Mulhouse. After that war, some firms and workers migrated west and south of the Vosges so as to remain in France, thus establishing new centres in the Meurthe, Mortagne and Moselle valleys, and at Belfort. There is intense specialisation but the future of these centres is doubtful.

The other traditional textile centre is the Lyons silk area (p. 440), where the city is as much an organisational as a manufacturing centre of silk, of which much is made outside the city in homes or small towns.

Artificial silk and other man-made fibre manufactures are increasingly important, and are located in the Northern textile area, in certain ports importing the raw materials of artificial silk (e.g. Dunkirk), in centres of the chemical industry making synthetic fibres (e.g. St. Fons south of Lyons), and in major urban centres such as Paris. Clothing manufacture is closely associated with these. While firms are becoming fewer and larger, and the mass production of woollen and cotton goods becomes more and more concentrated in the North, the artificial and synthetic products are being produced in more dispersed but still large factories.

INDUSTRIAL AREAS   The old basic heavy industries are on or near the iron ore fields, coalfields, and other mineral areas. They are also near sources of power, the early hydro-electric power areas of the northern Alps and Pyrenees, but now rather more elsewhere using supplies from the electrical grid e.g. at Toulouse, Paris and many other places. Sources of natural gas, first at Saint Marcet and then at Lacq, have brought industry to Lacq and to places on the gas grids (Fig. 73) such as Toulouse and Lannemezan. The long-distance crude-oil pipelines, of which that from Lavéra to Strasbourg is but the first, may have the same effect, as may the increasing production of electricity in atomic power stations. Industry is becoming more dispersed, cleaner, and more sophisticated in its output.

Yet certain industries such as cement and some basic chemicals will still tend to be tied to sources of raw materials. Rather similar in localisation, but not giving rise to planning problems, are the food-processing industries whose importance is growing as a result of the rising standards of living in France and elsewhere. These industries are important in Bordeaux, Toulouse, Marseilles, the Loire Valley, Paris, Dijon, Metz, Strasbourg, and in Normandy, to cite only examples. It must be added that water is an important raw material for many industries, especially in the manufacture of plastics, aluminium, rayon, paper, steel and tyres.

Many industries depend wholly or substantially upon imported raw materials, and so are often in or near ports—coastal or river. The oil-seed crushing works of Marseilles and Bordeaux are examples, as are their mineral oil refineries and associated petro-chemical industries.

As in other industrial countries, industries are still found where the initial locating factors have ceased to apply. The Lyons silk industry, the clothing industry of Berry (around Bourges), and the lock and tap manufactures of Vimeu (south of the Somme Estuary) are examples, while cotton has replaced the original wool industry of Rouen. New industries often take over disused works of other industries—a common feature in the older industrial areas and larger towns. Some industries are located as the result of personal connections or decisions, such as the Michelin tyre works in Clermont-Ferrand, although such factories survive only because the advantages of their sites outweigh their disadvantages.

Industries located in or near markets, of which Paris is so outstanding an example, are of increasing importance. This is a great metallurgical, chemical, food, and other consumer or semi-consumer goods industrial area. As explained on p. 428 the industrial attraction of Paris is so great that it has been thought necessary to try to divert industry elsewhere. Nevertheless, industry tends to locate as near as possible to this great market, where there is also skilled labour, ready information, and transport to all markets—indeed everything the modern industrialist needs.

By 'carrot and stick' methods some industries have been established in areas of unemployment, such as the western part of the Northern Coalfield (e.g. at Béthune), where old industries are static or declining. They have also been diverted to areas regarded as insufficiently diversified or industrialised like Brittany e.g. at Brest and Lannion.

Yet the most satisfactory areas are likely to be those that naturally attract industries. The Rhône Valley is probably the future industrial heart of France, for it has large and increasing amounts of power (hydro from the Rhône, the Alps and Central Massif; thermal from St. Etienne; atomic from Marcoule). It has the major port of Marseilles at the southern end and Lyons at the other—France's second and third cities, while there are excellent rail links with Paris. As the Rhône is being progressively controlled, so water transport will be further improved and cheapened. Moreover, the valley is attractive for residence, and people are easily encouraged to come from the poor, nearby Central Massif and southern Alps. Although much less favoured, the Rhine Valley may also attract more industries by its power from the Rhine, crude oil by pipeline from

Lavéra and the associated new refineries and petro-chemical works, the river port of Strasbourg, good access to Paris, and to nearby German markets of increasing importance through the Common Market.

Through her shortage of coal, France was at a severe disadvantage in the Coal and Steam Era of the Industrial Revolution. She is now well-placed in the Electrical Era, provided she can reduce her usually high costs of production. One way of doing this would be by a more rapid concentration of production, for so much of French industry is still carried on in small and ill-equipped factories; in 1962 two-fifths of all factories had 100 workers or less. Her increasing numbers of young people are likely to hasten this by insisting upon better conditions of employment. Nevertheless, French industry has made dramatic advances. By 1947 production had, in general, regained 1938 levels; by 1951 it had passed the maximum inter-war peak of 1926; and by 1964 had trebled the figure of 1938, especially through the prosperous energy and power, metal, vehicle, cement, electronics and chemical industries.

COMMUNICATIONS

France has an extensive and varied network of communications. Their patterns have been negatively affected by the obstacles of the Central Massif, Vosges, Jura, Alps and Pyrenees, and positively by the routeways mentioned on pp. 341–2. The coal and ironfields, and their associated industries, have been outstandingly important economic stimuli, while this highly centralised state has encouraged intense focusing upon Paris of road, rail and air routes. About three-quarters of French freight is carried by road, under one-fifth by rail, and almost all the rest by water. However, if long-distance traffic alone is considered, then one-quarter is carried by road, two-thirds by rail, and one-tenth by water.

Waterways

Although of relatively minor importance, these are discussed first because of their long use and association with the natural drainage. Almost all are in the north-east and east (Fig. 74). Much the greatest traffic is carried on the Seine below Montereau (ocean vessels also below Rouen), on the tributary Marne, Oise and its tributary the Aisne, all of which are improved natural waterways. Canals link the Aisne to the Meuse, the Oise to the Sambre and, more important, via the St. Quentin and Nord canals to the Scheldt, Scarpe and Lys, as well as the ports of Calais, Dunkirk and Antwerp. The Marne is connected by narrow and shallow canals with the Aisne, Meuse, Moselle, Sarre, Saône, and especially the Rhine, but traffic is less than on the Oise-St. Quentin-Nord-Scheldt waterways. The latter have so much traffic (despite the fact that most are limited to barges of 280 tons), mainly because they link Paris with the Northern Coalfield and the Channel ports. These areas produce products of relatively low value in relation to bulk and weight, such as coal, coke, pig iron, semi-finished steel and slag; or have need of such products as

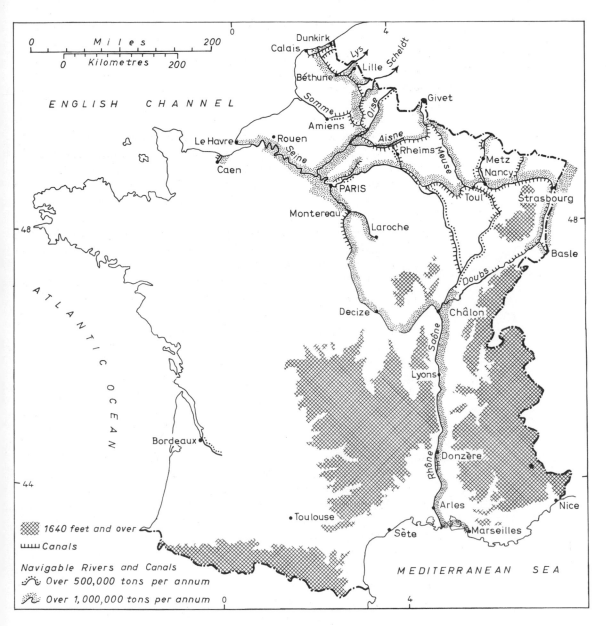

Fig 74 Major French waterways

sand, limestone, ores, cement, bricks and fuel oil. All are well suited to carriage by water. On the other hand, as coal becomes less important in industry the significance of these canals may decline, especially as competing crude oil and natural gas are increasingly carried by pipeline.

Next in significance is the Moselle Canal, opened only in 1964, but discussed since Roman times. Modern opposition by the German and

French railways, and Ruhr steel firms, was overruled in 1956–7 in favour of the project. This became essential to keep France within the European Coal and Steel Community, and to secure the return of the Saar to Germany; without the canalisation of the Moselle France would have been at a greater disadvantage compared with the Ruhr than before the creation of the Community. The Moselle can now take 1,500-ton motor barges drawing slightly over eight feet, and push-tow convoys of barges of up to 3,000 tons. Lorraine is at last well served by a major international waterway. The costs of bringing in Ruhr coal and coke, and of sending out iron and steel, have been halved compared with previous rail charges. However, Lorraine ore sales have not increased; indeed, imported haematite is made even more competitive with the local lean and phosphoric ores. Dunkirk and Antwerp may lose rail-borne Lorraine traffic, Strasbourg some water-borne, but Rotterdam gains Moselle-Rhine traffic. By 1968 the older Moselle Lateral Canal will be enlarged to the same specifications as far as Frouard, just north of Nancy.

The Rhine is of major importance upstream to Strasbourg, again for 1,500 ton barges, and most use the Rhine Lateral and Huningue (Grand Canal d'Alsace) canals to Basle. The small Rhine-Marne Canal with its equally poor links, all for 280 or 350 ton barges, have been mentioned. Small barges use the Marne-Saône and Canal de l'Est (Moselle-Saône), and there are schemes to build new canals between the Saône and Moselle or, more likely, between the Saône and Rhine. However, the Lavéra-Strasbourg pipeline takes the crude oil traffic, and the rest could be more cheaply and speedily handled by the forthcoming electrified Mulhouse-Dôle railway. On the other hand, Alsace-Lorraine traffic now passing through Rotterdam or Antwerp might use these southern canals for shipment through Marseilles, and these canals would strengthen Marseilles and Strasbourg's competitiveness in the Common Market.

The Saône-Rhône is the other significant long waterway, and it has been much improved by the several deviation canals constructed for hydro-electric power stations on the Rhône, so that it can now take large motor barges. Crude oil moves by pipeline but refined products travel by motor barges, as do imported phosphates, French sulphur, cement and salt. Some steel goods come south from Lorraine. The Saône carries more traffic than the Rhône because of its more even régime and gentler flow compared with that of the improved Rhône.

The major true inland ports are those of Paris and Strasbourg, each handling 5–6 million tons annually, Lyons (some 2 million), Denain and Aniche (coal ports west of Valenciennes) and Lille, each handling about one million tons.

Roads

The Romans built a remarkable network of roads focusing upon Lyons. Napoleon was mainly responsible for the present network of *routes nationales* fanning out from Paris (Fig. 75), and *routes départementales* focusing upon the chief towns of the *départements*. The present dense

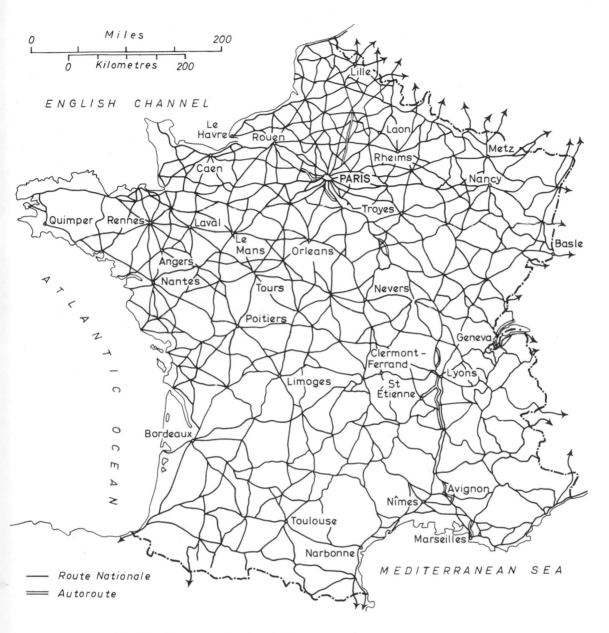

Fig 75 Routes nationales and autoroutes

network is little more than these roads—numerous but narrow, indiffer-
ently surfaced, less straight than in Roman times, and often lined by
trees originally planted to conceal troop movements but now a menace
to motorists. There are few town by-passes, so that densely peopled urban
areas are further congested and endangered by through traffic. Twenty-
five years behind Germany and Italy, France embarked in 1955 upon
building motorways. The results (Fig. 75) are proportionately less even

than Britain's in mileage, and certainly less effective, for there are few long stretches. The greatest achievements have been on the Riviera, the Rhône Valley, near Paris and Lille. The seven-mile-long Mt. Blanc tunnel into Italy, the largest road tunnel in the world, is also important.

Railways

Although the French railway network is less dense than that of the German Federal Republic, Belgium or the United Kingdom, it is the longest in Europe (excluding that of Russia). The original companies were given authority to build from Paris, and railways have notably

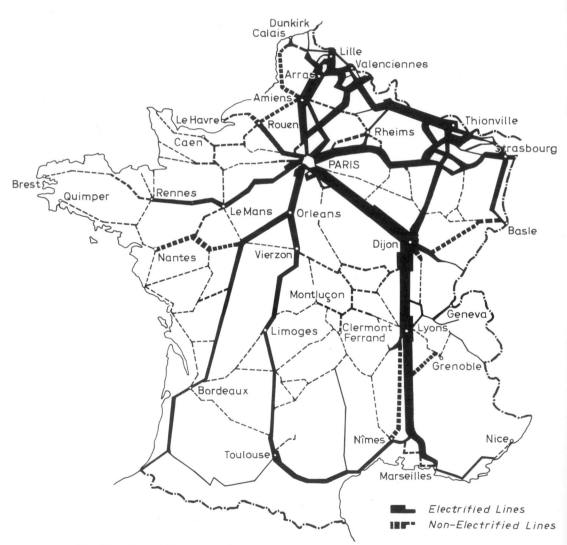

Fig 76   French Railways freight and passenger traffic
(Partly after *Annuaire Statistique de la France*)

reinforced French centralisation. The modest production, cost and indifferent quality of French steam coal, and the great hydro-electric power potential encouraged two of the original companies to develop power for railway electrification, first in the Alps in the early years of this century and then in the Pyrenees. By 1938, 2,090 miles had been electrified, including the trunk routes Paris-Bordeaux-Spanish border, Paris-Toulouse (except Brive-Montauban), and Paris-Le Mans. Between the wars the Michelin company developed self-powered auto-railers, or *michelines*, forerunners of diesel rail cars now common on minor or tourist lines, or at off-peak hours (Plate 76). Since the Second World War, 3,600 more lines of track have been electrified, and this after delays caused by formid-

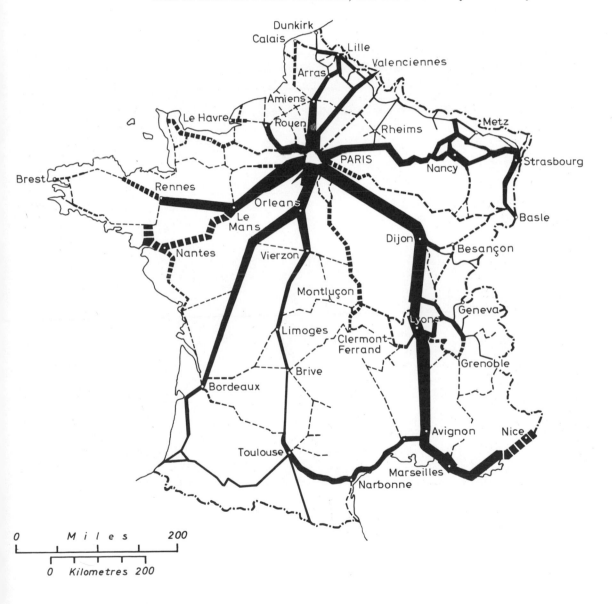

Plate 76　Two aspects of French railways.
Left : Villeneuve-Saint-Georges (just south of Paris, in the Seine Valley) is Europe's largest marshalling yard, and is operated electronically.

Right : A two-decker tourist diesel rail car on the Mediterranean coast.

able war damage. One-quarter of the mileage is now electrified, and over two-thirds of the passengers and freight are moved by electric traction (Fig. 76). Much of the rest is dieselised, using *michelines* rather than diesel locomotives with ordinary coaches.

The Second World War (unlike the First) affected every part of the system, which had been damaged by the enemy during invasion and retreat, and by the allies and *maquis* (French Underground Forces) during the German occupation. Of the pre-war rolling stock there survived only one-fifth of the locomotives and coaches, and two-ninths of the trucks. Most of the wagon-shops, locomotive depots and marshalling yards were ruined, so that repairs could not be quickly undertaken. Nearly 2,000 bridges were down, over one-third the important stations, most signal boxes and nearly one-tenth of the track mileage were destroyed. The need to reconstruct enabled complete modernisation (Plate 76) and stand-ardisation, the more so as the companies had been nationalised in 1938.

French railways have long advertised 65 trains a day maintaining an average of 65 m.p.h. over great distances; indeed, Paris-Lille, Paris-Strasbourg, Paris-Marseilles-Nice and Paris-Bordeaux are done at averages of 73 m.p.h. or over. Even the Provence freight express averages 61 m.p.h. with many stops for attaching further wagons. Car-carrying sleeper-car trains are run from Paris, the Channel ports, Lille, Belgium, the Netherlands and Germany to the French tourist areas, where the railways also run passenger coach tours.

It is not surprising that both passenger and freight traffic have increased since the Second World War, through the attractive efficiency of French rail travel, its tapered rates, the developing economy, rising tourist and transit traffic, the latter further helped by the Common Market.

Airways

Despite the eminence of France in world air transport, her domestic services are few. This is the consequence of centralisation in Paris, fast alternative means of transport, the compact shape of the country, low population, the paucity of urban clusters and industrial areas, the low income of substantial groups e.g. the peasants, and of numerous poor areas e.g. the massifs and mountains.

The 'Paris Airport' comprises both Orly and Le Bourget. It has less traffic than London but more than Frankfurt or Rome, and is about eighth in the world. By passenger-miles and freight-value it follows New York, Chicago and London.

Nice and Marseilles (Marignane) have substantial inter-continental traffic, while Toulouse, Bordeaux and Lyons have a little. Yet the latter cannot compete with Geneva airport, which serves a city and country much smaller than Lyons and France.

The remaining airports have mostly seasonal traffic, often of car-carrying planes, charter or cheap flights from Britain, Scandinavia, Germany and Benelux.

Ports

France has a long and varied coastline, facing several seas, and is adjacent to great maritime routeways. There are many natural harbours and several navigable estuaries, so that the establishment of numerous ports was easy. This was not the case on the coasts of Belgium, the Netherlands and Germany, where development had to be concentrated at few points. The major ports in these countries far surpass French ones; Rotterdam's trade is much greater than the sum of all French ports. The latter handle only one-third of French exports by weight; the rest travels over land boundaries, much of it to Antwerp which exports more French goods (especially iron and steel) than any French port.

No French port is of world stature, and all are rather too far west or south to have much transit trade, or to benefit greatly from the Common Market. Indeed, they are likely to lose further trade because of high port charges and poor handling methods. Increased state aid for improvements is being given, perhaps too late. Le Havre and Dunkirk have the best prospects, because of location, good reconstruction after fantastic war damage, and their great expanses of cheap land for dock and industrial expansion.

The major ports are Marseilles (Plate 88) and its associates (which handle about one-quarter of the total port tonnage of France); Le Havre one-fifth; Dunkirk (Plate 75), Rouen and Nantes–St. Nazaire each about one-twelfth; and Bordeaux about one-fifteenth. About two-fifths of the import tonnage is crude oil and one-third the exports are refined products, the proportions varying from port to port according to the location, size and character of refineries. This trade is likely to become even more preponderant. France must be able to accommodate the growing size of oil tankers and ore carriers, and in a few decades two or three ports will dominate the scene.

France has magnificently re-equipped her railways and increased their traffic, but has far to go in developing internal air services, improving the roads, ports and worthwhile waterways.

FOREIGN TRADE   France is not one of the world's great traders, nor does she earn substantial amounts from services (invisible exports). One-quarter to one-third of her trade is done with her partners in the European Economic Community—especially Germany, and one-sixth with those in the Franc Zone (former colonies). Manufactures naturally predominate in exports, particularly machinery, transport equipment (cars, diesel-locomotives, planes and aero-engines, etc.) and textiles, but foodstuffs and wine, chemicals, mineral and other raw materials, fuels (especially oil) are important. Major imports are transport equipment, manufactures, raw materials, fuels, foodstuffs and chemicals.

FURTHER READING   *General*
J. F. Gravier, *La Mise en Valeur de la France*, 1949.
P. Pinchemel, *Géographie de la France*, 2 vols., 1964.

Population
J. I. Clarke, 'Demographic Revival in France', *Geography*, 1963, pp. 309–11.

Agriculture
G. C. Weigend, 'Basis and significance of viticulture in south-west France', *Annals of the Association of American Geographers*, 1954, pp. 75–101.

Fuel and Power
B. S. Hoyle, 'Changes in the Durance Valley', *Geography*, 1960, pp. 110–113.
I. M. Thompson, 'A Geographical Appraisal of Recent Trends in the Coal Basin of Northern France', *Geography*, 1965, pp. 252–60.

Minerals and Industry

J. E. Martin, 'Location Factors in the Lorraine Iron and Steel Industry', *Transactions of Institute of British Geographers*, 1957, pp. 191–212.

J. E. Martin, 'Recent Trends in the Lorraine Iron and Steel Industry', *Geography*, 1958, pp. 191–99.

J. E. Martin, 'Developments in the Lorraine Iron and Steel Industry', *Geography*, 1961, pp. 242–5.

Atlases, Maps and Relief Models

Atlas de France

P. Gourou, *Atlas Classique—France et Union Française*

The main maps are the 1/50,000, 1/100,000 and 1/200,000 (the latter also in an Oro-hydrography edition and with Special District sheets). There are also relief models—on these scales.

The Regions of France

'*On ne peut comprendre la France si on ne part pas de cette marquetterie régional longuement mise en place*'. P. Pinchemel, *Géographie de la France*, Tome 1, 1964, p. 19.

The Hercynian Massifs
Hard, worn remnants of the oldest geological eras occur widely in France. Their evolution has been sketched on pp. 342–4; here the contrasts between and within the massifs will be described.

Armorica is the lowest in altitude, it has experienced no volcanism or glaciation, but the slightly drowned coasts are often rugged. The effects of the West Coast Marine climate are all-pervading and, because of usually impervious rocks, there are numerous streams. In Brittany, the Celtic imprint on the settlement and economy is vivid.

The Central Massif, more south-central in situation, is the highest and largest, and the greatest obstacle to transport. This massif is also the most diverse geologically and, consequently, in its scenery, soils and economic activities.

The Vosges, the Maures and Esterel (pp. 458) are the smallest and most uniform massifs; Corsica (pp. 459–60) is also small but less homogeneous geologically, and is further differentiated by insularity and history. The larger Ardennes (pp. 293–6) is only marginally within France.

The massifs are attractive scenically but provide generally difficult environments for agriculture, industry and transport. All are areas of rural depopulation, except for the tourist areas and large towns.

ARMORICA
The Breton words *Ar Mor* (*Armor* or *Arvor*) 'country of the sea' have been given to this low massif, France's only substantial peninsula and characterised by its two-pronged form. It includes not only Brittany, but western Normandy (le Bocage Normand), Anjou (le Bocage Angevin), the lower Loire Valley, and the Vendée (including le Bocage Vendéen). Brittany is the most distinctive in its physical variety and has a Celtic culture.

Granite, gneiss and schist face the seas, granite forming most of the headlands and islands, the other rocks the bays. There are pronounced contrasts between the coastal areas (*Armor*) and the interior (*Arcoët* or *Argoat* = wooded country), which have been kept very much apart by the sharp Silurian and Cambrian ridges of the Monts d'Arrée and Menez in the north, and the Montagnes Noires and Landes de Lanvaux in the south (Fig. 77). The interior is an alternation of gneiss and schist moorland plateau with basins of Carboniferous or Tertiary deposits. The climate is less maritime in the interior, except for the most westerly basin of Châteaulin. Settlement is in numerous small towns or villages around the coast;

mostly in dispersed farms or small hamlets in the interior. Near the coasts the fields are open, and becoming more open as hedges are being bull-dozed; in the interior they are hedged (*bocage*) and alternate with moorland. The density of settlement is far greater on the coasts than in the interior; because, as well as farming, there are opportunities for fishing and tourism (Plate 77). Rail services and roads are best developed on the coasts, although the Rennes Basin is a transport focus.

Fig 77   Armorica

Yet the coasts are not homogeneous, physically or economically. The northern one is most active in fishing, farming and tourism. From this coast cod-fishing fleets sailed to Newfoundland as early as the sixteenth century, but only St. Malo can accommodate the large trawlers (now fishing Arctic waters). It has good rail links and the shortest haul to markets. Elsewhere, many small havens are concerned mainly with shell fish and oysters. Around St. Malo, St. Brieuc, Paimpol and Roscoff small vegetable farms are typical. Benefiting from loess deposits and from long cultivation and continued application of seaweed and crushed shells, they produce early potatoes, carrots, peas, beans, cauliflowers, artichokes and onions. Poultry are also important. Otherwise, the farming is like adjacent parts of the interior.

More important, the north has been the great tourist coast, because of its scenic grandeur and the attraction of its tiny ports. Most tourist centres are enlarged fishing havens, but some are tourist creations. Dinard and St. Malo, respectively on the west and east sides of the Rance Estuary, are very different in historical evolution and function. In the past a family would, in different seasons, combine fishing, farming and the accommodation of visitors. With the decline in fishing, incomes now usually come from one or two sources. Although industry is rare, St. Brieuc has an electric steel works, foundries, France's largest brush works, kitchen equipment and car accessory manufacturers and many others. Industry was initiated here by the use of profits from the now-extinct cod fisheries.

The short west coast is enlarged by the deeply-penetrating rias of Brest and Douarnenez (Plate 77), developed on fault lines of weakness as well as by submergence. There is little tourism—the area is too remote and humid, but fishing and agriculture are important. This is near the northern limit of sardines, and Douarnenez is the largest French sardine-packing port. Mackerel, tunny and shell fish are also landed. Brest, the major French Atlantic naval base, is also a small commercial port trying to diversify its interests, despite an eccentric position, like that of Plymouth. The main market-gardening area is around Plougastel, long famous for strawberries but now more diverse in its output.

The southern coast has a softer climate, with early springs, and more flat land than the other coasts. It might have had far more market gardening had it faced Britain, earlier an important market. As it is, vegetable production is important only around Lorient and the west, where pea and bean cultivation has been encouraged by fish canneries to diversify their output. Otherwise, agriculture is similar to adjacent inland areas, cereals, potatoes and cider apples being especially important.

Slight drowning of the southern plain has produced vast shallow inlets, and there has been more recent coastal accumulation. This accumulation, the increasing size of ships, and the concentration of fishing have brought decay to many small havens, and have favoured the emergence of Concarneau and Lorient as the main fishing and canning centres. The same fish are landed as on the west coast, particularly tunny. Trawled fish are likewise important, and there are oyster and mussel beds as on the other

Plate 77   Harvest from sea and land in Brittany.
Left : Douarnenez roadstead with inshore and deep-sea fishing vessels, and pleasure boats. On land are small hedged fields.
Right : Artichokes at St. Pol de Léon, north-west Brittany.

coasts. Lorient, which began as the base of the French East India Company (hence the name), is also a general port and a naval base. In the past this southern coast attracted fewer tourists (except La Baule) than the northern one, but is now popular, especially for camping and caravan holidays.

The most westerly interior basin of Châteaulin, underlain by Carboniferous shales, has damp clays but the climate is mild. In this and the other basins, cattle and pig-keeping is important. The surprising amount of land occupied by roots and cereals is principally for animal fodder. In the Rennes Basin there are Tertiary limestones and light clays, as well as loess. These, together with the drier climate, better transport and greater proximity to markets favour more productive and varied farming. Sugar beet, cider apples and dairy cattle are also important. Rennes is the administrative, commercial and cultural centre of Brittany. The town has

printing, publishing and paper industries, food processing and the manufacture of agricultural equipment. Industries have also been directed here by the government e.g. the arsenal of long-standing and a newer car works. The most easterly basin of Laval (outside Brittany) is geologically similar to Châteaulin but is drier and nearer to markets. There is some emphasis on milk production, mainly for Camembert, Saint Polin and Port Salut cheese and for butter, as in the Cotentin Peninsula and the Bocage Normand.

The vale of the lower Loire is an alluvial belt some two miles wide, sheltered and warm; but whereas in the Paris Basin the vale is underlain by permeable limestone or sands, in Armorica impermeable rocks lie beneath. Thus, waterlogging of the otherwise excellent alluvium occurs.

Nevertheless, the same seed production, vegetable and flower gardens are found, albeit less productive. Meadows are more common, especially around the estuary. On the driest south-facing slopes vineyards produce the highly individual white Muscadet, Anjou rosé and Layon red wines.

Nantes is 32 miles upstream, where channels between islands have been reclaimed for docks and railway yards. In competition with Le Havre, Bordeaux and Marseilles the town has a long-standing trade in tropical produce, especially sugar, coffee, cocoa, bananas, oilseeds, tobacco and wood. These are processed in Nantes, as are local foodstuffs. Fertilisers and other needs for the agricultural hinterland are produced. Defence industries were directed here and, together with shipbuilding, attracted metallurgical firms. In interests, situation and problems there are affinities with Bristol. As with the latter, an outport has developed. For Nantes it is St. Nazaire, where bulk shipments of timber, cement and coal are received, where the largest ships have been built, and where thermal and atomic power station equipment is now made. Donges receives and refines oil, and has allied industries; Paimboeuf imports phosphates and pyrites. Nantes is the economic capital of southern Brittany and, with its Loire outports, the only real industrial region of Armorica. It has received government aid, like the semi-industrial towns of Lorient, Quimper, Brest, St. Brieuc, Dinan and Rennes. Natural gas from Lacq is available at Nantes, Vannes and Rennes, and increasing amounts of hydro-electric power.

The Vendée is France's most secluded mainland region. On the coastal dunes and marshes livestock are raised, and small ports land fish as in southern Brittany. The crystalline ridges of the Bocage Vendéen and the Gâtine have a livestock-based economy, while in the Jurassic areas cereals are more important.

Armorica has experienced heavy outward migration, comparable with that from Ireland and Cornwall. As in the latter there were once many copper and tin mines, and there are still quarries for slate (especially at Trélazé, near Angers) and for kaolin at Ploemeur (Morbihan), Plémat and Quessoy (south-east of St. Brieuc). But the peripheral situation, remote markets, small towns and general dispersion of settlement inhibit industrial development. Similarly, the small scale, diversity, scattered character and poor methods of much of the farming and fishing make difficult the necessary radical reforms. Even large-scale processing of local produce such as cider, butter and meat have made little progress.

THE CENTRAL MASSIF

This physically diverse massif, twice the size of Switzerland, yet with a lower population, has little unity. Although basically crystalline, it also has Carboniferous and Jurassic inliers, Tertiary basins, Tertiary and Quaternary volcanic outpourings. In the Cantal the effects of glaciation may be seen. Upheaval on the south and east from the Alpine movements causing internal fracturing (see p. 343) split up the massif and modified the earlier radial drainage pattern, directing it especially to the Loire and

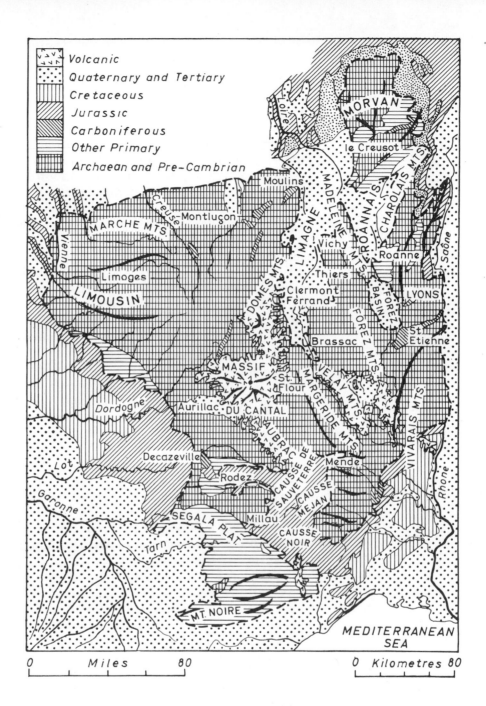

Fig 78 The Central Massif

Garonne. Earlier mighty rivers had washed acidic sands and gravels from
the massif and deposited them in Sologne (southern Paris Basin).

There has for long been migration from the generally poor massif to
the richer areas of the Paris or Aquitaine basins, the Saône-Rhône valleys
and the Mediterranean lands. To the rigours of the climate and the

paucity of resources has been added a scarcity of man-power in agriculture and industry. The area is deficient in means of transport, towns are few, and redevelopment is difficult.

The crystalline areas are exposed to rude climatic conditions, especially high humidity, wind and late frosts. Soils are poor and largely under pasture, fodder and subsistence crops like rye, oats and potatoes. Limousin, the most westerly region, is the more exposed to maritime influences by the Armorican trends of its Marche and Limousin ridges (Fig. 78). On the moors sheep predominate. Where there is grass cattle are more numerous, while in the highest areas there is reafforestation. Limoges is the regional centre, but its porcelain and shoe industries, based originally upon local china clay and leather, are declining.

On the east side of the massif the crystalline areas were subjected to the Caldedonian and Hercynian movements, so that their relief trends north-east to south-west. The north-easterly Morvan is another cattle-rearing area, as are the Madeleine, Forez, Vivarais, Haut Livradois and Margeride mountains, the last two also being well forested. The uptilted Cévennes have been dissected into separate east-west ridges by Rhône tributaries flowing east, and the west-flowing Lot and Tarn. Communications are difficult. There are remarkably isolated areas—in some of which Protestant villages have survived. There is more cultivation in the numerous valleys open to Mediterranean influences, as in the mainly Silurian areas of the Montagne Noire and Ségala, where the chestnut replaces the potato as a staple food.

Lying on the basement rocks are small Carboniferous basins (Fig. 72). Most have been mined for coal at high cost, and only a few are still significant (p. 365). However, they nourished iron, steel and chemical industries, which are still important at Le Creusot and St. Etienne (both of which originally had iron ore occurring with coking coal), Montluçon and elsewhere. St. Etienne is the largest town of the massif, but it is very peripheral.

The Jurassic karstic plateaux of Méjean and the Causse Noir (the most barren), of Comtal and Sauveterre (the most wooded), and others, are the poorest areas of the massif. Their plateau surfaces are remarkably level; dry—because of the extremely permeable limestone; stony, with only skeletal soils, except in the rare damp clay depressions (*sotches*). Sheep are kept for milk (Fig. 70 and Plate 78). This is also collected from as far away as other poor areas in the Pyrenees and Mediterranean, and is made into Roquefort cheese, caverns in the limestone at that town being used for maturing it. Sheep skins, local and imported, are treated at Millau. This town lies on the Tarn below its spectacular gorges (Plate 78). The valleys are sudden and deep; some are collapsed caverns of underground drainage. Fruit and nuts are cultivated on their narrow benches.

Plate 78 Canyons and dry pastoralism in the Causses.
Above : The Tarn gorges near La Malène.
Below : Flock of sheep kept for milk for Roquefort cheese. The town is in the distance, and the cheese is matured in its limestone caves.

The Allier, Loire and some other rivers are fault-guided, and part of their valleys are fault basins, mostly of Tertiary (Alpine) age. On the Loire are the basins of Le Puy, Forez and Roannais; on the Allier those of Langeac (Carboniferous), Brioude, Lembron, Issoire and the Limagne. This latter name is used to denote the basins collectively as *les limagnes*. Tertiary deposits predominate in them. There are also many lava flows which, though once in valleys, have by their great hardness often survived as higher plateaux (the phenomenon of inverted relief). Where lava occurs, the land may be stony, e.g. in the Le Puy Basin and on the west side of the great Limagne. Forez is still ill-drained and Roannais was formerly so, while all the basins have wide alluvial and marshy belts along the rivers. Otherwise, the limagnes are fertile and, being sheltered, are drier and sunnier than the uplands. Cereals and sugar beet were much grown until labour shortage caused some land to be put under pasture. The great Limagne has the most intensive agriculture, because of nearby markets. Fruit crops are important on the west wide on partly volcanic soils; the east margin, with siliceous soils, is pastoral.

Clermont-Ferrand, originally Montferrand and Clermont on separate volcanic buttes, but now interconnected by narrow streets and much hemmed in by old lava flows, is the regional focus and the second largest town of the massif. It owes its development very largely to the several Michelin works which developed here by chance and employ some 16,000 people.

The high volcanic areas are very diverse. The Monts Dômes or Chaîne des Puys, lying from north-south to the west of Clermont-Ferrand are well-preserved, recently-extinct volcanoes. Their lava flows and cinder fields are equally clear, while some lakes (e.g. Pavin) are crater lakes and some (e.g. Aydat) occupy lava-blocked valleys. To the south lies the giant extinct exploded volcano of the Cantal (Fig. 79). Puy Griou is the phonolithic cone remnant, while the Plomb du Cantal, Puys Chavaroche and Violent are high parts of the crater. Within this former crater are rich summer pastures where cattle are grazed for milk. This is made into

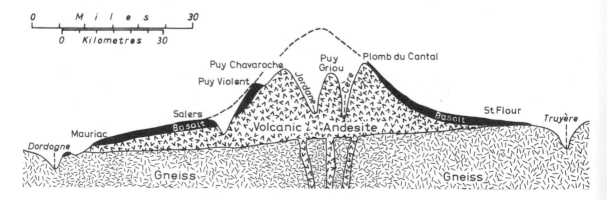

Fig. 79   Cross-section of the Cantal

Cantal, St. Nectaire and Bleu d'Auvergne cheeses in the upland summer huts. On the outer, western and eastern sides of the crater are, respectively, the Planèzes de Salers and St. Flour, fairly level basalt flows, with fertile soils, formerly under cereals, now partly pastoral. Valleys on the outside of the crater are glacially deepened, and under pasture and crops.

To the south-east of the Cantal is the Aubrac lava field, dissected like a herring bone on the wetter west, less eroded on the east. In the Le Puy Basin are phonolithic needles of former volcanoes (Plate 79); whilst to the west in Velay, and to the east in southern Vivarais, are their lava fields. Other flows reached the Rhône Valley near Montélimar, and the Mediterr-

Plate 79   Volcanic plugs or necks at Le Puy.
The last erupting material alone remains, the cone and crater of each having been eroded.

anean west of Sète at Mt. Agde. Almost all give richer though sometimes drier pastures than the crystalline areas.

The bases for industry are few, although coal resources are still significant. There are large hydro-electric power stations mostly on the upper Dordogne, on its tributaries, and on the Truyère, all on the west side of the Monts Dômes and Cantal, at the junction of volcanic and crystalline rocks. Rare and base metals were mined in the past, and tin and lead-refining industries survive using imported supplies e.g. at Limoges. Uranium is mined north of Limoges, and chemical industries are developing around its refining. Wolfram, kaolin, fluorspar, barytes, felspar, volvic and other building stones, and mineral waters are the bases of industries, but their significance is modest. Far more important are electric steel, metallurgical and chemical industries which evolved from the now extinct iron resources, and are usually on the coalfields of Le Creusot, St. Etienne, etc. As in Brittany some industries were established here for greater safety from invasion (e.g. Vichy's arsenal); some have been directed here under the policy of industrial decentralisation (e.g. aluminium at Issoire). The Moulins and Montluçon areas are likely to benefit in this way. Otherwise the problems of Armorica are repeated more acutely here because of the greater area and difficult communications.

THE VOSGES (FRANCE) and BLACK FOREST (GERMANY)

These small massifs are remnants of a larger one which took the full force of the northward thrust of the Alpine Orogeny, confined it, and, with the Bohemian Massif, diverted the Alpine movements to the east. Such was the strain, however, that deep internal faulting let down the Rhine Rift Valley in the centre (p. 343), and separated the Vosges and Black Forest. Both have steep edges on the south due to uplift by the Alps; both have steeper fault edges facing each other across the Rhine. East of the river, in Germany, is the tiny Kaiserstuhl, the only volcanic remnant. The massifs are mainly drained north-westward and north-eastward, down the direction of slope. This is partly the consequence of Caledonian and Hercynian folding, and partly the consequence of the Tertiary (Alpine) tilting. Glaciation carved cirques and deepened some valleys, certain of which were blocked by moraines to give lakes e.g. Gérardmer (Vosges).

The dominant granite gives rounded summits, seen typically in the Ballon d'Alsace (Vosges) and Feldberg (Black Forest). The highest parts are often peat bogs, moor or rough pasture, the steepest slopes are heavily wooded, the gentler and lowest ones are mainly under permanent pasture or fodder crops (Plate 32). Cheese (e.g. Munster in the Vosges) is an important product, whilst timber-using industries are common. Tourism is significant because of the attractive scenery e.g. Gérardmer (Vosges) and Titisee (Black Forest), and picturesque villages and towns e.g. Riquewihr (Vosges) and Freudenstadt (Black Forest).

The eastern fault margin of the Vosges and the western fault edge of the Black Forest retain narrow outcrops of Triassic and Jurassic sedimentaries. These outcrop in rapid succession on the steep slopes, loess also occurs, and downwash has been great, so that soils are mixed and fast-draining. The climate is of the Short Cold Winter type. The steep slopes are heavily cultivated for still, dry, white wines (especially on the French side which faces the ideal direction of south-east), with subsidiary hops (more important on the German side), tobacco, fruit and vegetables. The valley-exit villages of the Vosges give their names to famous wines (Plate 86).

On the eastern edge of the Vosges are also small silk and cotton industries, now mainly in Colmar and Mulhouse. Outliers using water power were established early in eastern Vosges valleys, but after the French lost Alsace–Lorraine in 1871 some firms moved across the new boundary (the watershed and linguistic divide) to Belfort, and to the Meurthe, Mortagne and Moselle valleys on the west of the massif.

On the west and north of the Vosges, and on the north and east of the Black Forest, the granite is covered by Bunter Sandstone (Fig. 82), giving level and forested country and siliceous soils. Such areas are extensive in the north in both countries. Between the southern mainly granitic Vosges and the northern low tabular Bunter Sandstone Vosges is the partly faulted, narrow and vital Saverne Gap (p. 341).

The Tertiary Folded Mountains

The folded mountains of the Alpine system are excellently represented in France not only by the Alps—themselves exceptionally diverse in France—but also by the very different Jura and Pyrenees. Although all are part of the same mid and late-Tertiary Alpine system, they differ in their sequence of folding and alignment, and also in their structure and composition. Further, they vary in height and width, and yet the high and wide Alps have such deep inter-penetrating valleys that they are more easily crossed than the lower Pyrenees. The much lower Jura are, for their relatively low altitude, a remarkable obstacle.

Although the traditional economies of pastoralism, forestry and home crafts, and the usually later ones of tourism, hydro-electric power and small-scale industry are common to all the folded mountains, their importance varies greatly, mainly because of differences of ease of access within and without to other areas in France and abroad. All have rich regional variety, often expressed politically in the past, and frequently still evident, e.g. in methods of land use.

THE PYRENEES

Aligned from the west-north-west where the Pyrenees (Fig. 87) give a rocky coast on the Franco-Spanish Atlantic border, to the east-south-east on the Mediterranean coast, the Pyrenees are some 250 miles long but rarely more than 50 miles wide. They rise steeply on the French side; less so on the Spanish one where, however, deeply cut plateaux do not help access. They are difficult to cross because the inter-penetrating valleys on either side do not often end near each other, because the passes are relatively high, and because deeply-trenched valleys are found only in the east where they do not facilitate crossings. The seaward extremities were early crossed by railways, although the eastern line has tunnels. The single-track twentieth century trans-Pyrenean lines from Oloron to Jaca and from Foix to Barcelona are spectacular but unremunerative. Almost the whole history of France and Spain has also been divisive, so that there is incomparably less trans-Pyrenean traffic than trans-Juran or trans-Alpine. About one-third of the Pyrenees are in France and, although the watershed is often the boundary, the Garonne rises in Spain, and the Segre in France.

The Alpine earth movements began in the Pyrenees, while later subsidences broke the link with the southern Alps and resulted in the characteristic promontories of the Eastern Pyrenees. As in the Alps there has been heavy glaciation, Gavarnie being a classic example of a glacial cirque; while Lannemezan, Ger and Orignac are type examples of outwash gravel fans.

Structurally, the Pyrenees fall into three parts: a central core of ancient Archaean and Pre-Cambrian rocks caught up in the Alpine movements and flanked by Primary and later rocks; an east-west frontal trench occupied by parts of the Garonne, the Gave de Pau (below Lourdes) and the Gave d'Ossau; and the outer Petites Pyrénées mainly of Cretaceous limestone obscured westwards by the Lannemezan Plateau (Fig. 87). However, in respect of general physical character and man's occupancy, the Pyrenees are sharply divided into four regions.

The Western, Atlantic or Basque Pyrenees

This is the French part of the Basque homeland, with its distinctive architecture (two or three-storied narrow wooden houses) and its own language. The coast is rocky southwards from Biarritz, with some fine resorts such as St. Jean de Luz, now also a tunny port.

From the Atlantic this part of the Pyrenees extends south-eastwards to the Somport Pass, and is composed mostly of Primary sandstone but it also has some Secondary limestone giving hummocky country rarely higher than 6,500 feet. The annual precipitation is 45–60 inches, the highest in the Pyrenees, and falling mostly as snow in autumn and winter. Previously this area was largely wooded with beech up to 2,600 feet, but much is now under pasture for dairy cattle and sheep. Most of the milk of the latter is taken the long distance to Roquefort by refrigerated road tankers, but some is mixed with cow's milk for local cheese. Aquitaine polyculture extends into the lower valleys, and there are small footwear and textile factories.

The Central, High or Gaves Pyrenees

From the Somport Pass to the upper Garonne, lies the truly alpine part of the Pyrenees, within which is the highest peak—the Pic du Midi d'Ossau, the great Cirque de Gavarnie, and the Gaves (a Basque word for 'torrents').

Timber is cut for domestic needs. Sheep and cattle still move between

Plate 80   Two aspects of tourism in the Pyrenees.

Above : The town of Bagnères de Luchon began as a Roman spa for the cure of soldiers who had contracted respiratory troubles in Britain, and remains an all-year-round resort.

Below : Superbagnères—reached by funicular railway from Bagnères de Luchon —is a winter sports resort. Note the ski lifts.

valley and upper slopes, but rarely into the plain in winter as in the past. Hydro-electric power was first developed by a railway company for the electrification of its lines. In consequence, there was less general application of hydro-electric power here than farther east. However, some is used in mining e.g. of lead and zinc, and in their refining at Pierrefitte-Nestalas in the Gave de Pau, and in electro-chemical works at Luchon in the Gave d'Ossau. There has long been tourism in erstwhile fashionable small spas, with such expressive names as Eaux Bonnes and Eaux Chaudes, but their large hotels are now little patronised. More fortunate is Bagnères de Luchon (where the Romans sent soldiers convalescent from service in Britain) with its wider valley and more diverse interests (Plate 80). It is linked by funicular to its winter sports station of Superbagnères, and thus it has more of a year-round season.

Garonne-Ariège Pyrenees

Between these two rivers is the widest part of the Pyrenees, lower than the previous region, but with as few crossings. It includes the semi-independent country of Andorra, which occupies a high basin, and is the last relic of many former basin or valley political units. To the north this part of the Pyrenees is paralleled by the Petites Pyrénées.

This region has rounded landforms and, very significantly, is transitional in climate and vegetation between mountain-modified West Coast Marine conditions and mountain-modified Mediterranean ones. Box, lavender and the cork oak appear, while varied crops are grown in the valleys. Formerly there were varied mineral resources, now largely exhausted. However, hydro-electric power has permitted the survival, with re-organisation, of specialised electro-chemical and electro-metallurgical industries. Thus there is the processing of local silica-bauxite for an abrasive at Lavelanet (south-east of Pamiers), and the mining of anhydrite and the manufacture of ammonium sulphate from it at Tarascon. In Pamiers, natural gas as well as hydro-electric power is used in alloy steel production, and gas is also used in the paper mills of the Salat Valley near St. Girons.

Eastern Pyrenees

East of Andorra the Pyrenees resemble a left hand, the open fingers of which represent divergent and generally north-east or east-trending ridges. The intervening valleys become increasingly broad towards the Mediterranean. Each valley has a regional name e.g. Vallespir of the upper Tech and Conflent of the Tet. Catalan peoples live on both sides of the border, in France as far north as Perpignan, and they have given a strong imprint in place names such as Espezel and Pradès. Catalan styles are evident in architecture and costumes.

A journey down a valley reveals a remarkable altitudinal-cum-climatic zonation. At the highest levels e.g. at Mont Louis in upper Conflent there is much pasture and only hardy crops. Lower down, pears are a famous speciality (Plate 81); then come the hardier bush fruits. Farther down are

Plate 81   Irrigated pears in Conflent.
This is a fairly high part of the Tet Valley, Eastern Pyrenees.

the richer fruits such as apricots, peaches and the vine; then come cereals, and an area by the Mediterranean devoted to the intensive production of very early vegetables often with irrigation.

As at the eastern end of the Pyrenees there is a rocky coast with promontories and beautiful coves. In these are picturesque Collioure, Port Vendres with a trans-Mediterranean shipping service, Banyuls with vineyards for its famous wine, and Cerbère at the border.

The Pyrenees and Aquitaine

In the past there was close contact between these two great regions, through the movement of livestock from the former to the latter in winter, and through the sale of timber. Hydro-electric power has been developed in this century in the Pyrenees, and some of it is used in Aquitaine, notably at Toulouse, Tarbes and Pau.

There are also vivid examples of regional-contact towns of two orders. First, there are the small valley-exit settlements, often former valley capitals such as (from west to east) Mauléon, Oloron, Laruns, Lourdes, Bagnères-de-Bigorre, St. Girons and Foix. They usually supported spring and autumn fairs and festivals, and early craft industries using local wood, wool and stone. Some crafts have survived, such as blanket and shoe manufacture at Oloron. Bagnères de Bigorre has not only retained and developed industry but attracts tourists. In general, however, employment in these towns is precarious.

Secondly, there are the larger piedmont towns of Orthez, mainly commercial, and Pau, no longer fashionable, but commercially and industrially lively in the kind of activities mentioned above. Tarbes, more a town of the nineteenth century, has a state arsenal, state-aided light aircraft industry, and railway-sponsored diesel-electric locomotive manufacture. In the east, Pamiers has somewhat the same characteristics as Tarbes but there Toulouse overshadows all.

THE JURA   Although the lowest in altitude of the three parts of the French Alpine system, the Jura have great individuality. They have given their name to one of the classical types of country. They have been and still are a major obstacle to transport. As with the other constituents of the Alpine system they are a frontier zone.

The Jura extend in an arc for some 200 miles, taper at either end, and are compressed between the Vosges-Black Forest blocks on the north-east, the Central Massif in the south-west and the Swiss Plateau to the south-east. The widest extension, or bulge of the Jura, is towards the gap between the massifs (Fig. 80).

At their extremities the Jura are crossed by the Rhine and Rhône, while on their flanks are the Belfort Gate, Saône Valley and Swiss Plateau. All are great routeways. Thus, although communications are difficult within the Jura, they lie near some of Europe's (indeed the world's) most important lines of movement. This is one reason for the persistence of small industries within certain areas.

The steepest edge of the Jura is naturally on the south-east, nearest the centre of the Alpine Orogeny, and overlooking the Swiss Plateau. The adjacent parts of the Jura are crumpled into acute anticlinal ridges and intervening synclinal valleys (Fig. 80). To the west are two or three success-ively lower plateaux, each with a clear edge, the westernmost terminating in the Revermont and le Vignoble overlooking the Saône Valley. The Jura were glaciated only in the extreme south-west, south of the Rhône.

The basic contrasts in the Jura are between the western plateaux and the eastern folded ridges. The Plateau Jura have a moderate rainfall, but are subject to rather continental extremes of temperature and violent winds. The plateaux are deeply trenched by rivers some of which, like the Loue, disappear. The limestone drains rapidly, while its soils are thin and poor. The density of settlement is very low, and the economy largely restricted to poor pastures for dairy cattle, whose milk is collected for Gruyère cheese.

Besançon, on an incised meander of the Doubs, is the old capital of la Franche-Comté but poor communications into the Jura denied to it the supreme role of a Jura regional centre. One-third of its employees are in the watch, clock and optical industries, of which it is the French centre. Sochaux, near Montbéliard, is the industrial complex of the great Peugeot car, cycle and domestic equipment firm, which has developed from eighteenth century family enterprises in steel production.

The ridges of the Folded Jura attract a heavy rainfall, and forest and pasture are widespread. There has also been severe erosion which has

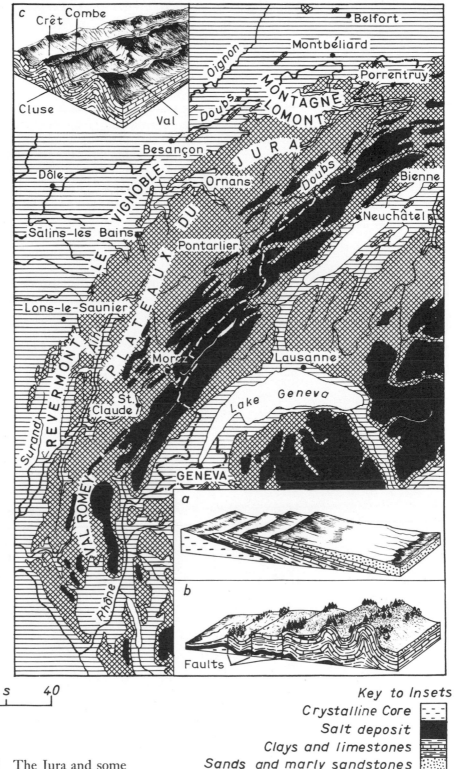

c

Crêt Combe

Cluse Val

Belfort

Montbéliard

Porrentruy

Oignon

MONTAGNE

Doubs

LOMONT

Besançon

J U R A

Dôle

Ornans

Doubs

Bienne

LE VIGNOBLE

Salins-les Bains

Neuchâtel

PLATEAUX DU

Pontarlier

Lons-le-Saunier

Ain

REVERMONT

Morez

Lausanne

St. Claude

Lake Geneva

Surand

GENEVA

Rhône

VAL ROMEY

a

b

Faults

Feet

3281 and over

1640

0

0   M i l e s   40

0   Kilometres   40

Key to Insets

Crystalline Core

Salt deposit

Clays and limestones

Sands and marly sandstones

Fig 80   The Jura and some
of their relief forms

opened up some anticlinal ridges into high *combes* with surrounding *crêts* (Fig. 80), while debris of sands, clays and limestone has accumulated in the valleys. In consequence, possibilities exist for both pastoral farming on the ridges and arable farming in the valleys.

The drainage pattern of the Jura is bizarre. Apart from disappearing drainage, there has been widespread capture; the most spectacular capture is of a stream which once joined the Rhine near Basle but is now the upper Doubs. In the Folded Jura synclinal valley rivers are joined by vigorous *ruzes* or side streams from the anticlinal ridges, or from the crêts and combes eroded in them. Gradually the ruze of one valley will meet and capture that of an adjacent one. A transverse narrow slit or gap forms called a *cluse*, of which there are some 70 in the Jura. St. Claude occupies one of these (Plate 82). Such towns were often fortresses; they now barely have room for industrial and urban renewal, or transport development.

Timber has been traditionally used a great deal for housing, for heating

and other domestic purposes. It is also used for carving into wooden clocks and toys, although briar rose wood is now imported for the famous St. Claude smokers-pipe industry (Plate 82). Milk is used for Gruyère cheese. Animal bone, celluloid and casein from milk were successively employed for making such items as toys and knife handles; plastics are now employed in their place and the articles made are more diverse. Parts of watches and clocks are made in homes or small workshops for assembly at Besançon and elsewhere. Morez is highly specialised in lens production for spectacles, photographic, projection and microscopic equipment. Its workshops also produce watch parts. Some 50 Jura villages have up to 200 industrial employees. Pontarlier, Morez and St. Claude (in the Folded Jura) and Champagnole and Lons-le-Saunier in the Plateaux Jura each have over a thousand industrial workers, while Besançon and Montbéliard have far more. Industry survives best in the towns, but it suffers from remoteness and high transport costs.

Plate 82   Industry in the Folded Jura.
Left : St. Claude, a great world centre for the manufacture of smokers' pipes.
Above : Making spectacles in a typical workshop at Longchaumois.

Most of the Alps south of Lake Geneva are in France, and they are her highest mountains. In Savoy and Dauphiné they lie in a north-south arc, but in Provence (where they were once the continuation of the Pyrenees) their trend is first from west to east and then from north to south towards the Mediterranean. In contrast to those of the Pyrenees, the structural divisions of the Alps form well-defined regional units (Fig. 81).

The Cretaceous and Jurassic Pre-Alps

From north to south, the principal regions are separated by the broad cluses of Cluses itself, Annecy, Chambéry and Voreppe (Isère). All are glacially-deepened, unlike the purely river-cut cluses of the Folded Jura. The beautiful lakes of Annecy and Bourget result from the blocking of two cluses by glacial débris.

Chablais experienced much over-thrusting, so that it is varied geologically, pedologically and scenically. It was also much affected by glaciation; its cirques of Fonts and of Le Fer-à-Cheval are surpassed in Europe only by that of Gavarnie. A pastoral economy, with some cultivation of fodder crops, survives because of the relative isolation of this area. Milk is collected by co-operative dairies for making Gruyère for sale, while Tome and Reblochon cheeses are made more for home consumption. There is much vital supplementary home industry. Around its lowland borders, fruit and vegetables are grown side by side with dairying.

Bornes is similar, but with more interest in forestry and tourism. Bauges lost migrants to the adjacent tourist and industrial centres offering far better livelihoods. Accordingly its pastures are often neglected, and are reverting to forest. The Grand Chartreuse is so eroded that anticlines have often disappeared, and the vigorous relief derives from synclines. Again the forest is gaining on pasture land.

The Alpine Furrow

This 120 mile-long trench extends from La Mure (south of Grenoble) in an arc to Albertville in the north-east and, after an upthrust, on to St. Gervais. It is known as Devoluy in the south, as Grésivaudan north-east of Grenoble, and as la Combe de Savoie near St. Gervais. To the east of the trench is the faulted edge of the High Alps; on this fault rivers and glaciers have worked to erode the furrow in which Liassic clays are exposed. Along its sides are alluvial cones, built by tributary hanging-valley streams, and these cones are sometimes sites for villages.

The trench is widest (over two miles) and most continuous in Grésivaudan. So sheltered is it and so warm are the summers, that maize, tobacco, the vine and fruits are all grown, as well as the hardier crops. Dairy cattle and poultry are also important. The result is a belt of intensive agriculture in otherwise largely pastoral, forested or unused lands. Only the flood plain of the rivers is avoided and little used. The trench is a natural routeway, the more so because it is joined by valleys leading from the heart of the Alps. Its hanging valley streams were the first to be used for hydro-electric power, beginning in 1869. The constantly increasing power resources are the

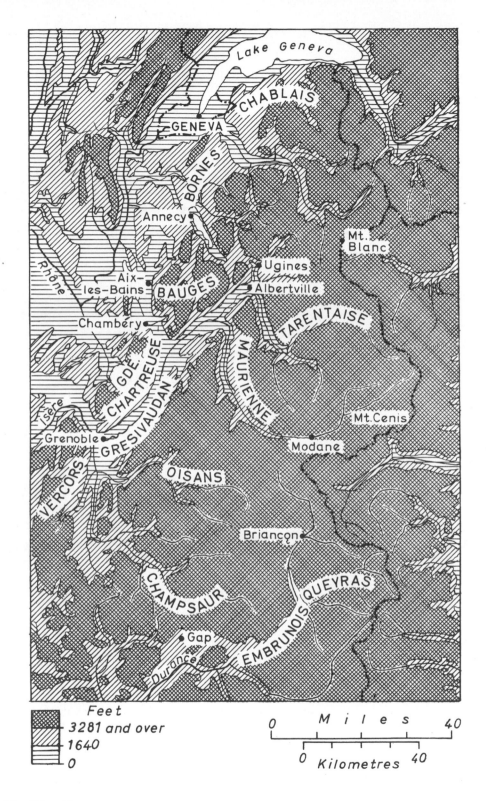

Fig 81 The Alps

Plate 83   Three aspects of Alpine development.

Above : Tourism in the High Alps. The Aiguille du Midi cableway takes passengers from the Chamonix Valley (below) at 3,379 feet up to 12,605 feet. From
near the summit of the Aiguille du Midi one can ski in the high Vallée Blanche,
even in summer, or the valley may be crossed by another cableway to the Franco-
Italian boundary at the Pointe Helbronner, 11,483 feet. From there another cableway descends to near Courmayeur in the Aosta Valley. Note the Bossons Glacier
of the Chamonix Valley, material washed out beyond it and its melt-water stream.
Most woodland is on this (south) side of the valley, as it faces north-west; whilst
on the other, sunnier side of the valley, woodland is restricted to steep slopes.
On the far side of the valley, on the right edge of the photograph, is an outwash
fan or cone under pasture, houses and hotels, facing south-east, and a part of
Chamonix. The entrance to the Chamonix-Courmayeur Alpine road tunnel is
below and to the left of the point from which this photograph was taken.

Top right : Specialised industry; an electric steel works at Ugines, in the north of
the Alpine Furrow.

Bottom right : Intensive agriculture in Oisans, the upper Romanche Valley.

basis of important electro-chemical and electro-metallurgical industries, as at Albertville and Ugines (Plate 83).

The focus for this and the high Alpine valleys is Grenoble, the Alpine regional centre, with a fast-growing population. Its earliest hand-industry was glove-making, originally using lamb and chamois skins; to-day, almost every kind of material is employed in factories. Cement, using limestone from La Grand Chartreuse and clay from the Alpine Furrow, and paper-making (located here partly because of pure water) also use local materials. As hydro-electric power was first developed nearby, it is not surprising that varied electrical equipment should also be made, or that there should be so many building firms in an area where hydro-electric power has been under development for a century, longer than anywhere else in the world. In view of the nearby arable area, excellent transport to markets, and the higher than average standard of living of its own population, the presence of food processing industries is understandable. Grenoble is also favoured by the state as a focus for industries that might otherwise have been located in Paris.

High Alps

These are the classical Alps of the tourist. In addition to old rocks thrust up in the Alpine orogeny, there are also sedimentaries. All are highly contorted, over-thrusted and eroded, especially by glaciation which persists around Mt. Blanc, in the Mts. de la Vanoise, and in the Pelvoux Massif. The many deep and transverse valleys are oriented broadly from east to west, and they show striking contrasts between the settled and more used *adret* or sunny northern side facing south, and the *ubac* or cold southern side which faces north and is usually forested.

The old economy in these valleys was a pastoral, arable and timber-cutting one, and it survives in remoter areas. The modern economies are exemplified in the specialised electro-chemical and electro-metallurgical industries of Maurienne (Arc Valley), which has one of Europe's largest aluminium works, and through which runs the Mt. Cenis trunk railway.

Serving these industries are many hydro-electric power stations, comprising the old small gravity schemes, and the newer large dams and reservoirs e.g. Tignes on the upper Isère. The latest developments have involved taking Isère water from below Moutiers by tunnel to the Arc; another takes water from the Arc at St. Jean-de-Maurienne to the Breda tributary of the Isère at Allevard; a third diverts Romanche waters under the Belledonne range also to the Isère. These will be among France's largest power stations.

Tourism is the other great development; railways made it possible on a large scale, e.g. at Chamonix near Mt. Blanc. The earliest centres were in the Pre-Alps at Aix-les-Bains, Annecy and Evian. The first two no longer attract mainly rich visitors, and now have discreet industry to provide employment (transformers at Aix, razor blades at Annecy). Some can attract visitors all the year, such as Megève in Savoy, famed for winter sports, yet beautiful and sunny in summer.

There has been a remarkable development of transport media for winter sports participants in such centres; first with funiculars, and later with cable cars (Plate 83), chair and ski-lifts. Again, these are most economic where there are two-season patrons, as at Chamonix. Such devices also provision high winter sports centres not lived in during summer, e.g. La Prieuré above Chamonix. More rudimentary lifts are also used by herdsmen for sending down milk (there are also milk pipe lines), and by foresters for despatching timber. The road tunnel from Chamonix to Courmayeur has put Chamonix and its area on a major trans-Alpine route. It may be that tourism will supplant almost all other economic activities in the High Alps, except industry. It and tourism are naturally mutually exclusive in their distribution.

The Provence Alps

South of Dauphiné, a little south of 45°N, the Alps have the Pyrenean west-east orientation in Upper Provence and in the western Maritime Alps, but then turn seaward. All are composed largely of Cretaceous and Jurassic rocks, except for Tertiaries in the middle and lower Durance Valley, and in the Aix-en-Provence, Marseilles and Nice basins. There are also the older Permo-Triassic rocks of the Draguignan depression, and the tiny Archaean and Pre-Cambrian massifs of the Maures and Esterel. The bare limestones and the dry summers of Provence make the greatest imprint on Upper Provence, the backdrop of the Mediterranean coastlands. These mountains are often grey or white, dry, and with little soil or water. With few resources but adjacent to the prosperous Riviera and Rhône Valley, they have few people and rare towns. They are too dry to have much but sporadic lavender cultivation and poor sheep pasture. Hydro-electric power potential is low because of the seasonal rainfall, although some had been developed at high cost on the Durance and Verdon rivers, as at Castillon (Fig. 90). The hot, dry, barren landscape and glare repel tourists, and the only minerals exploited are bauxite and lignite.

There are thus not only the three-fold structural and regional contrasts of the northern Alps of Savoy, but other contrasts between these and the southern Alps of Provence. Although the first also have limestones, these are well clothed with beech, sweet chestnut and spruce forest, and alpine and valley meadow grasses because of the evenly distributed precipitation. This, the higher relief and the geology most distinguish north from south, though there are other aspects such as the glaciation, the many valley route-ways, industries and the more varied economy of the northern Alps.

The Sedimentary Basins and Valleys
THE PARIS BASIN

The Paris Basin is the largest major physical unit of France. It occupies about one-quarter of the country, and extends for some 300 miles from west to east, and for 200 miles from north to south. It is also the largest structural basin in western Europe, and lies between the massifs of Armorica in the west, the Central Massif in the south, the Vosges in the east and the Ardennes to the north-east. Much of the history of France was enacted in the Paris Basin; it is also one of the richest agricultural areas in Europe.

The physical evolution is part of the story outlined in the previous chapter. The oldest deposits (Triassic) have been largely covered by later formations, so that they are exposed only in Lorraine, but the Liassic series, although best represented there, are also evident on the southern and western fringes. Each successive geological formation covers a smaller and more central part of the basin, so that an analogy has often been made with a stack of saucers of different sizes. The most widespread formations are the limestones—Secondary and Tertiary (Fig. 82).

The Tertiary Seas were far more extensive here than in Britain, and left in the centre of the basin extensive areas of limestones which are all-but-absent in the British Isles. They have had great importance in the development of near-level plains made rich by limon coverings. The stone is widely employed for building, most strikingly in cathedrals. The Tertiary seas retreated south-westwards, in which direction their deposits thin out. They are there disposed in a less orderly manner, and are increasingly the relics of shore-lines and lagoons.

The effects of the Alpine and Pyrenean earth movements have already been mentioned; the first accentuated the basin-like character especially on the east and south-east; while subsequent differential erosion of soft and hard layers has given the characteristic scarp-dipslope-clay vale topography, comparable with but higher than in south-east England. Pyrenean movements left north-west to south-east anticlines and synclines, the latter evident in some reaches of the Loire, the Seine below Paris, the now-eroded anticline of Bray, the Somme syncline, and the high edge of Artois, itself eroded in the terminal weald of Boulonnais.

Both movements caused rejuvenation of the drainage, the creation of the fan-like shape of the river-system, and its focusing upon the Paris area. This greatly enhanced the significance of the rivers for barge-navigation and the value of their valleys for routeways. There are, however, the peripheral rivers of the north and east (Meuse and Moselle); while the Loire flows into the south-west part of the basin, only to leave it again by flowing westwards. It is presumed that in Pre-Tertiary times the Loire flowed north-westward into the present lower Seine.

The widespread deposition of limon in Quaternary times in this non-glaciated basin has been of immense significance to agriculture and settlement. The relief is gentle or undulating, except for the escarpments. These are extremely pronounced features, often of defensive significance in the past, especially where they are breached by rivers, as at Bar-le-Duc. Now they are more commonly occupied by vineyards, especially for Champagne along part of the Tertiary *Falaise de l'Ile de France*.

The climate, as already noted, is a transition between the West Coast Marine and Short Cold-Winter types, and is a remarkable partner to the limon soils of much of the basin in presenting a fine environment for temperate agriculture. This, in turn, is helped by ease of transport and the market attraction of Paris.

There are, therefore, unifying factors in the geological evolution and basin-like structure of the region, with their associated landforms, relief and hydrographic pattern. Communications, a helpful climate, rich agriculture, diverse and growing industry, and the immense historical, political and economic influence of Paris on the basin all gather it into a unity.

Yet there are remarkable differences between the sub-regions or *pays*, by virtue of subtle variations in climate, relief, geology, soil, drainage, vegetation, human occupation and development. No region of comparable size in the world has such unity at large and such diversity in detail as the Paris Basin; none could be so expressive, so meaningful, and such a joy to study for a geographer.

The 'Pays' of the Tertiary Series

These are the regions of the centre of the basin (Fig. 82). The main formations, their age, and the regions in which they occur are shown below, in order from the youngest in the south-west to the oldest in the north-east.

Series	Age	Region
Sologne Sands	Miocene	Sologne
Beauce Limestone	Oligocene	Beauce, Hurepoix
Fontainebleau Sands	,,	Fontainebleau Forest
Brie Limestone	,,	Brie, Tardenois
Argiles Vertes	,,	Part of Marne Valley
St. Ouen Limestone	Eocene	Plaine de France
Beauchamp Sands	,,	Forests of Chantilly, Compiègne, d'Halatte, and Villiers-Cotterets.
Calcaire Grossier	,,	Soissonnais, Vexin Français
Bracheux Sands, etc.	,,	Outcrop in Falaise de l'Ile de France.

There is thus an alternation of limestone strata with sands and occasional clays, as the section (Fig. 82) further demonstrates. It must be emphasised

P

that in drawing the section the dip of the formations has been greatly exaggerated. As one proceeds from south-west to north-east, through the series chronologically and stratigraphically, *buttes-témions* (residual hills) are encountered. These remnants of younger formations remaining on older ones survive only where a resistant limestone crag withstands erosion. Therefore the first area in which buttes-témoins may be found is Brie, since only one important limestone is younger than Brie Limestone, namely Beauce Limestone. Consequently, in Brie there are some buttes-témoins composed of Fontainebleau Sands and Beauce Limestone. However, most of these residual hills are found on the next older limestone in the Plaine de France. Montmartre, which dominates northern Paris and is some 200 feet above the general surface, is a striking example. The foundations of the Basilica of Sacré Coeur are anchored in the capping of Beauce Limestone. Another butte is that of Passy in west-central Paris, but its cap is Brie Limestone; on it stands the Arc de Triomphe. The

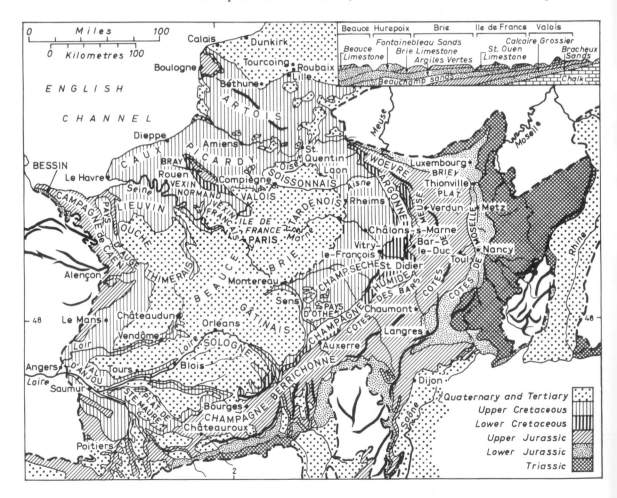

Fig 82 The Paris Basin and section of Tertiaries

great *Etoile* of roads radiate from it downhill in twelve directions. There are far larger buttes in the plains outside Paris to the north and north-east, often visible to travellers between Paris and the Channel ports.

Some of the limestones are exceedingly permeable, as is that of Beauce; some are remarkably impermeable, like that of Brie. Beauce is a very dry region; Brie a very wet one. The other limestones and their associated regions occupy an intermediate position. All are made fertile by a covering of limon, averaging three to six feet in thickness and of an orange-brown colour, more the former colour when dry, nearer the latter when wet. The limon thins out westward, so that there the regions are poorer. There are few river valleys in the youngest limestone but more in the others. Valleys are often rather deep and sudden, for once a limestone is breached, the underlying sands are quickly eroded. Thus there are deep valleys around Rambouillet, where the Beauce Limestone is very thin; while in the north-east towards Laon, the Calcaire Grossier is so dissected as to give a region of hillocks rather than a plain. The whole area terminates in a splendidly impressive scarp, the *Falaise de l'Ile de France*, extending in an arc from La Fère on the Oise to Montereau on the Seine.

On the limon-covered limestone plains are large (200 acres or 80 h. upward) tenant farms, mechanised and efficient, growing cereals, sugar beet, clover, lucerne, potatoes and some minor crops, and keeping livestock. By contrast, in the narrow valleys, on the sands, are small, often part-time or part-income market gardens, producing a rich diversity of vegetables, fruit and flowers for the Paris market. Where there are large, level outcrops of sands are large state forests, which have survived because they are on infertile acidic soils scarcely worth clearing, and were kept first as royal hunting domains and then as state forests. In them are occasional market garden farms, quarries of sand for glass making, châteaux for gracious summer living, and vast areas of recreation for Parisians. The main *pays* are now described.

Sologne. This lies south of the great elbow turn of the Loire and north of the Cher River below Vierzon. Some 160 feet of granitic pebbles, sands and clays lie over Beauce Limestone. They are acidic and largely covered with natural deciduous woodland, with additional planted conifers. Timber exploitation is the leading occupation of the sparse population. Cleared areas are under heath or support semi-subsistence cultivation of rye, oats, potatoes, and the keeping of a few cattle, pigs and chickens. Because of the clays, drainage is impeded and there are hundreds of lakes and ponds. Although the region is damp and unpleasant in winter, it is attractive in summer.

In the west the rivers have cut through the clays to the limestone so that there is better drainage, fewer lakes, and substantial vegetable and hardy fruit cultivation.

Beauce. Coincident with the Beauce Limestone, this is a dry and naturally treeless area locally, reminiscent of the Russian steppes or Canadian prairies. Fertility entirely depends upon the limon; where this is thin in the south-west and west is *La Beauce Pouilleuse* ('poor Beauce'). Farms are mostly of 500–800 acres (200–320 h.) in size, with 5–9 employees. Wheat is the main cereal, colza is important, and hybrid maize gives high yields. Sheep, once the typical livestock, are rarely kept partly because of the shortage of shepherds.

Plate 84   The near-level plain of Beauce.
A great cereal region. In the distance is Chartres Cathedral.

Central Beauce is devoid of rivers and the water table is often 280 feet (85 m.) underground. In the past this severely limited settlement; as a result villages were and still are few and settlement is highly nucleated. There are no towns in true Beauce; market centres grew up where Beauce meets a contrasted region. Thus Orleans and Blois are in contact with the Loire Vale and Sologne, whilst Vendôme, Châteaudun and Chartres border clay-with-flints country. Chartres is famed for its magnificent cathedral, built of Beauce Limestone with the offerings of Beauce farmers. Etampes adjoins the dissected Beauce Limestone region of Hurepoix. This has level cereal lands alternating with deep valleys, often occupied by pleasant outer suburbs of Paris.

Brie. Outcropping east of Beauce are the Fontainebleau Sands, and the great forest extends nearly as far as the Seine. East of the Seine and south of the Marne lies Brie, while north-east of the Marne is the geologically similar Tardenois. The chemical composition of the limestone is such that, on weathering, it yields a clay which impedes drainage, so that there are many lakes and ponds. In the past there were also forests, but because of the fertility of the uniformly limon-covered limestone, most have been cleared. Farms are from 500–1,000 acres (200–400 h.) in size, and grow the more humid-tolerant barley, sugar beet, potatoes and fodder crops. There is much pasture. Dairy cattle are important, Brie cheese being a famous speciality, though much milk goes to Paris. As cattle are important, more labourers are needed than in Beauce. In complete contrast with Beauce the population is both more numerous and more dispersed, excess water being the problem here.

The north-east is variously known as Haute Brie, Brie Pouilleuse or Brie Humide; as these names imply, it is higher, poorer because of the absence of limon, wetter and more wooded. Yields are lower, farmers poorer, the Paris market more remote, and the population density less. Tardenois is akin to this part of Brie, and almost all under small farms.

Plaine de l'Ile de France, and Valois. The St. Ouen Limestone, exposed between the Marne, Seine, Oise and the forests on the Beauchamp Sands, is of average permeability. On it stand numerous buttes-témoins, capped by Brie or Beauce limestones, especially Montmartre and several north-west to south-east trending groups north-east of Paris. Steep slopes of the buttes are often wooded; otherwise the plain has few trees and little superficial drainage. The agriculture would, if mainly influenced by the physical environment, probably be like that of Beauce. Instead it is much affected by the Paris market on its doorstep, and so dairy herds are kept and there are large market gardens. The region has also been much affected by suburban and industrial development.

Soissonnais and Vexin Français. The Calcaire Grossier is of average permeability and its pays are farther from the Paris market than are Beauce, Brie or the Plaine de France. So there are no outstanding physical or economic encouragements here to any particular aspect of the general farming pattern.

Soissonnais has several wide, deep valleys. Laonnais is so dissected as to be largely an assemblage of hills, on one of which stands the old fortress and cathedral town of Laon. Here, as there are more sands than limestone, vegetable farming is the rule.

There are, thus, sharp differences in scenery and land use between the several limestone plains; and between plain and valley. The varying permeability of the limestones affects vegetative cover, settlement pattern and land use, even the suitability of the limestone itself for building; while the thickness of limon largely controls natural fertility. There are immense contrasts between farms of the plains and those of the valleys, and in the varying impact of the Paris market.

Falaise de l'Ile de France. From the Oise, in a great semi-circle round to the Seine, lies the steep, east-facing Tertiary erosion scarp. At its base or associated with outliers are Laon, Rheims, Epernay and Montereau.

Between the Aisne River and the Marshes of St. Gond south-west of Epernay, the middle slopes of the scarp are covered by the almost continuous Champagne vineyards (Fig. 71 and Plate 71), occupying 34,000 acres (13,600 h.), mostly in small holdings. The area within which the product may be so called is limited by law to this scarp (which produces most of the output), to the river bluffs downstream from the scarp, and to outliers. The vine is at its northernmost economic limit; farther north there is insufficient sunlight. To the south-west the scarp is so aligned that moist south-westerlies penetrate too deeply. The vineyards are limited to the gentle middle and lower slopes, where there is least risk of temperature inversion. In addition, these slopes offer the greatest admixture of soils, due to the downwash of limestone, sands and clays from several minor formations not mentioned above. The Chalk beneath quickens drainage, provides the natural lime the vine needs, and allows faster absorption of warmth and its longer retention. The Chalk has been excavated since pre-Roman times for stone, and early and newer galleries provide storage facilities. Rheims and Epernay are the centres of the champagne trade. In the former are five large firms; one alone has some twelve miles of cellars and 25 million bottles maturing. Both towns are honey-combed with underground storage galleries. The large companies may have a few vineyards but buy most of their needs from the small vineyards. There are also many small champagne firms.

Both towns have long histories. Rheims was the centre of the pre-Roman Rèmes tribe, became the Roman Durocortorum, and the coronation town of almost all French kings. It was also a medieval fair town. Dry routeways over the chalk helped travellers, and Rheims was well sited for visitors from Flanders, the Rhinelands, Burgundy and Paris. The Marne-

Aisne Canal, railways and roads have accentuated its nodality as a route centre. Epernay has had a more purely defensive role, controlling the Marne Gap. Both towns have ancient woollen industries depending originally upon supplies from sheep runs of the chalklands to the east. The food industries of Rheims (e.g. biscuits) were likewise originally dependent upon wheat from the same area. Rheims also has metallurgical industries concerned e.g. with cars and domestic electrical appliances. It has been chosen by the state as a centre for industries that might otherwise have been sited in Paris.

Paris

This urban jewel is at the very centre of the Paris Basin, be the centre defined topographically, hydrographically, or mathematically. Towards it converge many streams and valleys; around it are some of the richest areas of French agriculture. The long centralising tendencies of French governments have left it without rivals or subsidiary capitals like Edinburgh, Belfast and others in the United Kingdom, the state capitals in the U.S.A., or commercial rivals such as New York to Washington, Milan and Turin to Rome.

The site of Paris lies above the confluence of the Oise, but below those of the Marne and of the once-significant Bièvre. The ancient trackway from Orleans to Flanders could cross the Seine here without also crossing the Marne or the Oise at their widest points. The Seine crossing was further

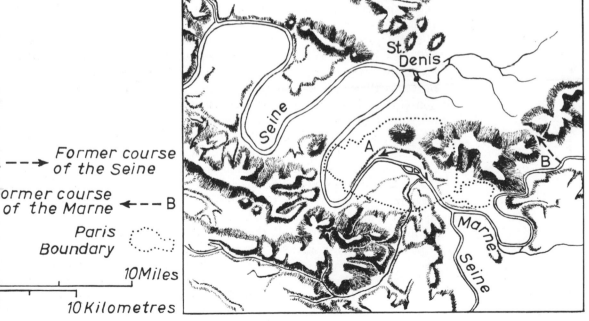

A - - → Former course of the Seine

ormer course of the Marne ← - - B

Paris Boundary

10 Miles

10 Kilometres

Fig 83   Situation of Paris
(After Demangeon)

facilitated by islands. These are of recent geological date, for the Seine previously flowed at the foot of the Belleville-Ménilmontant and Montmartre heights to rejoin the present course near the Trocadero (Figs. 83–4). At this time the Marne flowed north of Paris, through the St. Denis Plain, to join the Seine near the present site of St. Denis. But in a more snowy or more pluvial period, when the Marne had more water and so more force, it cut a new course, with incised meanders, to effect its present confluence with the Seine. The latter, with the additional water and strength, cut the present more direct course through the site of Paris, but the immaturity of this course is evidenced by the islands, previously seven but made into two by man. The abandoned course of the Marne was marshy, and for long unused except for annual fairs, but its plain has been occupied by industry, railway yards and poor housing since the mid-nineteenth century, when steam pumping made drainage possible. The former course of the Seine in central Paris may still be seen in sudden dips in northward-running roads in north-central Paris, and on the east the old course is occupied by the Canal St. Martin. In older days it was occupied by the moat of early city walls. In times of flood the Seine has tended to re-occupy this old course; it is because of this that the Seine is now so substantially embanked in Paris.

The Seine islands facilitated defence as well as crossing. The Parisii tribe established themselves on one or more of them shortly before the birth of Christ. When the Romans arrived, the governor had, by tradition, to live among the conquered people, and here the Temple was also built. But the Roman officials had their villas on the slopes above the left bank where the Calcaire Grossier gave drier conditions. Here also was built the arena, still used as a children's playground.

The departure of the Romans and the advent of the Franks led to a withdrawal to the islands in the fourth century A.D. Here Clovis established his court in the sixth century, and the Capets at the end of the tenth; thereafter Paris owes most to royal direction. The western isle (a combination of two islands) became the ecclesiastical centre with the construction of Notre Dame on the ruins of the Roman Temple, and of the Sainte Chapelle, as well as the first royal palace and buildings for administration— a function still retained. At first produce was brought mainly by river and soon came to be unloaded on the right (northern) low bank, which became the commercial quarter. The markets are still there, though scheduled for removal. Following disagreements with the ecclesiastical authorities the infant university under Richard de Sorbon established itself on the butte or hill of the left bank, the so-called *Montagne de Sainte Gènevièvre* (the Patron Saint of Paris). This is the Latin Quarter, so called because instruction in the university was originally in Latin. There were residential colleges here until they were destroyed in the French Revolution; a renaissance occurred in the twentieth century with the building of the extensive University City on the southern side of Paris.

Paris was successively enclosed by walls (Fig. 84), first by Philip Augustus who in 1180 enclosed the northern commercial and southern

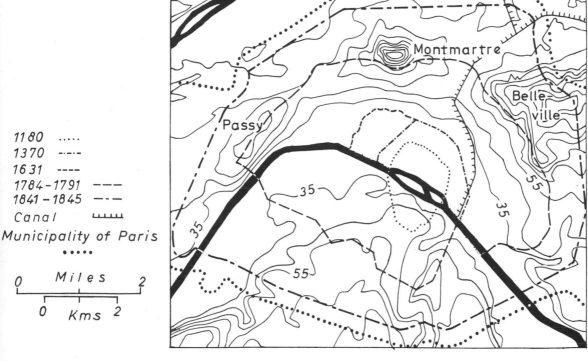

1180 ......
1370 -·-·-
1631 ----
1784 – 1791 ———
1841 – 1845 —·—
Canal ⊔⊔⊔⊔⊔
Municipality of Paris
·····

0 Miles 2

0 Kms 2

Fig 84   The site of Paris
(After Demangeon)

university suburbs. About 1370 Charles V enlarged the fortifications on the north side, using the line of the old marshy course of the Seine as a moat, and the Bastille and Louvre as bastions. Under Louis XIII the walls were extended in 1631 from the St. Denis Gate to the site of the present Place de la Concorde, to guard the then new royal palace of the Tuilleries, built to replace the Louvre.

Louis XIV had all walls pulled down and replaced by the Grands Boulevards, the first of many wide avenues in Paris. Although building was prohibited outside the walls, it was not entirely prevented, and so at the end of the reign of Louis XVI, between 1784 and 1791, the tax-collecting Fermiers-Généraux constructed a building and tax-control wall at the then limits of the city. These walls were demolished and replaced by the Boulevards Extérieurs at the time of Napoleon III by his Paris Prefect—Haussmann (see below). The last walls were erected in 1841–5, and survived until 1920–30. Their line is the limit of the Municipality of Paris (which also includes the Bois de Boulogne and Bois de Vincennes).

In the nineteenth century the canals and railways were brought into Paris. The Canal St. Martin followed the old course of the Seine, up to then still unused marshes. The Est and Nord railways established termini in the level area between the buttes of Belleville on the east and Montmartre on the north, while the Ouest (later Etat) company established St. Lazare between the buttes of Montmartre and Passy. The Paris-Lyons-Méditerranée and Paris-Orléans companies brought their lines down the Seine to the Lyons, Austerlitz and Orsay (now abandoned) stations near the river, whilst another line came up the river to the Invalides station (now the Air Terminal). As in London, the terminii were built near the limit of the then built-up area—the line of the 1841–5 walls.

Under Napoleon III, Haussmann enlarged the Champs Elysées, the Place de la Concorde, and the Grand Boulevards (Madeleine, Capucines, Italiens, etc.). He built the Boulevards Extérieurs (Kléber, Friedland, Haussmann, Grenelle, etc.) and others giving access to each railway station. Squares and the Bois de Boulogne and Bois de Vincennes were improved, and broad avenues made to and within the Bois. All were constructed with an eye to the relief, many afford fine views, all have added to the charm of Paris and eased the circulation of traffic. Along them were built the characteristic six-storied apartment blocks, often with shops below, entered by an inconspicuous door usually leading into an interior courtyard with one or more staircases or lifts, all superintended by that characteristically French person the *concierge*, or caretaker of residents and their letters.

Before the administrative enlargement of Paris under Napoleon III the city had $1\frac{1}{4}$ million inhabitants; after it, $1\frac{3}{4}$ million. By 1940 the population exceeded 2 million, so that Paris had become the most densely peopled town and capital in the western world. The railway age, mechanised barge traffic, the development of industry in the St. Denis Plain and the highly centralised and too-numerous civil service, together with the fashion of living in central Paris, all encouraged its growth.

The *Métro* was built nearer to, on or above ground, because of the frequent outcrop of limestone in Paris compared with London's soft clay. The lines have a grid-iron pattern, unlike the radial one in London; and the Métro runs essentially within the limits of the last walls and administrative limits of the Paris Municipality. A uniform fare operates, and the usual possibility of returning home for lunch makes for intensive usage and four rush hours. Like the several walls, it further encouraged the concentration of population within the cheap-travel area, a concentration twice that of London, four times that of New York, and containing within the municipal area 2.8 million people, or over 83,000 pcr square mile excluding the Boulogne and Vincennes Parks.

Like other large cities Paris has its characteristic quarters, the core Cité, with the old commercial centre to its north, and the Quartier Latin to the south. Immediately to the west is the St. Germain quarter, centre of publishers, bookshops and the resort of writers. Passy was a fashionable residential area until the mid-thirties; offices and embassies now occupy many of its spacious houses. Montmartre, for all its exoticism or eroticism, still has some of its not-so-distant village character.

Commerce and industry are fairly sharply localised in Paris. Publishing, originally dependent upon the adjacent university, has been mentioned.

The Gobelins state tapestry works was established on the banks of the Bièvre to use its clean, soft water (having flowed through Fontainebleau Sands); later dyeworks and laundries came as well. The Bièvre, now more of a sewer, is no longer used industrially, though many factories remain along its course. Fashion houses are mostly around the former royal palaces, whose clientèle they originally served.

The heavy industries are in two main locations, though the localising factors of access to river, canal or rail-borne supplies are the same. Those that need, or were early enough in their establishment to obtain abundant, cheap flat land are in the St. Denis Plain at St. Denis and Aubervilliers, immediately north of the municipal area and of Montmartre. They include the production of transport equipment, engineering works, boiler-making, chemical, paint and glue manufacture. Some, like the latter, use residues from the nearby abattoirs. Many car, engine and engineering works are located on the Seine below central Paris e.g. Renault's oldest factory at Boulogne-Billancourt (Plate 85), as are the power and gas stations. The

Plate 85   The Renault works at Billancourt, south-western Paris.
This is the older of Renault's main works, the more modern large one being at Flins, east of Mantes, on the Seine. Billancourt employs some 37,000 people and the works cover 300 acres. Renault have eleven works in France.

main centres are Suresnes, Puteaux, Courbevoie, Gennevilliers (a river port) and Argenteuil.

Paris suffers acutely from the constricting effects of its former walls and the centralisation of French administration. It is the supreme centre of every facet of French life, not to forget tourism. One-fifth of the employees, one-third the executive grades, two-fifths of the higher administrative and professional cadres of France are in Paris. So are one-third of the female employees, over a quarter of the doctors, two-thirds of the car registrations, and four-fifths of the newspaper sales.

After the Haussmann era there was no further re-development; indeed suburbs grew in an unplanned and disorderly fashion. Not until 1932 was some regional planning instituted in the area within about 22 miles of Notre Dame. In the continuously built-up area there are 7.4 million inhabitants or 15,600 per square mile. It is estimated that in A.D. 2000 Paris will have at least 12 million people, taking account only of the excess of births over deaths, and ignoring inward migration, hitherto greater than the natural increase. If Paris grows no faster than the rate of French towns as a whole it will have 16 million; if it grows at recent rates it could have 25 million.

Faced with these possibilities, industrial licensing began in 1950, and since 1959 there has been control over both the expansion of existing industries and the establishment of new ones. However, most still seek sites as near as permissible to Paris. More urban competitors to Paris are needed, perhaps other cities of over a million (of which there are none in France but several in France's neighbours) and certainly better regional centres (p. 351). The Master Plan for Paris envisages eight new towns with industries, sited between Pontoise and Meaux to the north of the city, and between Mantes and Melun to the south-west, so recognising the attractiveness of the Paris area to modern industry and people.

The 'Pays' of the Secondary Series

Beyond the central Tertiaries are the more or less concentric rings of the Secondary series, exceptionally well displayed on the east, less so on the west and often masked by deposits from the retreating Tertiary Sea on the south-west and south of the basin (Fig. 82). The succession resembles that to the west-north-west of the Tertiary edge of the London Basin.

Six types of region may be distinguished as associated with Chalk, the most widely outcropping formation in the Paris Basin.

1. *Pure Chalk*. The Champagne Sèche (Pouilleuse) is the perfect example of this. It is a plain about 35 miles wide from west to east, and 100 miles in an arc from north to south, limited northward by the Oise, south-westward by the Seine, westward by the Tertiary scarp, eastward by Champagne Humide (Fig. 82). There is but a thin covering of soil over the chalk, and almost no limon. The region has great similarities with Salisbury Plain, and this was likewise once a land of sheep runs. The towns of Rheims and Châlons-sur-Marne still have small woollen industries,

Series	Age	Region
Chalk	Cretaceous	Champagne Sèche (Pouill-euse)
Chalk with super-ficial deposits	—	Varied regions (pp. 430–2)
Upper Greensand (Gaize)	,,	Argonne
Gault Clay	,,	Champagne Humide
Portland Limestone	Jurassic	Côte du Barrois (des Bars)
Kimmeridgc Clay	,,	Meuse Valley Commercy-Verdun
Corallian	,,	Côte(s) de Meuse
Oxford Clay	,,	Woëvre, La Vallée, Pays d'Auge
Oolitic Limestone	,,	Briey Plateau and Côtes de Moselle; Langres Plateau and Côte d'Or; Campagnes de Caen, Argentan & Alençon
Liassic Clay	,,	Moselle Valley, Vallée Noire, Bessin
Rhaetic Limestone	Trias	Côte Virine (cut by Moselle tribs.)
Keuper Marls	,,	Saulnois and Pays des Etangs
Muschelkalk (Calcaire coquillier)	,,	West of Epinal and east of Sarre Valley from Sarrebourg to Sarre-Union
Bunter Sandstone	,,	St. Avold Plateau, Warndt Forest, Mts. Faucilles

while at Troyes these have developed into a major knitwear industry. As with Salisbury Plain the poorest areas, or *savarts*, with little or no soil cover, are used for military exercises.

In the eighties of the last century there were substantial plantings of Black Austrian Pine and lesser ones of Sylvester Pine, which altered the appearance of the region, but added a resource of timber. More recently, heavy applications of fertilisers and the use of mechanical cultivation have made Champagne Sèche into a wheat land, though without subsidiary root crops because of the shallow soils, and with few livestock because of the scarcity of labour. The pine areas are being reduced as mature trees are cut but not replaced because of the success of wheat cultivation.

The rivers have wide flood plains, avoided by road and rail which keep—like the settlements—to their fringes, but are adventurously farmed for vegetables and small fruits. The towns, apart from their textile and associated industries, are important transport foci.

2. *Chalk with Tertiary overlays.* Tertiary sands and clays cover the chalk in south-eastern Picardy (west of the Oise) and the Plateau de Ste. Maure south-east of Tours on the Loire. Tertiary sands over the fast-draining Chalk give dry woodlands of good recreational but poor farming value.

3. *Chalk with Clay-with-Flints.* This is a familiar type of country in Britain in the Chilterns and North Downs. In the Paris Basin it is found in the Pays d'Othe, Sancerrois north of Bourges, the Gâtine de Touraine (north of Tours) and continuing north-east into Thimerais and north-west into Ouche. The clay gives a damp country with many ponds, lakes and woods, typified by the adjective *gâtine*. The soils are fertile but forests were hard to clear, and drainage and cultivation were difficult in the past. Now with mechanised farming and liming these regions give good yields, especially of root crops.

4. *Chalk with Clay-with-Flints and Limon.* These deposits occur on the Chalk in Artois, Caux (between Le Havre, Dieppe, Bray, the Andelle and Seine rivers), in the adjacent Vexin Normand and in western Normandy around the Somme Estuary. They are more fertile than the previous group, because of the limon, but are otherwise comparable. They support mostly large mixed farms, very diverse in their outputs.

Rouen lies 78 miles up the Seine at the head of sea navigation. This has remained possible by dyking and training the deep channel, so that at high water there are now depths of 35 feet. However, so deeply incised is the river and so sharp its meanders, that these limit the size of ships to those not too long to turn in them.

The right bank terrace above the flood plain was settled in pre-Roman days, and Rouen was an important Roman town, and the Norman capital. It has had maritime interests since the earliest days of ships, especially with northern Europe and Britain, importing timber and derivatives and, formerly, much coal. The latter has given way to mineral oil, now brought in by pipe-line from downstream refineries. As mineral oil no longer appears as an import, Rouen has a much lower tonnage than before, but excluding mineral oil imports it is the leading French port in terms of tonnage. As a river port it is second to Strasbourg. Rouen has 12 miles of maritime quays and eight miles of river ones.

Rouen formerly had a hand woollen industry (Elbeuf—upriver—is still a wool manufacturing town), turning later to linen, then to cotton-spinning. The long connections with timber make interests in artificial fibres easy to understand, and there are clothing industries. Specialist steel, engineering and ship-repairing works originally depended upon imported British coal or coke. There are also diesel engine, cable and refrigerator factories. Chemical industries use imported phosphates and pyrites, paper works take timber and pulp, and there are oil refineries.

The town, its industries and influence, have spread up valleys in the Chalk. The old heart of the town was severely damaged in the Second World War, and Rouen had to do some painful economic reorientation in the face of scarce coal imports immediately after that war.

Le Havre, on the north side of the Seine estuary, is the modern successor to Harfleur on that side and Honfleur on the opposite bank. Le Havre was born of the need for deeper water for larger ships on the North American route, and is France's main port in this trade, for passengers and goods. It is second only to Marseilles in tonnage cleared, and has very modern facilities because of the utter destruction of its terminal in the Second World War. Berths for 150,000 ton tankers are available. There are also vast areas of new housing near the docks.

It is a major importer of fuels (mineral oil especially, but some coal), cotton, timber and pulp, chemicals, oil seeds and coffee. In the latter two goods it is, with Dunkirk, a northern competitor to Bordeaux and Marseilles. In general, Le Havre is in competition with London, Antwerp, Rotterdam and Hamburg.

Industries are less varied than at Rouen, younger in age and more modern in product (refineries are typical), while the alluvial areas extending 15 miles eastward and two miles wide are being reclaimed for a vast industrial estate. Car and chemical works are on it, and the aim is to copy the Rotterdam Europort, as well as to attract industries from Paris, or to entice others to settle here rather than in the Paris area. Le Havre could be very attractive, with cheap land, government help, and plenty of water and labour.

5. *Chalk with Limon.* Such regions occur in central Picardy and most of contiguous Artois. These are undulating regions, have numerous streams with wide flood plains (used for market gardening), and are very fertile. Agriculture has benefited from new ideas, as these regions are historic passage-ways from Paris to the Channel ports, Flanders and the lower Rhinelands. There are also excellent communications with large markets in the Northern Coalfield, Paris, Rouen and Le Havre. Cereals, rootcrops,

fodder crops, dairy and beef cattle are typical outputs. Large sugar-beet factories process the beet crop, and there are many textile and metallurgical industries, off-shoots from the northern industrial area, Paris and Rouen. To keep labour, agriculture must remain efficient and remunerative; in general it has succeeded.

Amiens is very much the dominant urban centre with textile, engineering and many consumer-goods industries. Severely damaged in both wars, it has been rebuilt on modern lines and has established industrial estates on which tyre manufacture is prominent.

6.   *The wealds of Bray and Boulonnais.* These eroded anticlines have, in a small area, a rich variety of outcrops from the Chalk down through the Jurassic series, a diversity which is responsible for remarkably varied land use and crops. On the limestones, cereal, root and forage crops are grown; on the clays there is more pasture for cattle (cream cheese and butter are important at Neufchâtel in Bray). On the steep slopes cider-apple and other fruit trees are often grown.

It remains to describe briefly the type regions of Secondary rocks older than Chalk.

Argonne. This high forested ridge of the Upper Greensand has been most significant as an obstacle to east-west movement, often to invaders. Steep, and with deep V-shaped valleys, it has only one passageway—at Clermont-en-Argonne.

The Clay Vales. Whether these be of Gault Clay as in Champagne Humide; of Kimmeridge Clay like part of the Meuse Valley; of Oxford Clay as in the Woëvre, La Vallée of Burgundy or the Pays d'Auge of western Normandy; or of Liassic Clay like the Moselle Valley, the Vallée Noire of Berry, or of Bessin in western Normandy, all are dominantly pastoral lands. They produce milk, butter or cheese, the latter two especially in Normandy (Pont l'Evêque, Port Salut and Camembert cheeses). Root and fodder crops are also important for feeding dairy cattle and for fattening beef cattle sent into these regions. They are necessarily damp, and have much superficial drainage and woodland.

Limestone areas. The dip slopes and scarps of the Côtes de Meuse and Côtes de Moselle in the east, the Champagne Berrichonne in the south, and the Campagne de Caen in Normandy are the most important of such regions. Cereals, root and fodder crops are typical but yields are usually less than in the Tertiary limestone plains. Livestock are again important, fruit trees and the vine have some significance on south-east facing slopes, but high or steep areas are often wooded. In the Moselle plateau and scarp and in the Campagne de Caen Jurassic iron ores are mined, and in Lorraine there is much heavy industry (pp. 370–3, and Plate 74).

Many of the towns are former fortresses guarding gaps in the scarps, such as Bar-le-Duc, Bar-sur-Aube and Bar-sur-Seine in gaps of the Côte du Barrois (des Bars); Verdun behind (west of) the Corallian Côte de Meuse; Metz and Nancy (the old Lorraine capital) adjacent to the Côte de Moselle. Toul lies between the last two scarps, and east of a dry gap formerly occupied by an upper Meuse tributary until it was diverted to the Moselle.

In the Champagne Berrichonne the various limestones and clays outcrop in quick succession. The southerly position permits the cultivation of additional crops e.g. maize, but former semi-isolation has retarded agricultural techniques. Bourges, with a fine cathedral, was the capital of Berry, and originally used local iron ores. Some engineering industries persist. Vierzon also used these ores and charcoal from Sologne; it now makes agricultural machinery with Lorraine steel.

The Campagne de Caen is a level Oolitic limestone plain, dry but fertile because of a limon covering thicker than in the other Jurassic areas. The stone is excellent for building; it was much used in southern English cathedrals. Iron ores are worked, as in Lorraine, and there is some associated industry (p. 372). Caen is the local regional centre, with industry encouraged by the Caen-Ouistreham Canal. The town was devastated in 1944, and rebuilt on modern lines.

Triassic areas. The most important outcrops are the Rhaetic Limestone, Keuper Marls, the Muschelkalk Limestone and Bunter Sandstone, all of which outcrop only in Lorraine. The agriculture of the undulating clayland of the Keuper Marls is dominantly pastoral, but with its fodder and other crops has more arable farming than the other clay vales because of the nearby markets of industrial Lorraine. Rock salt is obtained from the series, and is a vital raw material for local and other chemical industries. The Bunter Sandstone is still largely wooded (forests of St. Avold, Warndt and Houve) because of acidic soils, heavy rainfall, much wind and a shorter growing season on this high eastern margin.

THE BRUSSELS BASIN

Artois forms a clear edge to the Paris Basin, and falls sharply to the flat Brussels Basin. Between Artois and the Franco-Belgian border, the sand-dune coast and the Ardennes, are French Flanders and other segments of the Brussels Basin.

Calais and Dunkirk have been developed on a coast inimical to ports. The first owes its origin principally to proximity to Britain and to lace and other textile manufactures. Dunkirk was developed after the rest of the area was acquired by France in the seventeenth century to provide a French port for the region, previously served by Antwerp, and canals were built to divert trade to Dunkirk. The new port benefited greatly from the opening of the French Northern Coalfield and the rise of its dominant industries of iron, steel, chemicals and textiles, all of which need bulk imports of raw materials. Dunkirk also handles some Lorraine and Rhineland traffic, in minor competition with Antwerp and Rotterdam. West of the port are France's first coastal integrated steel works and an oil-refinery, while there is hope of attracting other large works to the plentiful cheap flat land (Plate 75).

Maritime Flanders, Interior Flanders and Hainaut are comparable in character and farming with these areas in Belgium. The difference lies in the development in France of the coalfield east of Béthune, which has added mining and industry to an area of intensive farming. The main industries have been mentioned above; the textiles are north of the coalfield, in Lille and especially in Roubaix-Tourcoing on the border, in the latter two originally to attract Belgian labour. The other industries are on or near the coalfield.

THE RHINE RIFT VALLEY (France and Germany)

This great trench lies between the crystalline massifs of the Vosges and Black Forest in the south, and the much lower Bunter Sandstone covered Hardt and Odenwald in the north. The valley extends from Basle to Mainz some 150 miles (240 Km.), and is some 20 miles (32 Km.) in width. It results from the collapse during the Alpine Orogeny of the centre of a single massif.

Gulfs of the Mediterranean first occupied the trench and left their deposits. These include potash (the consequence of evaporation of sea water in a shallow side lagoon) at Nonnenbruch near Mulhouse, and oil at Pechelbronn north of Strasbourg. However, the Tertiary deposits have been largely masked by later fluvial ones, resulting mainly from the Rhine.

Fluvo-glacial deposits were also carried into the rift valley from Vosges, Black Forest and Alpine glaciers, and give occasional ill-drained areas or sticky soils. The Rhine and the Ill also have wide flood plains or *Ried* ('wet forest'), drained in the case of the Ill, still marshy in the case of the Rhine.

The lower pebble terraces of the Ill and Rhine are still largely forested e.g. the Harth Forest east of Mulhouse on Rhine terraces, and Nonnenbruch Forest west of Mulhouse on Ill ones. The higher terraces were ancient routeways (Strasbourg was a 'bourg' on the greatest western one), and they are still followed by roads, railways and the Rhône-Rhine canal.

In the north of the valley, beyond Strasbourg and Karlsruhe (Germany), the river terraces have been built by streams from the infertile Bunter Sandstone of the northern Vosges, Hardt and Odenwald. In the far south, the Sundgau, south of Mulhouse, was the valley of the Rhine when it was a tributary of the Saône. The Sundgau is now the Rhine-Ill-Doubs watershed, and the Ill has dissected the old Rhine terraces to give an area of confused topography and drainage, and generally poor agriculture.

On the mixed soils of the terraces and of the fringes of the massifs is a thick mantle of loess, highly beneficial to agriculture. Moreover, the climate is markedly continental, of the Short Cold Winter type, with a rainfall maximum in July and high summer temperatures. The farms are small, with dispersed fields, and 'polyculture' of the vine, hops, tobacco, fruit, vegetable and fodder crops (Plate 86). Where there is less shelter from the west the climate is damper e.g. south of Mulhouse and north of Strasbourg; there poorer pedological conditions are emphasised by difficult climatic ones.

The great importance of rift valley routeways, and the diversity of

Plate 86 The Rhine Rift Valley.
A view south-eastwards over the vineyards of Ammerschwihr, a valley-exit village on the eastern edge of the Vosges. Beyond lie the pasture lands of an upper terrace of the Fecht River, and then the wooded *ried* of its flood plain, within the Rhine Rift Valley.

resources on the plain, in the foothill vineyards, and in the massif pastures and woodland encouraged the development of French towns such as Mulhouse, Colmar and Strasbourg, and German ones such as Freiburg and Darmstadt. In Alsace the establishment in the eighteenth century of a cotton print industry (copying Indian styles) was the result of overseas contacts by Calvinists with capital and access to abundant labour. Concentration of the industry has been necessary, so that it is now mainly in Mulhouse and Colmar.

Strasbourg is the largest French city in the valley. Until the First World War it was essentially an administrative, commercial and military centre, with food, beer and other consumer-goods industries. Under the Germans it could not compete for Rhine traffic with Ludwigshaven and Mannheim, but after it returned to French rule in 1918 the port was developed, and the beer, meat-conserving and tobacco industries also benefited. It has several machine-tool and engineering firms, which are favoured by good access to the Lorraine and Ruhr steel producers. The port administration has encouraged the milling of cereals and trade in cellulose, while the Lavéra (Marseilles)–Strasbourg–Karlsruhe pipeline feeds two refineries and petro-chemical industries. Coal and coke are received by water from the Ruhr; oil products, potash and manufactured goods go down the Rhine. Relatively little is carried by either the Rhine-Marne or Rhône-Rhine canals, except via the Grand Canal d'Alsace and Huningue sections taking traffic to Basle. Strasbourg faces some uncertainty through the probable declining use of Lorraine lean iron ores in favour of imported richer ones, and their transport on the canalised Moselle; but the town is well sited for chemical, especially fertiliser, industries. It is also the seat of the Assembly and Council of Europe.

THE SAÔNE-
RHÔNE CORRIDOR

This is one of the world's greatest passage ways. It was first part of the 'amber road' between the Baltic and the Orient, and as early as the fourth century B.C. became the route along which tin from Brittany and Cornwall was carried to supply the Greco-Roman bronze industry.

The valley is a structural depression which developed as the result of successive pressures and tensions of the Alpine Orogeny against the resistant Vosges and Central Massif. At first the valley was occupied by a gulf of the Mediterranean as far as the site of Lyons, and by a lake to the north; ultimately the gulf retreated and the lake was drained. In Pleistocene times the area was occupied by Alpine glaciers penetrating through the cluses of the Pre-Alps. Glacial melt waters resorted the older deposits, and also left glacial ones. This great bulk of diverse materials has pushed the Saône and Rhône rivers westward, while the formidable amount of water has caused great leaching of these deposits, although there has been some recompense with post-glacial limon deposits. In general, however, the soils are poor, but the Mediterranean-Cold Short Winter transitional climate (pp. 345–8) and the location are so good that this is an important area agriculturally, especially for cultivating fruit, vegetables and the vine.

The location is good because road and rail give easy access to the whole of the Paris Basin (including Lorraine), the Rhine Valley, Switzerland, Italy via the Mont Cenis tunnel, Marseilles, the Riviera and Italy by a second route, the Aquitaine Basin, St. Etienne and Le Creusot.

The river is the subject of integrated development by the Compagnie Nationale du Rhône. Large power stations have been constructed across diversion canals, navigation has been vastly improved, and irrigation brought to 160,000 more acres (Figs. 85 and 90). Industry of the most modern kind has been attracted (pp. 366–7, 377).

Upper Saône Basin

This is the widest part of the corridor; it extends as far south as Châlons-sur-Saône, and is limited by steep though low bluffs. On the west are the

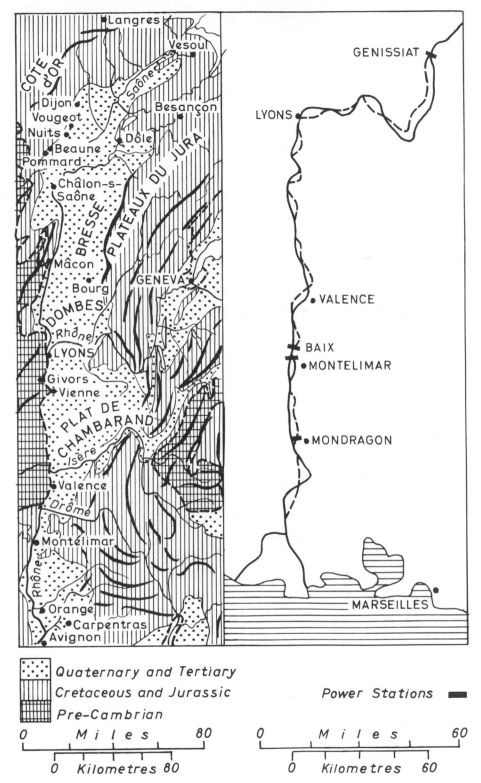

Fig 85 The Saône-Rhône Corridor and Rhône power sites

famous Burgundy vineyards, no more than a mile wide but extending from Dijon first through the Côte de Nuits and Côte d'Or, with mixed soils over Jurassic limestone. Along them are such world-famous villages or châteaux as Vougeot, Vosne-Romanée, Nuits-Saint-Georges, Beaune, Pommard, Volnay and Meursault. The vineyards continue through the ordinary-quality area of la Côte Châlonnaise, into the better one of la Côte Mâconnaise, finally ending southward in the ordinary-quality Beaujolais. Cane fruits, cherries and peaches are also important crops.

In the basin the Saône and its tributaries have left a great series of terraces and wide flood plains. These are mostly under woodland or pasture, but market gardening is important on the more fertile terraces near to good transport or towns. Cereals and fodder crops are dominant off the terraces.

Dijon, the old Burgundy capital, is a rail and road focus, and also has some barge traffic. The town is more commercial than industrial, and the industries are intimately connected either with nearby agriculture or with transport equipment.

Bresse

This area was occupied by the Tertiary lake, which left blue marls, but Bresse also has fluvial deposits of sand on the north, and windborne limon on the east; while there are the usual wide alluvial plains and river terraces. Farms are almost all under 25 acres, intensively cultivated with cereals and other fodder crops for feeding the famous *poulets de Bresse*, and the less-known piglets and dairy cattle.

Dombes

Compared with Bresse this is a poor land because of boulder clay, moraines, glacial or fluvial gravels and sands, and because of the low humus content of the soils. There are still thousands of lakes, some of which are fish-farmed for two years, and then drained and cropped for a similar period. Reclamation and settlement of the area has proceeded around the edges, often for country homes and 'suitcase farming' for Lyons people. Farms are larger than in Bresse—they should be on such poorer soils—and the country is best suited to dairying. However, labour shortage on this doorstep of Lyons has encouraged beef cattle keeping, with market gardening very near Lyons, and poultry-farming towards Bresse. There are also some silk mills.

Lyons (Fr. *Lyon*)

This, the third city of France, lies half way along the Saône-Rhône corridor, at the confluence of these rivers. Here a settlement was founded in 42 B.C. on the high western bluff of Fourvière, overlooking the right bank of the Saône and two miles above the confluence (Fig. 86). Lugdunum was the capital of Roman Gaul, but thereafter the town had a border position successively in Burgundy, Provence, the Holy Roman Empire and France, until Savoy was acquired in 1860. This is one reason why it

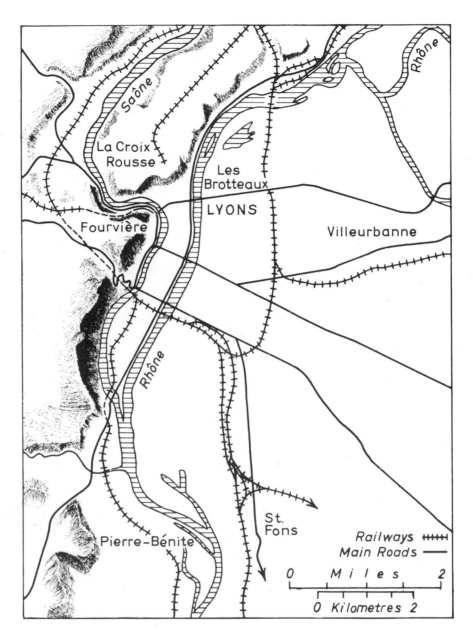

Fig 86 Lyons

for long fell short of being a regional capital. However, its nodal position caused it to have an annual fair from 1420, still continued in its international fair. Lyons had an early development of banking and other financial activities, which Paris has since taken over, though the name Crédit Lyonnais lives on.

Lyons has a major role in ecclesiastical life, civil administration, education, transport, commerce and industry. It is best-known for its silk industry, although this is no longer pre-eminent. The craft was introduced by Italian refugees, and in 1450 Charles V gave the town a monopoly of silk manufacture and control, although it was later withdrawn. Silk worms were formerly raised in Vivarais and the Cévennes until cheaper silk could be imported from the Orient after the opening of the Suez Canal in 1869; meanwhile, the local mulberry trees had been attacked by disease. Since then the industry, though changed, has remained, principally because of facilities in the city for technical education, the availability first of steam and then electric power, good transport connections, and the presence of inter-connected industries. There are about a thousand silk establishments, mostly small, in the high Croix-Rousse district north of the confluence. There have always been many out- or home-workers (now one-third), as well as the 4,000 other silk establishments now outside Lyons. Certain types of silk are, indeed, produced elsewhere: muslin in Ardèche, satin in Voiron (north-west of Grenoble), and voile in Tarare (north-west of Lyons). Lyons was sensibly quick to develop artificial silk, being the first to manufacture it (in 1900). Since then Lyons has played a prominent part in making most artificial fibres. It was prominent in the wool trade in the fifteenth and sixteenth centuries, and retains interests in most textiles.

The textile trades encouraged the early growth of machinery-making for them, and later for the railway, electrical and other industries. Tin-plate manufacture is important, there is a large truck and earth-moving equipment firm employing 15,000 (the largest employer), as well as big cable, computer, and household equipment industries.

The silk industry also encouraged the development of vegetable dyes and, later, the chemical dyestuffs industry. Now a wide range of chemical industries is represented, including man-made fibres, pharmaceuticals, photographic chemicals and papers, insecticides and paints. There are seven large chemical works in the southern suburb of Saint Fons. The common urban industries of food and tobacco, furniture, wood working, leather, shoes, glass and paper are well represented.

Lyons has benefited from plenty of incoming labour from poor nearby mountainous areas, as well as ease in employing home workers in its poor environs. When something other than man-power was required or possible, wood, coal and electric power were successively available. As large-scale industry developed, cheap flat land has been available to the south-east. Water supplies—so often critical elsewhere—have been plentiful, a great point for the chemical industries. These have also benefited by cheap river transport, now much improved, and by the advent of the natural gas and oil pipelines.

Lyons is a great railway, road and river transport centre, and a link between the Rhône and Saône navigations has at last been constructed, with a power station at Pierre Bénite (Fig. 86). Rather surprisingly, Lyons airport is not important, being over-shadowed by Paris, Geneva and Marseilles. The disadvantages of the town are its individualism, the small size of most industries, a housing shortage severe even by French standards, and the shadow which Paris casts even as far as this.

Below Lyons are successive plains, separated by gorges where the river cuts through westward projections of the limestone Pre-Alps. Thus there are the plains of Givors, Vienne, Valence, Montélimar, Pierrelatte, Orange and Avignon. In the first two are the poor, wooded and pastoral glacial Terres Froides and Plateau de Chambarand; otherwise these pebbly, gravelly or sandy areas, with some limon, are usually intensively cultivated away from the Rhône flood plain. Irrigation is increasingly available, especially through the Compagnie Nationale du Rhône. There is usually polyculture, since all the temperate and almost all Mediterranean crops can be grown. There is some emphasis on either the vine, fruits (especially peaches) and vegetables; and on milk near towns if labour is available. Thus peaches are important near the river in the Valence Plain, and to its north are the famous vineyards of Tain l'Ermitage. To the south the soils are not rich but the warmer climate helps early vegetable crops; protection must, however, be given by cypress windbreaks against the north-westerly mistral, and heaters are often used in cold weather. There are numerous small towns, such as those mentioned above, which have synthetic textile, chemical, electric steel alloy and cement works, many of which use Rhône water in great quantities. Pierrelatte, near the Donzère-Mondragon (Bollène) hydro-electric power station (Fig. 85) is France's most costly and complex industrial unit, making radio-active isotopes. It lies between the natural and artificial courses of the Rhône where unused flat land, unlimited water, and huge quantities of power were available without fear of breakdown because of being able to call on Central Massif and Alpine production. There are associated chemical works and nearby, at Marcoule, is France's first commercial atomic power station.

This area is, therefore, not only at the meeting point with the Mediterranean climate, its crops and its culture, but has the traditional and the ultra-modern in industry. Here is, perhaps, the industrial centre of to-morrow's France. It benefits from plenty of space, power, an oil pipeline, excellent road and rail facilities, is near the port of Marseilles, and is attractive to labour.

THE AQUITAINE BASIN

Like the Paris Basin, that of Aquitaine has varied deposits from the Secondary to Quaternary eras. The drainage pattern is broadly similar, with the central system of the Garonne and its numerous, mainly right bank tributaries. This system is flanked by the Charente in the north and the Adour with its many tributaries in the south-west. Agriculture is again very important—here much more so than industry, which is largely restricted to Toulouse, Bordeaux and Lacq.

Yet there are more contrasts than similarities with the Paris Basin. The Aquitaine Basin is much smaller, and is triangular in shape. It lacks the concentric geological arrangement of much of the Paris Basin, and the scarpland topography so characteristic of much of that basin is almost absent. The Pyrenean movements have left important traces, although they were sharply confined by the Central Massif; the main ones are the central 'gutter' of the Garonne, and the north-west to south-east alignment of the Secondary formations in the north-east of the basin. There are also fewer Tertiary limestones, as the Tertiary seas were shallower but, in consequence, Tertiary sands are well represented, as in the Landes.

The Aquitaine Basin has a number of its own characteristic formations, such as molasse (also spelt mollasse) a heterogeneous deposit derived from limestones and sandstones, and washed down from the Pyrenees into the centre of the basin. Bands of Tertiary limestone occasionally occur in it. There are also highly dispersed *faluns* of shells and sands, commonest south of the Garonne, but never extensive. Furthermore, the rivers come from prolific gathering grounds—the Central Massif with its rapid run-off and the Pyrenees with their annual snow-melt. Floods on both groups of rivers are common, and may be disastrous in the lower Garonne if spring storms occur in the Central Massif as snow melts in the Pyrenees. The rivers have left many terraces because the swollen torrents of the Pleistocene snow-melt era re-cut the valleys. Terraces are important settlement sites in this land of frequent floods. They are also used by rail and road, and often occupied by the vine. Lastly, the great deltaic fan of Lannemezan and smaller fans to the west are the consequence of deposition by gigantic post-glacial Pyrenean floods.

The basin is rather isolated by the Central Massif from the rest of France, and by the Pyrenees from Iberia, although the Poitou and Naurouze sills provide easy routeways to the Paris Basin and Mediterranean lands. It is not surprising that this part of France has somewhat lagged behind in general development, and that rather archaic methods survive in agriculture and in small industry.

The climate is transitional, as explained on p. 348. In general, it enjoys the advantages of the Mediterranean without its disadvantages. Winters are short and mild; the growing season is thus long, and the Mistral does not occur. Summers have sufficient rain to avoid the necessity of irrigation.

Agricultural potential in this southern area is plainly greater than in the Paris Basin. Maize will ripen, there is no great climatic danger to the vine, and fruits such as table-grapes, melons, peaches and apricots do well, as does tobacco. Yet all the crops of the Paris Basin may also be grown. Furthermore, there are continuing if weakening contacts with upland farms in the Central Massif and the Pyrenees which sell cattle for fattening in the lowlands. The very diversity of possibilities has, however, been somewhat of an economic disadvantage. Farmers have tended to practise polyculture, growing a little of many crops. They have specialised insufficiently, although there are signs of change.

THE SECONDARY LIMESTONE REGIONS

Aunis and northern Charente. The north of the basin is a region of transition between northern and southern France. Although mostly underlain by

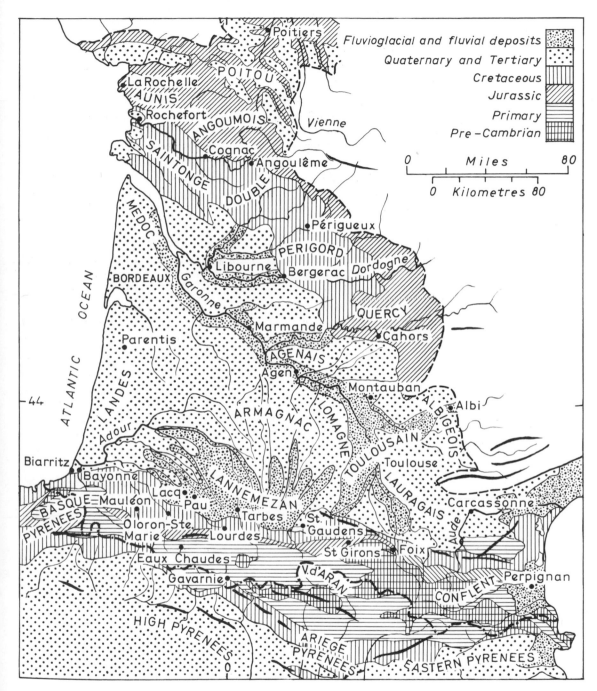

Fig 87 The Aquitaine Basin and Pyrenees

Jurassic limestones, there are usually coverings of Tertiary sands and clays, while there are extensive coastal marshes (as in coastal Saintonge). The Charente is one of France's great livestock regions, where dairy cattle are kept (Fig. 70). Milk is processed into butter, but partly into cheese, usually in co-operatives which are the oldest in France, but are now mostly small and inefficient. There is much permanent grass, but also substantial cereal and sugar beet cultivation to provide a rotational element as well as fodder.

La Pallice and La Rochelle have the most sheltered and deepest water of any western French port, yet they have declined by comparison with either the Loire ports of Nantes and St. Nazaire, or with Bordeaux. La Rochelle was a Huguenot centre and so was neglected by the state in the past, and the railways provide better services to the other ports. The trade of La Rochelle is similar to them. So are the industries, for the most part, but timber working is also important, and the state is encouraging industry to become established here.

The Jurassic limestone regions of Angoumois and Quercy. These landscapes are undulating in the north, but rather more level, bleaker and even karstic in the south-east, where the rivers are deeply incised, such as the Lot below Cahors. The soils are thin and poor. The best are the red-brown ones of the dry valleys, or the alluvial soils of the present valleys.

Woodlands are the main though slender resource. Chestnut trees are exploited for wood and tannin rather than for nuts; walnut trees for timber, nuts and oil; pine trees for paper, sawn timber and, less so, for resin. Farms are rare clearings in the woodlands, and are little more than poor cereal, grass and other fodder producers for their few cattle and numerous sheep. In Quercy and other causses truffles are still routed out from the roots of oaks by pigs. Vineyards appear on valley slopes, especially around Cognac where they provide wine for distillation to brandy. Greengages, apples and pears are important in the valleys, as is tobacco.

The Chalk limestone regions of Saintonge, Double and Périgord. These regions are lower than the Jurassic ones, have softer land forms, and generally better conditions, though the economies are much the same. Périgueux, Angoulême, Cognac, Saintes and Rochefort are market towns.

THE TERTIARY LIMESTONE REGIONS

Entre-deux-Mers and Agenais. These are the small areas of the basin with mainly Tertiary limestone, although in Agenais it is so dissected as to be discontinuous. In the more northerly area the limestone is continuous but often covered with sands, clays and limon, and is a most important wine-producing area (St. Emilion, Entre-deux-Mers, and Les Côtes). Agenais is more significant for table grapes, plums for drying to prunes (between Agen and Villeneuve-sur-Lot), and peaches (north of Moissac and the Aveyron). Most Agenais farms have under 25 acres and they can be much smaller. A great variety of early vegetables and specialities is grown, such as early potatoes, leeks, carrots, onions, melons, artichokes, peas, dwarf (French) beans, gherkins and tobacco.

MOLASSE REGIONS   *Marmande, Montalbanais, Albigeois, Toulousain and Lauragais.* Although Tertiary limestone occurs in these regions and as cuestas in the east, the areas are characterised by highly mixed molasse soils. These soils, together with the gently undulating relief, good drainage and central situation have helped them to become some of the most productive and varied agricultural lands in France, even in the world. Diversity of output is again characteristic, but cereals and tomatoes are especially important, as are poultry and livestock. The Central Massif rearing area is near, a source of female calves for dairying, and of older males for fattening; while Bordeaux and especially Toulouse offer good markets for the produce.

OTHER REGIONS   *The deltaic fans of Lannemezan, Ger and Orignac.* These are dejection cones of pebbles deposited by past and present rivers when flowing at higher elevations and with greater volumes than now, and beginning with the elevation of the Pyrenees in mid-Tertiary times. They are poor pasture or heath lands.

Lomagne, Armagnac and Chalosse. Though again composed of molasse, these regions have been deeply trenched by rivers with very asymmetrical valleys, steep on the right or east banks, and gentle on the left or west banks. It is thought that this asymmetry is due to more rapid ice and snow-melt on the westward facing eastern sides at the end of the glacial eras. The gentler slopes have a light soil or *boulbène*; it is easy to work, poorer than the molasse because of leaching, but excellent for the vine.

These are again regions of polyculture but with considerable emphasis on cereals including hybrid maize; while Armagnac produces a brandy of that name. In the Adour Valley below Aire geese and ducks are confined in small spaces and dark buildings to enlarge their livers used in making pâté de foie gras. But all these regions keep poultry and cattle, so that fodder crops and grassland are common, while fruit orchards have been established by farmers who left Algeria at independence. These areas suffer from summer water shortages. The Alaric Canal below Tarbes and the Saint-Martory Canal above Toulouse supply water to the north-west and north-east fringes, and new works will help the south-central areas.

Within this otherwise rural environment the exploitation of natural gas, sulphur and oil at Lacq, and the associated industries of aluminium smelting and petro-chemicals, have led to the creation of a new town (Mourenx), a new economy and a new landscape (Plate 73).

The Landes. This great triangular region between the Atlantic, the Garonne and Chalosse is the largest in Aquitaine, the most strongly individualised and the most uniform. Rising above 300 feet only in the eastern apex, it is otherwise low and flat, with thick deposits of Tertiary and Quaternary sands. Formerly swampy because of an impermeable alio or iron pan, it has been drained, its scenery changed, and a major resource provided by the planting after 1857 of maritime pines. These now cover two-thirds of the area (Plate 87). At first the forest was worked for pitch and turpentine, pit props for French and British coalmines, railway sleepers, and for flooring. All these products and outlets have declined—there are now substitutes for pitch and turpentine; there are fewer coal mines—and most use steel props; steel railway sleepers are also in vogue; and cork, plastic and stone mosaic floorings are more used in France, whilst tropical wood parquet is preferred in Britain.

The timber is now used largely for making packing paper, for which there are some six factories employing about 3,500 workers. To be economic these factories must be large, and the largest brings in additional timber from outside. A state company is buying up areas for conversion to firebreaks and agriculture, and improving the rest of the forest. There has always been some poor semi-subsistence farming, plus a little tobacco and maize for sale, and the rearing of calves. Sheep and pigs, once important, are now few. Some lignite is quarried for power generation (p. 365).

La Côte d'Argent. From Biarritz northwards is a young emergent coastline which has sealed off former river outlets except the Bassin d'Arcachon—

Plate 87   Timber in the Landes.
Timber is now mainly used for packing paper.

an oyster fishery. Otherwise there are lagoons behind semi-active dunes, partially fixed by marram grass. Although difficult of access before the car age, this is a fine holiday coast for young families. Around the Etang de Parentis is France's largest oilfield (p. 367).

Alluvial plains and river terraces. Lower valleys are usually wide because rivers have cut easily into the dominantly soft rocks. In most valleys there are the terraces so characteristic of Aquitaine (Fig. 87); thus in Toulousain the Garonne terraces are over 15 miles wide on the left bank, and the river also flows in a wide flood plain. Similar series of terraces are typical of the Garonne-Tarn confluence zone, and above Agen, around Marmande and La Réole. Likewise, they are well seen on the Ariège at Pamiers, on the Tarn, on the Lot below Villeneuve, on the Dordogne from above Bergerac, and on the Isle. The terraces of the lower reaches have finer silts, richer soils, and often have limon coverings as well; while the terraces of the upper reaches are usually pebbly and acidic. This is especially true of the rivers fed by past glaciers e.g. the Adour and the several *gaves*.

The significance of the higher terraces for safer settlement and lines of communication in valleys subject to severe flooding has been mentioned, as also the use of terraces for cultivation of the vine, fruits and vegetables. Holdings are characteristically small (under 5 acres) and intensively worked. Typical areas are those around Albi, Gaillac, Montauban and Moissac on or near the Tarn; Agen and Marmande on the Garonne; Villeneuve-sur-Lot; and Bergerac on the Dordogne.

The Bordelais Vineyards

The vine is the principal crop of the basin; in the Gironde department it occupies about one-third of the cultivated area, and almost all its communes are dominantly planted or concerned with it (Fig. 71).

The great impetus to wine production was given during the English occupation from 1154–1453. Although the soils are varied and thus suited to different grapes and wines, and the area has easy transport of its produce by river and sea, coastwise and for export, it suffers from excess humidity. This encourages mildew and oidium which can be countered only by expensive spraying, which may introduce too much sulphur to the soil. Destructive spring storms and late frosts are further problems, especially north of the Dordogne. Windbreaks on the western sides of fields are often required against stormy Atlantic weather in Médoc, Graves and Sauternes.

River terraces are much planted in the latter three areas, and on the Côtes de Blaye opposite Médoc, in the Premières Côtes de Bordeaux opposite Graves, on the slopes of the Dordogne in Entre-deux-Mers and above Fronsac, around Bergerac, Cahors, Moissac and Gaillac. The best vintages tend to be produced above the valley floor, yet in sight of water, for this reduces summer temperatures and scorching. The vine is, however, much grown away from water and river terraces, notably in limestone areas such as central Entre-deux-Mers and, less so, in molasse areas.

The larger producers are responsible for one-third the output, although the largest château has only 910 acres (364 h.). They tend to be dominant where the vine itself is the major crop. Red wine is no longer the main production, average quality wine is on the ascendency, and is often produced by large new managements or by small producers helped by co-operative stocking or marketing. The luxury product areas of Haut Médoc, Graves and Sauternes have been affected by urban competition for land, and by conversion to market gardening or pasture lands for dairy supplies to Bordeaux.

Toulouse and Bordeaux

These cities lie at either end of the Aquitaine Basin, and should be contrasted with the single great focus of Paris in its basin.

Toulouse. The Toulousain is a natural focus of routes between the Atlantic and the Mediterranean via the Garonne and the Naurouze Sill or Carcassonne Gap, and of routes from the north towards the south-east and south-west. The precise location of Toulouse is below the Ariège-Garonne confluence on an outcrop of limestone which permitted fording of the single river.

The town developed first on a river terrace related to the old valley—now dry—of the Hers-Mort between Pech David on the south side and Calvinet on the north. In 1347 the first walls enclosed the town on both banks. The larger medieval extensions of Saint Sernin on the north, Saint Etienne on the east, Carmes on the south, and Saint Cyprien on the west have left strong imprints. The University was the second to be founded in France.

The nodality of the town was increased by the seventeenth century Canal du Midi and the later Garonne Lateral and Brienne canals. Although narrow and encumbered by numerous locks these canals carry mineral fuels, cement, paper pulp and chemicals. The railways did much more to strengthen the town, roads have helped further, and the aerodrome, once more important, is regaining traffic with summer charter flights and car-carriers. The city is a regional centre for the south-east of the basin, the central and eastern Pyrenees, and for the south-west of the Central Massif.

Yet in the middle of the last century its population was only 90,000 and highly concentrated. Substantial suburbs did not develop until after the Second World War, since when there has been much building, and Toulouse has grown fast. Of all French cities, only Toulouse and Le Mans grew between 1936 and 1946, both receiving refugees from elsewhere in France. After the war most of these left but other people came in, especially Frenchmen from North Africa. Two-thirds of the present population have come from outside—approximately equally from surrounding areas and from the rest of France or abroad.

Toulouse has the second highest proportion of people employed in Tertiary occupations of any French city. Its commerce in cloth and leather are relics of ancient trades, and it is a great agricultural collector or distributor of local and imported foodstuffs.

Industry is poorly represented, with but two-fifths of the workers. Only three establishments employ over 1,000 workers. There are numerous small metallurgical works, printing, textile and clothing, paper-finishing works, and one substantial shoe factory. All have roots in the past.

The relative remoteness of Toulouse from France's threatened boundaries encouraged the establishment of three state armament and explosive works here before the First World War. This consideration, together with cheap hydro-electric power from the Pyrenees, led to a state-assisted nitrogenous fertiliser works in 1924. There are now others making fertilisers and sulphates from gypsum obtained from near Tarascon-sur-Ariège. These also use natural gas and sulphur from Lacq, and some 3,000 workers are employed.

Distance from the eastern boundary, flat land and usually clear skies encouraged the establishment of aircraft works of which Sud Aviation is best known, and employs some three-quarters of the 11,000 aircraft workers.

Toulouse is representative of some of the newest French industrial developments, some encouraged to locate here by the state, yet like Bordeaux the town is handicapped by a somewhat peripheral situation in France.

Bordeaux

Like Toulouse, Bordeaux began on an outcrop of dry limestone, adjacent to an elbow turn of the Garonne, but at Bordeaux it is on the left bank, by the deepest upstream water. Here was a Roman city, with a temple where the cathedral now stands.

During the three centuries of English rule much wine was shipped to Bristol and London. Later the town traded rather with the Baltic lands, but its second great era came with the first French empire in America and the West Indies. Many of its finest buildings date from that time. Another great era, now perhaps declining, has been its trade with North, West and West-Central Africa, as well as some continuing trade with the Americas. The growth of processing industries in Africa has affected such imports as groundnuts and a diminution in their crushing here. Independence for these countries also tends to reduce cargo and passenger traffic through Bordeaux, and passenger traffic is further reduced by air competition. Nor does France (still less the Aquitaine Basin) need to import much coal, and pit-props are little exported.

Bordeaux must re-adjust so as to develop trade with Europe, but it is badly sited for this. Nor does Bordeaux have much of an industrial hinterland. The population of the municipal area has remained at a quarter of a million since the beginning of the century, although the agglomeration has nearly half a million people. Bordeaux seems to lack the relative dynamism of Toulouse although, like it, Bordeaux has received government aid for redevelopment.

The city has grown in concentric rings, using up as much space as a British rather than a French city. It is, for example, remarkably spacious compared with Paris, but its bungaloid *echoppes*, built from 1870–1914, have covered vast areas without adding beauty or housing many people per acre. New housing blocks of 12–20 stories have been built since the Second World War. They were formerly unknown in this mainly marshy, sandy environment, and are often ill-sited amid industry or near the docks, away from open spaces and other facilities.

Bordeaux is the outstanding wine centre of France. It blends, bottles and re-distributes wine, nourishes subsidiary industries making apéritifs, spirits and vinegar, and makes bottles, corks, boxes and printing labels. Other local crops are used in flour milling, biscuit making and fruit conserving, etc.

Cement manufacture is based on Tertiary limestone from Entre-deux-Mers, the Ambès oil refinery refines local oil from the Etang de Parentis as well as imported crude oil, and paper is made from local timber. 'Bordeaux mixture' (an anti-mildew spray) and fertilisers (super-phosphates from Moroccan phosphate) are manufactured for the agricultural hinterland.

Another typical group of industries are those processing tropical foods or beverages—groundnut oil extraction, sugar and rum, coffee, cocoa and chocolate, soap and tropical timber trades. In addition, there are industries common in large towns (beer, shoe, and clothing manufacture), and specific port industries such as shipbuilding (critically reduced) and repairing, engine and boiler-making, and paint manufacture. As at Toulouse, relative situation helped to bring in an aircraft industry—though it is now much less important than at that town.

Across the river La Bastide has many of these industries, often the more noxious ones, so that it presents a dismal urban scene. There are specialised outports at Bassens for wood, coal and cereal handling; while Ambès, Blaye and Pauillac have refineries. Mineral oil is, indeed, the largest import by weight and value.

The peoples of Aquitaine face formidable problems of re-adaptation—from a too diverse to a more specialised, capitalised and remunerative agriculture; from industries too small in scale, and too orientated to old trades connected with the now-changed Africa; or too unresponsive to new local resources such as natural gas, oil and sulphur. There are real difficulties—distance from the industrial and populated areas of France, legal difficulties of changing land-systems sometimes based on share-cropping (métayage), or of concentrating farms and industries. The people often know what is needed but see no way to effect the remedies.

MEDITERRANEAN FRANCE

Thus far France has been divided regionally mainly on grounds of structure and geology, but lastly another criterion is used—that of climate, because it gives a distinctive imprint to lands near the Mediterranean. The virtual drought of summer is very largely the cause of the great tourist industry of the eastern sector of the coast, but it imposes upon farmers either the need for growing drought-resistant crops or the use of irrigation.

Cattle can rarely be kept commercially, although sheep are still common. Terracing to gain land and conserve water is also a feature of the agricultural landscape.

There is great structural and geological variety, as in other major regions, but everywhere there is the close proximity of the almost tideless sea, and of plains and mountains, especially east of the Rhône Delta in Provence. Here and there on stony limestone outcrops are remnants of *garrigue*, with scattered prickly thistle and gorse, and aromatic plants such as thyme, lavender, sage and rosemary. On siliceous soils there is the

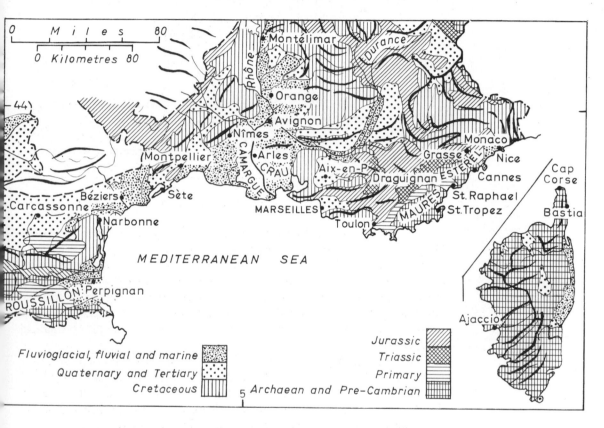

Fig 88 Mediterranean France.

closer brushwood of the *maquis*, with its rock roses, heathers, ferns, foxglove and lupins. Its typical trees are the cork oak, parasol pine and chestnut. More widespread, because more tolerant of differing soils, are the olive, most oaks and cypress. There are many introductions such as the agave, cactus aloe, various palms and eucalyptus. Plants commonly have thorns for protection against animals; whilst to control transpiration they are either aromatic, or have shiny, narrow or hairy leaves. Roots are long to gather all possible moisture during drought.

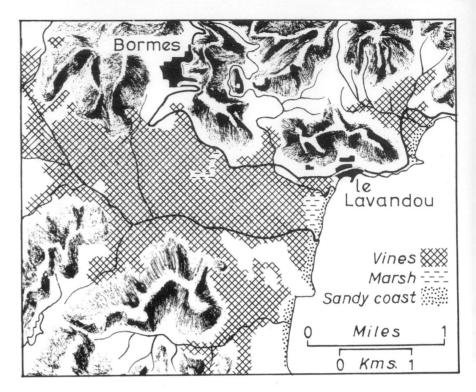

Fig 89   A Mediterranean plain with old and new settlement sites.

The Tyrrhenian and Central Massifs confined and moulded the Alpine Orogeny, giving a west-east trend to the Provence Alps (originally linked to the similar-trending Pyrenees), while the Mercantour Massif of the Alps enforced a north-south trend to the seaward extremities of the Maritime Alps. Farther south great nappes lay against the eastern edge of Tyrrhenia; when it split and foundered, the Maures, Esterel and western Corsica survived as remnants, whilst eastern Corsica has remains of the nappes in its schists.

The Provence Alps are dominantly limestone, either Jurassic or Cretaceous. They have been severely eroded, are more or less devoid of soil, and covered only by poor grass or aromatic shrubs. Windswept in winter, the Provence Alps reflect the sun in a glare in summer, especially on the *Plans* or Causses plateaux. These mountains are unattractive scenically and have few resources, except for bauxite quarried or mined around Brignoles, poor sheep pastures, and sporadic cultivation of lavender. Most people have left Haute Provence for the more rewarding Durance or Rhône valleys and especially for the coast.

North of the Maures and Esterel lies a Permo-Triassic depression, a convenient routeway for road and railway between Toulon and Cannes, while its red soils are largely cultivated with vineyards. Otherwise, the Mediterranean plains are former Mediterranean gulfs of Tertiary or Quaternary age, with soils lighter in colour and texture, usually fairly intensively cultivated, in the past for cereals, the vine and olive; now rather for table fruits, vegetables, flowers and the vine (Figs. 71 and 88).

Settlement was originally highly nucleated and located above the malarial plains on sites capable of defence against Barbary and other pirates, and where water was obtainable. In the last century-and-a-half, as these problems have disappeared, and railways and more roads were built, some old settlements have spread down to the plain (Fig. 89). Many new ones have developed there, mainly for tourists, while lowland agricultural settlement is now fairly dispersed. Houses commonly have rather flat roofs with pink tiles, windows have shutters, and open doorways have bead curtains or plastic streamers to admit a breeze but exclude flies. Walls are thick for interior coolness.

Diet and cuisine are different. Olive oil is used in place of butter; there is much use of garlic; *bouillabaisse*—a fish stew—is a famous dish; and fish, vegetables and fruit figure largely in the diet. The pronounced Midi accent and the slower pace of life, especially around mid-day, add distinctiveness to these lands.

Roussillon and Languedoc

West of the Rhône, drift of material from that river has smoothed an earlier sunken coast. The lowest areas nearest the sea e.g. the salanques of Roussillon are often saline; if uncultivable they are known as Aspre. Where irrigation is possible in Roussillon there is intensive *huerta*-style cultivation. Fruit trees such as peaches, apricots, cherries, early apples and pears, and the vine are grown on the baulks, often with onions or garlic beneath them. Temperate crops such as cauliflowers, cabbages, carrots and peas are planted on the north-facing sides of the baulks; the less hardy tomatoes, artichokes, asparagus and melons on the south-facing ones. The huerta is protected from the north-westerly *Tramontane* wind (akin to the Mistral) and the south-easterly *Marinade* by hedges. There is much cooperative marketing, efficient rail transport has helped growers to secure profitable markets in and outside France, whilst there is much local conserving.

In Languedoc the diverse cultivation of the small huertas gives way to vine monoculture on large estates for ordinary red wine, which has replaced the older cereal and olive cultivation on the plains of Biterrois (around Béziers) and the Costière (around Arles). However, there has been overproduction of wine and there is a need for alternative crops, which can be met only by providing irrigation, agricultural improvements, and processing industries.

The Compagnie Nationale du Bas-Rhône-Languedoc was founded in 1955 to provide this irrigation on another 400,000 acres (160,000 h.) as far west as the Aude River. Water is taken from the Rhône just above Arles and pumped to the Costière along a 110 mile (175 km.) canal (Fig. 90). Where there was mostly the vine, usually unirrigated, there are now irrigated and intensive farms similar to the huertas of Roussillon. Villages and canneries are being built, and the coast is being developed for tourists by the same state company. The market and route centres of Arles, Nîmes, Montpellier, Béziers and Narbonne will also gain, and be less exclusively

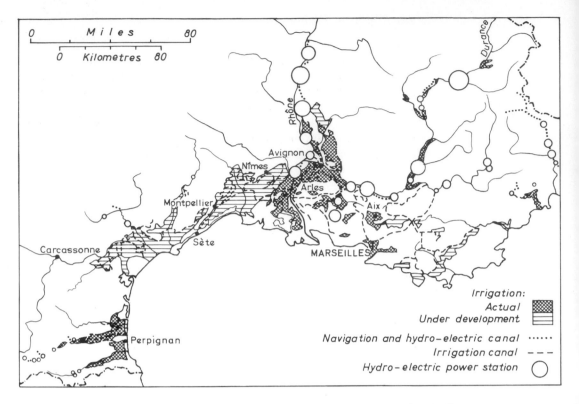

Fig 90 Irrigation, navigation and hydro-electric power in Mediterranean
France.
The size of the circles is proportional to the capacity of the power stations.
(After Carrère, Dugrand and Graves)

concerned with wine. Sète, likewise engaged in that trade, also imports
phosphates for fertiliser manufacture, and oil for refining. This port is
likely to gain from the agricultural renaissance of Languedoc.

Camargue

The Rhône Delta, though still having huge lagoons and marshes
(sansouires), is less desolate than formerly. Flamingo, herds of bulls, and
flocks of sheep remain, but the scene is dominated by rice. This is grown
on large estates, hulled in a central mill, and makes France more or less
self-sufficient in the crop, albeit at high cost.

Crau

This is the former Durance Delta, now partly covered by the Camargue.
The Crau is pebbly, was formerly grazed by sheep or under the vine, but
is being increasingly irrigated on the north and east for olive, almond
and fodder crops. On the south-east industries are extending into the
Crau from the Etang de Berre.

Western Lower Provence

From east of the Crau to the Maures and Esterel the sharp, craggy, mainly Jurassic limestone mountains are aligned from west to east, greatly impeding communications. Thus the railway and canal tunnel under the Estaque ridge north-west of Marseilles, the main roads skirt it, and lesser ones have tortuous routes over it.

Marseilles (Fr. *Marseille*). Given the Saône-Rhône and Mediterranean routeways, a port was likely to develop on or near the Rhône outlet. In the past Aigues Mortes and Arles in the delta were more important than Marseilles, which was even by-passed by Roman roads but triumphed when it was able to build piers to accommodate large ships.

The tiny west-east inlet of Le Vieux Port, the first cove east of the Rhône free of silt, was settled by Greeks some six centuries before Christ. The town flourished when Mediterranean and Near East trade was important, but barely held its own during the rise of the Americas. It revived with the opening to European trade of North Africa, with the cutting of the Suez Canal and increased trade with the Orient, with the development of the French Empire in Africa and Asia, and with the building of the railway through the Rhône-Saône Valley.

Yet Marseilles has had to counter formidable environmental problems. In 1511 the first finger-piers projecting into deep water were opened north

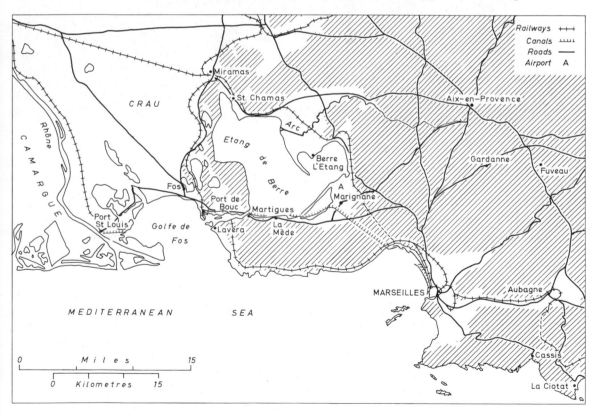

Fig 91   Marseilles. High ground indicated by hatching.

Plate 88   A view from the north-west of Marseilles and its harbour.
The town is severely constricted by the bleak limestone Provence Alps and space is at a premium. The first settlement was around a cove below the hill now surmounted by Notre Dame de la Garde towards the right front of the picture (see Fig. 91). The harbour has been built at the expense of the sea, by constructing the protective breakwater and finger piers from the shore. Rubble has been used to make the flat land on the left.

of the Vieux Port. Since then finger quays have been built extending nearly five miles north-westwards, with a projecting mole parallel to the coast—all won from the sea because of the shortage of soft, flat land near sea and city (Plate 88). Land access to the port is difficult because of the proximity of high and rugged mountains around the tiny Tertiary basin occupied by the city. Railways have many tunnels and severe gradients. Urban and industrial development have also been severely constricted.

Fortunately, the Etang de Berre, north of the Estaque ridge and linked to Marseilles by a 1,500 ton barge canal, with a $4\frac{1}{2}$ mile tunnel under the ridge, has developed as a newer industrial zone, with several oil refineries, petro-chemical and vegetable-oil works (Plate 89). Lavéra, at the entrance to the Etang, can take tankers of 75,000 tons, but larger ones lie off and discharge through pipelines. The development of the Middle East and Saharan oilfields greatly encouraged the establishment of refineries and the Lavéra port development. These, in turn, encouraged the construction of a 34 in. pipeline from Lavéra to Karlsruhe and intermediate towns—especially Strasbourg—which also have refineries based on this supply.

Plate 89   Port de Bouc, Lavéra and the Etang de Berre.

Port de Bouc (left foreground), and Lavéra oil refinery (right centre)—the terminal of a pipeline to the Rhinelands—are in the foreground. Beyond the railway bridge lies Martigues, either side of the eastern end of the Etang de Caronte and at the entrance to the large Etang de Berre. On its south-west side (right) is La Mede, an older oil port. From the south-east corner the Rove Canal (partly under the mountains) connects with Marseilles. On the south-east and north-east of the Etang de Berre are industrial outliers of Marseilles, requiring access by water and flat land, e.g. chemical works and oil refineries, as well as Marignane—Marseilles airport.

R*

Yet even around the Etang de Berre industrial development suffers from the proximity of mountains around one-half the perimeter, and from insufficient water supplies. Canal communication to the Rhône is so poor that barges usually cross the Fos Gulf and enter the Rhône by a short canal to Port St. Louis. On the gulf another oil port to accommodate tankers of over 100,000 tons, a refinery and a petro-chemical complex are being developed, and France's second integrated steelworks on a coast (the first is at Dunkirk) may be built here.

Meanwhile, Marseilles, France's second city, is by far the leading Mediterranean port, and vies with Le Havre as the first port of France. However, this is only possible because the annexes around the Etang de Berre have such vast petroleum imports; other imports have tended to remain static. They are mainly tropical and other foodstuffs, vegetable oils, rubber, mineral oils and chemicals. The city processes, packs and re-exports many of these. Exports by weight are, unusually for a French port, as heavy as imports (exclusive of oil), and consist of local fruit, wine, and manufactured goods.

Certain industries were founded on local supplies e.g. soap on olive oil although imported vegetable oils are now used. Yet it is the Etang de Berre industries and petroleum imports that have been the salvation of Marseilles, for the port has suffered competition from ports with a quicker turn-round like Rotterdam, from the relative decline in trade with former colonies, and from fast-disappearing passenger traffic. On the other hand, Marseilles stands to gain from the varied developments in the Rhône Valley.

East of Marseilles are deep and narrow bays (*calanques*) in the limestone. This is sometimes quarried for building stone and for cement, as at Cassis, an activity which has spoilt the fishing haven-cum-tourist resort made famous by the author Mistral and the artists Vlaminck and Matisse. La Ciotat has combined tourism and shipbuilding more successfully, although the latter is declining. Some towns are pure resorts, like Bandol. Toulon, the largest town, is essentially the French Mediterranean naval base and has a fine double harbour, but there is some commercial shipping and shipbuilding.

The Maures and Esterel

These have rounded land-forms and maquis vegetation. Permanent settlements are rare, although holiday homes are numerous. The coast is not sharply indented, and main roads and the railway skirt these massifs.

Cote d'Azur

The French Riviera is characterised by north-south promontories of the uplifted limestone Maritime Alps. Between are narrow valleys e.g. of the Var, or small plains e.g. of Nice. Here are the world-famous resorts of Cannes, Nice, the Principality of Monaco (Plate 90), and others. They were aristocratic winter resorts before the First World War; since the Second World War they have become mainly summer resorts for all. They

Plate 90   The Mediterranean coast and the Maritime Alps.

This view shows most of the Principality of Monaco, with the palace and museum on the peninsula, the harbour of La Condamine, and Monte Carlo, the casino being obscured by the pine branch. Note the typical scarcity of flat land.

are rarely affected by the Mistral in winter, because of their easterly position, and protection is afforded by promontories and the mountainous hinterland. Scenery and colour, climate and easy access—initially by rail (Plate 76) but now more by car or air (Nice Airport)—have made these towns famous, but increasingly congested.

Corsica

The physical evolution and divisions of this 'mountain in the sea' (Ratzel) have been described on p. 452. The location of Corsica has given it a strong Mediterranean imprint in climate, vegetation and cultural characteristics, while its relief looks more Alpine than Hercynian. It rises abruptly from the sea, and communications are difficult, except through the several small Tertiary or Quaternary basins. Most of these lie between the two main physical divisions—Hercynian Corsica on the west and south, and the Nappe-Schist zone of the north-east. It is the latter which has so alpine a character, because of its origin. Yet Hercynian Corsica is also highly dissected along its north-east to south-west trending ridges, with their deep, intervening gorges leading to the rugged and sunken west coast. The north-eastern one is emerging and smooth.

Corsica was for long isolated geographically and politically—an isolation only now being partially offset by tourism. There is some specialised agriculture e.g. the vine (for among other wines the apéritif Cap Corse), artichokes, citrus, and the keeping of sheep for milk for Roquefort cheese. Emigration has long been formidable, although French emigrès from North Africa have settled, and introduced capital and new agricultural methods.

The Mediterranean lands are some of the most distinctive in France. For long poor agriculturally, Languedoc could become a French California with the irrigation developments, rationalised marketing and processing. Tourism is likely to become increasingly the major activity, and could develop greatly in Languedoc and Corsica. Discreet industry based upon Rhône power (or, later, atomic power), good communications and the attractiveness of the area to labour, is likely to develop where allowed; the International Business Machines factory at Nice is a pointer.

CONCLUSION France is a classic example of diversity—the physical diversity of geology and scenery, of climate, soil and vegetation; the diversity of agricultural and industrial output, of technique and scale. Equally evident are the contradictions and complexities of the French economy—the ultra modern and the incredibly archaic, and the uneven development of productive areas. Around the diversity and contrasts have been the tight reins of centralisation, restricting and frustrating local initiative.

Almost too late have come dramatic changes. The demographic revolution has made France a country of young as well as of old people. Tremendous physical reconstruction has transformed many towns and the railways. The undersized and too numerous départements have been grouped for planning purposes, and the spread of Paris is being regulated. The integral development of the Rhône Valley and of Bas Languedoc has been undertaken on grand scales.

Natural gas from Lacq has brought great industries to its source, and its national grid has revivified industries far away. Hydro-electric and atomic power are transforming the Rhône Valley into an industrial area of the Late-Electrical Age. Agriculture is being transformed in Languedoc, whose coast is being developed for mass tourism. Meanwhile, the Riveria flourishes as never before from international tourism and discreet industries. The canalised Moselle and the European Parliament at Strasbourg are symbols of the integration of France and her neighbours and, one may hope, of Europe.

FURTHER READING
General Regional Studies of France
C. Chabot, *Géographie Régionale de la France*, 1966.
M. Le Lannou, *Les Régions Géographiques de la France*, 1964.
F. J. Monkhouse, *A Regional Geography of Western Europe*, 2nd Edit., 1964.
J. F. Gravier, *L'Aménagement du Territoire et l'Avenir des Régions Françaises*, 1964. *Studies of several regions.*
La France de Demain Series:
R. Nistri & Claude Prêcheur, *La Région du Nord et du Nord-Est*, 1959.
A. Blanc. E. Juillard, J. Ray & M. Rochefort, *Les Régions de l'Est*, 1960.
J. Labasse & M. Laferrère, *La Région Lyonnaise*, 1960.
P. Barrère, R. Heisch & S. Llerat, *La Région du Sud-Ouest*, 1962.
P. Flatrès & J. Trebert, *La Région de l'Ouest*, 1964.
P. Etienne & R. Joly, *La Région du Centre*, 1961.

The Hercynian Massifs
Simone Derruau & André Fel, *Le Massif Central* (*Que Sais-Je?*), 1963.
James Bird, 'Scale in Regional Study: Illustrated by brief comparisons between the Western Peninsulas of England and France', *Geography*, 1956, pp. 25–38.
J. W. House, 'A Comparative Study of the landscape of the Plateau de Millevaches and the Western Cévennes', *Transactions of the Institute of British Geographers*, 1954, pp. 159–180.

The Sedimentary Basins
P. George & P. Randet, *La Région Parisienne* (*France de Demain*), 2nd Edit., 1964.
J. F. Gravier, Paris et le Désert français, 1958.
B. Chapman, 'Baron Haussmann and the planning of Paris', *Town Planning Review*, October 1953, pp. 177–192.
Peter Hall, *The World Cities*, 1966.

The Mediterranean Lands
P. Carrère & R. Dugrand, *La Région Méditerranenne* (*France de Demain*), 1960.
J. M. Houston, *The Western Mediterranean World*, 1964.
A. Randeau, *La Corse*, 1964.
Swanzie Agnew, 'Rural Settlement in the Coastal Plain of Bas Languedoc', *Geography*, 1946, pp. 65–77.
Swanzie Agnew, 'Cultural Heritage of Bas Languedoc', *Geography*, 1951, pp. 44–50.
N. J. Graves, 'Une Californie Française. The Languedoc and Lower Rhône Irrigation Project', *Geography*, 1965, pp. 71–3.
Ian Thompson, 'The Revival of Corsica', *Geographical Magazine*, 1966, pp. 898–908.

By R. J. Harrison Church

Conclusion

Almost every page of this book speaks of the diversity of physical and human conditions in Europe—the mosaic continent. Here is one of the salient contrasts with so many of the other continents, with their usually more uniform terrain, human occupancy, and style of development. It is rare indeed to travel far in North-West Europe without encountering major changes in scenery, soil, climate and vegetation.

The human scenery is likewise as varied in its architectural styles and layouts, language, political and social organisation, agricultural policy, organisation, scale of production and output. Almost every possible type of farm and of agricultural practice has been noted in this book—peasant, tenant—large and small, métayer, cooperative and state farm. In their size farms vary from a fraction of an acre to over a thousand acres, from virtual monoculture to polyculture, from intensive to extensive, from dairying on polderland to dairying on summer alp. One common feature, however, is the rarity and declining significance, compared with several other continents, of subsistence agriculture, and the great possibilities still of increasing and intensifying outputs, notably in southern France.

Industrial organisation is likewise as varied in respect of age, organisation, size and output. Virtually every known fuel or motive force is employed, not forgetting the natural hot water and steam of Iceland, the natural gas of the Netherlands, the North Sea and France, as well as imported gas and the use of nuclear power. Yet in the use of oil and natural gas Europe still lags behind Anglo-America, and depends a great deal upon coal and hydro-electric power. Industrial location is strongly influenced by both of these, as well as by the attraction of large clusters of population and good transport, but political control of industrial location is significant in most of the countries studied. So, too, are integrated schemes of development e.g. of the Rhône for power, navigation and irrigation. More exciting are the international projects such as the international oil pipe lines, the Anglo-French Concord aircraft, Franco-German coal and petro-chemical collaboration at Carling in Lorraine, and many more.

Europe, especially North-West Europe, has the greatest trade per acre or *per capita* of any in the world. Much of it is internal and intra-European especially with the development since the Second World War of Benelux, Comecon, the European Coal and Steel Community, the European Economic Community and the European Free Trade Area. The unified Scandinavian Airline System (grouping Norwegian, Swedish and Danish private and public capital), the international oil pipelines, the canalised Moselle, the luxurious Trans-Europe Express trains and Eurobuses, are further steps to greater mutual trade and personal mobility.

Europe is a peninsula of peninsulas, in which maritime influences have penetrated more profoundly than in any other continent. Europe has the longest coastline, per area, of any continent, a remarkable number of harbours capable of development as ports, and easy access to rich fish resources.

Much of European history is the story of struggles between maritime and continental powers and indeed concerns maritime enterprise itself. This continues to be vital to several countries studied in this book, notably Norway and Denmark. Yet the importance of land transit trade is no less significant to Switzerland and the Netherlands.

Europe has a longer history of development by man than any other continent except Asia, and Europe is certainly the most intensively developed continent. There is a long story of trial and error, an understandable respect for experience and tradition, for the husbanding of resources and capital, and a questioning of the need for most changes. There is, inevitably, a greater problem of obsolescence than in newer countries and, after the loss of man-power and the destruction of resources in war, a greater shortage of capital.

Europe has recovered remarkably from wars, but the rift between communist and non-communist continues to impoverish it, by restricting trade and obstructing transport. Germany remains divided, and the effect upon such towns as Lübeck, Hamburg and especially Berlin, is grievous.

With these restrictions on intra-European trade, the problems of renewal of equipment, and the decline in certain natural resources especially of the rare and base metals, Europe must depend more and more upon human initiative, ingenuity and invention. These are well seen in such difficult environments as Scandinavia and Switzerland, and in industries such as electronics and petro-chemicals. Europe must necessarily continue to modernise and specialise to maintain its standing and its standard of living. It must also achieve even greater unity to maximise the rational development of its resources and widen its markets.

By R. J. Harrison Church

Statistical Appendix

Countries are listed in the order of treatment in this book.
United Kingdom statistics are given for comparison.

A. AREA, POPULATION AND TOWNS[1]

Country	Population	Census Date	Annual Increase	Area in sq. m.	Area in sq. km.	Density /sq. m.	Density /sq.km.
Finland	4,446,222	1960	0·8	134,804	337,009	36	14
Sweden	7,495,316	1960	0·6	179,917	449,793	44	17
Norway	3,591,234	1960	0·8	129,688	324,219	29	11
Iceland	143,973	1950	1·9	41,400	103,000	5	2
Denmark	4,585,256	1960	0·7	17,217	43,043	286	110
German F.R.	53,977,418	1961	1·3	99,189	247,973	588	226
German D.R.	15,940,469	1964	−0·2	43,158	107,896	387	149
Switzerland	5,429,061	1960	2·1	16,515	41,288	369	142
Luxembourg	314,889	1960	0·9	1,034	2,586	330	127
Belgium	9,189,741	1961	0·6	12,205	30,513	798	307
Netherlands	11,461,964	1960	1·4	13,445	33,612	939	361
France	46,520,271	1962	1·3	218,810	547,026	229	88
United Kingdom	52,708,934	1961	0·7	86,498	244,030	575	222

Population of capital cities, and of towns of over 200,000 inhabitants[2]

Finland (1963)

Helsinki	482,390

Sweden (1965)

Stockholm	793,714
Göteborg	418,600
Malmö	245,803

Norway (1964)

Oslo	484,711

Iceland (1964)

Reykjavik	77,220

Denmark (1964)

Copenhagen	694,479

German Federal Republic (1964)

Bonn	142,818
Hamburg	1,856,530
Munich	1,182,411
Cologne	841,682
Essen	728,819
Düsseldorf	702,006
Frankfurt am Main	694,435
Dortmund	653,260
Stuttgart	635,340
Bremen	584,640
Hanover	566,323
Duisburg	495,641
Nuremberg	467,735
Wuppertal	422,381
Gelsenkirchen	378,062

(*continued*)

---

[1] United Nations, *Demographic Yearbook*, 1965.

[2] Comparable statistics for agglomerations of all these towns are not available.

ᴀʀᴇᴀ, Pᴏᴘᴜʟᴀᴛɪᴏɴ ᴀɴᴅ Tᴏᴡɴs (continued)

Bochum	359,147	*Luxembourg* (*1964*)	
Mannheim	323,972	Luxembourg	77,254
Kiel	270,247		
Oberhausen	259,804	*Belgium* (*1964*)	
Wiesbaden	259,586	Brussels	170,802
Karlsruhe	252,526	Antwerp	247,156
Brunswick	240,190		
Lübeck	237,865	*Netherlands* (*1964*)	
Krefeld	218,015	Amsterdam	868,173
Kassel	213,217	The Hague	601,134
Augsburg	209,814	Rotterdam	732,232
Hagen	200,621		
West Berlin	2,197,408	*France* (*1962*)	
		Paris	2,790,091
German Democratic Republic (*1964*)		Marseilles	778,071
Berlin (East)	1,071,462	Lyons	528,535
Leipzig	595,203	Toulouse	323,724
Dresden	503,859	Nice	292,958
Karl-Marx-Stadt	293,549	Bordeaux	249,688
Halle	274,402	Nantes	240,028
Magdeburg	265,141	Strasbourg	228,971
		Saint Etienne	201,242
Switzerland (*1965*)			
Berne	170,100	United Kingdom (1964) has 23 towns	
Zürich	438,800	over 200,000	
Basle	212,700		

B. ᴀɢʀɪᴄᴜʟᴛᴜʀᴇ, ᴀɢʀɪᴄᴜʟᴛᴜʀᴀʟ Pʀᴏᴅᴜᴄᴛs, Fᴏʀᴇsᴛʀʏ, Fᴏʀᴇsᴛ Pʀᴏᴅᴜᴄᴛs ᴀɴᴅ Fɪsʜɪɴɢ

Land use[3]

Thousand hectares 1964.

	Total Area	Arable	Permanent Pasture	Forest	Built up, waste, etc.
Finland	33,701	2,728	88	21,761	9,124
Sweden	44,979	3,304	525	22,505	18,645
Norway	32,422	849	168	7,026	24,379
Iceland	10,300	1	2,279	3	8,017
Denmark	4,304	2,740	328	438	798
German F.R.	24,688	8,411	5,710	7,146	3,421
German D.R.	10,789	5,015	1,420	2,942	1,328
Switzerland	4,129	422	1,743	981	983
Luxembourg	259	72	65	86	36
Belgium	3,051	939	732	601	779
Netherlands	3,361	977	1,291	288	805
France	54,703	20,828	13,281	11,963	4,632
United Kingdom	24,403	7,439	12,225	1,778	2,961

[3] This and the following three tables from F.A.O., *Production Yearbook*, 1965. Letters 'n.a.' in certain tables indicate 'not available'.

AGRICULTURE (continued)

Percentage of population in agriculture

	1930–44	1945–64
Finland	57	35
Sweden	33	14
Norway	35	19
Iceland	57	38
Denmark	29	17
German F.R.	27	11
German D.R.	22	18
Switzerland	21	11
Luxembourg	n.a.	15
Belgium	17	6
Netherlands	21	11
France	36	20
Eng., Wales, Scot.	6	6

Tractors in use

Number 1964

World	12,955,000
Finland	121,400
Sweden (1963)	168,600
Norway	68,749
Iceland	7,340
Denmark	162,362
German F.R.	1,106,899
German D.R.	117,714
Switzerland	66,000
Luxembourg	7,100
Belgium	61,377
Netherlands	111,701
France	952,718
United Kingdom (1963)	389,250

Combine Harvesters

Number 1964

World	n.a.
Finland	15,000
Sweden	34,700
Norway	8,176
Iceland	10
Denmark	26,922
German F.R.	109,000
German D.R.	13,833
Switzerland	n.a.
Luxembourg	1,068
Belgium	5,133
Netherlands	n.a.
France	92,219
United Kingdom (1963)	61,481

Indices of agricultural production[4]

1952/3–1956/7 = 100

Country	1963/4
Finland	130
Sweden	99
Norway	105
Denmark	118
German F.R.	127
German D.R.	n.a.
Switzerland	107
Belgium–Luxembourg	122
Netherlands	118
France	126
United Kingdom	132

Meat production Thousand metric tons 1964	Beef and Veal	Pork	Mutton and Lamb	Total
World	32,400	29,100	6,000	67,500
Finland	98	67	2	167
Sweden	157	215	2	374
Norway	58	55	15	128
Iceland	2		11	13
Denmark	156	688	1	845
German F.R. (1962)	1,114	1,748	15	2,877
German D.R.		not available		
Switzerland (1963)	115	137	3	255
Luxembourg	13	12		25
Belgium	231	256	2	489
Netherlands	273	n.a.	6	n.a.
France (1963)	1,661	1,216	117	2,994
United Kingdom	876	831	256	1,963

[4] This and following tables from United Nations, *Statistical Yearbook*, 1965.

AGRICULTURE, etc (continued)

Butter production

Thousand metric tons 1964

World	n.a.
Finland	104
Sweden	80
Norway	39
Iceland	2
Denmark	156
German F.R.	491
German D.R.	175
Switzerland	30
Luxembourg	5
Belgium	82
Netherlands	90
France	435
United Kingdom	28

Cheese production

Thousand metric tons 1964

World	n.a.
Finland	35
Sweden	57
Norway	43
Denmark	124
German F.R.	360
German D.R.	47
Switzerland	73
Luxembourg	1
Belgium	31
Netherlands	213
France	500
United Kingdom	111

Beer production

Thousand hectolitres 1964

World	483,600
Finland	996
Sweden	3,010
Norway	1,067
Iceland	18
Denmark (1963)	4,786
German F.R. (1963)	59,156
German D.R.	13,772
Switzerland	4,580
Luxembourg	519
Belgium	11,330
Netherlands	4,964
France	20,252
United Kingdom	48,442

Wine production

Thousand hectolitres 1964

World	272,000
German F.R.	6,610
Luxembourg	162
Switzerland	906
France	61,568

Timber production

Million cubic metres 1964

	Total	Coniferous
World	1,956	953
Finland	46	35
Sweden	48	42
Norway	8	7
Denmark	2	1
German F.R.	27	18
German D.R.	6	5
Switzerland	4	3
Belgium	3	2
France	45	14
United Kingdom	4	2

Sawn wood production

Thousand cubic metres 1964

	Coniferous	Broad Leaf
World	279,938	76,418
Finland	6,891	93
Sweden	9,345	160
Norway	1,640	11
Denmark	330	360
German F.R.	7,054	1,745
German D.R.	1,605	380
Switzerland	1,210	114
Luxembourg	36	24
Belgium	325	315
Netherlands	82	238
France	5,150	2,655
United Kingdom	266	729

AGRICULTURE, ETC (continued)

Mechanical wood pulp production
Thousand metric tons 1964

World	20,805
Finland	1,594
Sweden	1,220
Norway	898
German F.R.	642
German D.R.	250
Switzerland	137
Belgium	109
Netherlands	152
France	442
United Kingdom	240

Chemical wood pulp production
Thousand metric tons 1964

World	53,090
Finland	3,736
Sweden	5,146
Norway	900
German F.R.	725
German D.R.	400
Switzerland	113
Belgium	62
France	916
United Kingdom	40

Newsprint production
Thousand metric tons 1964

World	15,765
Finland	1,079
Sweden	652
Norway	291
German F.R.	202
German D.R.	97
Switzerland	100
Belgium	98
Netherlands	155
United Kingdom	762

Fishing
Thousand metric tons 1964

World	51,600
Finland	63
Sweden	372
Norway	1,608
Iceland	973
Denmark	871
German F.R.	624
German D.R.	225
Belgium	59
Netherlands	388
France	780
United Kingdom	975

C. MINING

Indices of mining
1958 = 100

	1964
Finland	155
Sweden (1963)	130
Norway	136
German F.R.	105
German D.R.	117
Luxembourg	95
Belgium	92
Netherlands	116
France	107
United Kingdom	95

Coal production
Thousand metric tons 1964

World	1,996,900
Sweden	84
Norway	442
German F.R.	142,704
German D.R.	2,340
Belgium	21,305
Netherlands	11,480
France	53,030
United Kingdom	196,734

MINING (continued)

Lignite production

Thousand metric tons 1964

World	749,400
Denmark	2,195
German F.R.	110,945
German D.R.	256,926
France	2,241

Iron ore—iron content

Thousand metric tons 1964

World	281,230
Finland	307
Sweden	16,220
Norway	1,290
German F.R.	2,796
German D.R.	490
Switzerland	36
Luxembourg	1,887
Belgium	19
France	19,805
United Kingdom	4,479

Bauxite

Thousand metric tons 1964

World	29,510
German F.R.	4
France	2,433

Natural gas

Millions of cubic metres 1964

World	n.a.
German F.R.	2,336
Belgium	66
Netherlands	899
France	5,090
United Kingdom	178

Crude petroleum

Thousand metric tons 1964

World	1,410,100
Sweden	81
German F.R.	7,673
Netherlands	2,270
France	2,846
United Kingdom	129

Salt

Thousand metric tons 1964

World	n.a.
German F.R.	6,415
German D.R.	n.a.
Switzerland	182
Netherlands	1,596
France	3,873
United Kingdom	6,745

Potash

Thousand metric tons 1964

World	9,950
German F.R.	2,553
German D.R.	1,857
France	1,983

Sulphur

Thousand metric tons 1964

World	23,900
Finland	2,242
Sweden	485
Norway	1,030
German F.R.	611
German D.R.	42
France	273

D. INDUSTRY

Indices of industrial production (1964)
1958 = 100

	All Manufs.	Manufacturing				
		Food Drink Tob.	Text. and Cloth.	Chems. Coal Pet. Prods.	Basic Metals	Metal Prods.
Finland	162	142	138	199	227	160
Sweden (1963)	141	121	131	144	163	147
Norway	141	110	123	178	164	136
Denmark	157	148	147	173	—	168
German F.R.	152	130	140	209	139	154
German D.R.	151	129	126	160	145	180
Switzerland			Not available			
Luxembourg	127	119	36	108	133	88
Belgium	153	126	142	162	148	161
Netherlands	152	126	137	178	n.a.	163
France	138	n.a.	119	184	128	141
United Kingdom	130	118	105	157	128	127

Production of cotton yarn
Thousand metric tons 1964

World	n.a.
Finland	19
Sweden	20
Norway	5
Denmark (1963)	9
German F.R.	383
German D.R.	81
Switzerland	39
Belgium	94
Netherlands	76
France	300
United Kingdom	245

Production of wool yarn
Thousand metric tons 1964

World	n.a.
Finland	8
Sweden	12
Norway	8
Denmark (1963)	5
German F.R.	118
German D.R.	31
Switzerland	2
Belgium	62
Netherlands	23
France	147
United Kingdom	254

Production of woven cotton fabrics
Thousand metric tons 1964

World	n.a.
Finland	14
Sweden	21
Norway	4
Denmark (1963)	6
German F.R.	264
German D.R.	n.a.
Switzerland	n.a.
Belgium	86
Netherlands	n.a.
France	227
United Kingdom	n.a.

Production of woven woollen fabrics
Thousand metric tons 1964

World	n.a.
Finland	3
Sweden	5
Norway	2
Denmark (1963)	2
German F.R.	61
German D.R.	n.a.
Switzerland	n.a.
Belgium	39
Netherlands	n.a.
France	76
United Kingdom	n.a.

INDUSTRY (continued)

Production of continuous and dis-
continuous rayon fibres
Thousand metric tons 1964

World	3,317
Finland	24
Sweden	36
Norway	24
German F.R.	297
German D.R.	141
Switzerland	24
Belgium	38
Netherlands	57
France	148
United Kingdom	248

Production of super phosphates
Thousand metric tons 1964

Finland	514
Sweden (1963)	517
Norway	53
Denmark (1963)	738
German F.R.	381
German D.R.	684
Switzerland (1963)	26
Belgium (1963)	122
Netherlands	1,122
France	684
United Kingdom	514

Production of continuous and
discontinuous man-made fibres
Thousand metric tons 1964

World	1,685
Finland	1
Sweden	1
Norway	1
German F.R.	140
German D.R.	17
Switzerland	17
Belgium	8
Netherlands	33
France	93
United Kingdom	126

Production of nitrogenous fertilizers
Thousand metric tons 1964

World	16,500
Finland	74
Sweden	71
Norway	319
Iceland	7
German F.R.	1,289
German D.R.	334
Switzerland	30
Belgium	346
Netherlands	527
France (1963)	913
United Kingdom	595

Production of sulphuric acid (100%)
Thousand metric tons 1964

World	n.a.
Finland	356
Sweden (1963)	475
Norway	108
Denmark (1963)	13
German F.R. (1963)	3,316
German D.R.	937
Switzerland	159
Belgium	1,348
Netherlands	976
France	2,702
United Kingdom	3,185

Production of plastics
Thousand metric tons 1964

Finland	2
Sweden (1963)	72
Norway (1963)	48
Denmark (1963)	16
German F.R.	1,745
German D.R.	204
Switzerland	n.a.
Belgium	n.a.
Netherlands	274
France	611
United Kingdom	881

INDUSTRY (continued)
Production of main petroleum products
Thousand metric tons 1964

	Motor Spirit	Light Oils	Heavy Oils
World	299,700	243,900	415,500
Finland	405	367	918
Sweden (1963)	440	650	1,366
Norway	424	858	1,553
Denmark	667	720	1,457
German F.R.	9,000	6,788	32,093
German D.R.	1,462	2,024	
Switzerland	163	367	298
Belgium	1,864	4,163	4,283
Netherlands	2,769	6,025	10,943
France	8,771	4,817	26,731
United Kingdom	8,794	12,185	27,212

Production of metallurgical coke
Thousand metric tons 1964

World	274,500
Sweden	375
German F.R.	43,350
German D.R.	1,048
Belgium	4,398
Netherlands	4,514
France	13,941
United Kingdom	17,127

Production of cement
Thousand metric tons 1964

World	414,000
Finland	1,572
Sweden	3,567
Norway	1,512
Iceland	108
Denmark	1,858
German F.R.	33,632
German D.R.	5,767
Switzerland	4,322
Luxembourg	204
Belgium	5,846
Netherlands	2,873
France	21,542
United Kingdom	16,966

Production of pig-iron and ferro alloys
Thousand metric tons 1964

World	299,300
Finland	639
Sweden	2,336
Norway	885
Denmark	75
German F.R. (1963)	23,015
German D.R.	2,260
Switzerland	30
Luxembourg	4,191
Belgium	8,047
Netherlands	1,947
France	16,082
United Kingdom	17,551

Production of crude steel
Thousand metric tons 1964

World	424,200
Finland	355
Sweden	4,392
Norway	615
Denmark	396
German F.R. (1963)	31,597
German D.R.	4,392
Switzerland	345
Luxembourg	4,559
Belgium	8,731
Netherlands	2,646
France	19,780
United Kingdom	26,651

INDUSTRY (continued)

Production of aluminium
(excluding scrap)
Thousand metric tons 1964

World	4,920
Sweden	32
Norway	262
German F.R. (1963)	209
German D.R.	40
Switzerland	64
France	316
United Kingdom	32

Ships built
Thousand gross registered tons 1964

	General	Tankers
World	10,264	5,529
Finland	161	27
Sweden	1,021	784
Norway	409	256
Denmark	242	130
German F.R.	890	397
Belgium	103	58
Netherlands	226	56
United Kingdom	1,043	420

Production of motor vehicles
Thousands 1964

	Cars	Comm. Veh.
World	16,770	4,940
Finland	—	2
Sweden (1963)	147	21
German F.R.	2,650	254
German D.R.	93	12
United Kingdom	1,832	456

E. ENERGY

*Consumption of energy from all sources
per capita*
Kilogrammes of coal equivalent

World	1,542
Finland	2,387
Sweden	4,320
Norway	3,527
Iceland	3,725
Denmark	3,955
German F.R.	4,230
German D.R.	n.a.
Switzerland	2,483
Luxembourg and Belgium	4,566
Netherlands	3,278
France	2,933
United Kingdom	5,079

Production of electric energy

Million kwh	Total	Hydro
World	3,104,400	n.a.
Finland	13,636	8,501
Sweden	45,247	43,022
Norway	43,942	43,778
Iceland	681	653
Denmark	7,425	—
German F.R.	161,081	12,114
German D.R.	51,032	536
Switzerland	22,864	22,663
Luxembourg	1,443	32
Belgium	20,800	114
Netherlands	22,975	—
France	93,779	34,715

F. Transport

Motor Vehicles in use
Thousands 1964

	Cars	Comm. Veh.
World	128,420	31,920
Finland	376	90
Sweden	1,666	122
Norway	416	129
Iceland	25	7
Denmark	675	231
German F.R.	8,014	957
German D.R.	n.a.	n.a.
Switzerland	839	89
Luxembourg	56	10
Belgium	1,159	222
Netherlands	1,059	220
France	8,800	2,023
United Kingdom	8,264	1,666

Rail traffic
Millions 1964

	Passenger km.	Ton km.
Finland	2,038	4,863
Sweden	5,267	12,919
Norway	1,716	1,888
Denmark	3,490	1,550
German F.R.	37,218	59,037
German D.R.	17,378	39,113
Switzerland	8,569	5,022
Luxembourg	231	671
Belgium	9,075	6,863
Netherlands	7,854	3,885
France	37,910	65,260
United Kingdom	31,984	26,168

Merchant shipping
Thousand gross registered tons 1964

	General	Tankers
World	153,000	50,563
Finland	964	—
Sweden	4,308	1,465
Norway	14,477	7,664
Iceland	130	—
Denmark	2,431	884
German F.R.	5,159	839
German D.R.	502	—
Switzerland	164	—
Belgium	796	—
Netherlands	5,110	1,638
France	5,116	2,209
United Kingdom	21,490	8,002

Sea-borne shipping   Vessels: thousand net registered tons
                       Goods: thousand metric tons   Both 1964

	Vessels entered	Vessels cleared	Goods loaded	Goods unloaded
Finland	9,670	8,888	19,617	12,474
Sweden	15,916	11,286	21,428	29,554
Norway	12,333	15,800	25,755	13,185
Iceland (1963)	n.a.	n.a.	385	741
Denmark (1963)	28,562	n.a.	4,555	20,235
German F.R.	68,249	45,346	17,776	76,530
German D.R.	n.a.	n.a.	2,286	6,103
Belgium	48,028	37,547	18,570	40,199
Netherlands	83,010	49,430	28,212	113,692
France	79,024	46,601	17,995	96,401
United Kingdom	103,858	57,827	34,332	152,104

TRANSPORT (continued)

Civil aviation, domestic and international, on scheduled routes by each nation's airlines (1964)
Thousands

	Kilo- metres	Pass. km.	Ton km.	Mail Ton km.
World	3,700,000	171,000,000	3,920,000	910,000
Finland	11,955	311,157	4,251	1,287
Sweden*	33,154	1,419,610	36,610	9,310
Norway*	21,199	997,616	22,066	5,897
Iceland	10,285	652,544	2,844	856
Denmark*	15,961	783,339	21,521	4,918
German F.R.	58,800	3,149,941	97,633	19,660
Switzerland	42,422	2,142,949	46,419	10,786
Luxembourg†	570	10,504	63	10
Belgium	30,487	1,626,520	48,823	5,241
Netherlands	60,889	3,008,199	151,503	13,102
France	115,807	6,696,545	152,675	39,664
United Kingdom	221,391	10,868,220	245,900	57,874

* Apportionment of Scandinavian Airlines System
† International only

G. TOURISM

Foreign visitors
Numbers 1964

Finland	n.a.
Scandinavia	9,809,054
German F.R. (1963)	5,603,357
Switzerland	5,842,248
Belgium (1963)	4,696,000
Netherlands	1,761,541
France	10,250,000
United Kingdom	2,458,000

H. EXTERNAL TRADE

Imports and exports
In million U.S. dollars 1964

	Imports	Exports
World	180,600	172,200
Finland	1,505	1,291
Sweden	3,853	3,672
Norway	1,982	1,290
Iceland	131	111
German F.R.	14,613	16,215
German D.R.	2,380	2,670
Switzerland	3,610	2,647
Luxembourg and Belgium	5,922	5,590
Netherlands	7,057	5,808
France	10,069	8,993
United Kingdom	15,589	12,357

Index

(Bold type indicates the more important references.)